DISCARD

PRAISE FOR *VEGANOMICON*

--------------- ◆ ---------------

"Spending time with [Moskowitz's] cheerfully politicized book feels like hanging out with Grace Paley. She and her cooking partner, Terry Hope Romero, are as crude and funny when kibitzing as they are subtle and intuitive when putting together vegan dishes that are full of non-soggy adult tastes. Do look for an excellent roasted fennel and hazelnut salad, bok choy cooked with crispy shallots and sesame seeds, hot and sour soup with wood ears and napa cabbage and a porcini-wild rice soup they say is 'perfect for serving your yuppie friends.'"—NEW YORK TIMES BOOK REVIEW

"Exuberant and unapologetic, Moskowitz and Romero's recipes don't skimp on fat or flavor, and the eclectic collection of dishes is a testament to the authors' sincere love of cooking and culinary exploration."—SAVEUR

"[T]his slam-bang effort from vegan chefs Moskowitz and Romero is thorough and robust, making admirable use of every fruit and vegetable under the sun."
—PUBLISHERS WEEKLY

"Full of recipes for which even a carnivore would give up a night of meat."
—SAN FRANCISCO CHRONICLE

"It's no shocker that the very same urban chefs who had you inhaling vegan butter-cream frosting during your free time have crafted the next revolution in neo-vegan cuisine."—PHILADELPHIA CITY PAPER

"*Veganomicon* not only offers tons of mouth-watering ways to put 'veg' back into your vegan diet with actual produce, but also tutorials that gave me confidence to start improvising on my own."—BUST

"*Veganomicon* is user-friendly, packed with tips and instructions for a wide range of cooking techniques."—NEW YORK SUN

"*The Betty Crocker's Cookbook* of the vegan world. It's one more step in the quest to prove that vegan food really doesn't taste like cardboard when you know what you're doing."—BITCH

"Seriously good with broad appeal."—WASHINGTON POST

"These two very real and very sassy food-obsessed women have put together a cookbook that you wish your mom cooked from when you were growing up. The recipes are seriously delicious and, for the most part, uncomplicated."
—BUFFALO SPREE

VEGANOMICON

10TH ANNIVERSARY EDITION

VEGANOMICON

10TH ANNIVERSARY EDITION

THE ULTIMATE
VEGAN COOKBOOK

ISA CHANDRA MOSKOWITZ & TERRY HOPE ROMERO

Go
hachette
BOOKS

New York

Hachette Go
Hachette Book Group
1290 Avenue of the Americas, New York, NY 10104
HachetteGo.com
Facebook.com/HachetteGo
Instagram.com/Hachette Go

Printed in Malaysia. First edition published in 2007.

Originally published as Da Capo Lifelong Books
First Hachette Go Edition 2020

Hachette Books is a division of Hachette Book Group, Inc.
The Hachette Go and Hachette Books name and logos are trademarks of Hachette Book Group, Inc.

The publisher is not responsible for websites (or their content) that are not owned by the publisher.

The Veganomicon V was designed by Vivian Ghazarian and Matt Bouloutian.

Vegan Mayo is from *The Superfun Times Vegan Holiday Cookbook: Entertaining for Absolutely Every Occasion* by Isa Chandra Moskowitz, copyright © 2016. Reprinted by permission of Little, Brown and Company, a division of Hachette Book Group, Inc.

Editorial production by Christine Marra, *Marrathon* Production Services. www.marrathoneditorial.org

Interior design by Laura Palese
Food styling by Kate Lewis

Library of Congress Cataloging-in-Publication Data has been applied for.

ISBN: 978-0-7382-1899-1 (hardcover)

ISBN: 978-0-7382-1900-4 (ebook)

IM

10 9 8 7 6 5 4 3 2 1

IN MEMORY OF
AMY SIMS

CONTENTS

THE RECIPES 42

SNACKS, APPETIZERS, LITTLE MEALS, DIPS & SPREADS 42

BRUNCH 76

SALADS & DRESSINGS 96

SALADS 97

ONE-POT MEALS & STOVETOP SPECIALTIES 260

PASTA, NOODLES & RISOTTO 286

SAUCES & FILLINGS 310

VEGANOMICON 2007–2017

DECADE OF VEGRESSION

TERRY'S INTRO

Sitting down to reread the *Veganomicon* introduction Isa and I crafted over ten years ago, initially I thought, "Throw it out! Gimme a fresh start!" I'm glad I soon got over that impulse. Even though we were just entering our cookbook-writing career at the time, there is still a lot of wisdom packed into a few sassy pages.

I smile when I read through the lines about how much we've grown since 2007. Although *Veganomicon* is absolutely the product of an urban upbringing, Isa for a short while did have an honest-to-gosh suburban kitchen in Omaha (one that I enjoyed very much baking pies in during our summer of wrapping up *Vegan Pie in the Sky* and with a view of picket fences, green lawns, and sprawling vegetable gardens). I graduated myself from the omnipresent New York rental apartment kitchen (good-bye lopsided stovetop, crooked plywood cabinets, and never the luxury of a dishwasher) to a co-op apartment in Queens populated with appliances I bought myself. Never could I have imagined the joys of scrubbing the insides of a refrigerator I actually own.

Our love of obscure pop culture and blatantly urban aesthetics aside (you can practically hear us complaining about hauling groceries up the subway entrance stairs), I think we made it abundantly clear our stance on vegan eating was for everybody. Everybody = the "newly minted since watching *Earthlings*" vegan, the battle-hardened eating-nutritional-yeast-by-the-spoonful since-1985-vegan, or just the adventurous omnivorous cook curious about seitan. Years later, I still hear stories from old friends and new acquaintances about the dog-eared copy of *Veganomicon* that's been hanging out in their kitchen for years. I get texts and Facebook messages with photos of a copy of *Vcon* (nickname since the start) propped up on a bookstore shelf in Tokyo, atop flatmate's fridge in Berlin, or used for pressing tofu in a long-lost college buddy's kitchen in Berkeley (nothing like a big fat hardcover vegan cookbook that can double as a tofu press). *Veganomicon*—a title our metalhead friend Dro devised, which hinted at the vast, epic place vegan food would occupy in the culinary universe ten years later—no longer is whispered only on vegan message boards. It's now a household word, and occasional kitchen tool, the vegan culinary world over.

Then and now, we've appreciated every kind of chef who's cooked from this book. No matter how many "vegan points" they've amassed or how many meals they cook a week, *Vcon* is for anyone looking to eliminate meat and animal products from their diet one meal at a time. But we don't judge; we get that people are busy. We never preach. And we know you microwave frozen bean burritos for breakfast or eat cereal doused with almond milk for dinner and damn well enjoy it. For most of my own cookbook writing career I've been engaged in one full-time day job or another. Outside of developing recipes for cookbooks, there's forever a new recipe I'm working on that needs refinement, so there's rarely time to cook only for the pleasure of it. Sometimes it's cereal for supper, even for cookbook authors.

Not only have we changed, but the guerrilla vacant-lot garden of vegan food of 2007 has exploded into a vibrant and fascinating edible landscape in 2017. Americans now love vegetables! Tech money–funded meat substitutes are served in fancy destination restaurants, next-level gourmet veggie burgers baffle (still, really?) mainstream meat-eating food writers but are commonplace, and Brooklyn is home to a vegan cheese shop dedicated to selling artisanal vegan cheeses prepared with the same attention and care as their dairy-based counterparts. And beautifully, vegan cookbooks are not a fad, but a staple in any bookstore or public library.

Vegan food = normal food still has a long way to go, but what a glorious and exciting time it is to go vegan . . . be it for a day, a week, a year, or we hope, the rest of your life.

What keeps me going still are the countless stories from fans across the world about how a few *Veganomicon* recipes changed not just what's for dinner, but changed minds and hearts. "Going vegan," a.k.a. to stop eating animals and products derived from animals, doesn't mean missing out or feeling deprived. It means cupcakes, lasagne, wholesome weeknight dinners with family and meaningful, no-bullshit-no-standing-in-lines homemade brunch with friends.

The care and attention stirred into making great food can go beyond those who eat that meal. Make a vegan meal and in a small yet impactful way you opt out of the system that exploits animals, the ecosystem, and our health. Make a great vegan meal to share and show others that chocolate chip cookies or tacos can be vegan and taste awesome, too. I'm so proud that ten years of *Veganomicon* have helped light that way. Here's to ten or more years of kicking ass and cooking up the resistance.

Terry, Queens, May 2017

ISA'S INTRO

In the past ten years I've been (almost) all over the world. Sometimes packing up all the cats and straight-up moving, sometimes just exploring little vegan corners of the planet. I've lived in the vegan mecca of Portland, Oregon, where croissants and donuts cascaded out the doors of cruelty-free bakeries and vegan pizzas were flung high and proud in almost every pizzeria.

I dined at fancy French restaurants in actual France. Had the best Thai food ever in Melbourne. And stuffed my face on jerk tofu in the Caribbean.

And then, just to make life interesting, I relocated to Omaha Nebraska, where . . . not so much. But I lived there for six years, learning to garden (and drive), and watching as vegan awareness grew and grew. So much so that a new food hall had a few fabulous veggieful menu items at each turn, including homemade burgers, tofu bowls, and incredible slices of Sicilian pizza.

All of this makes it so interesting to revisit *Veganomicon* right now. Especially the introduction, which is just as true today as it was ten years ago. Vegan food is normal food. And its numbers are growing and growing. What does the future hold ten years from now, when Terry and I are all Grey Gardens and writing the twentieth-anniversary edition?

Keep cooking, keep innovating, keep making vegan food not only normal, but extraordinary. In ten years, let's hope that we are the standard and there are nonvegan options at the food hall for those people who just haven't caught up yet.

Isa, Brooklyn, May 2017

INTRODUCTION

◆

Veganomicon. What does it mean? Is it the economic
theory of eating tofu hot dogs? Maybe an all-meatless convention?
Or the book of the vegetable-undead?

No, no, it's none of those. It's the doorstop of a cookbook that you hold in your precious hands with over 250 recipes that since 2007 really have become some of the most requested recipes by both vegans and nonvegans alike. It's been around just long enough that we've met full-grown adult plant eaters who tell us this was the book that taught them how to make vegan meals in high school, creating a whole generation of then vegan-curious teens who are now vegan-forward grown-ups. We're like the J. K. Rowlings of vegan cookbook authors: just substitute the mountains of money with piles of chickpeas, and that's us. But even back then we knew a big vegan cookbook needed a big vegan name (to be safe, don't read this cookbook backward at the stroke of midnight), and teaching the world to say "vee-gahn-NOM-ikon" has been almost as fun as instructing the masses on how to unlock the secrets of great homemade vegan food in their own kitchen.

This is the book that was the proverbial flax egg before the unchicken and it set the stage for cookbooks from Isa and Terry for years to come. While we've both gone on to write dessert books together and our own separate books focused on brunch, veganized Latino food, salad, and weeknight meals, people are always excited to talk about this one.

The *Veganomicon* is a big, bold vegan cookbook that doesn't hold back any punches. But don't be scared; she's still quite a softy. She's like a love song ('80s power ballad, with some light '70s rock and a touch of postpunk angst) to our favorite things about vegan cooking—its diverse, delicious flavors and limitless possibilities.

But enough with the pop-culture references; what the heck is it, really? Well, it's a good old-fashioned, all-purpose cookbook. And when we say "all-purpose" we mean it. You'll soon master the art of homemade seitan, unlock the mysteries of tofu, and know what the hell to do with tempeh. Savory sauces, tasty grains, and loads of vegetables will round out your vegan feast. Or if one-dish meals are what you're after, we'll take care of you with hearty casseroles, luscious pastas, nourishing soups, and filling full-meal salads jam packed with protein and rockin' textures . . . we mean business when it comes to stick-to-your ribs food.

Many of the recipes were written for everyday meals, in hopes that you won't even need to look at the recipe again after making it a few times. You know, the kind of chow you can whip up any night of the week with your pantry staples and some seasonal produce. But you can also trust this cookbook when you're looking for an extravagant spread to impress, say, your in-laws, your meat-lovin' grandma, or the mayor of your town when she stops by.

Besides giving you recipes, we've included lots of basic cooking information. Maybe you already know how to roast pumpkin, soak beans, and toast millet. In that case—awesome! (Then you can just be like, "Shut up, Isa and Terry!" and move on to an adventurous coconut Bundt cake or pasta enhanced with avocado.) But we also wrote this book with the beginner cook in mind, or maybe the forgetful cook who can't be bothered to memorize grain-to-water cooking ratios or the baking time for sweet potatoes. So, we've included preparation guides for beans, grains, and veggies (see pages 28–41).

RECIPES WE WISH WE GREW UP WITH

"How do you come up with a recipe?" is a question we get from time to time . . . why nobody believes us when we mutter things about sacrificing beets under the full moon, we'll never guess. Instead, be content in knowing that we are tireless and slightly obsessed foodies. There's not a vegetable we don't adore (except a certain so-called baby corn), nor a spice that doesn't take up precious real estate in our spice racks.

It helps that we call the greatest city in the world our home. New York City is a supermarket of almost every flavor of ethnic cuisine. We can't help but be inspired by it. It's what we're thinking about when munching on crispy yet soft scallion pancakes or tucking into a saucy eggplant rollatini, when digging into a sub sandwich bursting with tangy barbecued seitan or scooping up that last bit of hummus with freshly baked pita bread. We get flashes of inspiration after finally putting down that huge canvas bag on the kitchen floor; the one filled with gorgeous Brussels sprouts still on the stalk, creamy yellow ears of corn, or voluptuous butternut squash from the farmers' market, all grown within a few dozen miles of the city and lugged home for a few more on the subway.

During the course of developing recipes and writing *Veganomicon*, we kept coming back to this phrase: Recipes you wish you'd grown up with. These meals were not born in spotless, stainless-steel, made-for-TV kitchens. The recipes that await you in *Veganomicon* were created by two women who cook, live, and eat in real, urban kitchens. Since we're both apartment dwellers still to this day, these are lessons learned from waging wars with temperamental gas burners, moody old ovens passed down from apartment rental to rental, and tiny little cabinets bursting with pots, gadgets, and groceries. This is food made while chatting with significant others, gossiping with friends, and shooing nosy pets off the countertops. In other words, this is kind of food you make and eat while life happens.

LET THEM EAT TEMPEH

Fans of our no-budget, filmed in Isa's little red kitchen in Park Slope, early 2000s cooking show *The Post Punk Kitchen* and *Vegan with a Vengeance* were hungry, and they let us know. We learned not only did they want vegan good, but they were starved for both new ideas for preparing whole foods and for new takes on old favorites: tastier tofu scrambles, better bean burgers, the perfect cheeseless mac 'n' cheese, and for the green thumbs out there, what-in-the-world-do-I-do-with-all-this-zucchini?

We didn't make this cookbook alone. Well, by definition, we wrote it together so already we weren't alone. The results are our shared wisdom knitted from years of eating a bazillion meals and engaging in conversations about food with vegans—and aspiring vegans too—of all stripes. It taught us that no matter how long it's been since you've stopped eating hamburgers—be it eight months or eight years—the common question seemed to be, "What else is there for dinner/lunch/breakfast/midnight snack/Groundhog Day party?" besides tofu hot dogs or pasta and jarred sauce?

This book also owes a huge debt to our secret fleet of recipe testers scattered across the globe like poppy seeds on a bagel. Thanks to the miracle of the Internet, we've had the support of this tireless bunch of testing maniacs cooking and giving us feedback for many months during this book's development. Each recipe has been tested by several people, from new cooks to old hands, from teenagers, grad students with day jobs, stay-at-home dads to globe-trotting grandmothers. Their feedback and guidance informed this cookbook every step of the way.

VEGAN FOOD = NORMAL FOOD

And there is a larger reason why we wrote this book. Our mission in life is to prove that vegan food doesn't have to be repetitive, difficult, bland, or inaccessible. So, let us bore you for a few moments with our culinary philosophy.

There are some people who think that the way we eat is the way it always has been and the way it always will be. Yet to look at the history of food is to see that cuisines are in constant flux, traveling all over the world and taking root from one continent to the next. The foods that are currently available to us influence our entire culinary identity, and that identity is ever shifting. For example, we think of Italian food as loaded with tomato-y goodness, yet the tomato was not widely used in Italy until the eighteenth century, which in the grand scheme of things is a pizza throw away from present times. Just like that, our definition of what makes a complete, satisfying meal can forever change. In today's world, average folks are evolving and learning that dinner need not be defined by a big ol' chunk of meat surrounded by a few bits of overboiled vegetables.

The beauty of this culinary whippersnapper—vegan cuisine—is that it draws influences from every part of the world to create an entirely new way to eat. And we explore the dickens out of that in the *Veganomicon*: stuffing samosa filling into baked potatoes, throwing apples into green chile, tossing lemongrass into risotto. Tradition always starts somewhere, and we hope that something in these pages will inspire a few new seedlings of tradition to take root.

With love (once again) from Queens & Brooklyn,
Terry and Isa

ABOUT THE ICONS

⸺⸺⸺ ◆ ⸺⸺⸺

You might be wondering what all those cute little icons right at the beginning of each recipe mean. Behold, the mystery revealed! With just a flick of the eye muscle, you'll know whether a recipe is gluten-free, low-fat, or soy-free. You'll also know whether you can just shop at Giganto-Mart or need to make an additional stop at the Organic Natural Wonderland grocery before cooking dinner—plus an approximation of how long things will take once you've procured all your ingredients.

Soy-Free: Recipe doesn't contain tofu, tempeh, soy milk, soy sauce, or any other typically soy-derived product.

Gluten-Free: No wheat, vital wheat gluten, or other gluten-containing flours or grains, such as rye. All the major gluten offenders have been accounted for in these recipes, although we can't vouch for cross-contamination or ingredients that must say "gluten-free" to be truly celiac friendly (e.g., oatmeal). Several recipes marked gluten-free call for soy sauce; be sure to use tamari or gluten-free soy sauce.

Lower-Fat: Usually less than 2 tablespoons of oil in the entire recipe, so we figure it's got to be lower in fat overall.

Under 45 Minutes: We're experts at the two-hour recipe, but we know that you busy types want to know how long it will take you to do something. Of course, the 45 minutes doesn't include time spent yapping on the phone and running into the living room to watch some television. Many recipes with this icon take just 30 or even 15 minutes to prepare.

Supermarket-Friendly: A lot has changed in the decade since writing this cookbook, and now the nooch (slang for nutritional yeast and so much better sounding anyway) is located two steps away from the deodorant in many supermarket chains. But we kept this icon as an ode to the time when whole wheat pastry flour was not right next to the multipack of toilet paper and giant tin of cinnamon.

These days we don't need to make an additional trip to pick up very "vegan" ingredients at a natural foods store.

However, if you're still living in the '90s, this icon means *most* regular old grocery stores should do the trick. Our view on "supermarket friendly" might differ from yours, but to gauge this accurately we made sure that the supermarket closest to Isa's house in Omaha had all the items on the shelves. With that in mind, recipes featuring tofu and non-dairy milk are included in this icon, but agar and nutritional yeast, for example, are not.

STOCKING THE VEGANOMICON PANTRY

⸺⸺⸺ ◆ ⸺⸺⸺

For your shopping convenience, here's a list of ingredients that feature in these recipes. We call these "pantry" items, but really what we mean is that they are ingredients that we always keep on hand; that way, there is never "nothing to eat." This isn't a list of every ingredient in the book, just some of the ones we can't live without. You may already have a few, or a lot, of these pantry staples already stored away on your kitchen shelves and in your cabinets. If you encounter an ingredient that is new to you, take advantage of the opportunity and try out a recipe or two with this new ingredient. Who knows, you might find yourself wondering how you ever cooked anything without mirin, chickpea flour, or basmati rice!

CANNED GOODS

Beans: A whole dinner can start with just one can of beans. Keep a can or two of the following on hand, but don't limit yourself to: chickpeas, black beans, kidney beans, navy beans, cannellinis, black-eyed peas, and pintos.

Coconut milk, canned or shelf stable: Nothing beats the creaminess coconut gives to bisques and curries. *Nothing.* There are a lot of canned coconut milk options on the shelves right now, including reduced-fat or "lite" coconut milks that just include more coconut water and less of the good stuff, the coconut cream. We find that the consistently best-tasting one (and the best coconut milk for your money) is pure Thai full-fat coconut milk. Read those labels and avoid any coconut milk with added thickeners, gums, stabilizers, or sugar. One more important thing: Coconut milk should not be confused with the new coconut-based beverages that are similar to almond, rice, soy, etc. milk, and they are not interchangeable.

Pureed pumpkin: We use it in a few entrée-type dishes, but it's also great to have around for baked goods on the off chance that you're not in the mood for chocolate. Be sure that the only ingredient is pure solid-packed pumpkin and that the label doesn't say "pumpkin pie mix."

Tomatoes: Most often our recipes call for crushed tomatoes, but we also keep canned whole tomatoes and plain tomato sauce on hand. For tomato paste, we prefer the kind that comes in a tube. We usually just go for the cheapest brand we can find, unless we're cooking for company—then we buy those fire-roasted ones and deplete our hedge funds. (P.S. What's a hedge fund?)

FRIDGE STAPLES

What is a fridge but a climate-controlled cold pantry? Following are things that a vegan fridge can't be without. Some start out in the pantry but need to be refrigerated once opened.

Applesauce: Sure, it's a nice treat to just eat out of the jar with a spoon, but it's also a great ingredient for baked goods, especially for low-fat baking. If you don't like to collect half-eaten, moldy jars of applesauce in the fridge, we suggest keeping a pack of those little cups of applesauce for kids' lunch boxes with your baking supplies; they're the right portion for your average batch of muffins or pancakes.

Capers: The briny taste of caper berries is the secret ingredient in quite a few of our recipes. They're usually relegated to

a garnish in Mediterranean cuisine, but we branch out and use them blended up in dips and salads as well.

Dijon mustard: Sometimes the tangy bite of mustard is just what sauces, casseroles, and salad dressings need to make them complete. Sometimes it isn't. But for those times when it is, keep your fridge stocked with whole-grain Dijon mustard.

Jams and jellies: We use these to add yumminess to baked goods, either in the batter or as a spread or as a filling, as in the Jelly Donut Cupcakes (page 396). And you don't need us to tell you to eat PB&Js! What flavors do we consider staples? We have at least raspberry, strawberry, and apricot in our pantry at all times.

Miso: Everybody's favorite fermented Japanese paste. The standard kind you'll find in most American supermarkets is made from soybeans and rice, but there are dozens of other varieties out there—brown rice, chickpea, barley—all with their own unique properties and flavors ranging from sweet or winey to earthy or fruity. We often use miso the same way vegetable broth is used—to give soups, stews, and gravies an intriguing backdrop. The recipes in this book use either white (or sweet) miso, which is a blond sort of color and has a mild, slightly sweet flavor, or brown rice miso, which is rich and full bodied. Store miso in an airtight container.

Nondairy milk: Use whatever kind floats your boat, be it soy, rice, almond—even hazelnut, and more recently coconut-based milk beverages. As long as it's not an overly sweetened or flavored milk, you can use any of these milks interchangeably in all recipes.

Tempeh: A fermented soybean patty or cake. Often made with other grains and beans folded in for more flavor, textures, and nutrition, too. Doesn't sound all that appealing, now does it? But, trust us, when treated right—and the *Veganomicon* will make sure that you do treat it right—tempeh is a succulent and welcome addition to your diet. Isa's mom swears by it.

Tofu: Some people like to pronounce it toFU, we think in an effort to make it sound bad. Well, nice try, haters, tofu is here to stay! For *Veganomicon* purposes we suggest keeping on hand a block or two of refrigerated water packed (a.k.a. Chinese style) firm and extra-firm tofu for savory recipes, and a few packs of shelf-stable silken (Japanese style) firm and soft tofu for desserts.

Vegan mayo: If you are not using our recipe for mayo (page 123) and just want to grab something off the shelf, Isa suggests that Veganaise is the absolute best vegan mayonnaise you can buy. Both homemade and store-bought brands are naturals for some salads and dressings, and of course, for sandwiches. Terry, however, enjoys many of the new and exciting vegan mayo developments since 2007, including Just Mayo and the chickpea water–based miracle that is Fabanaise; try out all the new vegan mayos and pick your favorite for making recipes in this book. We live in interesting times where the cutting edge of vegan food is in mayonnaise technology; who would have imagined such a thing?

Vegan yogurt: Just like mayonnaise, vegan yogurt is experiencing its own revolution. As of this writing, soy yogurt has fallen out of fashion while coconut-, cashew- (cashewgurt is now a word!), and almond-based yogurts are all the rage. For the purposes of this book, seek out plain and preferably unsweetened vegan yogurts to use in recipes. As different yogurts have different formulas, you may have to experiment with a few brands to find the right yogurt for the right job.

HERBS & SPICES

Loosely defined for culinary purposes, an herb is the leaves of a plant (as in thyme or dill) and a spice is anything that isn't the leaf, such as the root (ginger), fruit (chile), seeds (cumin), berry (allspice), or bark (cinnamon) of a plant.

The spice rack is the heart of the vegan kitchen, and getting to know your herbs and spices is a fun and magical journey. It's smart and easy to let regional cooking be the first steps in this adventure. You probably already know that Italian cooking relies on the flavors of thyme, oregano, and rosemary, whereas Mexican cooking often uses cumin, coriander, and chile. As you familiarize yourself with the tastes and aromas of your collection, you can begin to branch out and try combinations that, while probably not unknown to man, might be unknown to you.

The recipes in this cookbook don't shy away from herbs and spices, and we hope that as you cook from it, your spice rack will become as overflowing and varied as ours are. To that end, don't worry just because you see coriander seed on a recipe list and don't happen to have any. Either try the recipe without it and get some seeds for next time, or flip to a recipe that you do have all the ingredients for and build your arsenal as you go along. Instead of obtaining your spices in expensive glass jars from the grocery store, find a source for bulk herbs and spices, which are often cheaper than prepackaged spices. Indian, Middle Eastern, or Chinese markets are great for this, and often health food stores have a nice bulk selection. If all else fails, you can order online from many sources, including Penzey's (www.penzeys.com).

Here is a good list to get you through most *Veganomicon* recipes. Those marked with an asterisk are what we consider essentials and should be the first items you obtain. With the exception of basil, whose strength and taste are hugely different in fresh and dried forms, fresh herbs can be used interchangeably with dried in most any recipe.

The basic guide to go by is 1 teaspoon of dried herb/spice = 1 tablespoon of finely chopped fresh herb/spice, but taste as you go to make sure the flavoring does not overpower the recipe. For best results and flavor, use purchased ground herbs/spices within a year or by the expiration date. Please throw out that five-year-old, beat-up can of ground black pepper! The flavor just won't be there anymore.

Dried Herbs

Basil	Oregano*
Dill	Rosemary
Marjoram	Tarragon*
Mint	Thyme*

Spices, Ground or Whole

Caraway seeds	Mustard, ground/mustard powder
Cardamom pods	
Cayenne pepper, ground*	Mustard, black, brown, or white, whole seeds
Celery seeds, whole	Nutmeg, whole
Cinnamon, ground* and sticks	Paprika (Hungarian if you can find it)
Cloves, ground and whole	Red pepper flakes
Coriander, whole seeds	Black pepper, whole* (grind in a pepper grinder)
Cumin, ground* and whole seeds	White pepper, ground
Curry powder (we like to have a variety)*	Saffron (expensive, worth it, and a few strands go a long way)
Fennel seeds, whole*	
Garam masala	

BAKING BASICS

Always having the right sugars, extracts, and powders handy means that fresh muffins and cookies are just a few mixing bowls away.

Agar powder/flakes: A magical seaweed that, when boiled in a liquid, forms a kick-ass vegan alternative to gelatin. We feel like we're forever talking about the wonders of agar, but that's a small price to pay for the world to know what they're missing. Fun fact: agar "gelatin" can firm up at room temperature, unlike that stuff made from animal bones (but it will cool faster if refrigerated). Purchase agar in either powdered or flake form.

The powder is by far the easiest form to use and considerably more concentrated than the flakes, so if you're new to agar, please use powdered for an easier, happier life. If you must use flakes, they will need to soak in the liquid they will be melted in for about 10 minutes before heating. Agar can be found in well-stocked health food stores or Asian groceries. Roughly 1 teaspoon (or slightly less) of agar powder is equivalent to 1 tablespoon of agar flakes.

Agave nectar: Agave is the majestic cactus used to make tequila of all stripes in Mexico. And it just happens that the sap (before distilling) is a tasty, syrupy stuff that's sweeter than sugar and entirely agreeable in dressings, drinks, desserts, and baked goods. Not to make any revolutionary health claims, but it seems that some people with certain sugar intolerances can handle agave nectar with ease. More and more regular supermarkets are carrying agave these days, but if yours doesn't, try a health food store.

Baking powder and baking soda: The wonder twins of chemical leaveners that are the key to success with vegan baked goods. Baking soda (sodium bicarbonate) is an alkali ingredient that releases leavening carbon dioxide when it is combined with moisture. Baking powder is baking soda plus an acid salt (such as cream of tartar). When double-acting baking powder is combined with an acidic ingredient (such as vinegar or lemon juice), you get the chemical reaction that makes your cakes and muffins rise, first when wet meets dry and again when the batter goes into the oven. Are you still awake? Have fresh boxes in your pantry at all times.

Extracts: Vanilla extract, the Cadillac of extracts, is one you'll most often be using. So, it's worth spending a little extra to get the real stuff—stay away from anything labeled "artificial" or "vanillin." It's hard to imagine any baked good without a hint of vanilla; it pulls all the ingredients together and provides that bakery-fresh aroma. If you love to bake, it's recommended that you pad your baking supplies with a few extra extracts. Others we use in this book include almond, anise, hazelnut, and coconut, but it never hurts to add other extracts to your collection, such as lemon, mint, or raspberry.

Liqueurs: Back to the booze again! Liqueurs have been used to flavor all kinds of food for centuries, but we mostly use them when baking. Hazelnut and coffee liqueur are our hands-down favorites, the ones we use most often in our dessert recipes. Unless you live in a state where it's legal to sell hard alcohol in the supermarket, you'll find flavored liqueurs at the liquor store.

Maple syrup: Isa calls this "the taste of freedom" because she spends too much time in Vermont. Pure maple syrup can be expensive so we use it sparingly, not just for baking but to give a hint of sweetness wherever needed. But it isn't just for the elite. Budget-minded people like us are never fooled into buying a little expensive bottle of the "grade A" stuff. "Grade B" syrup, a little darker in color but just as flavorful, works just as fine for you, me, and true democracy. Don't forget to refrigerate after opening.

SUGARS

Yes, we're guilty of using sugar. While we love whole wheat, sugar-free raisin bran muffins as much as the next guy, we also know that life often requires fluffy cupcakes, chocolate chip cookies, and pumpkin crumble pie. Adding sugar is also much cheaper than baking with maple syrup or agave all the time, not to mention far more predictable when it comes to getting the results you want with baked goods. Happily, lots of organic, vegan-friendly sugar options are easily obtainable these days:

Brown sugar: Also called muscovado sugar when it is raw and unrefined, typical brown sugar is refined sugar with a little bit of the molasses left in or added back to it. Opt for organic.

Confectioners' sugar: A combination of finely ground sugar and cornstarch, also called powdered sugar. We use confectioners' sugar to create glazes and frostings.

Granulated sugar: When we call for "organic sugar," we always mean granulated. We use interchangeably evaporated cane juice or organic evaporated cane juice, such as Florida Crystals, or brands that specifically say "beet sugar" on the packaging. "Cane sugar" is typically made with the use of animal products in the form of bone char in the processing, so some vegans avoid it.

Turbinado sugar: A coarse, unrefined, steam-cleansed sugar that has bigger crystals (for example, Sugar in the Raw). We use turbinado wherever a little crunch is desired. You can also use it in place of regular sugar, but results may vary.

All-purpose flour: You should always have a sack of unbleached all-purpose flour the size of a small child around. Even if the cupboard is bare, you'll be able to whip up some pancakes or muffins. Even though we mostly use flour for baking, we've also been known to use it to thicken sauces and make tempura.

Arrowroot powder: This fine white powder—ground from the roots of a tropical vine—is ideal for thickening sauces and soups, particularly if a clear, nonopaque appearance is desired. Arrowroot also helps bind and provides a crisp texture in baked goods.

Chickpea flour: A pale yellow flour, sometimes called garbanzo flour, made from ground chickpeas. Look for it in most health food stores and Indian grocery markets (where it is called gram flour or besan). Imparts a sweet, nutty, beany (some might even call it "eggy") flavor to baked goods and sauces. It's especially good for crepes and flatbreads.

Cornmeal: We use it in some recipes to add a little crunch, particularly to baked goods. And having some around in case of a corn bread emergency is not a bad idea.

Cornstarch: Also used to thicken, at half the price of other starches. Plus, it adds crispiness and structure to baked goods.

Tapioca flour: Our starch of choice for thickening custards and fruit pies, available at health food stores. This is a fine powder; do not use granular or pearl tapioca as a substitute.

Whole wheat pastry flour: Whole wheat pastry flour (not to be confused with ordinary whole wheat flour) is just as finely milled as white flour, but not all of the bran and germ has been processed out of it, making it a healthier, more fiberific choice. It is difficult to detect a *very* significant difference between whole pastry and regular old all-purpose flours, but whole wheat pastry flour can make baked goods a bit denser and healthier tasting, so we often do an equal mix with all-purpose.

Vital wheat gluten: The naturally occurring protein in wheat that makes it all happen; it's what gives wheat dough its characteristic stretch and makes seitan (sometimes called wheat meat) so toothsome. We also use it in combination with beans in several recipes to give a chewier, meaty texture. Look for organic brands at your health food store, usually in the baking section. We recommend Arrowhead Mills brand above others if you have a choice.

Canola oil: Short for "Canada oil" and formerly known as "rapeseed oil," this oil is now politically correctly named, available most everywhere, and a fine choice for multipurpose use. Mild in flavor, it's perfect for baking and cooking when a neutral-tasting oil is desired. Look for "high-heat" canola oil for use in sautéing and grilling. Canola oil also provides you with a healthy dose of essential omega-3 fatty acids.

Coconut oil, refined/unrefined: Poor coconut oil has been typecast in the role of a nutritional bad guy for too long. Non-hydrogenated coconut oil is perfectly healthy consumed in small amounts. For curries and coconutty baked goods we like unrefined oil for its luscious coconut aroma and delicate flavor. It's a favorite of ours when cooking Indian- and Southeast Asian–inspired cuisine. For times when we want less coconut flavor, such as in simple piecrusts, but all the buttery richness, we reach for refined coconut oil, so keep a jar of both in the pantry!

Grapeseed oil: A light, nearly colorless oil made from pressed grape seeds. We love it in salad dressing because it has the thickness and body of olive oil, but a neutral taste. While it isn't an essential thing to have, it should be the first item you purchase once you've decided to broaden your oil horizons. It's a bit pricier than canola oil but not as expensive as olive oil, and it's available in most health food stores and, increasingly, in regular old supermarkets.

Olive oil: There's a reason people have been cultivating this stuff for thousands of years. Olive oil is so good for you, plus its rich, earthy, and fruity flavor is essential in cooking all things Mediterranean and Middle Eastern. We use extra-virgin for almost everything, but the purist might want to use

WHAT IS A FATTY ACID AND WHY IS IT ESSENTIAL?

Without getting into words that we cannot pronounce, our body needs fats, not only to store energy but to absorb vitamins and protect our vital organs from disease (unless you don't consider your brain a vital organ). We naturally produce some of the necessary fats, but others need to be obtained from our diet. The very base of our existence, our cells, are largely composed of such fatty acids, making these, well, essential!

cheaper virgin or blended oils for frying (even though people have been shallow-frying in good olive oils for as long as it's been made, it can be used for longer or deeper frying. The key is to use low to medium heat, never, ever high heat!).

Peanut oil: Another stock oil in our pantries, peanut oil is a must when cooking many things Asian, as it's often that little touch of authentic flavor that is missing from homemade stir-fries and curries. Its high smoke point also makes it perfect for frying.

Toasted sesame oil: Unlike other oils, toasted sesame oil is not for frying or cooking but instead adds a yummy and fragrant roasted sesame taste to finished dishes and salad dressings.

PANTRY SUNDRIES

Why say "other stuff" when you could say "sundries"?

Dried beans: It's worth making a pot of beans every now and then; we keep on hand the usual suspects that are also listed in the canned section. They're incredibly economical and the flavor is superior to the canned stuff. It's helpful to buy them in bulk and store them in one-pound increments for quick and easy measuring and cooking. Quick-cooking beans, such as lentils and split peas, are an absolute, economical must for soups during those cold winter months when you're saving up all your money to buy a sled or pay for your health insurance. (For information on specific beans, see our bean-cooking section, page 40.)

Grains: Ditch that dusty old box of instant rice! We keep a variety of whole grains in airtight jars in our cupboards, and use them in lots and lots of *Veganomicon* recipes. (See page 37 for how to cook some of our favorites.)

Nutritional yeast: Not to be confused with brewer's yeast or any other kind of yeast, "nooch" (as we call it) is great to add an umami (savory) taste to sauces or just to sprinkle on rice and beans. We don't use it in too many *Veganomicon* recipes because it's hard to find and people tend to love it or hate it. Most commonly, this mustard-colored yeast comes in flake form, and that is what we call for in our recipes. But sometimes you'll find it in powdered form, which is just ground-up flakes. If you can only find the powdered kind, reduce every ¼ cup called for by a tablespoon.

Nuts: Always have slivered or sliced almonds and walnuts on hand for pesto and to create texture in casseroles and sauces. Nuts are also great toasted in salads, breaded on tofu, and of course for all kinds of baked goods and desserts. If you are going to be storing them like a human squirrel for months and months, keep them in the freezer. Other nuts we like to have around: cashews, hazelnuts, pecans, peanuts (which are actually a legume), and pine nuts.

Seeds: Any seed that goes on a bagel should also have a place in your pantry. Toasted sesame and black sesame seeds go a long way toward providing flavor to our dishes, as well as adding drama to the presentation. Pumpkin seeds are a favorite, too, loaded with good-for-you zinc and great tasting in pestos and in salads. We also keep flaxseeds in the refrigerator, either in ground or whole form, for baking and sometimes for sprinkling onto our oatmeal.

Pastas: Keep around a few boxes of pasta of all shapes and sizes. We don't need to remind you what it's good for! (See our pasta section, page 287, for different types that we like.)

WINES & VINEGARS

A snotty person once said that you shouldn't cook with any wine you wouldn't drink. We say "Pfft!" The wines you'll find in any supermarket marked simply "cooking wine" are just fine. But whether you use the cheap stuff or a $60 Australian Riesling splurge, a shot or two of wine can elevate that sauté from just homemade to near restaurant quality. There's really nothing like wine when it comes to drawing out the flavors of seared and sautéed vegetables (particularly mushrooms), herbs, and oils. We use white wine most of the time, but red and sherry are good choices to have around, too. For the straight-edgers out there, we don't mean to alienate you. Nonalcoholic wine (and beer) or vegetable broth can be substituted in these recipes. Although deglazing a pan (page 27) just isn't the same without it, it can be done. Also included here are a few vinegars that we use often.

Cooking wine, red and white: Like we say, cooking wine doesn't have to be anything fancy, even that box o' wine that shows up at ironic trailer-trash parties in the hip section of town will do. Just make sure it is dry, which just means not sweet. A bottle of cooking sherry will also take you places and adds that particular sweet, mellow flavor some recipes just call out for.

Mirin: A Japanese rice cooking wine. It has a thick, almost syrupy texture. A little goes a long way in adding a deep, complex flavor and aroma to stir-fries, soups, stews, and marinades. It's a little pricier than most fruit-based cooking wines, but nothing quite tastes like it. We recommend steering clear of any mirin with added sugar, salt, or other flavorings.

Apple cider vinegar: We use apple cider vinegar in our baked goods because of its mellow taste and acidity. Apple cider vinegar not only reacts with baking soda to help things to rise, it also makes our baked goods tender.

Balsamic vinegar: We don't douse our foods in it, but the deep, winelike taste of balsamic vinegar works wonders in marinades or to pull together a bowl of soup.

Brown rice vinegar: A very mild vinegar that's great in Asian food and nice to know in salad dressings.

Wine vinegar: Red wine, white wine, or champagne, your go-to vinegar for adding tangy zing to savory foods and sauces.

KITCHEN EQUIPMENT

◆

All you really need to cook is a knife, a pot, and a big spoon. But this is the twenty-first century, after all, and we're often taken in by shiny new things, so we have way more equipment stuffed into our tiny kitchen than it can possibly handle. Rather than regale you with stories about how our lives have been changed by our two-chamber automatic ice-cream maker, we've compiled a little info about the basic tools we use every day. Gadgets are great fun, but our mango slicer mostly collects dust. We're beginning to think it might be useless.

Here's some consumer wisdom we've had drilled into our head: if you can't afford to buy a quality, well-made kitchen tool, you may be better off without it. Sure, you can buy a peeler at the everything-for-a-dollar store, but will it take the skin off a butternut squash? No. Better to save up the $8.95 you'll need for that sturdy all-purpose one the kitchen store sells. It'll last forever. The same goes for pots and pans and knives and mixers and whatever else. A caveat, though: more expensive does not necessarily mean better! Since this is the technological age, weed through consumer reviews on such shopping sites as Amazon.com to see which ones are best.

CHOPPING & PREP TOOLS

Because having a stove is great if you intend to cook something, but unless you plan on living on whole boiled potatoes, you're going to need just a few prep tools.

Knives: We know it's been said many times, many ways, but the only knife you need is a good chef's knife. Period. If you're still chopping vegetables with a sad little steak knife you borrowed from your mom's cutlery tray, stop it this second and go out and buy a real knife. A good knife has a solid feel, comfortable grip, and can be sharpened when it gets dull. Dull knives are dangerous! They slip off tomato skins and cut your finger. Buy the best knife you can afford; decent knives can be purchased for under $30 at discount stores, but if you've had a sudden windfall of cashola, it doesn't hurt to, as we said in 2007, drop a Benjamin on a really spiffy one.

Now that you have a good knife, you'd better learn how to use it. You could take some classes or watch a few hundred hours of *YouTube videos*. Let the knife do the work—it wants to!

Besides the chef's knife, we only really bother with a serrated-bladed bread knife and a little, sharp paring knife. The bread knife is great for slicing bread, of course, but it's also a miracle worker for slicing very soft tomatoes and sushi nori rolls. The little paring knife can come in handy for reckoning with sprouting potatoes or making radish roses, if for some reason you go insane and need to make those. You can go with slightly lesser quality when it comes to purchasing these guys.

Cutting board: We don't want to hear about you chopping on dinner plates or directly on the countertop. Any official cutting board will do . . . oh, except those glass ones; no one wants to hear a knife "clink" on glass; what a bad idea. We prefer wood over plastic ourselves, especially for Instagram purposes, and particularly fancy those new bamboo cutting boards. They're *très chic*, tougher than Thelma and Louise, and totally renewable (since that bamboo grows like a weed).

Vegetable peelers: The truly sadomasochistic chef (or Isa's grandma) loves to peel vegetables with a paring knife. Even our copy editor says she does it with those two-for-one dollar knives she's had for eons. For everyone else, there are a plethora of peelers to choose from. We're partial to the Y-shaped rather than the old-fashioned straight variety, but do what makes you happy. Get the sharpest, sturdiest one you can, with a large, comfortable handle. If you are only going to purchase one, make it the serrated kind. If you skipped the opening paragraph we'll say it again: it's a good idea to spend just a little extra on these, since nothing sucks more than a dull vegetable peeler (with a teeny, miserable handle) when you've got 8 pounds of apples to skin.

Food processor: Wonder of wonders, miracle of miracles! Saver of time, conservator of energy! So easy! So convenient!

How did I ever survive without you? Every well-equipped kitchen has a food processor in it. You can't live without one, right? Sort of. You *can* do without, but when you are staring at the latkes recipe with a tear in your eye, wondering how in the world you will fit shredding 5 pounds of potatoes into your busy day of video games and knitting circles, you need to get yourself a food processor. If you can't afford one right now, then get married simply so you can put this on your wedding registry.

Not only will the proper attachments shred and slice everything for you, but nothing can really replace a food processor in the kitchen when it comes to transforming tofu, vegetables, beans, and so on into smooth and silky purees. The quality is rather flexible when it comes to choosing a food processor, so go for whatever fits in your budget and literally fits on your countertop. Those combination blender/food processor gadgets are kinda small but work great.

Blender: Speaking of blenders, it's not absolutely necessary to have a standing one for the recipes in this book, but it's pretty awesome for the occasional peanut butter banana smoothie or to puree soups and sauces.

High-speed blender: Ten years ago we never could have imagined suggesting that you need a $400 blender. And we still wouldn't say "need." In fact, none of the recipes in this cookbook requires one. BUT. Wouldn't it be nice if you could get smooth and creamy cashew cream in thirty seconds? So, you know, put it on your registry. Or max out your credit card. When you feel your life is on the right path, all your student loans are paid off, and maybe you *don't* need that weekend AirBnB cabin by the lake, then a high-speed blender, such as Vitamix or Blendtec, might be for you.

Immersion blender: Sure, we just said that a blender is not a necessity here. BUT, this handheld version of that old standby is worth every penny, which is not a lot of pennies since they're surprisingly inexpensive. Often in this book we give you two choices: you can wait for your stew or soup or whatever to cool a bit and then puree half of it in a blender or food processor, then add it back to the pot, or the much-more-appealing second choice—simply whip out your immersion blender and puree. If you want to dabble even further in immersion blender magic, look for ones that come with a selection of attachments for whisking and grinding spices or coffee.

Box graters and Microplane graters: Box graters are a kitchen staple that attack carrots, celery, and jicama with ease. We suppose that you could also grate vegetables with

A FEW BASIC KNIFE SKILLS

The more you chop, dice, and slice, the better your knife skills will get. It helps to know the correct way to hold a knife, but really practice and intuition are what make almost perfect. We say "almost perfect" because the skills are constantly evolving and we're always figuring out new stuff and what works for us. That said, it doesn't hurt to have a little practical guidance, and since minced garlic and diced onions are included in most all of our recipes, here are a few tips for getting them prepped quickly while keeping your fingers intact.

Garlic

Wet your hands and your knife before beginning. That will keep the garlic from sticking to your fingers and the knife. Break off a few cloves and lay your knife blade squarely over a clove. Use the palm of your hand to give the clove a whack. That should crush the clove and loosen the skin. The papery skin should slip off easily once it's been whacked. Discard the skins and continue smashing as many cloves as you need.

Once you have skinned all the cloves, bunch them up on the cutting board. The quickest and easiest way to mince is to use a seesaw rocking motion. Use your writing hand to grasp the blade and use your other hand to rest on top of the blade to provide balance. Rock the knife back and forth steadily, stopping once in a while to bunch all the garlic up again, because it will spread out as you are mincing. When you have this method perfected, you should be able to mince a whole bulb of garlic in two or three minutes.

Onions

First, slice off the top and bottom of the onion. Then, slice the onion in half lengthwise. Now the skin should come off easily. Once the skin is removed, place the onion cut side down. With your fingers safely curled in, grasp the onion at the bottom to hold it in place. Slice the onion widthwise, trying to keep the slices intact. Then turn the onion and slice lengthwise.

Isa swears that if she breathes through her mouth, she never cries from cutting up onions. Try it for yourself and see if she's lying and crazy or not.

that food processor, but it seems more work than necessary to clean it if you're grating just one carrot to toss into a salad. The zester on those things is mostly useless, though, which is why we recommend you get yourself a Microplane grater. Then finely shredded mounds of citrus zest and freshly grated nutmeg shall be yours!

Mandoline: Just a note about these—mandolines are ominous-sounding, human-powered contraptions that can transform a pile of carrots or pound of potatoes into slender, completely uniform shreds in mere minutes. They are also the kind of medieval instrument one might encounter should one have the terrifying experience of going to a Renaissance fair. With a mandoline it's possible to quickly grate, slice, shred, sliver (and julienne!) any firm vegetable or fruit into a plethora of perfect shapes that would take you hours of tedious work with a knife. Handle with care please and always use the provided vegetable gripper tool because mandolines are armed with a deadly serious blade that does all that work for you. Absolutely not necessary for cooking, but something to consider should you want to live off of hash browns and shredded salads.

Tofu press: How serious are you about tofu? Enough to know you like to eat it often? Well, year after year, week after week, day after and so forth of pressing tofu with cutting boards and bricks and bean cans and endless towels inspired us (or at least Terry) to buy a tofu press. There are a few options to choose from but choose any and the investment is worth it if you like firm tofu that drinks up marinades for better frying, roasting, and other dishes where soggy tofu is not wanted. Browse online for a design and price that works for you and say good-bye to heaps of wet towels and countertops covered in tofu water forever.

Enough prep work. It's time to move on to the fun stuff.

POTS & PANS & OTHER FOOD COOKING VEHICLES

When we were starving artists we cooked with a found rusty wok and ate off of upside-down Frisbees. Times have changed.

Skillets: A.k.a. sauté pans, a.k.a. frying pans. We're big fans of good old cast iron for skillet cooking, not to mention that cast iron has the added benefit of being able to be popped into the oven for additional browning, making a potpie or the best corn bread you'll ever eat. A 10- or 12-inch cast-iron skillet is all you really need, and while cast-iron pans require a little more care (no tossing in the dishwasher), preseasoned pans (brands such as Lodge) are inexpensive, ready to use, and will pay for themselves in a few batches of scrambled tofu or cornbread.

Cast-iron pans are the best but you might want something lighter around, too. It's hard to beat stainless-steel pans for bombproof functionality; no matter what you burn in 'em, you can get it off with a little elbow grease, and none the worse for wear (except possibly your elbow).

While a bit controversial (due to the nasty chemicals used to make their surface nonstick), nonstick pans are handy for their nonstickiness. If you must use one, choose a high-quality pan made with the new "eco" or "ceramic" coatings with a very smooth, nearly shiny surface. These will cost more than the old-school cheap and dented college dorm–style Teflon skillet. No metal should ever touch any kind of nonstick pan, so while you're shopping, get a few good-quality silicone or wooden utensils to use with it. If you do scratch old-fashioned Teflon or another nonstick coated pan, it's rendered useless, and if you get it too hot (like 500°F hot, which is really easy to do if you're forgetful), it gives off fumes extremely toxic to your parakeet and your canary and probably rather awful for you. And extra toxic fumes suck, even when you breathe them every day living in New York City. So, why do you still have nonstick pans?

The Great Big Soup Pot: The name says it all. Look for a large 6- to 8-quart pot that's preferably stainless steel with a good stout bottom. Accessories (e.g., a steamer basket) are nice. The Great Big Pot and a skillet are the bare essentials, but if you've got the scratch (and space) you'll find that it's great to have a . . .

Cast-iron grill pan: For grilling! Nothing can beat it. Unless you have a Weber in your kitchen, which is a really bad idea. So, go get a grill pan; they're cheap! Since you're on a shopping spree, you might as well get a . . .

Crepe pan: But only if you're going to make crepes. And you will make crepes (you just don't know it yet). See page 95 about our recommendations, but in general, stick to steel or cast-iron varieties. Run away from any goofy, infomercial-style gadgets that expect you to dip an electrical object into runny crepe batter.

Casserole dish: Is it for cooking? Is it for serving? You can have it both ways! You can use a cast-iron skillet instead if it's all you got, but you'll love having a deep, enameled, cast-iron casserole dish that you can sauté your ingredients in first, top with some dough, and then shove into the oven to finish. Yeah, you can casserole your heart out with a glass or (gasp!) metal one, but the cast-iron ones are really fun to use and look pretty, too. Also good for lasagne!

The spray bottle: Our good friend the spray bottle of oil can help you use less oil when cooking, so he makes a few cameo appearances throughout recipes in the book. We're not talking about that aerosol stuff that you buy in the supermarket, but an actual bottle that you fill with the oil of your choice. You can buy the pump kind, such as a Misto, where you have to pump the top with air (kind of like how a Super Soaker works), but you can also just buy a plastic spray bottle, usually available in housewares stores in the gardening section.

More pots and pans! Okay, we lied in our introductory paragraph. You can never have enough. If you're getting a food processor on the wedding registry plan, go ahead and throw a set of pots and pans on the list. Or just buy 'em when they go on sale. More is more! Lots of discount stores carry good-quality pots and dishes that will last you the rest of your life with little care. Get the heavy-bottomed variety—give 'em a knock on the bottom to make sure they're thick and solid. If they sound like a gong and feel thin, skip them. Light-bottomed pans will burn your onions and cook unevenly. We're big fans of pots that come with a few steamer baskets of assorted sizes.

BAKING TOOLS

You can resist that castle-shaped Bundt pan for as long as you like, but if you want cookies and cupcakes, you'll need a few essentials. Not that castle-shaped Bundt cakes aren't essential for all you Renaissance Fair enthusiasts.

Baking sheets: The classic, 11 x 17-inch, slightly rimmed jelly-roll pan will serve you well roasting just about any vegetable—just line the bottom with baking parchment or aluminum foil first, or you'll never get them clean again. You can also use

it for baking jelly rolls! Nonrimmed cookie sheets work for roasting, too, but you risk having the juices run off and burn to the bottom of your oven.

Baking tins: This is where you can go all freestyle with your bakeware collection. Large muffin tins, medium-size muffin tins, little bitty cutie muffin tins . . . go crazy! Hate muffins (and don't have a soul)? Then, don't get muffin tins. But maybe you fancy Bundt cakes, so go get the best Bundt cake pan you can afford. And don't forget a standard loaf pan, unless you want to live a monklike existence free of banana bread. In general, we don't care for silicone bakeware, but we understand if all those pretty colors lure you in.

We had to go and bring up baking, didn't we? Well, then you'll also need this stuff:

Mixing bowls: These are for more than just baking—you'll use them for everything. You might as well buy a set, since it's nigh-impossible to buy them separately, but you'll be happy you did. The stainless-steel ones are tops in our book, although plastic will do. Glass or ceramic ones are great as well, but your cat will knock them onto the floor and cause disaster, so only get them if you're allergic to cats.

Measuring cups and spoons: Psychic chefs can use the power of their mind to determine ½ cup of nutritional yeast or ¾ teaspoon of vanilla. For the rest of us, a sturdy metal or high-quality plastic or stainless-steel set of measuring cups and spoons will do. Bonus: a stainless-steel tablespoon makes a cool MacGyver-style melon baller.

Kitchen timer: In our carefree youth, we would put some cookies to bake in the oven, then go call a friend, play with the cat, take a nap, or do whatever people did before there was YouTube. Okay, maybe we're exaggerating about the nap, but the resulting charcoal cookies would make us take note that maybe getting a kitchen timer would be a good idea. Older and wiser, we've learned to relax a little and let the timer do all the work of reminding us to do something. Nothing fancy required, as long as you keep a plastic one away from the stove so it doesn't melt. If you happen to be a cheapskate with a cell phone, most cell phones have a timer feature.

Oven thermometer: How much do you trust your oven? Unless you have one of those fancy top-of-the-line superexpensive ovens (and even if you do), trust us, your oven is lying to you. Buy an oven thermometer; they're cheap and will save you burnt cookie heartache or the perils of soggy cakes with undercooked centers.

(Extra Credit) Wire cooling racks and parchment paper: A few wire racks for sliding on warm cookies, breads, and muffins will help your precious handy work avoid soggy bottoms in favor of firm bottoms. A roll of parchment paper (even better, one presliced into sheets) for lining baking sheets will save you the heartbreak of anything ever sticking to the bottom of a pan again.

STANDARD UTENSILS

Spatulas: Shop around for a thin, flexible, metal spatula that suits you. You'll use it for frying and sautéing in cast iron and aluminum, as well as for flipping pancakes and transferring cookies to cooling racks. A wooden (bamboo, preferably) spatula with an angled edge is great for stirring sauces and soups, and for sautéing in enamel or nonstick cookware.

Tongs: Tongs are great for flipping tofu on the grill, sautéing greens, mixing salads, and retrieving the olive oil cap that you dropped into the soup. Choose a sturdy pair of long-handled stainless-steel kitchen tongs (not the weird and dainty salad-lifting kind) and for cooking in pans with delicate surfaces a pair of silicon-tipped tongs.

Slotted spoon: It's the spoon that's not a spoon, because it doesn't hold anything! Maybe it sounds like the ultimate rip-off, but a slotted spoon is damn handy when fishing out ravioli from a boiling pot o' water.

Pasta spoon: That really creepy looking spoon-thing with teeth is a superhero when it comes to grabbing lumps of linguine or spools of spaghetti.

Ladles: Sometimes ladles make you feel like you're pouring out the finest French soup, sometimes they make you feel like you're in a soup kitchen. Either way, you need a ladle because that tablespoon isn't going to get that soup into the bowl anytime soon.

Fork and spoon: You may laugh, but this humble dynamic duo from the cutlery drawer will come to the rescue in your darkest hours. Forks make great mini whisks in a pinch (just don't use them for stirring anything in a nonstick pan), and spoons are experts at seeding squash and portioning out flours.

OTHER STUFF

Barely a day goes by where the salad spinner doesn't see some action. And that's not because we're eating salads every day; salad spinners are geniuses at washing leafy greens, herbs, mushrooms, berries, green beans, and any smallish, numerous fruit or vegetable. Not to mention it doubles as an extra colander and additional large bowl to hold annoyingly large vegetables and greens. Speaking of colanders, you need one. You should get a fine-mesh strainer, too, for straining stuff and sifting flour. A citrus reamer can squeeze the juice out of a lime much, much better than your hands ever will. A whisk is nice to have also. But the bottom line is that you will cook best with the equipment you are most comfortable with. Spend as much time as you need in the housewares aisle, handling your future equipment and seeing what feels best to you. If you prefer one handle to another, don't discount this as something trivial. And if you have a hand-me-down skillet from your best friend's mother, and love cooking with it, well then, keep it and cook on.

COOKING & PREPPING TERMINOLOGY

"Sweating" mushrooms doesn't mean we're trying to make them admit some dark secret. It's just one of a few cooking terms we like to throw around here, because they're a lot easier than writing out things like "partially cover and allow to steam until tender." Here are a few terms to know that will have you cooking like a master chef (almost):

Bias: Often we say to slice something on a bias—say, carrots, for example. This means to cut diagonally instead of straight down or across. This is usually specified when the cut makes a big difference to the texture of the food, or in situations where it will be more aesthetically pleasing. This way, instead of people barely noticing that you sliced a carrot, they will gasp in admiration of your damn fine-looking carrots.

Blanch: A quick boil, when you don't want to cook your veggies all the way but just get them a bit softened up, usually because they will be cooked further somewhere down the line.

Blend: Stirring the contents of a bowl, pot, or pan to combine all of the ingredients. Usually done at a vigorous pace and sometimes done in a blender (obviously).

Braise: Briefly sautéing a piece, or pieces, of food to lightly sear or brown the outside. Then a small amount of liquid is poured over the hot food; often it's a seasoned vegetable broth or alcohol, but water works also. The food is then covered and allowed to steam just enough to make the food tender. An easy way to think about braising is a cross between sautéing and steaming.

Caramelize: To cook, usually over moderate heat for an extended period of time, until the sugars naturally present in the ingredients, or actual sugar, begins to brown.

Chop: Cutting things up any which way. Although most recipes will give you a general size to shoot for, when we say simply to chop something rather than *dice* or *julienne* or another more specific term, it usually means that it doesn't much matter what the shape is.

Deglaze: After your vegetables (usually garlic and onions) are cooked, adding liquid to the hot pan to lift up anything stuck to the bottom. This is a great way to make sure that all the food and flavors are incorporated into the entire dish, rather than turning into burnt bits and getting sacrificed to the bottom of your pan. Deglazing also makes a great sizzling noise that makes you feel like a real chef.

Dice: Chopping vegetables or other items into uniform cubes. When we say "uniform," we don't mean that you should whip out a tape measure; just aim to get them as alike as you can. Typically, dicing is done in rather small pieces, about ½ inch or less.

Fold: Gently stirring in a single ingredient into a larger mixture or batter, usually done by stirring the bottom batter over the added ingredient with a large spoon or spatula. The idea is not to overmix the main batter or mixture, rather to evenly incorporate the new ingredient without disturbing the overall texture.

Grate: Scraping food along the surface of a shredder or Microplane grater to yield fine shreds or particles of food.

Grill: Cooking marinated vegetables or proteins over a heated metal outdoor or indoor grill. The food is often turned several times to ensure it's completely cooked and the exterior lightly caramelized.

Julienne: We will take our carrots in matchstick form, thank you. We rarely julienne anything else, except for a cucumber here or there for a sushi nori roll.

Mince: Using a knife, chopping vegetables or herbs into very small particles, around ⅛ inch across or even smaller.

Process: Basically our lazy way of saying use a food processor or blender to puree something.

Puree: Blending the heck of out something in a food processor or blender.

Reduce: Simmering a sauce or soup on a stovetop until some of the water has evaporated. Usually done with the pot uncovered or partially covered. Reducing will eliminate some of the total volume of the sauce and help intensify the flavors.

Roast: Baking food in an oven until the exterior has browned or caramelized and the interior is fully cooked. When roasting vegetables and protein foods, it's often necessary to rub the exterior with an oil to prevent its drying out entirely.

Rough chop: When you don't care how the ingredients look that much, you just want to chop 'em up quickly. For instance, an onion that's just going to end up pureed or herbs that are going to be pesto anyway.

Roux: A cooked paste of flour and oil. When a roux is carefully cooked and stirred, it begins to brown, forming a tantalizing, full-flavored base for soups and stews. In addition to providing flavor to these dishes, it also is an effective thickening agent.

Sauté: Frying food in a skillet or pot, while stirring occasionally, with the addition of a fat.

Sear: To cook at high heat for a short period of time so that the outside of a food gets browned but the inside doesn't cook as much.

Slurry: A mixture of liquid and starch (usually flour, cornstarch, arrowroot powder, or tapioca starch) that's used to thicken soups and stews. The reason for making a slurry is that you can't add starch to hot things directly or it will clump up. Once the starch has been broken down in the water, it thickens a dish nice and evenly. We use this method a lot, so figured we might as well let you know the proper culinary term.

Sweat: In a heated skillet, partially covering a sautéed food and letting it steam in either its own juices or added liquid until tender.

Whisk: Quickly stirring a liquid ingredient, or combination of ingredients, to mix and lightly beat in a little air. Usually done with a whisk, but often a dinner fork will do just as nicely.

HOW TO COOK A VEGETABLE

(or, the art and science of transforming edible roots, shoots, leaves, and fruits of an array of plants with critically applied heat, oils, and seasonings so that they will be eaten with great pleasure)

---------- ◆ ----------

Dear Veganomicon,

I don't know where to begin. I've been eschewing meat and dairy products for years but I can't bring myself to eat vegetables. They are often so bland and flavorless I presume that if I ate my napkin I might acquire the same amount of fiber, without the "ick" factor of having to eat something green. But I have heard that there are some advantages to eating these things that grow in the dirt. Whatever should I do?

Yours truly,
Cautious of Carrots

Okay, we've never received a letter like that, now or ten years ago when we first imagined what a resentful but dutiful vegetable eater would confess to us if they could. Everything has changed regarding how vegan and nonvegan chefs and eaters think about vegetables. "Vegetable forward" they sometimes call it: chefs in star-bedazzled restaurants serving up cauliflower as steaks or everyday home cooks putting kale in smoothies, roasting carrots like sausages, or sneaking parsnips into desserts. It's official: people like vegetables!

However, we know that they are *still* out there, reckless vegans and would-be vegans who are pulling the green and orange blocks out of the bottom of the food pyramid and replacing them with things fried, sugary, and bready. We don't blame them. We blame society, or more exactly a society composed of limp, boiled broccoli; iceberg lettuce salads; and canned mushrooms. And probably an unfortunate childhood of boiled Brussels sprouts (a tragedy for such a beautiful veg) or undercooked, rubbery eggplant. For those of you who love vegetables, this will be a tribute to everything glorious about the delicious part of the plant kingdom. At the very least, it will get you excited about roasting an extra bulb of garlic or two next time you fire up the oven.

Learning how to cook vegetables so that they're flavorful, enticing, and exciting is about the best thing you can do to help spread the word about veganism, hands down. This chapter is organized according to different methods to coax the most flavor out of your veggies, to give you the skills to last a lifetime. Notice we're not a big fan of boiling (except for the occasional root vegetable, but even then done with great care). It's so last century and kind of a mean thing to do to vegetables, if you think about it.

GRILLING VEGETABLES

Vegetarians are sometimes at a loss for what to put on the grill. It's often a sad toss-up between the oddly orange-hued tofu hot dogs or frozen disks of veggie burgers. We know this is a crazy thought but how about . . . vegetables?! Grilling brings out so much flavor in vegetables that you don't even need to dress them up too much. So pretty to look at and toothsome, perfectly grilled vegetables are like the spring break of parties in your mouth. A little olive oil and salt and you're good to go, or if you're feeling especially inspired, some garlic and lemon juice never hurt. You don't have to limit your grilling skills to the outdoors or miss out because it's snowing outside—a cast-iron grill pan works wonders on the stovetop as well.

Asparagus: Grilled asparagus is at once chewy and crispy, savory and sweet.

> **Prep:** Remove the rough end of the stems. Place in a plastic bag. Add enough olive oil to coat, and a few minced garlic cloves. Close the bag and rub all over to make sure the asparagus is coated. Let it sit for 10 minutes or a few hours—whenever you are ready to grill. When you are ready to grill, sprinkle with a little bit of coarse sea salt.

> **Grill:** Turn every few minutes and brush with olive oil if it looks like it's getting dry. It's ready when the tips turn slightly charred—but before they turn shriveled—about 5 to 7 minutes.

Bell peppers: The pepper of choice for the grill is the red bell pepper, for its sweetness and meatiness, but you can go with orange, yellow, or even purple if you can find it. Green bell peppers are simply not quite ripe red bell peppers, so they are a little bitter, but if that's your thing, go for it.

> **Prep:** Carve out the pepper stem with a paring knife. Remove the stem and seeds, and peel out as much of the white stuff on the inside of the skin as you can. Cut each pepper in half. Brush each side with olive oil.

> **Grill:** Place, skin side down, on the grill and flatten with a spatula as much as you can. Let cook

TOOLS FOR OUTDOOR GRILLING

Metal tongs: Tongs are like an extension of our arms if there's a grill within fifty feet. Don't bother trying a spatula; tongs are the tool of choice for flipping your veggies with precision. Simple, cheap metal ones will do, but you can get exotic with silicone-handled, heavy-duty tongs.

Spatula: So, you don't need a spatula for turning vegetables, but it doesn't have to join the unemployment line just yet. Spatulas are great for flattening things out on the grill to ensure even cooking. Just be sure to get a really long-handled one for the grill, or use the little guy used for flipping pancakes if your hands are made out of asbestos.

Pastry brushes: Kitchen supply stores sell pastry brushes that are just a little too dainty and precious for our tastes, not to mention more expensive. So, we use the kind of fat, round, nylon brush that you can find in a hardware store. Grill like a *Veganomicon* author and keep two at your side: one for brushing the grill with oil and one for brushing the veggies with oil or marinade during cooking.

Metal skewers: For some reason, grilling vegetables in kebab form makes them 76 percent more fun to eat, according to our studies. You can also use wooden skewers, but to make sure that they don't burn: soak the wooden skewers in water beforehand for at least an hour. Get those freeloader picnic guests to assemble bite-size veggie chunks onto skewers while you make the marinades or just work on your fierce tan. See Kebab Advice, page 32.

Lidded plastic containers: They make for easy transport of your veggies, and you can shake them to coat your veggies in oil or marinade with no worries.

Large, resealable plastic bags: For some vegetables, such as asparagus, it's difficult to find a container that's the right size. Hence bags.

Aluminum foil: You always need it for something. It's almost a mystery how aluminum foil saves many a grilling day.

The grill: We don't live in the suburbs, so generally the perfect grill for us is the permanent, for-the-people kind you'll find in the park (a good a reason as any to leave the house on a Saturday before eleven a.m., just to lay claim on the good ones), or anything under thirty bucks. The great part about cooking veggies is that it takes a fraction of the time the meaty stuff does, so you really don't need that monster grill that costs as much as a down payment on a car.

until the skin is very charred; depending on the heat of your grill this can take anywhere from 8 to 15 minutes. Once the skin is good and charred, flip the pepper over for just a few more minutes.

We like to get sneaky and cook other kinds of peppers on the grill when nobody's looking. Turn your head for just a minute and we've put whole, unpeeled jalapeños or serranos on the grill. Turn them a few times and make sure they get nicely charred and blistered, then sock them away in a covered plastic container. You'll then have roasted chiles on hand to chop up and toss into any salsa, and therefore instantly become a salsa superhero.

Corn: We don't think it's necessary to make a case for corn on the cob; everyone loves it.

Husk-on grilling prep: Pull back the husks as far as you can without ripping them off or damaging them. Pull the silk away from the corn and then close the husks back up. Soak the corn in a big pot of water for at least half an hour. The water softens the kernels as well as provides moisture that steams the corn and helps it to cook faster. Push the husks aside and brush the corn with oil and sprinkle with salt. Close the husks back up.

Grill: Place the whole ears on the grill and turn often for about 20 minutes. The corn is ready when the kernels are soft and release moisture if pressed.

P.S. If you're cooking with a campfire, get all outdoorsy and bury prepared, presoaked corn (make sure to keep plenty of the husk on!) in the hot ash and glowing coals of the campfire. Turn the corn once or twice. Depending on how hot your fire is, check the corn after about 10 minutes. Don't forget it or you'll have corn charcoal!

THE #1 TOOL FOR INDOOR GRILLING

Cast aside your fears and get a cast-iron grill pan!

We probably say this about ten times throughout the book, but since this section is specifically about grilling, it would be remiss not to mention it here. You absolutely need to get one! Once you have procured this, the most important purchase you will ever make in your life, then you can follow these same directions for outdoor grilling, only you will be indoors.

Bare naked grilling: This method gives you blackened bits of corn that you may love! Remove the husks and stringy bits completely. Coat with coconut oil and a bit of salt. Place on the grill over low heat, turning often, until blackened in spots. About 10 minutes.

Eggplant: We love grilled eggplant as much as the next guy, but we're the first to admit that it's been much abused by the delis and restaurants of the world in the name of "vegetarian" food. We've all been there: the only meatless thing on the menu is that grilled vegetable sandwich, usually featuring a huge blob of tasteless, rubbery "grilled" eggplant. Cast aside those fears; the eggplant grilled at home by you will banish those blues forever.

Prep: Eggplant is great sliced in numerous ways; the stylish bias, completely lengthwise for huge eggplant "steaks," or the widthwise circular slice. Slices can be a little bit thicker than for summer squash, about ¾ inch. Remember to brush liberally with olive oil.

Grill: Grill for 5 to 7 minutes, then flip and grill for another five to seven. Brush often with oil as eggplant loves to drink that stuff up and tends to stick to the grill easier than other veggies do.

Leeks: Adventurous types might enjoy throwing whole leeks on the grill. They have a great fresh oniony flavor and chewy texture that is fun and satisfying to eat.

Prep: Trim both ends of each leek, then slice—starting from the green end—to about halfway through the white part. Completely cover in water and allow to soak about 5 minutes, shaking to ensure than any sand or grit is washed away from the leeks. Coat liberally with olive oil.

Grill: Grill for 5 to 7 minutes, or until soft and slightly charred. Sprinkle with salt after they are grilled.

Onions: Onions are excellent additions to your portobello burger or grilled veggie sandwich. We love using large, candy-sweet Vidalia onions but any big, preferably yellow, onion will do.

Prep: Slice off tops, remove the skin and cut into thick slices—a little under ½ inch should do. Keeping each slice intact, brush with olive oil.

Grill: Grill for 5 to 7 minutes, or until soft and slightly charred. Flip often, using the tongs to keep the rings together.

EGGPLANT: TO SALT OR NOT TO SALT?

We've been fence sitters on this issue for a while, but we've decided to err on the side of caution and tell you to salt the eggplant. Does salting eggplant really leach out the bitterness? Yes, even though eggplant is now bred to be less bitter. On the pro-salt side, the salt really does tenderize the eggplant, so why not take the extra time to do it? So even though we do recommend it, we aren't tyrannical in our belief and you can skip this step if you feel like it. If you're lucky enough to pick eggplant straight out of the garden, you'll likely find that superfresh eggplant doesn't need salting, but that slightly wrinkly, not-so-fresh specimen in the supermarket produce section may benefit from a little salting.

Portobello mushrooms: Who needs burgers? Portobellos are nature's own burger: big, juicy mushrooms that just beg to be grilled and placed between a bun. You could go through a whole song and dance with balsamic vinegar and soy sauce, but this is just about the basics. A little olive oil and garlic lets the mushroom flavor shine through.

Prep: Remove the stem (see tip). Wipe clean with a damp towel. Drizzle and brush generously with olive oil and sprinkle with salt.

Grill: Place, gill side down, on the grill. Sprinkle with a little coarse sea salt. Let the portobellos cook for about 10 minutes, then flip over and cook for another five, brushing with olive oil if they look dry. Depending on the heat of your grill and the size of your mushrooms, you may need to cook for another 5 to 10 minutes, flipping every so often. The mushrooms are ready when they are soft and dark. The center should be tender and release moisture when you press down with a spatula.

Tomatoes: Use big, fat beefsteak tomatoes, and be careful not to overcook them, lest they turn into marinara right on your grill. Sprinkle with salt and pepper, drizzle with olive oil. Grill on high heat just until grill marks appear, about 3 minutes. Flip and grill for another two.

Cherry tomatoes are great as kebabs! Place them on skewers and brush with lots of oil and some salt. These don't take very long, maybe only 2 to 3 minutes, tops, so don't go wandering over to finish off the last of the guacamole when these babies are on the grill.

PINEAPPLE

Pineapple is not a vegetable, you say (well, neither are tomatoes, but . . .). You haven't lived until you've tasted pineapple fresh off the grill. No, really, maybe you're a vegan zombie looking for BBQ tips or something. Anyway, to the humans out there, freshly sliced pineapple—coated with a little vegetable oil—is totally asking to be grilled, for 3 to 4 minutes each side. The sugars caramelize into a sweet heaven on the outside while the insides remain juicy. Serve warm, either with barbecue sauce–covered items or as a dessert with fresh berries and your favorite nondairy ice cream.

For some really good times, place a whole, peeled, unsliced pineapple on the outdoor grill. Lightly oil it and turn it occasionally to caramelize each side. This is especially a good idea if you have lots of hot, smoldering coals left over (after the main grilling) and don't want to waste them. Better than a stupid roasted marshmallow, if you ask us. It's fun to slice hot off the grill (use a big knife and pierce it with a fork so it doesn't fly off the cutting board), kind of like a big old holiday roast made just out of, you guessed it, pineapple.

Zucchini or summer squash: Zucchini really takes to the grill and rewards you with those perfect grill lines you see in magazines. For best results, use young to middle-aged squash, avoiding those really huge, old zucchini that are nothing but tough skin and lots of seeds.

Prep: Cut off the stems. Slice on a bias (angle) into just less than ½-inch slices. The reason for cutting on a bias is so that you get nice big slices that won't fall into the grill, but it also has the added benefit of being a nicer presentation. Brush with olive oil.

Grill: Cook one side for 3 to 4 minutes. Check the bottom to see whether your grill marks have appeared. When they have, brush with olive oil, flip over, and cook for a few minutes more. The squash should be tender but not completely falling apart. Remove from the grill and lightly salt.

Other vegetables: Maybe someday you'll have the burning desire to grill a sweet potato or a rutabaga. And who are we to stop you? In general, it's helpful to keep in mind that whatever you put on the grill should ideally: (a) be completely cooked in fewer than 10 to 12 minutes, and (b) not fall apart when put under such intense heat. Generally, it helps to keep vegetables sliced less than ¾ inch thick. Root vegetables should be precooked—usually by boiling—until just tender but not cooked all the way, then sliced into ½-inch-thick pieces. Same applies to winter squash; just make sure not to overcook it before putting on the grill. Use plenty of oil to protect against sticking, and have ready a spatula if anything appears to be too fragile or soft to handle with tongs.

ROASTING VEGGIES IN THE OVEN

Roasting simply means to cook something with indirect dry heat for a moderate amount of time. The wonderful thing about this method is that, whereas boiling leaches the flavor out of our food, roasting concentrates the flavor, as well as crisps and caramelizes the outside. Most any vegetable can be roasted and all that is needed is some oil, salt, and pepper. And of course, a little garlic never hurts. The other bonus is that the cook has to do very little work while the veggies are cooking. So, we often complete our meals with a hodgepodge of roasted veggies. This way, while the stovetop might be seeing a lot of chaotic action, there is an oasis of serenity down below as our little friends do their thing and roast away.

The following are not so much recipes as guidelines for some of our favorite roasted vegetables. You'll notice, throughout the book, we demand that you serve something

GETTING THE STEM OFF A PORTOBELLO

Now, this is sort of an art, as many a portobello has been ruined by untrained hands that either rip or pull too hard or crush the delicate cap. So, forgive us if this is just too much detail about how to remove a stem from a mushroom (but if you had seen all the carnage that we have, you would understand our precautions). Place the portobello, stem side up, on a flat surface. Place your fingers gently on the underside just outside the stem, to secure it. Using your free hand (which should be your writing hand), place your fingers at the base of the stem and gently turn the cap inward. This may take a few turns until you feel it giving; it's sort of like gently jiggling your key in a lock. When the stem gives, you should be home free and can just gently turn until the stem comes off. You don't have to do this every time; once you get a feel for the portobello, you will be able to just pull a stem off in the blink of an eye.

KEBAB ADVICE

Maybe you didn't ask for it, but we've got it. Our basic kebabs generally consist of peppers, whole mushrooms, onions, and zucchini. Prep the peppers by blanching them, then cut them into inch-thick slices. Chop the zucchini and onions into ½-inch slices and leave the mushroom whole. If you need to add cherry tomatoes, fine, but make separate little skewers just for them. They cook far faster than other vegetables and will end up falling off the skewers and into the fire before the other vegetables are done.

For heartier fare, add chunks of seitan or pressed tofu. Place it all into a plastic bag or container, coat with olive oil and a few pinches of coarse sea salt, and squeeze a lemon over it. For the professionally lazy, we'll even let you use your favorite bottled oil and vinegar dressing as a no-effort marinade. Let them sit for about 15 minutes, then place on skewers, alternating vegetables and seitan. Cook for 7 to 10 minutes, turning every few minutes and brushing with oil. Drizzle with Miso Tahini dressing (page 325) for optimal yumminess.

So, now that you have the basics of grilling down, it's time to serve these babies up. If you are going the sandwich route, it's a good idea to grill the bread as well—why not? Fire is free. If not using hamburger buns, we like to use chewy vegan peasant bread. Simply brush with oil and lightly grill each side until faint grill marks start to appear. You can also opt for garlic bread. It's simple—just puree two cloves of garlic with ½ cup of olive oil, brush onto bread, and grill. Once your bread is grilled, spread with Basil-Cilantro Pesto (page 325), pile on veggies, and enjoy!

You can also serve grilled veggies on top of a cold pasta or rice salad; the combination of hot and cold foods is the best thing in the whole world. Grill some extra vegetables and save the leftovers just for this or a dozen other reasons: to put on pizza, blend into hummus (page 74), sneak into the Roasted Eggplant and Spinach Muffuletta Sandwich (page 142), finely dice and sprinkle into a bean soup, and so on.

with roasted this or that, so we figured that it was only right that we let you know how to do it. First we give you the basic prep and cooking time, but you decide what kind of herbs and flavorings (if any) that you want to use. Go lightly with dried spices and add them before cooking. If using fresh herbs, toss them in about 5 minutes before the veggies are done cooking. We suggest a 13 x 17-inch rimmed baking sheet; spread your veggies in a single layer so they cook evenly and perfectly.

Asparagus: When roasted, asparagus's rich flavors get really concentrated. The entire vegetable achieves a certain succulent texture that only happens with roasting. You'll notice, throughout the book, that we ask you to serve lots of things with roasted asparagus, and that is not because we work for the National Asparagus Council, it is just because we love it that much. (On a side note, is the NAC hiring?)

Oven temperature: 400°F

Prep: Remove the rough stems. Drizzle and coat the asparagus with olive oil and sprinkle with salt and freshly ground black pepper. Place on a lightly greased baking sheet. If you like, add minced garlic 5 minutes before the asparagus is done, and mix it in with tongs.

Roast: 15 to 20 minutes, depending on the size of the asparagus. The tips should be a bit crispy and the stems should be lightly browned and crinkly.

Complements: Tarragon, thyme, crushed fennel seeds, rosemary, a drizzle of balsamic vinegar, or fresh lemon juice.

Fancy it up: Because we worry that you might not be eating enough capers, why not try tossing in a few tablespoons of capers along with the asparagus in the roasting pan?

Brussels sprouts: This is the recipe that will take you from nose-turner-upper to fork-digger-inner. Roasting Brussels sprouts brings out their nutty flavor.

Oven temperature: 400°F

Prep: Remove the rough knobby stem; slice the sprouts in half lengthwise. Drizzle and coat with olive oil and sprinkle with salt and freshly ground black pepper. Place, cut side down, on a baking sheet. If you like, add minced garlic 5 minutes before the Brussels are done and mix in with tongs.

Roast: 15 to 20 minutes, depending on the size of the sprouts. The cut side should be browned and crispy in places.

Complements: Fresh herbs (e.g., mint or chives), creamy dressings (e.g., ranch)

Cauliflower: Roasting cauliflower is a popular way to serve up this vegetable in a variety of Mediterranean cuisines. Like Brussels sprouts, cauliflower has an aromatic nutty flavor when roasted, which makes sense since they are in the same family.

Oven temperature: 400°F

Prep: Slice the head of cauliflower in half and remove the leaves. Slice into bite-size chunks.

Drizzle and rub with olive oil and sprinkle with salt and freshly ground black pepper. Place on a lightly greased baking sheet.

Roast: 15 to 20 minutes, using tongs to turn them halfway through cooking

Complements: After cooking, add chopped fresh parsley and drizzle with fresh lemon juice, if you wish. It's great with hummus and tahini, too.

Fancy it up: Make a yummy Indian side dish by adding a teaspoon each of crushed cumin and coriander seeds before cooking.

Eggplant: Oven-roasted eggplant is so versatile and dare we say "meaty" that you'll find a way to work it into pastas, sandwiches, curries, salads, and more. Especially nice when you're feeding a mixed crowd of meat- and plant-eaters. Simply slice the eggplant any way that you please (but keep the skin on). Cutting crosswise into ½-inch-thick rounds creates a good, all-purpose shape; ¼-inch-thick lengthwise slices rule for hero-style sandwiches and layering in casseroles. We recommend salting eggplant before cooking it (see sidebar "Eggplant: To Salt or Not to Salt?" on page 30 and final tip of the Eggplant Rollatini recipe on page 245).

Oven temperature: 350°F

Prep: Remove the stems. Slice as described above, or cut into ½-inch cubes for use in a soup or salad. If you want to go with salting the eggplant, rub each slice with kosher salt and place in a colander; put the colander in the sink. Let sit for 20 to 30 minutes, allowing any excess liquid to sweat out. Rinse each slice and pat dry with a kitchen towel. Whether or not you salted the eggplant, rub the slices with olive oil and sprinkle them with freshly ground black pepper (if you salted them, there is no need for salt here; if not, sprinkle with salt now). Place on a baking sheet.

Roast: 15 to 20 minutes. You may want to spray with a little oil intermittently to prevent the eggplant from drying out. The slices should be lightly browned.

Complements: Tarragon, thyme, crushed fennel seeds, rosemary, oregano, a drizzle of balsamic vinegar, or fresh lemon juice. Or go in a Middle Eastern direction and sprinkle on ground cumin and paprika.

Fancy it up: Top roasted eggplant with lightly sautéed chopped garlic, sliced black olives, fresh parsley or dill, and drizzles of high-quality olive oil.

Whole eggplant: Roast a whole eggplant in its skin? Are you mad? Mad about tender, melt-in-your-mouth eggplant, maybe. Take a small to medium-size eggplant, prick little holes all over it with a fork, place it in a "cradle" of foil on a baking sheet, and bake it at 400°F for 25 to 35 minutes, or until it's collapsed and easily pierced with a fork. The resulting interior (don't eat the charred skin) is creamy, delicate, and delicious scooped away from the exterior and mashed with a little olive oil, fresh lemon juice, salt, and a touch of cumin. Use as a dip with toasted pita triangles, cucumbers, and carrot spears.

Green beans: If roasting a green bean sounds weird to you, then get ready to question everything you thought you knew and bite into a crisp 'n' chewy, yet tender 'n' roasty green bean. These are especially lovely tossed into a pasta or potato salad.

Oven temperature: 400°F

Prep: Trim the tops. Drizzle and coat with olive oil and sprinkle with salt and freshly ground black pepper. Place on a lightly greased baking sheet. If you like, add minced garlic 5 minutes before the beans are done, and mix it in with tongs.

Roast: 12 to 15 minutes

Complements: We prefer these plain and unadulterated.

Peppers: Roasting peppers at home will make you feel like you're on a cooking show. A show so fabulous that you can film in your pajamas and nobody will say anything because you're famous for your breathtaking roasted peppers. If you want to roast just one, see page 35.

Also, roasted peppers are particularly perfect for placing on pizzas (say that 5 times fast).

Oven temperature: 425°F

Prep: Cut the peppers in half lengthwise and remove the stem and seeds. Coat lightly with olive

---

HOW TO PREPARE YOUR ROASTING PAN

Parchment paper can be a baking sheet's best friend when roasting vegetables. It isn't completely necessary, but it does help to protect your sheet and to make sure that your veggies don't stick.

oil (a spray bottle works great for this) and place on a lightly greased baking sheet.

Roast: 20 to 25 minutes, or until the pepper is collapsed and skin is dark brown in spots

Note: Most of the time people remove the skin before eating, but that isn't exactly necessary if your peppers aren't charred beyond belief. We actually like the way the burnt parts taste. If you would like to remove the skin, place the peppers in a paper or plastic bag the moment you remove them from the oven. Close the bag and this will steam the peppers. When they have cooled for about 30 minutes, the skins can be peeled away easily.

Potatoes: When in doubt about what to eat for dinner or brunch, there's always roasted potatoes. Leave the skin on for taste, texture, and fiber too, hurray!

◆

ROASTING GARLIC

Some articles from the '80s, such as stirrup pants and banana hair clips, are best left to theme parties and buzz-feed quizzes. However, the wonderful roasted garlic that was everywhere during that decade is here to stay, if we have anything to say about it. It's so mellow, sweet, and simple to make. There's no excuse not to work roasted garlic into everything from salad dressings to hummus.

If you can tease up some "mall hair," then you can make roasted garlic. Take one or more whole, unpeeled, and unseparated bulbs of garlic. With a heavy, sharp knife, slice off approximately ½ inch of the entire top of the bulb, exposing the insides of the garlic cloves. Drizzle about 1 tablespoon of olive oil onto the top of the bulb, making sure the cut cloves are covered with oil and some oil sneaks into the spaces between the cloves. Wrap tightly in foil and bake at 375°F for 20 to 30 minutes, or until the cloves are very soft and turned a deep golden color. For slightly caramelized cloves, unwrap the tops of the bulbs and let them roast for 8 to 10 additional minutes.

It may seem like a big waste to heat up the oven just to roast a few cloves of garlic. Sometimes we use our toaster oven. Other times, if we know we're going to have the oven fired up for an hour or more (when making a casserole or roasting other veggies), we'll wrap up some garlic and sneak it into the oven even if we have no particular roasted garlic in mind, just to have it on hand. Roasted garlic, if stored in a tightly sealed container, should keep for about a week.

◆

Oven temperature: 425°F

Prep: Cut into ¾-inch chunks. Drizzle and coat with olive oil and sprinkle with salt and freshly ground black pepper. Place on a lightly greased baking sheet.

Roast: 45 to 55 minutes, turning occasionally. If you like, add minced garlic 5 minutes before the potatoes are done cooking and mix it in using tongs.

Optional complements: Potatoes go well with just about any herb you can think of: rosemary, thyme, sage, and on and on down the spice rack.

Fancy it up: What's even better than roasted potatoes? Roasted French fries, also known as "French Bakes" by maybe fifteen people. Cut potatoes into fry shapes (about ½ inch wide and ¼ inch thick); toss with a little oil, salt, and spices of choice. Lightly grease a baking sheet with oil. Spread out your fries in a single layer, leaving a little space between them. This will ensure that the fries properly roast and get crunchy instead of steaming. Bake at 425°F for 15 minutes, flip, and bake for another 8 to 10 minutes, or until they are slightly puffed, brown and crisp. Eat ASAP, dipped in ketchup, vegan mayo with a little Dijon mustard blended in, or BBQ sauce, as they get a little bit tough when they start to cool.

Root veggies and tubers: Carrots, beets, turnips, sweet potatoes, parsnips—you name it—bring it on! Your oven can take these rock-hard roots and tubers and transform them into candy-sweet, tender nuggets in lovely shades of orange, magenta, and cream.

Oven temperature: 400°F

Prep: Peel the veggies and slice off their stems. The shapes you cut are pretty much up to you, although ¾ inch across in any direction is a pretty good size to aim for. Drizzle and coat with olive oil, then sprinkle with salt. Place on a lightly greased baking sheet. You can also slice into ¼-inch slices for chips, in which case you should reduce the cooking time by 10 minutes.

Roast: 35 to 45 minutes, flipping once about halfway through cooking. The roots should be tender and easily pierced with a fork, the outsides should be browned and even lightly caramelized.

Complements: Rosemary and thyme or sweet spices, such as cinnamon, nutmeg, and allspice.

Fancy it up: Add a light coating of maple syrup

HOW TO ROAST A PEPPER ON THE STOVETOP

Sometimes you want just one roasted pepper. And you want it fast. The best way to go about this is roasting a whole, unsliced pepper directly on top of the stove, on a gas burner over high heat (DON'T use an electric burner; if that's all you have, use the oven method instead). Go ahead; the pepper can take it. Use tongs to rotate the pepper as its skin starts to blacken and blister. When about 75 percent of the pepper is done roasting, pick it up with the tongs and drop it into a paper bag or a large, heatproof bowl. Crimp the top of the bag or tightly cover the bowl with a dish or some plastic wrap. Allow the pepper to sit for at least 10 to 15 minutes. This step not only lets it cool enough to be handled but also allows the steam escaping from the pepper to loosen its skin. After it's cooled for a while, gently peel away as much of the skin as possible. It's okay if bits of charred skin remain on the pepper; they're full of flavor and have that exciting barbecued look. Slice, seed, and proceed as usual.

and minced ginger before cooking for a hint of sweetness.

Tomatoes: Roasting tomatoes brings out all their flavor and sweetness. Save your beautiful vine-ripened type tomatoes for a sandwich or salad, but when you have tomatoes that aren't as juicy, such as plum tomatoes, then roasting is the way to go. A bonus is that they make your kitchen smell like the most inviting restaurant in Little Italy. Roasted tomatoes in sandwiches, along with a portobello (page 161) would be nice, or use them as the base for sauces and soups.

> **Oven temperature:** 350°F
> **Prep:** Remove the stems. Slice into ½-inch slices. Place on a lightly oiled baking sheet, drizzle with olive oil, and sprinkle with salt.
> **Roast:** 50 minutes to an hour, or until the skin is a bit crinkled
> **Complements:** Oregano, thyme, or really any herb you might find in a Simon and Garfunkel song.

Winter squash: Although steaming may be more convenient, roasting most winter squashes and pumpkins brings out their sweet flavor as no other cooking method can. You can roast squash whole, in its skin, and serve it in large luscious pieces, or cut it into small caramelized pieces, so we will give you directions for both ways.

For big pieces of whole roasted squash:
> **Oven temperature:** 400°F
> **Prep:** Remove the stem. Split the squash in half lengthwise. Remove the seeds and use a spoon to scrape out any stringy bits. Place, cut side down, on a lightly greased baking sheet.
> **Roast:** 45 minutes to an hour, depending on the size. The outside peel of the squash should be easily pierced with a fork when it's done cooking. Slice into more manageable (but still large) pieces to serve. Leave the skins on for a more dramatic presentation; if the skin is not edible, just peel it off while eating.

For smaller, caramelized pieces:
> **Oven temperature:** 400°F
> **Prep:** Remove the stem. Peel off the skin. Split the squash in half lengthwise. Remove the seeds and use a spoon to scrape out any stringy bits. Cut into ¾-inch pieces. Drizzle and coat with olive oil and sprinkle with salt. Place on a lightly greased baking sheet.
> **Roast:** 25 to 30 minutes, turning twice during cooking. The squash should be tender, browned, and lightly caramelized on the edges.

For both methods
> **Complements:** Rosemary, sage, thyme, or sweet spices, such as cinnamon, allspice, and nutmeg.
> **Fancy it up:** Before cooking, add a light coating of pure maple syrup. Sprinkle with crushed coriander seeds and minced ginger.

Zucchini or summer squash: "*Oy gevalt!* I've got *ferkakte* zucchini up to *mayn kepele!*" How many times have you uttered these words, amazed at your newfound grasp of Yiddish? Roasting to the rescue, once again. Get ready for succulent summer squash that will rock your *tuchus*.

MASHED SQUASH TO THE RESCUE

If you're (God forbid) tired of mashed potatoes or just in need of a sweet change, use our whole-roasting method for winter squash and make mashed squash instead. Just remove the skin, and mash or puree with a little pure maple syrup, salt, and ground cinnamon.

Oven temperature: 425°F

Prep: Remove the stem. Cut widthwise into ½-inch pieces; try to slice at a diagonal for a nice presentation. Drizzle and coat with olive oil and sprinkle with salt and freshly ground black pepper. Place on a lightly greased baking sheet. If you like, add minced garlic 5 minutes before the zucchini is done.

Roast: 25 to 30 minutes, turning once halfway through cooking

Complements: Dill, rosemary, thyme, tarragon, or parsley. Drizzle with balsamic vinegar or fresh lemon juice once done cooking.

SIMPLE STEAMING

Steaming should be thought of as boiling for the new century. No longer will we tolerate flaccid, drab-green vegetables when they should be crisp, flavorful, and their truer shades of brilliant greens. Steaming is also really easy; you can easily steam any vegetable without fancy equipment. A large soup pot with a lid is all the bare-bones gear you need. If you do have a steamer basket, though, then great! (There are recipes in this book where it will come in handy.) There is definitely no need to clutter up the kitchen counter with special plug-in electric steamers or other food-steaming contraptions.

We're not too crazy about dried herbs on steamed veggies, but adding fresh herbs about three minutes before the veggies are done steaming is never a bad idea. Try parsley, dill, thyme, oregano, or tarragon on any of these veggies. You can also drizzle them with any of our sauces in the sauce chapter (pages 310–329).

Directions for preparing a steamer pot for any kind of veggies: Fill a large soup pot with 2 to 3 inches of cold water, fit your steamer basket into the pot, cover, and bring to a boil. Once the water is boiling, place the veggies in the steamer and cover. If you don't have a steamer basket, no worries; just fill the pot with 2 to 3 inches of water, cover, and bring to a boil. Once the water is boiling, place the veggies directly into the boiling water and cover. We call this boil/steaming, or stoiling—but no one else does, so never say the word aloud.

Asparagus: What's better than crisp-tender asparagus in the height of spring? Okay, maybe there are a few other things, but shhhh . . . we're totally grooving on steamed asparagus right now.

Prep: Remove the rough stems.

Steam: 8 to 14 minutes, depending on thickness. Asparagus should be bright green and still crisp.

To serve: Drizzle with Dill-Tahini Sauce (page 325) or Cheezy Sauce (page 326).

Broccoli and cauliflower: Since this is what everyone thinks vegans live on, why not prove them right?

Prep: Cut into medium-size florets.

Steam: 10 to 12 minutes, tossing with tongs a few times.

To serve: We love these with Dill-Tahini Sauce (page 325).

Dark, leafy greens: A little bit of boiling water is really the best, lazy way to cook up quickly a bunch of collards or kale. It makes you feel really healthy, too, and levels you up in the vegan echelon.

Prep: Wash and chop the greens into bite-size pieces.

Steam: 10 to 14 minutes. Toss the greens with tongs as they start to wilt. In the South, it's popular to keep on boiling these greens to form the famous delicacy of "pot liquor"; but being north of the Mason-Dixon Line, we just like 'em bright green and with a little bit of crunch left in them.

To serve: A simple and old-school hippie restaurant way to enjoy steamed greens is sprinkled with plenty of sesame salt (known as gomasio, which is just a blend of crushed, roasted sesame seeds and sea salt), with maybe a touch of fresh lemon juice or a sprinkle of malt vinegar. We also like them with Citrus-Date-Sesame Sauce (page 327).

Green beans: Nothing scares a green bean more than being

◆

SHOCKING!

It might not be apparent, but even after you've turned off the heat, vegetables will continue to cook. The steam that's working its way out of the vegetables will still continue the cooking process, and if you're not careful it might turn those perfectly steamed asparagus spears to mush. If you're not planning on serving vegetables immediately, or plan on serving them cold or at room temperature, quickly run them under cold water for about a minute. This is called "shocking" the vegetable, which sounds pretty cool. Transfer to a colander and allow to drain.

◆

boiled to death and canned. Fortunately, we grew up on gently steamed green beans before they were the "in" thing.

Prep: Trim off the ends.

Steam: 8 to 10 minutes, depending on size, tossing with tongs a few times

To serve: Sprinkle with coarse salt and enjoy. Or try with Mustard Sauce (page 312).

HOW TO COOK A GRAIN

---------- ◆ ----------

There's a reason that grains were found in the tombs of the Egyptian pyramids as well as at the base of our food pyramid: they're packed with so many nutrients, vitamins, minerals, fiber, and even protein, all while being low in fat.

But grains aren't just life-giving sustenance. They're also a culinary jewel, adding notes of nuttiness, earthiness, and sometimes even floral hints to round our meals out. And their affordability will make you wanna do an infomercial about them. The following is by no means a comprehensive list of grains. There are hundreds of edible ones worldwide; these are just some that we consider essential and that are easy to find.

We give you the simplest preparation methods to serve four people, but feel free to double the quantities; however, anything more than double, you will have to adjust the amount of water used. A good rule of thumb is to remove ¼ cup of water for every multiple increment above doubling. So, if you are quadrupling the recipe, subtract ½ cup of water.

You'll notice that some of these preparation methods are simply to boil and simmer the water and grain together, whereas some are steamed by pouring the water over the grain and covering tightly. Still others benefit most from being toasted and then boiled. As we said, these are the simplest preparation methods for grains meant to be served as side dishes, but of course we include all of these grains in more adventurous recipes throughout this book.

An easy way to punch up the flavor and get the most out of your grains is to use vegan vegetable broth instead of water (for homemade broth, see page 223) or throw a vegan bouillon cube into the mix. A 2-quart pot is just right for all of these recipes. The most economical way to purchase grains is to buy from the bulk bins of health food stores or co-ops, but all of the varieties listed also come in boxes or bags at well-stocked grocery stores. Store grains in airtight jars and keep out of direct sunlight, and they will stay fresh for years—an important thing to remember for when the revolution comes.

With the exception of oats and couscous, you'll want to rinse everything on this list before cooking. To rinse, place in a very large bowl and cover with lukewarm water. Swish around with your hands, drain in a fine-mesh strainer, and repeat until the water is no longer cloudy. Drain very well following your last rinse. This washes off starches or dustiness or anything weird and ensures that your grains cook up fluffy and awesome.

Bulgur: A parboiled grain made from wheat, thus it has a very pure wheat taste. It's wonderful in Middle Eastern and Mediterranean meals. Like couscous, it's steamed, but it's a whole food that's full of fiber. We especially love bulgur chilled and used in salads.

Cooking time: 30 to 35 minutes

To serve 4: 1 cup rinsed and drained bulgur, ¼ teaspoon salt, 1⅓ cups water

Cook: Place the bulgur and salt in a pot with a tightly fitting lid. Bring about 2 cups water to a boil in a teapot. Measure out 1⅓ cups of water and pour over the bulgur. Cover and let sit for about 30 minutes. The bulgur should be tender but chewy. Fluff with a fork and serve.

Couscous: Although couscous has a culinary role similar to that of a grain and it is derived from grain, it definitely is not one unto itself; it's actually more similar to pasta. It's made by rolling moist wheat and flour in a wide, shallow bowl until the characteristic pebblelike couscous shape is formed. Because it's so filling, cooks so fast, and tastes so yummers, this African staple has become a permanent fixture in the American diet. Its neutral taste and fluffy texture make it extremely versatile for any meal, sweet or savory. There are lots of different flavors of couscous on the market, such as pesto or sun-dried tomato, but we prefer regular or whole wheat.

Cooking time: 10 minutes

To serve 4: 1 cup couscous, ¼ teaspoon salt, 1 cup water

Cook: Place the couscous and salt in a pot with a tightly fitting lid. Bring about 1½ cups water to a boil in a teapot. Measure out 1 cup of water and pour over the couscous. Cover and let sit for about 5 minutes. The couscous should be soft. Fluff with a fork and serve.

Kasha and buckwheat: Yes, it has the word *wheat* in it, but it's gluten-free. Favored in Eastern European recipes for centuries, kasha is the whole, toasted kernels (also known as groats) of the buckwheat plant. In its untoasted form, buckwheat is also used to make soba noodles in Asian cuisine. But when toasted, buckwheat groats are strictly called kasha. Kasha has an intense earthy taste that may remind some of the smell of wet autumn leaves, but we savor its complex, hearty flavor and deep color. It goes well with other savory earthy foods, such as mushrooms and beets, and you'll feel like a Russian princess if you eat it covered in mushroom gravy. Also look for silky buckwheat flour, great in pancakes and essential for Buckwheat Blini (page 59) and Buckwheat Crepes (page 94).

Cooking time: 20 to 25 minutes

To serve 4: 2¼ cups water, ¼ teaspoon salt, 1 cup kasha

Cook: Bring the water and salt to a boil in a heavy-bottomed pot. Lower the heat to very low, add the kasha, cover, and simmer for about 20 minutes. The kasha should be tender but chewy and all the water should be absorbed.

Millet: Nothing says "health food" like millet. It's one of the more flexible grains. Lightly boiled, it makes for a nice, fluffy dish, as in Mexican Millet (page 173), and when boiled even further you get a soft porridge that can be served soft or molded (like polenta). One of the oldest cereal crops there is, some variety of millet exists on almost every continent and has been popular on and off for thousands of years—maybe its time has come again, and you can say you were eating it before it sold out! It has a slightly sweet, mellow taste that goes well with any meal that brown rice would complement, so add it to your grain rotation tout de suite. Millet doesn't have to be dry-toasted first, but the flavor and texture really benefit from it, so we give you those directions here.

Cooking time: 30 to 45 minutes

To serve 4: 1 cup millet, 2 cups water, ¼ teaspoon salt

Cook: Preheat a heavy-bottomed skillet over medium heat. Put in the millet and toast for about 10 minutes, stirring very often, until the millet has turned a few shades darker and smells toasty. Transfer the millet to a pot with a lid, add the water and salt, cover, and bring to a boil. Once boiling, lower the heat to very low and simmer for 20 to 25 minutes, or until soft. Fluff with a fork and serve.

Oats: Of course, you're familiar with oats. We prefer what's called "quick-cooking" or "rolled" oats, which are different than the magic instant stuff that's been sweetened and flavored beyond recognition. Quick-cooking oats are whole oats that have been cut smaller so that they, you guessed it, cook quicker! Not just for breakfast, we use oats in baked goods and to add bulk to things like veggie burgers. Since you wouldn't serve oats as a side dish, we'll just give you directions for making simple morning oatmeal.

Cooking time: 5 to 10 minutes

To serve 4: 2 cups water, 1 cup rolled oats, ¼ teaspoon salt. Optional: a pinch of ground cinnamon and a handful raisins or other chopped dried fruit, pure maple syrup, nondairy milk

Cook: Bring the water to a boil in a lidded pot and add the oats, salt, and cinnamon and fruits, if using. Lower the heat to low and cook, uncovered, for about 5 minutes, stirring often, until the oats are creamy. Remove from the heat, cover, and let sit for a few minutes. Add a touch of pure maple syrup and nondairy milk if desired.

Polenta: Polenta has been called many things, each more insulting than the last: cornmeal mush, grits, porridge. But it got a new lease on life in the '90s when foodies started referring to it by its proper name and charging $20 a plate for it. Polenta can be served soft, as a comforting addition to soups and stews, and molded into fancy shapes (e.g., isosceles triangles), then grilled or broiled. Or, serve it alongside your scrambled tofu for breakfast—we won't pretend to be above that. This recipe is for soft and creamy polenta to serve as a side dish, not the kind that you mold.

Cooking time: 35 minutes

To serve 4: 5 cups water, ½ teaspoon salt, 2 tablespoons olive oil, 1 cup polenta

Cook: Bring the water and salt to a boil in a pot with a lid. Add the oil. Pour the polenta in very slowly, stirring with a whisk as you pour. Lower the heat to a simmer and cook for 12 to 15 more minutes, stirring often. Turn off the heat and cover for 10 minutes, stirring occasionally.

Quinoa: Cultivated by the Inca for hundreds of years, the mystique of quinoa (pronounced "keen-wah") has been taken down a few notches by its placement alongside Uncle Ben's at many American supermarkets. Quinoa comes in red and light brown varieties (which taste exactly the same to us) and has a slightly bitter (in an arugula good way), nutty taste. There's even exciting, firmly textured black quinoa, perfect for your next goth quinoa bowl dinner party. We use it often in pilafs, salads, and the occasional muffin. It's especially attractive when cooked; the individual grains look a bit like couscous but the germ forms a pretty translucent ring around each one. Adorable. Quinoa is also a complete protein, which has recently made it something of a darling to the vegan community and health-conscious foodies.

Cooking time: 20 to 25 minutes

To serve 4: 2 cups water, 1 cup rinsed and drained quinoa, ¼ teaspoon salt

Cook: Place all the ingredients in a heavy-bottomed pot, cover, and bring to a boil. Once the mixture is boiling, lower the heat to very low and simmer for about 15 minutes. The quinoa should be translucent and the germ ring should be visible. Fluff with a fork and serve.

Rice: With the exception of the frozen continents, rice has been a staple food for every culture, each with its own laws about how it should be cooked and served, so no matter what directions we give you, someone somewhere will think we're wrong. If you have your own rice-cooking method handed down to you from your great-grandmother and handed down to her directly from God, please don't let our silly instructions to stand in your way. We don't have rice cookers because every inch of our counter space is precious real estate, so we give you directions for stovetop cooking here. The secret to not burning the rice is very, very, very low heat.

The difference between brown and white rice is that brown rice has not had the bran removed from it, so it is much healthier—more fiber, more vitamins, and more necessary fatty acids. Brown rice has a nuttier flavor and chewier texture, which is often desirable, but in some dishes where a more neutral flavor (read: less healthy rice) is desired, we use white rice. White rice also cooks much faster and is softer and fluffier. Rice is often labeled as long or short grain.

"Long-grain" not only refers to the shape of the rice, but to the stickiness of the starch content. Long-grain rice is less sticky and often used in fried rice and pilafs. Medium-grain rice is relatively sticky and used in paella and risotto. Short-grain rice is the stickiest kind, and used for sushi. Sometimes short-grain rice is called "glutinous" rice, but the reason for the quotes is that this rice actually doesn't contain any gluten, it's just supersticky. The brown varieties of this rice will always be less sticky than the white.

Dozens of rice varieties are available to us these days, such as black rice and red rice (both unmilled and unpolished rice with the bran intact), but here are a few of the basics that we keep on hand for any rice situation that comes our way. As with other grains, remember to rinse your rice before cooking.

Arborio rice: The favorite rice of Italy, Arborio rice is what gives risotto its succulent creaminess. We love to experiment with different herbs and vegetables to create all manners of risotto, but we don't suggest serving it alone as a side dish because the effort of all that stirring isn't worth the return if you're just cooking it plain, so try our risotto recipes on pages 304 and 305.

Basmati and jasmine rice: We like using both brown and white versions of these two fragrant long-grain rices. If you've never made either jasmine or basmati, you'll marvel at the wonderful buttery, popcornlike aroma both produce when cooking. The real beauty of these rices is that they make you feel like you actually put some thought and effort into dinner, when really all you did was turn on the faucet and the burner. They're perfect for Indian and Thai meals, but we like them with most anything that's a little bit sweet and fragrant, including BBQ and Mexican food.

For brown varieties:

Cooking time: 45 to 50 minutes

To serve 4: 2 cups water, 1 cup rice, ¼ teaspoon salt

Cook: Place all the ingredients in a heavy-bottomed pot, cover, and bring to a boil. Once the mixture is boiling, lower the heat to very low and simmer for 40 to 45 minutes. Fluff with a fork and serve.

For white varieties:

To serve 4: 1½ cups water, 1 cup rice, ¼ teaspoon salt

Cook: Place all the ingredients in a heavy-bottomed pot, cover, and bring to a boil. Once the mixture is boiling, lower the heat to very low and simmer for 15 to 20 minutes. Fluff with a fork and serve.

Brown rice, short-grain: The healthy stuff. Nutty, chewy, and slightly sweet, short-grain brown rice is a nutritious staple and will make you feel as balanced as if you've just done three hours of hot yoga.

Cooking time: 45 to 50 minutes

To serve 4: 2 cups water, 1 cup rice, ¼ teaspoon salt

Cook: Place all the ingredients in a heavy-bottomed pot, cover, and bring to a boil. Once the mixture is boiling, lower the heat to very low and simmer for 40 to 45 minutes. Fluff with a fork and serve.

Wild rice: All-American and not really a rice, wild rice is actually a delicious grain from a marsh grass. Mmm. Marsh grass. The rice is long and a sleek black color and the texture is deliciously chewy. Its earthy flavor pairs wonderfully with mushrooms and autumnal dishes.

> **Cooking time:** 55 to 60 minutes
>
> **To serve 4:** 2½ cups water, 1 cup rice, ¼ teaspoon salt
>
> **Cook:** Place all the ingredients in a heavy-bottomed pot, cover, and bring to a boil. Once the mixture is boiling, lower the heat to very low and simmer for 55 to 60 minutes. Fluff with a fork and serve.

White rice, long grain: Because sometimes you just want plain old white rice. These directions are of the everyday long-grain kind, often fortified with vitamins. While not especially loaded with nutrition naturally, it still pairs well with certain Latin and Asian dishes.

> **Cooking time:** 15 to 20 minutes
>
> **To serve 4:** 1 cup water, 1 cup rice, ¼ teaspoon salt
>
> **Cook:** Place all the ingredients in a heavy-bottomed pot, cover, and bring to a boil. Once the mixture is boiling, lower the heat to very low and simmer for 15 to 20 minutes. Fluff with a fork and serve.

◆

COMPLETE PROTEINS

Everyone has heard the term *complete protein*, but we're willing to wager that vegans hear it more than the rest of the world. Next time people ask you the million-dollar question, "But where do you get your protein?" turn the question back at them and ask them which essential amino acid they are most concerned about. Most likely they will have no idea what an amino acid is, essential or otherwise, but you will. Proteins are made up of amino acids, many of which our body produces all on its own. Essential amino acids are the ones that our body cannot synthesize without the help of the food we eat. So, when we refer to proteins as complete proteins, it just means that all ten of the essential amino acids are present. Contrary to old vegetarian thinking, essential amino acids consumed separately over the course of a day or so combine in our body to form complete proteins—so it is not necessary to turn cartwheels to consume all of them in a single meal.

◆

HOW TO COOK A BEAN

---------- ◆ ----------

You can't beat canned beans when it comes to convenience, especially when you have tiny kitchens as we do. But dried beans are way, way cheaper, and there's a certain amount of satisfaction that comes from doing it the old-fashioned way. Some say the flavor of homemade beans is far more delicate and always lower in sodium (or sodium-free) than the canned stuff is.

Long story short: dried beans can be substituted for canned in any of our recipes, but be ye warned: preparation is everything. Dried beans (except for lentils and split peas) need to be soaked before cooking! If you are working with dried lentils and split peas, then proceed right away as directed in the recipe and live your life without a bean-soaking care in the world.

We prefer a nice, leisurely overnight soak, but we will also allow the quick cooking (or boil the hell out of them) process.

THE SOAKING METHOD:

Put your dried beans in a pot with plenty of water (the water should come up about 6 inches above the beans), cover, and stash in the fridge until the next day (at least 12 hours).

After the beans have soaked, drain the water, then replace with fresh, cold water (roughly 3 cups of water to every cup of soaked beans; better too much than too little) and bring to a boil in a pot with a lid. Once the beans are boiling, lower the heat to a simmer—if you leave them at a boil, they will turn to mush—and cook with the pot's lid slightly ajar so that steam can escape.

How long will depend on the bean; see our guidelines but note that different factors, such as how old the bean is and how dry it is, will affect cooking times. Add a teaspoon of salt to the pot about twenty minutes before the beans are done.

Once the beans are nice and tender, drain and use as called for in the recipe. One cup of dried beans will give you roughly 3 cups cooked.

As a resource to you, dear reader, we've compiled this mini encyclopedia of common beans and their common uses. Of course, there are so many fun and wonderful beans out there in the bulk bins, we recommend buying the funnest, funkiest you can find, but this is just to get you started. Cook a pound of beans at a time, storing in the fridge, and using that week. Bean on!

Adzuki beans: Sometimes called aduki, sometimes called azuki, besides being incredibly fun to say, these shiny little deep red beans are fast cooking and nutritious. A popular bean in Japan and China, they have a delicate flavor that's both sweet and nutty. They're used in both savory dishes and sweet desserts (even ice cream). They also come in black, for your inner Goth.

> **Cooking time:** 1 hour
>
> **Recipes:** Acorn Squash, Pear & Adzuki Soup with Sautéed Shiitakes (page 212)

Black beans: Billions of burritos can't be wrong. Black beans may very well be the most popular bean in vegetarian cooking. Essential if you're cooking anything in many Latin American and Caribbean countries, it's a true workhorse of a bean, good in just about everything from breakfast to dinner and even as a sneaky ingredient in sweets.

> **Cooking time:** 1½ hours
>
> **Recipes:** Black Bean–Vegetable Soup (page 210), Acorn Squash & Black Bean Empanadas (page 56), Black Bean Burgers (page 134), Quinoa Salad with Black Beans & Mango (page 107), Grilled Yuca Tortillas (Black Bean variation) (page 47)

Black-eyed peas: These beans got soul. Tasty and cute, they're cream-colored beans with their namesake black spot that watches your every move. We like them worked into barbecue-themed foods and anything particularly saucy and/or spicy in American Southern, Caribbean, and African cuisines.

> **Cooking time:** 1 hour
>
> **Recipes:** BBQ Black-Eyed Pea–Collard Rolls (page 268), Black-Eyed Butternut Tostadas with Chipotle Pumpkin Seed Salsa (page 133)

Cannellini beans: See kidney beans.

Chickpeas (a.k.a. garbanzos): These adorable, round, pale beige beans have a rich and nutty taste that never fails to satisfy and works wonders in so many dishes. These are also known as ceci beans (Italy) and chana dal (India). Responsible for the miracle that is hummus, and also falafel and too many curries to mention.

> **Cooking time:** 1½ hours
>
> **Recipes:** Chickpea Cutlets (page 206), Chickpea-Quinoa Pilaf (page 165), Chickpea-Noodle Soup (page 218), Fresh Dill–Basmati Rice with Chard & Chickpeas (page 169), Chickpea &

Roasted Eggplant Stew (page 274), A Hummus Recipe, remastered (page 74)

Great northern beans (a.k.a. white beans): See also navy beans. We can't really discern a difference between great northern and navy beans, except that great northerns are a bit bigger. Both are creamy and mild-tasting in a good way, in that they work in most anything where a bean is needed, are dependable, and take on the flavor of whatever sauce or vegetables they're cooked with. They're both wonderful beans to blend into dips and spreads.

> **Cooking time:** 1½ hours
>
> **Recipes:** Escarole with Capers & White Beans (page 152), Rustic White Beans with Mushrooms (page 179), White Bean Aioli (page 66), Asparagus Quiche with Tomatoes & Tarragon (page 242), Sun-dried Tomato Dip (page 70), Manzana Chili Verde (page 263)

Kidney beans: A large, tender bean that's ideal stewed (such as in gumbo or jambalaya) or served at room temperature in salads. They're a natural, protein-rich addition to vegetable and pasta soups, too. Cannellini beans are a variety of white kidney bean, all the rage in Italian dishes: their flavor is significantly milder and texture mushier than red kidney beans.

> **Cooking time:** 1 hour
>
> **Recipes:** Jamaican Yuca Shepherd's Pie (page 248), Plantain & Pinto Stew with Parsnip Chips (page 278), Seitanic Red & White Bean Jambalaya (page 262), Spaghetti & Beanballs (page 289), Bulgur, Arugula & Cannellini Salad (page 109)

Navy beans (a.k.a. white beans): This little white bean is the star of a most American of bean dishes, baked beans. More or less all-purpose and very utilitarian, in that military kind of way. See also great northern beans.

> **Cooking time:** 1 hour
>
> **Recipes:** Cheater Baked Beans (page 184), Tomato-Rice Soup with Roasted Garlic & Navy Beans (page 211), as well as any of the great northern bean recipes.

Pinto beans: The backbone of Native American cuisine (along with corn) in many parts of the New World, this pale pink bean works well whole or pureed. It takes well to rich, complex seasonings and the addition of vegetables. Tex-Mex cuisine just wouldn't be the same without a creamy side of refried pintos.

> **Cooking time:** 1½ hours
>
> **Recipes:** Plantain & Pinto Stew with Parsnip Chips (page 278)

CHAPTER ONE

SNACKS, APPETIZERS, LITTLE MEALS, DIPS & SPREADS

"Who really makes appetizers at home?" we asked ourselves, in the midst of creating the following recipes.

Everyday cooking usually doesn't require a little extra snack to precede a weeknight dinner or weekend brunch. But, sometimes you might just crave an appetizer as your meal—small on size but big on flavor—and who are we to argue with that?

Of course, there could be the chance occasion when you're planning on eating dinner in something other than a T-shirt and flip-flops and to have guests over who are unaccustomed to seeing you in such finery. That's where appetizers step in. Keep hungry stomachs in check with a few Spicy Tempeh Nori Rolls or Walnut-Mushroom Pâté while you slave away in the kitchen preparing the main event. For a casual evening meal, in this age of "small plates," serve a spread of four or more appetizers for friends and family to nosh. Tell them it's like they're eating at a Michelin-starred restaurant, one that employs only you and features your cats working front of house. And certainly you don't need an excuse to craft a batch of grilled tortillas stuffed with creamy yuca filling or a platter of dainty Broccoli-Millet Croquettes, even if it's just for yourself.

-------------- ◆ ---------------

Here's our recipe for the sushi rolls that starred on the very first episode of our homemade zero-budget cooking show back in 2003, *The Post Punk Kitchen*. A decade later, it's appeared at countless parties and potlucks, lunch boxes, and weeknight dinners, and will become a supercelebrity in your kitchen, too. There are a few steps to preparing nori sushi rolls, and the actual assembly of rolls might be a bit of a learning curve, but once you get the hang of it, you'll be dialing in substantial homemade vegan sushi instead of reaching for the bland, boring take-out stuff. This is the roll to serve omnivorous friends who crave fish-free sushi beyond cucumber and avocado: engaging bites of spicy, creamy, crunchy sushi goodness.

Don't miss out on the luscious variant fillings: create the ultimate sushi platter and serve two or more at your next sushi soirée, or invite your guests/friends/enemies (not for long) over early and have a sushi-rolling party. Enough with the chitty-chat; let's roll!

Prepare the rice: Combine the rice plus 1¼ cups of cold water in a heavy-bottomed, 2-quart pot or saucepan with a lid. Bring the water to a boil over high heat and stir the rice just once. Lower the heat to low, cover the pot, and cook the rice for 20 to 22 minutes. Cook until the rice is completely tender and all the liquid has been absorbed.

Empty the hot rice into a large glass or ceramic mixing bowl. Sprinkle with the rice vinegar, sugar, and salt. Use a wooden spoon or rice paddle to gently fold the vinegar into the hot rice. Taste the rice: it should have a mellow "seasoned" vinegar flavor with a hint of sweetness. If it tastes too bland, add an additional dash of vinegar and mix. Cover the hot rice with plastic wrap and set aside to cool while preparing the filling. Sushi rice should be a little warm when you work with it (never ice cold) and have a hint of warmth when eaten (so, always prepare sushi rice just prior to serving rolls).

Prepare the filling: While the rice is marinating, dice the tempeh into 1-inch cubes. Place in a small saucepan, cover with 2 inches of water, cover the pot, and bring to a boil. Simmer the tempeh for 3 minutes, then drain. Transfer the tempeh to a mixing bowl and crush the cubes a few times with a fork. Add the mayonnaise and chile–sesame oil and mash into a chunky salad; taste and add more chile–sesame oil if desired.

To assemble: In a shallow cup, combine ⅓ cup of water and a tablespoon of rice vinegar, and keep near your sushi workstation. Follow these steps to assemble the nori rolls. Remember, your first attempt at shaping a roll may suck (but still taste great), and you'll get better with practice:

1. Place a nori sheet on a bamboo mat. Moisten your hands with the vinegar mixture, scoop a scant 1 cup of rice into your hands, and gently pat it together, like forming a loose snowball. Gently yet firmly pat onto the bottom two thirds or so of your nori sheet. Spread the rice to the very edges of the nori roll. The layer of rice should be less than ⅓ inch thick.

NORI ROLLS

MAKES 4 ROLLS, SERVING 3 TO 4
PEOPLE / TIME: 40 MIN

Sushi rice:

1 cup sushi rice

2 tablespoons brown rice vinegar (do not use regular white vinegar)

1 teaspoon organic sugar

Generous pinch of salt

Spicy tempeh filling:

½ (4-ounce) package tempeh

2 tablespoons Vegan Mayo (page 123) or commercially prepared vegan mayonnaise

1 teaspoon hot chile–sesame oil (also called hot pepper–sesame oil), or to taste

For assembly:

1 tablespoon brown rice vinegar

4 sheets nori seaweed

1 ripe avocado, peeled, seeded, and sliced into ¼-inch-wide strips

1 scallion, white part discarded, sliced lengthwise into narrow strips

1 tablespoon toasted or black sesame seeds if used inside the roll, or ¼ cup if used as a coating for inside-out rolls

----
NOTE

Look for brown rice vinegar, hot chile–sesame oil, nori seaweed, and black sesame seeds at a Japanese or Asian grocery or in the ethnic foods aisle of big-box grocery stores. If you can't find the hot sesame oil, a little regular toasted sesame oil with a pinch of cayenne will get you there.

VARIATIONS

PEAR AND TEMPEH ROLL: Substitute ½ recipe (about 1½ cups) of Creamy Asian Pear and Tempeh Salad (page 118) for the spicy tempeh filling.

Other Fillings, Made Simple and Snappy:
Here are a few alternative fillings that have been a hit with our veggie sushi fans everywhere. It's so easy to prepare one or more of these when whipping up a batch of Spicy Tempeh Nori Rolls. Be an interesting person and serve interesting sushi!

ELEPHANT ROLL: Stuff the sushi rolls with 2 tablespoons of roasted chopped peanuts and a few slices of ripe avocado per roll.

"YAMROOM" ROLL: For each roll, fill with 2 tablespoons of mashed sweet potato (about 1 small sweet potato, peeled and boiled), 1 to 2 dried or fresh shiitake mushrooms simmered in ½ cup of water, 2 tablespoons of soy sauce and a dash of mirin (Asian cooking wine). Sprinkle the filling with toasted sesame seeds before rolling.

SPINACH SESAME: Lightly steam ½ pound of well-washed, fresh spinach, squeeze to remove any excess water, and chop finely. Toss with 1 teaspoon of toasted sesame oil, 1 tablespoon of sesame seeds, a sprinkle of sea salt, and a dash of rice vinegar. Fill and roll as directed for the Spicy Tempeh Nori Rolls.

2. Place about 1½ tablespoons of Spicy Tempeh, three strips of avocado, and some scallion strips across the center of your rice, laying or spreading them horizontally to each side of the nori to create a strip of filling about 1 inch wide—the less filling, the easier the sushi will be to roll. You'll figure it out.

3. Pick up the mat and gently roll up that sushi, starting from the rice-topped end; try to keep your grip relatively tight, for a firm roll. When you've reached the seaweed-only end, pat the dry nori gently with a little bit of vinegar water to seal the roll. Gently press the length of the roll a few times with your hands to seal it all up.

4. Slice your roll into 1-inch pieces with a very sharp, serrated knife. Arrange on a decent looking platter and serve with little dishes of soy sauce, prepared wasabi, and some slivers of pickled ginger. That's it! Now go make a hundred more of 'em.

◆

INSIDE-OUT ROLLS

Maybe you've been rolling your own for a while, or you just need to look like a master sushi chef right now! Then inside-out rolled nori rolls will get you the attention you so deserve, and with less stress than you might expect.

Simply prepare your nori roll as directed, spreading the seasoned rice onto about two thirds of the toasted nori sheet. Place a sheet of plastic wrap on top, gently slid your hand underneath the bamboo mat and rest your other hand on top of the plastic wrap. Then in one quick motion . . . flip everything upside down! Remove the bamboo mat from underneath and place on your countertop. Place the nori and rice—plastic wrap side down—on the mat. Place your fillings as usual on the nori, taking care that it's the side without the rice underneath it. Now carefully roll, using the bamboo mat to firmly press the roll together. Make sure to gently peel away the plastic wrap as you roll.

For best results, roll your spiffy inside-out rolls in fun things, such as toasted sesame seeds, black sesame seeds, toasted nori flakes, or Japanese ground-up red pepper. If a nori wrapper rips a bit at the edges, don't worry; once it's rolled, you won't be able to tell.

◆

Somewhere between a panino and a quesadilla are these hearty grilled sandwiches: we skip the cheese and pile in a filling of creamy, garlicky mashed yuca. We love the filling as is, but go crazy over additions like roasted red peppers, sautéed corn kernels, fresh spinach, or sweet potatoes with black beans. If we had an outdoor grill, we'd brush them with a little extra olive oil in the summertime for a tasty addition to standard BBQ fare. These are best served with Tropical Avocado Salsa Fresca (page 322) or any kind of salsa, fresh pico de gallo, and of course, Guacamole (page 73).

The filling can be made a day in advance, or even better, have a container of filling and some tortillas on hand for quick suppers or filling, nutritious snacks.

Prepare the yuca filling first: Bring 3 quarts of water to a boil in a large soup pot. Add the yuca and cook for 20 to 25 minutes, or until tender and the flesh flakes easily when pierced with a fork, then drain. When the yuca is cool enough to touch, remove and discard any thick, rubbery skin from the outside of the roots or fibrous core from the center. Gently mash with your fingers and set aside.

Place the oil and garlic in a cold cast-iron skillet. Cook over medium heat, stirring constantly, for 2 minutes, or until sizzling and fragrant. Add the bell and jalapeño peppers and cook, stirring occasionally, until the peppers are very soft, 6 to 8 minutes. Remove from the heat, let cool for a few minutes, then pour over the mashed yuca. Stir in the lime juice, salt, and white pepper, mashing the mixture even more, until everything is combined (using your hands is okay). If making any of the variations, add those ingredients and mix thoroughly. Taste the mixture and adjust the salt content to taste.

To assemble: Preheat a griddle or cast-iron skillet over medium heat. Brush a tortilla lightly with olive oil and spread with a generous ½ cup of filling, covering half the tortilla all the way to the edges. Fold in half, gently pressing the tortilla together, and brush each side with a little olive oil. Place in the heated skillet and grill—flipping once—pressing down on the tortilla with a spatula until the outsides are nicely toasted and filling is piping hot. Remove from the heat, cut in half, and serve immediately with salsa and Guacamole (page 73).

TIP

Yuca (pronounced "yoo-ka") is also known as cassava or manioc root; you may have already met it in the form of tapioca. It grows exclusively in the tropics but can be found in most any Latino market or a supermarket that carries tropical produce. Yuca is a totally different plant from yucca, a cousin of agave, but chances are, if what you see is in chunks, it's yuca (however it's been spelled). Yuca is very inexpensive and found where most root vegetables are stocked in large supermarkets. The woody, hard tubers can be time consuming to peel and chop. If your supermarket serves a Latin American community, take a peak in the frozen aisle for peeled frozen yuca cut into easy-to-cook pieces (usually in 1- to 2-pound bags). It's a huge time saver!

-45-

GRILLED YUCA
TORTILLAS

SERVES 4 TO 6 / TIME: 40 MIN

Yuca filling:

1 pound yuca, peeled, chopped into 4-inch chunks, and each chunk quartered

3 tablespoons olive oil

6 cloves garlic, minced

1 small yellow or red bell pepper, seeded and cut into small dice (about 1 cup)

1 jalapeño pepper, finely chopped

1 tablespoon fresh lime juice

½ teaspoon salt, or to taste

Pinch of ground white pepper

Optional additional fillings:

½ cup of one or more:

Sautéed corn kernels

Diced roasted red pepper (pages 28, 33)

Sautéed mushroom

Sliced black olives

Olive oil, for brushing

4 to 6 (8-inch) flour or whole wheat tortillas

VARIATIONS

SWEET POTATO–BLACK BEAN: ½ cup of mashed sweet potato (about 1 very small sweet potato, peeled and boiled), ½ cup of cooked black beans, ½ teaspoon of ground cumin.

SPINACH-CILANTRO: ½ cup of cooked, chopped spinach, squeezed to remove excess water (half a 10-ounce package of frozen chopped spinach is perfect), ¼ cup of chopped fresh cilantro leaves, ½ teaspoon of ground coriander.

PINTO, CORN & JALAPEÑO
QUESADILLAS

SERVES 8 / TOTAL TIME: 45 MIN,
not including time for cheese to set /
ACTIVE TIME: (30 MIN)

Cheese:

1½ cups cashews, soaked overnight or boiled for 20 minutes

½ cup water

1 roasted red pepper, seeded (see pages 28, 33)

2 tablespoons nutritional yeast

2 tablespoons mellow white miso

1 tablespoon fresh lemon juice

2 teaspoons onion powder

1 teaspoon ground turmeric

1 teaspoon salt

¼ cup organic unrefined coconut oil, melted

Filling:

2 tablespoons olive oil

4 jalapeño peppers, seeded and thinly sliced

3 cloves garlic, minced

2 cups corn kernels (fresh is best)

8 ounces cremini mushrooms, thinly sliced

¼ teaspoon salt

¼ cup chopped fresh cilantro

1 cup cooked or canned pinto beans, drained and rinsed

For assembly and serving:

Spray olive oil, for pan

8 (8-inch) flour tortillas

Guacamole (page 73) or diced avocado (optional)

So, maybe you're looking to put the "ques" in "quesadilla." Then this is the recipe for you. Cashew cheese gets all melty and creamy in between the grilled tortilla, giving you that authentic quesadilla experience. If you don't have a grill pan, it's still yummy in a large skillet. But the grill pan is worth it because grill marks and smokiness!

Make the cheese: Drain the cashews and place them in a blender along with the water. Pulse until pureed. At this point the mixture will be a little gritty; that's okay. Just get it as well pureed as you can without adding the other ingredients just yet. Scrape down the sides often.

Add the red pepper, nutritional yeast, miso, lemon juice, onion powder, turmeric, and salt and blend again until well incorporated. Now add the melted coconut oil. This is where it's important to blend until the cheese is smooth and not gritty. It may take a few cycles if you don't have a high-speed blender, so be patient, give the motor a rest often, and blend until completely smooth. Use a touch more water, if needed.

Transfer to a tightly sealed container and set aside for at least 3 hours or overnight.

Make the filling: Preheat the olive oil in a large skillet over medium heat. Sauté the jalapeño and garlic in the oil for about 1 minute, being careful not to let it burn. Add the corn and mushrooms, and sprinkle with the salt, then toss to coat in the oil and garlic. Cook for 5 to 7 minutes, stirring occasionally, until the corn is lightly browned.

Mix in the cilantro and let wilt. Add the pinto beans and cook just to heat through, being careful not to mush. Transfer to a bowl. If there is any extra liquid in the pan, just leave it there or it will dilute your quesadillas.

To assemble: Lightly oil a grill pan and heat over medium heat.

Take two tortillas and spread a few tablespoons of the cheese on one side of each to about ¼ inch of the edges.

Place about ⅓ cup of the filling on top of one of the tortillas, then place the other, cheese side down, to close.

Cook each side for about 3 minutes, until grill marks appear and the cheese spread is melty. Continue to assemble and cook the other quesadillas.

To serve: Use a pizza cutter to slice each quesadilla in half or into quarters. Top with your favorite pico de gallo and guac, if using.

Rice noodles make the perfect canvas for velvety butternut squash, crunchy pumpkin seeds, and fresh herbs. Don't be intimidated by working with rice paper wrappers; it's easy once you get the hang of it, and rolling fresh spring rolls is a skill that will last a lifetime. Before you begin, you will want to lay a very clean, slightly damp kitchen towel (or a layer of paper towels) on your counter; rice paper wrappers can be slippery and the towel makes a great work surface.

We've included a simple soy dipping sauce recipe, but for a sublime and really fall-like experience, pair these with Cranberry-Chile Dipping Sauce (page 324).

Prepare the rolls: Preheat the oven to 400°F. Place the butternut squash cubes on a baking sheet and rub them all over with the oil; drizzle on another teaspoon if you need to.

Arrange the cubes in a single layer and roast for 15 minutes. Remove from the oven, toss, and cook for 10 more minutes, or until tender and slightly caramelized. Transfer the squash to a plate to cool.

While the squash is cooking, prepare the noodles. There are usually directions on the package, but just in case: Bring a large pot of water to a boil, then turn off the heat, add the noodles, and cook off the heat just until tender. It could be between 3 and 10 minutes, depending on your noodles. Just stir and check very often and get them drained as soon as they are ready, so that they don't break apart. Drain in a colander and run cold water over them to prevent further cooking. Set aside until ready to use.

To assemble: Fill a large pie plate or bowl with very warm water; tap water works just fine. Place two rice paper wrappers in the water at a time, completely submerged, and let sit for about a minute, until they have softened.

Handle each wrapper gently as you place it on your work surface. Place about ¼ cup of rice noodles in the lower third of the wrapper, leaving about 1½ inches of margin from the far edges on either side (you'll be folding those in). Place a layer of butternut squash above the noodles. Sprinkle with the cilantro and pumpkin seeds. If some of the seeds get stuck to your fingers, just dip them in the water. To roll, snugly fold the left and right sides of the wrapper over the filling. Lift the bottom of the wrapper over the filling and tuck it underneath the filling, then roll firmly but gently. Place the rolls, seam side down, on a plate and cut in half when ready to serve.

Prepare the dipping sauce: Mix the dipping sauce ingredients together in a small bowl and stir rigorously to dissolve the sugar. Serve with the rolls.

TIP Roasting the squash in cubes gives them a nice caramelized crunch on the outside that you wouldn't get if you just roasted the squash whole.

BUTTERNUT SQUASH & PUMPKIN SEED
RICE PAPER ROLLS

MAKES 12 ROLLS / TIME: 1 HR 15 MIN

Rolls:

1 pound butternut squash, peeled, seeded, and cut into ¼-inch cubes

2 to 3 teaspoons olive oil

4 ounces vermicelli rice noodles or rice sticks

12 (8-inch) round rice paper wrappers

1 cup fresh cilantro, torn into bite-size pieces (Thai basil makes a nice variation)

⅓ cup roasted, salted pumpkin seeds, chopped coarsely

Dipping sauce *contains soy:

2 tablespoons soy sauce

3 tablespoons rice vinegar

1 tablespoon Asian hot chile oil (or more to taste)

2 teaspoons toasted sesame oil

2 tablespoons organic sugar

GREEK ZUCCHINI TOMATO
FRITTERS
with Fresh Herbs

SERVES 4 TO 6 / TIME: 45 MIN

1 (1-pound) package firm tofu, squeezed to remove extra water, then crumbled

¼ cup ground walnuts (see tip)

1 clove garlic, minced

3 tablespoons fresh lemon juice

1 tablespoon tomato paste

2 teaspoons dried oregano

1 teaspoon salt

Generous pinch of freshly ground black pepper

½ cup vegan bread crumbs, plus an additional ⅓ cup for coating

¼ cup chopped fresh dill

¼ cup chopped fresh mint

½ pound zucchini, grated and squeezed to remove excess water (about 1 cup)

1 pound seeded, finely chopped tomatoes (about 1 heaping cup), drained to remove excess liquid

Olive oil, for frying

Just as enticing but way cheaper than a vacation on Santorini Island, these veggie-loaded Greek-inspired fritters are bursting with chunks of fresh tomato, dill, and mint. The addition of zucchini creates a tender and light texture. These are absolutely sublime served along with Mediterranean-Style Cashew-Cucumber Dip (page 71). You can easily make this lovely summertime appetizer into a meal by serving with salad greens dressed with olive oil and fresh lemon juice. For the fry-o-phobe, we give you alternative baking instructions as well for turning these into tasty baked patties.

In a food processor, pulse together the tofu, ground walnuts, garlic, lemon juice, tomato paste, oregano, salt, and pepper into a thick, chunky mixture (do not overblend). Taste and add more salt and pepper if necessary. Scrape the tofu mixture into a large bowl, using a spatula, and mix in the bread crumbs, dill, and mint. Your mixture should have the consistency of a thick cookie dough; if it's too moist, add more bread crumbs (by the tablespoon). Gently fold in the grated zucchini and chopped tomatoes.

Have ready layers of paper towels or a large, clean paper grocery bag for absorbing the oil after frying. Heat a ¼-inch layer of olive oil in a large, heavy-bottomed skillet (preferably cast iron) over medium heat. To test the oil, sprinkle a pinch of bread crumbs into the pan. If bubbles form rapidly around them, then the oil is ready.

Using 2 heaping tablespoons of mixture per fritter, drop each fritter into the bread crumbs and roll gently to coat. Flatten to about 1 inch thick. Fry the tomato fritters for 4 to 6 minutes on each side, or until golden brown, turning very carefully (these are delicate, so a thin spatula works well for this). Drain on paper towels and let cool for about 5 minutes before serving.

Serve sprinkled with more fresh dill or dusted with additional dried oregano.

Alternative baking option: Preheat the oven to 350°F and line a large cookie sheet with parchment paper. Lightly oil the paper with olive oil and arrange the bread crumb–coated patties on top, placed about 1 inch apart. Spray or gently brush the tops of the patties generously with olive oil. Bake for 25 to 30 minutes: at around 12 minutes, remove from the oven, flip each over, and spray or brush with more olive oil. Bake until the patties are golden and firm to the touch.

TIP   Can't find ground walnuts? Measure ⅓ cup of walnut halves or pieces into a food processor and pulse like hell, scraping the sides of the bowl frequently.

You can shape the uncooked fritters a day in advance, keep them covered in the refrigerator, and fry them just prior to serving. They can also be lightly sautéed in a little olive oil to reheat.

These are like potato pancakes, but instead of making them with the traditional potato, we make them perfectly autumnal by using beets, carrots, and sweet potatoes. It's pure fall harvest heaven! You're going to want a food processor to shred all these vegetables or else autumn will be over by the time you're done prepping. Serve with applesauce or Horseradish-Dill Sour Cream (page 318), or both.

Have ready layers of paper towels or a large, clean paper grocery bag for absorbing the oil after frying.

Combine the shredded veggies in a large mixing bowl. Add the shallot, flour, cornstarch, salt, pepper, and fennel seeds. Use a wooden spoon to mix everything well; the flour mixture should evenly coat all the veggies. Add ¼ cup of water and stir again, until all the flour is dissolved.

Preheat a heavy-bottomed nonstick or cast-iron skillet over medium-high heat. Pour a ¼-inch layer of olive oil into the pan. Let the oil heat for about 2 minutes.

Form the beet mixture into balls the diameter of a quarter, then flatten into 1½-inch medallions. Fry the medallions in batches for 5 minutes; turn over and flatten them a bit with a spatula. Fry for another 3 to 4 minutes. Transfer to paper towels to drain. Serve ASAP.

TIP   Replace the flour with matzo meal to make these Passover friendly.

AUTUMN
LATKES

MAKES ABOUT 24 LATKES /
TIME: 40 MIN

2 cups peeled, shredded beets (about 3 average-size beets)

1 cup peeled, shredded carrot (about 1 average-size carrot)

1 cup peeled, shredded sweet potato (you guessed it, 1 average-size sweet potato)

1 shallot, chopped finely (about ¼ cup)

½ cup all-purpose flour

¼ cup cornstarch

½ teaspoon salt

Several pinches of freshly ground black pepper

1 teaspoon fennel seeds, chopped

Olive oil, for panfrying

POTATO
LATKES

MAKES ABOUT 18 LATKES /
PREP TIME: 15 MIN
with a food processor, a lot longer without /
COOKING TIME: 1 HR

2½ pounds russet potatoes, scrubbed

1 medium-size yellow onion, peeled

¼ cup potato starch or cornstarch

½ teaspoon salt

½ teaspoon freshly ground black pepper

2 cups matzo meal

Lots of vegetable oil, for frying

- - - - - - - - -
NOTE
- - - - - - - - -

In Brooklyn we pronounce latke *lat-kuh*, but in
other parts of the country we've heard *lat-key*,
which sounds really cute. Both pronunciations
are correct, so go with whatever suits you.

This is the perfect recipe for the traditional Jewish fried potato pancake.
Crispy on the outside and tender on the inside, these guys are sure to please
everyone at the Hanukkah table. Because they are made with matzo meal,
they're good for Passover as well. If you non-Jews among us are like "Han-
nuwha?" and "Passwhatover?" don't worry about it, just make up a batch the
next time a need for fried potato-y goodness arises. Serve with applesauce
and Horseradish-Dill Sour Cream (page 318). The recipe doubles perfectly,
so make enough for the *meshpuchah* and then some.

Have ready a brown paper shopping bag or paper towels for draining the oil from
the latkes. You may also want to have the oven on at 200°F to keep the latkes
warm until you're ready to serve. If serving immediately, just have a baking pan
covered with aluminum foil ready to keep the finished ones warm after they've
been drained.

If using a food processor, use the grating blade to shred the potatoes and the
onion. If shredding by hand, use a grater to shred all the potatoes. Dice the onion
as finely as possible.

In a large mixing bowl, using a wooden spoon or your hands (we use our hands;
it's faster), mix the potatoes and onion with the potato starch until the potatoes
have released some moisture and the starch is dissolved, about 2 minutes. Add
the salt and pepper and stir. Add the matzo meal and mix well. Set aside for about
10 minutes. The mixture should become liquidy yet sticky.

In the meantime, preheat a large, preferably cast-iron but definitely nonstick skillet over medium heat, a little bit on the high side. Pour a ¼-inch layer of vegetable
oil into the pan. The oil is hot enough when you throw a bit of batter in and bubbles rapidly form around it. If it immediately smokes, the heat is too high and you
should lower it a bit. If the bubbles are really lazy, give the oil a few more minutes
or raise the heat a bit.

With wet hands (so that the mixture doesn't stick), roll the batter into golf ball–
size balls. Flatten into thin, round patties. Fry about four to six at a time; just be
careful not to crowd the pan. Fry on one side for about 4 minutes, until golden
brown. Flip over and fry for another 3 minutes.

Transfer to the paper towels and proceed with the remaining latkes. Once latkes
have drained on both sides, place in a baking pan and keep at 200°F or cover with
aluminum foil to keep warm.

Somehow, forming anything into a croquette makes a meal very impressive, even though it is an easy thing to do. Millet and broccoli are cooked together with garlic, tarragon, and red pepper, formed into squat little cushions, and lightly panfried. These make a great vehicle for the White Bean Aioli (page 66) or Dill-Tahini Sauce (page 325). They are delicately flavored, so definitely include a sauce when you serve. Round out the meal with roasted asparagus and red peppers (pages 28, 33, 35).

Make ahead: Prepare the millet and broccoli a day in advance. Then, you only need about 20 minutes to finish preparing this dish.

Preheat a small pot over medium heat. Sauté the garlic in the oil for about 30 seconds. Add the tarragon, red pepper flakes, black pepper, and salt and mix for a few seconds. Add the millet and stir constantly for about 3 minutes to toast it. It should turn a shade darker. If it doesn't, don't sweat it too bad; just proceed with the recipe. Better that than you burn the garlic.

Add the vegetable broth and cover; bring to a boil. Once the mixture is boiling, lower the heat to a simmer, cover, and cook for 10 minutes.

Mix in the chopped broccoli, cover, and cook for about 7 more minutes. Uncover and cook for another 10 minutes, stirring often. Once the water is mostly absorbed, turn off the heat but leave the pot on the stove, covered, to continue to cook for another 10 to 15 minutes. At that point, all of the water should be absorbed and the millet should be mushy if you push down on it with a spoon. It's very important that the millet be well cooked or else the croquettes could fall apart, so if it doesn't seem fully cooked, let it sit for an additional 5 or 10 minutes. You are looking for a polenta-like consistency.

Transfer to a mixing bowl and let cool for about 10 minutes, then place the bowl in the fridge to cool the rest of the way, for about 45 minutes or so. Give it a stir now and again to speed up the cooling process. Don't skip or skimp on this cooling step or your croquettes will turn to millet mush in the skillet.

Once cooled, tightly form the millet into golf ball–size balls. Press them down in your hands to flatten just a bit, then roll the sides between your hands to form tire-shaped croquettes.

Heat a thin layer of olive oil in a large nonstick or cast-iron skillet over medium heat. Cook the croquettes in batches for 3 to 4 minutes on each side. They should be golden brown with a few darker spots. Serve immediately.

BROCCOLI-MILLET
CROQUETTES

1 tablespoon olive oil, plus more for panfrying

2 cloves garlic, minced

1 teaspoon dried tarragon

½ teaspoon red pepper flakes

Several pinches of freshly ground black pepper

½ teaspoon salt

1 cup millet

2½ cups vegetable broth, purchased or homemade (page 223)

4 cups broccoli, tops and stalks, chopped very finely into pea-size or smaller pieces

------
TIP

When you chop the broccoli florets, they will probably crumble a lot. That is fine; just throw the crumbled tiny bits in with the rest of the broccoli.

ACORN SQUASH & BLACK BEAN
EMPANADAS

MAKES 12 EMPANADAS /
TIME: 2 HRS 30 MIN, lots of it inactive

Pastry:

2 cups all-purpose flour

¼ cup cornmeal

2 tablespoons organic sugar

1 teaspoon salt

½ teaspoon baking powder

½ cup refined coconut oil, softened

2 teaspoons apple cider vinegar

½ to ¾ cup very cold water

Filling:

1 acorn squash (about 1½ pounds)

Nonstick cooking spray, for pans

2 tablespoons olive oil

1 average-size red onion, sliced into 1-inch pieces

2 jalapeño peppers, sliced thinly (remove seeds if you don't want these too hot)

2 teaspoons coriander seeds, smashed (see page 161 for how to crush)

2 cloves garlic, minced

1 teaspoon ground cumin

½ teaspoon salt

1 cup cooked black beans, drained and rinsed

2 tablespoons fresh lime or lemon juice

2 teaspoons pure maple syrup

Most Latin American and Spanish-speaking countries have their own variation of empanadas, but they are all basically a savory stuffed pastry. We make our empanadas into triangles as a matter of efficiency, because we hate cutting circles and then having scraps to reroll. If you want to do circles, more power to you! The flaky crust has a hint of cornmeal, which makes this empanada dough especially tasty. Plus, the nutty flavor of acorn squash goes great with black beans. Serve these with Tropical Avocado Salsa Fresca (page 322), Guacamole (page 73), or Sour Cilantro Cream (page 319).

Preheat the oven to 400°F.

Prepare the pastry: Combine the flour, cornmeal, sugar, salt, and baking powder in a large mixing bowl. Add the coconut oil by the tablespoon, but you don't need to be precise about this. You just want to add it in small chunks, cutting into the flour with each addition. Cut in the coconut oil until the dough is crumbly and pebbly, as if you are making a piecrust.

Combine the vinegar with ½ cup of the cold water. Add to the dough in three batches, gently mixing it in with a fork, until the dough holds together when pinched. If need be, add up to ¼ cup more water.

Gather the dough into a ball and knead very gently a few times until it holds together. Sprinkle a clean work surface with flour, then roll out the dough into a rectangle about 8 inches long and 5 inches wide.

Place baking parchment on a cutting board (make sure the parchment is bigger than the cutting board because you are going to use it to roll out the dough later). Gently lift the dough onto it. Cover with plastic wrap and refrigerate for at least an hour.

Meanwhile, roast the squash: Cut it in half lengthwise and use a tablespoon to scoop out the seeds and stringy parts. Spray a baking sheet with nonstick cooking spray. Place the squash, face down, on the prepared baking sheet and bake for about 50 minutes, until it is easily pierced with a fork. When the squash is cooked, remove it from the oven and place, cut side up, on a plate to cool. Keep the oven at 400°F if you are making the empanadas now.

Make the filling: Preheat a large skillet over medium-high heat. Sauté the onion and the jalapeños in the olive oil for 5 to 7 minutes, until softened. Meanwhile, peel the skin from the squash and cut the squash into ¾-inch chunks.

Add the coriander seeds and garlic to the pan and sauté for a minute more. Add the cumin, salt, and a few splashes of water (about 2 tablespoons). Add the squash and cook for about 5 minutes, stirring often to coat. It's okay if the squash doesn't retain its shape perfectly. Add the black beans and heat through. If the mixture looks dry, add a few more splashes of water. Lastly, add the lemon juice and maple syrup and stir. Turn off the heat and prepare the empanada dough.

Spray a baking sheet with nonstick cooking spray and set it aside. Now grab your dough from the fridge and remove the plastic wrap. Slide the dough off the cutting board, keeping the paper underneath it. Roll out the dough into a 9- to 12-inch rectangle. Trim the edges to make it an even rectangle. Slice the dough into 3-inch squares—four cuts across and two cuts lengthwise.

Take a square and roll it out a bit more, to about 6 inches square (but you don't have to be precise about it). Arrange it so that a corner is pointing toward you. Place about 2 tablespoons of filling in the lower half of the dough, leaving about ½ inch of space at the bottom point. Fold over the dough so that it is in the shape of a triangle. You may need to pull it a little bit; just do so carefully so as not to rip it. Pinch together the seams with a fork or your fingertips and place on your baking sheet. Continue forming the rest of the empanadas.

Bake for 25 to 30 minutes, until golden brown. Serve warm!

PANKO-STUFFED
MUSHROOMS

**MAKES ABOUT 20 STUFFED
MUSHROOMS / TIME: 45 MIN**

22 big cremini mushrooms, rinsed and
    patted dry

1 tablespoon peanut oil

1 cup finely diced daikon

3 cloves garlic, minced

3 tablespoons mirin

½ teaspoon salt

½ teaspoon ground white pepper

1½ cups vegan panko

1 tablespoon toasted sesame oil, plus more
    for pan and garnish

½ cup finely chopped scallion, plus more for
    garnish

3 tablespoons toasted sesame seeds

TIP

To toast sesame seeds: Preheat a small, dry pan
over medium-low heat. Pour in the sesame
seeds and toast them, stirring often, for about
3 minutes. Once they are browned, immediately
remove them from the pan to prevent burning.

These little guys are different from your run-of-the-mill Italian-style stuffed
mushrooms since they're flavored with Japanese stuff: sesame, mirin, and
scallions. Panko is a Japanese bread crumb that ten years ago might not have
been on every grocery shelf but these days it's on the TGIF menu, so it's safe
to say you'll be able to find it. Daikon provides a little crunch but you can sub
water chestnuts or maybe celery if you roll that way. We like the way DIY-
toasted sesame seeds look on these because they provide some color contrast,
but you can buy them toasted if you prefer. Black sesame seeds would look
cool as well.

Preheat the oven to 350°F.

First, remove the stems from the mushrooms. An easy way to do this is to cup one
in your writing hand, stem up, and gently but firmly twist and pry the stem out.
Then, use a small spoon to remove any remaining stem. Do not discard the stems;
chop them up small and set them aside. It's common to break a mushroom or
two, which is why the recipe calls for twenty-two mushrooms but stuffs twenty.
If one breaks and can't be used, just chop it up along with the stems. If you have a
mushroom stem–removing talent and manage not to break any, then finely chop
the two extras anyway.

Preheat a large skillet over medium heat. Pour in the peanut oil and sauté the
chopped mushroom for about 3 minutes, until some moisture has released. Add
the diced daikon and cook for 5 more minutes, stirring often. Add the garlic and
cook for a minute longer.

At this point, lots of moisture should be released from the mushrooms. Add the
mirin, salt, and white pepper and cook for about 2 minutes.

Turn off the heat. Add the panko in ½-cup batches and stir, alternately adding the
sesame oil and splashes of water (up to 4 tablespoons) until all the bread crumbs
are moist. The mixture should be crumbly but, when you press some between
your fingers, it should hold together. Mix in the chopped scallion and adjust the
salt to taste.

Grease a baking sheet with a little sesame oil. Stuff each mushroom with the filling: place a little of the filling into the mushroom crevice and then add another
tablespoon on top of that, pressing firmly to form a mound. Place each stuffed
mushroom, stuffing side up, on the prepared pan.

Bake for 20 minutes. To serve, sprinkle the toasted sesame seeds over the mushrooms and drizzle with a little sesame oil, if desired. Garnish with extra chopped
scallion. If you are going for a fancy plating, place a few mushrooms on a handful
of raw spinach leaves.

Blini are light, savory, yeasted pancakes laced with Eastern European goodness, mostly in the form of buckwheat flour. They are small and bite-size, similar to silver dollar pancakes, and make a great appetizer. This recipe is a little time consuming because you have to make the pancakes in small batches, so you may only want to serve it for special occasions. But it's really worth the trouble, we promise. Serve with thick Mushroom Gravy (page 322) and Horseradish-Dill Sour Cream (page 318) and top with fresh chopped parsley.

Measure the milk into a measuring cup and add the vinegar to it; set aside to curdle.

Mix the sugar and water in a large glass or plastic mixing bowl. Add the yeast and stir briefly. Leave the bowl in a warm place and let the yeast foam up; it usually takes about 3 minutes.

Meanwhile, add the ground flaxseeds to the milk and stir well.

In a separate large mixing bowl, combine the buckwheat and chickpea flour, salt, and olive oil. Pour in the milk mixture and mix until smooth. Add this batter to the yeast mixture and mix again until smooth. Place a towel over the batter and leave it in a warm, draft-free place for about an hour.

Preheat a large nonstick skillet over medium heat. Give the batter a stir—it shouldn't be bubbling over the bowl, just slightly bubbly. When the pan is hot, spray with nonstick cooking spray. Carefully pour about 1½ tablespoons of batter into the pan to form a blin (pancake); you can usually fit about five at a time, but take care not to overcrowd; if you can only fit four, then so be it.

The tops of the blini should bubble up and set within 90 seconds (if they do not, then either the heat is not high enough or the pan hasn't had time to heat up properly). Flip each blin and cook for another 90 seconds. Both sides should be a dark, flecked golden brown.

If you are serving them within 30 minutes, you can place them on a plate covered with aluminum foil. If they are for later on, place on a baking pan and keep in a 200°F oven until ready to serve.

BLINI

MAKES ABOUT 36 BLINI /
TIME: 1 HR 30 MIN, lots of it inactive

1½ cups unsweetened nondairy milk, at room temperature

2 teaspoons apple cider vinegar

1 tablespoon organic sugar

½ cup warm water

1 (¼-ounce) envelope active dry yeast

1 tablespoon ground flaxseeds

½ cup buckwheat flour

½ cup chickpea flour

½ teaspoon salt

2 tablespoons olive oil

Nonstick cooking spray or olive oil spray, for pan

- - - - - - - -
TIPS
- - - - - - - -

Use an ice-cream scoop to efficiently pour the blini batter. Measure 1½ tablespoons of batter into it once to get an idea of how much batter that is, and then just eyeball it for the rest of the blini.

Use the thinnest spatula you can to flip the blini. Since you'll be using a nonstick pan, a very thin, flexible heatproof rubber spatula makes all the difference in the world.

EVERYDAY CHIPOTLE-VEGETABLE
TAMALES

MAKES ABOUT 3 DOZEN
TAMALES / TIME: 1 HR 25 MIN,
for assembling and steaming

2 (6-ounce) packages corn husks, for at
least 36 husks plus more husks for making
strips to tie ends of tamales

Tamale dough:

4 cups masa harina flour

2 teaspoons baking powder

½ teaspoon salt

½ cup mild-tasting olive oil, semifrozen until
cloudy and the consistency of soft sorbet

4 cups vegetable broth, purchased or
homemade (page 223), or equivalent
prepared vegetable bouillon, warmed

Chipotle bean filling:

2 tablespoons olive oil

1 large onion, diced small

1 clove garlic, minced

1 red bell pepper, seeded and diced

1 small carrot, peeled and diced

1 (15-ounce) can pinto or black beans,
drained and rinsed

1 cup frozen corn kernels

¼ cup vegetable broth, purchased or
homemade (page 223)

2 chipotle peppers in adobo sauce, minced,
plus 2 tablespoons of adobo sauce (use a
7-ounce can of chipotles in adobo sauce
for this)

3 tablespoons tomato paste

1 teaspoon ground cumin

½ teaspoon salt, or to taste

Tamales are special: they are holiday food, fiesta-forever food, and like so many holiday foods may take some extra effort but are so damned delicious the payoff is epic. With a title like "everyday" we hope you can make a little extra space during those ordinary times and appreciate the extraordinariness that is a snack or meal of humble homemade vegetable tamales.

This tamale recipe is as flexible as you want it to be; add fresh corn kernels, roasted chopped chiles, or scallions to the dough if you feel like it. Small bits of seasonal vegetables such as zucchini, pumpkin, poblano chiles, and even a little leftover sautéed seitan would be welcome. You need a large steamer basket for this recipe, so stop and make sure you have one right now. Sure, you could use a small steamer basket, but then you'll have to make these in two batches and it will take you longer. But there's no rush; it's time to make the tamales.

Although preparing the dough and filling is straightforward, tamale assembly can be tedious work. Enlist the help of a friend or two with promises of heaps of tamales to look forward to later and provide lots of chips, salsa, and Guacamole (page 73) while you work to keep ravenous tamale-seekers at bay.

Place the corn husks in the largest pot you've got (no need to separate them just yet). Cover them completely with hot tap water and allow to soak for at least 20 minutes, until the husks are soft and pliable. Keep covered in water the entire time the recipe is prepared, until ready to use.

Prepare the tamale dough: Combine the masa harina, baking powder, and salt in a large bowl, or if you have a standing mixer, use this to prepare the tamale dough (it will come out the fluffiest using a standing mixer, really!). Scoop the semifrozen olive oil into the bowl and use a pastry cutter or a fork to mash the oil into the dough to form a sandy texture. Form a well in the center of the mixture and pour in about a third of the warm broth. Beat the mixture in an electric mixer for about a minute, then add the remaining broth in two batches and continue to beat until a moist, fluffy dough forms and the sides of the bowl are clean. Cover the bowl with plastic wrap or a damp towel and set aside.

Prepare the filling: In a deep 12-inch skillet, heat the olive oil over medium-high heat. Sauté the onion and garlic for 3 minutes, or until softened. Add the bell pepper and carrot and sauté for 3 minutes, then add the beans, corn, broth, chopped chipotles and adobo sauce, tomato paste, and cumin. Sauté and simmer until most of the liquid evaporates, 5 to 7 minutes. Salt to taste and allow to cool before assembling tamales.

Recipe Continues

Dried corn husks for tamales, masa harina flour, and chipotles in adobo sauce can all be found where Latin American groceries are sold or in your local Mexican market. Note that there's NO substitute for masa harina, a specially milled corn flour made from corn processed with slacked lime (not lime fruit) for a unique flavor and speedy cooking consistency: don't even think of using regular cornmeal. If you've ever eaten a tortilla chip or a corn tortilla, you already know how special tasting masa harina is!

To assemble: Depending on the size of the individual corn husk, you expect to use one to two husks per tamale. There are almost as many ways to wrap a tamale as there are tortilla chips eaten daily in America; we like the following method for its simplicity and classic tamale form.

Take a corn husk and lay it flat; spread about 2 tablespoons of dough off center, leaving a 1½-inch space from the top and bottom of the husk. Pat the dough to about ¼-inch thickness and a roughly oblong shape. Spoon a heaping tablespoon of filling in the center of the dough. Lifting both edges of the corn husk, fold the dough over the filling. Now, tuck one edge of the corn husk under the opposite edge of dough and firmly roll any remaining husk to form a tube: make sure to completely encase the filling in both the dough and the corn husk to prevent anything from spilling out while steaming. Tie both ends securely with either heavy-duty kitchen string (maybe try different colors for different flavors), or simply tear an extra corn husk lengthwise into thin strips and use those as ties.

Loosely pack the tamales, standing them right side up (not stacked on top of one another) in a large steamer basket. Leaving room is important as the tamales will expand while steaming! Steam for 35 to 40 minutes. The tamales will expand and feel firm to the touch when done. To test the tamales, remove one from the center (metal tongs are great for grabbing hot tamales), unwrap, and test the dough: it should feel firm and have a consistency similar to reheated cooked polenta. Remove from the heat and allow to cool slightly before serving: we think it's most fun to let your guests unwrap their own tamales.

Serve with your favorite salsa and Guacamole (page 73) or for the whole enchilada, serve with rice (page 39) and beans.

When you want all the spicy goodness of a samosa but don't want to go through the trouble of making a dough, enter Samosa Stuffed Baked Potatoes. Serve these as a precursor to the Stir-fried Chickpea & Cauliflower Curry (page 282) or really any Indian dish. You can also have two halves for an entrée and serve with Sautéed Spinach & Tomatoes (page 149). Top with 5-Minute Mango Chutney (page 323) and you've got yourself a meal!

To bake a potato, in case you don't know how: Preheat the oven to 400°F. Poke the potato with a fork about eight times and wrap in aluminum foil. Bake for about an hour, until easily pierced with a fork. When done, unwrap and let cool.

Slice the cooled baked potatoes in half lengthwise and scoop out the insides, leaving about ¼ inch of potato in the skin. The easiest way is to hold the potato in the palm of your nonwriting hand and use a teaspoon to scoop the potato into a bowl. Go slowly and carefully so as not to break the potato, but you don't have to be a perfectionist about it. Mash the potatoes with the milk and set aside the skins.

Preheat the oven to 400°F.

Heat the coconut oil in a large skillet over medium-high heat. Add the mustard and coriander seeds. The mustard seeds should begin to pop; if they don't pop in a minute or two, turn up the heat. Let the seeds pop for about a minute (put a lid on them so you don't get splattered), add the onion and carrot, and sauté for 7 to 10 minutes, until the onion begins to brown.

Add the garlic and ginger and sauté for a minute more. Add the cumin, turmeric, and salt with a splash of water, stir well, then add the potatoes, mixing everything well. Add a little extra water if it looks too dry. Cook until the potatoes are heated through, then add the peas and cook until those are heated through. Add the lemon juice to taste and stir to incorporate.

Brush or spray the inside of the potato skins with a little bit of oil. Then, scoop the filling into the skin, pressing gently to hold the filling in place.

Line up the potato halves on an ungreased baking sheet and bake for 20 minutes. You can garnish with some chopped fresh cilantro, if you are so inclined, and serve.

SAMOSA STUFFED
BAKED POTATOES

**MAKES 8 POTATO HALVES /
TIME: 20 MIN,** once potatoes are baked

4 large russet potatoes, scrubbed, baked, and cooled (see headnote)

¼ cup unsweetened nondairy milk; vegetable broth, purchased or homemade (page 223); or water

3 tablespoons refined coconut oil, plus more for brushing potatoes

1 teaspoon yellow mustard seeds (or whatever kind you've got)

1 teaspoon coriander seeds, crushed (see page 161 for how to crush)

1 small yellow onion, cut into small dice (about 1 cup)

1 medium-size carrot, cut into small dice (about ¾ cup)

2 cloves garlic, minced

2 teaspoons grated fresh ginger

2 teaspoons ground cumin

½ teaspoon ground turmeric

½ teaspoon salt

½ cup frozen peas, rinsed

Juice of ½ lemon

Chopped fresh cilantro, for garnish (optional)

CREOLE
STUFFED
PEPPERS

**SERVES 8 AS A SIDE OR 4 AS A MAIN /
TIME: 55 MIN**

4 large bell peppers

2 tablespoons olive oil, plus more for
   casserole dish

1 medium-size yellow onion, chopped finely

2 jalapeño peppers, cut in half, seeded
   (if you don't want too much heat), and
   sliced finely

1 cup finely diced carrot

4 cloves garlic, chopped finely

2 dried bay leaves

1 teaspoon dried oregano

1 teaspoon dried basil

2 teaspoons sweet paprika

3 sprigs fresh thyme

1 teaspoon salt

1 (15-ounce) can diced tomatoes

2 (15-ounce) cans black-eyed peas, drained
   and rinsed (about 4 cups, cooked)

¼ cup chopped fresh parsley

These peppers are stuffed with a mildly spicy mixture of black-eyed peas and veggies. We don't know that much about Southern cooking besides what we've gleaned from too many hours of watching the Food Network, but we used the basic herbs and spices from Creole cooking—paprika, oregano, and thyme—so we think these earn the right to be called Creole. Choose peppers that aren't oddly shaped and that look like they would be good for cutting in half and stuffing. Serve with Messy Rice (page 174) and Hot Sauce–Glazed Tempeh (page 202). They also go well with mashed potatoes and Jalapeño-Corn Gravy (page 329).

Preheat the oven to 350°F and grease a 9 x 13-inch casserole dish with a little olive oil. Bring a large pot of water to a boil.

Cut the bell peppers in half lengthwise through the stem end. For aesthetic purposes, try to leave the stem intact on one side; if you can't manage it, no love lost. Remove the seeds and membranes. Submerge the bell peppers in the boiling water and cover. Let them boil for 5 minutes, then drain them immediately and rinse with cold water to cool them down a bit.

Meanwhile, heat the oil in a large skillet over medium-high heat. Sauté the onion, jalapeños, and carrot for about 10 minutes. You want the veggies to brown, especially the carrot. If it looks like the veggies are steaming rather than browning, then raise the heat a bit. Add the garlic about 5 minutes into the cooking process.

Add the bay leaves, the other herbs and spices, and the salt; sauté for 1 more minute. Add the tomatoes and peas, stir and cover, and cook for 10 minutes. If it seems too liquidy, then remove the cover and cook long enough to reduce some of the liquid. Mix in the parsley.

Remove the bay leaves and thyme sprigs. The mixture will be hot, so we find it's easier to just remove the herbs while filling the peppers; just be on the lookout for them.

Spoon a little less than ½ cup of the veggie mixture into each pepper half. Again, the filling will be hot, so be careful while you are handling it. Place the pepper halves in the prepared casserole dish and bake for about 25 minutes.

Don't let the simple ingredients fool you—this is a delicious, full-flavored dip, perfect for spreading on vegan crackers or pita bread. We use only a touch of garlic here because raw garlic tends to overpower things, so taste first before deciding there isn't enough.

Bring a small pot of water to a boil. Boil the carrots for 7 to 10 minutes, or until soft. Drain and let cool just until they are no longer steaming.

Place the sunflower seeds in a blender or food processor and process into crumbs. Add all the remaining ingredients and blend until smooth, scraping down the sides of the processor as you go.

Taste for salt and adjust the spices and lemon. Transfer to a covered container and refrigerate until ready to use (at least 30 minutes).

VARIATION

CARAWAY-PARSLEY-CARROT DIP: Omit the curry and cumin. Place ½ teaspoon of caraway seeds in the food processor along with the sunflower seeds. Add ½ cup of loosely packed fresh parsley after everything has been blended and pulse until it is chopped finely.

CURRIED
CARROT DIP

MAKES 2 CUPS DIP /
TIME: 25 MIN, plus chill time

1 pound carrots, peeled and cut into ½-inch chunks

¼ cup roasted sunflower seeds (salted are okay; just add less salt)

2 teaspoons olive oil

½ teaspoon minced garlic

1 teaspoon curry powder

½ teaspoon ground cumin

¼ teaspoon salt

1 tablespoon fresh lemon juice

Snacks, Appetizers, Little Meals, Dips & Spreads

WHITE BEAN
AIOLI

MAKES 1½ CUPS AIOLI /
TIME: 10 MIN

1 (15-ounce) can navy or great northern beans, drained and rinsed

2 tablespoons fresh lemon juice

¼ teaspoon salt

Several pinches of freshly ground black pepper

¼ cup olive oil

6 cloves garlic, chopped

Traditionally, aioli is a garlicky mayonnaise, but we love this version made of white beans, olive oil, fresh lemon juice, and lots and lots of garlic. It's great for serving with grilled or roasted vegetables; for spreading on sandwiches, bruschetta, or pitas; or as a creamy topping on burgers. The garlic flavor is very strong, so a little goes a long way.

Combine the beans, lemon juice, salt, and pepper in a blender or food processor and puree until smooth, scraping down the sides of the bowl to get everything.

Preheat a small pan over low heat. Cook the garlic in the oil for about 3 minutes. You want just to gently heat it, not brown it.

Add the garlic and oil to the mixture in the blender and puree. Taste for salt, pepper, and lemon, and adjust to your liking.

Transfer to a container, cover, and refrigerate until ready to use.

For dip sophisticates, this pâté has a deep, complex flavor, made woodsy and slightly sweet from the roasted chestnuts. This dip tastes especially good on melba toast or some such type of cracker. Make a few extra roasted chestnuts just for nibbling on, because you're going to want to.

Roast the chestnuts: Preheat the oven to 425°F. Slice a little slit in the shell of each chestnut to prevent them from exploding in the heat. Place the chestnuts on a dry, rimmed baking sheet and roast for 25 minutes. Remove from the oven and place in a kitchen towel. Let cool a bit and then bunch the edges of the towel together, tightly wrapping the chestnuts and crushing them to loosen their shells. Open the towel and peel the shells and inner skins from the chestnuts.

Meanwhile, prepare the lentils: Place them in a small pot with the 2½ cups of water and the crushed garlic. Cover, bring to a boil, then lower the heat to a simmer. Simmer for 30 minutes, until all or most of the water is absorbed and the lentils are very tender.

Remove as much of the garlic as you can from the lentils. Place the lentils in a food processor or blender, along with the chestnuts. Blend a bit, adding ½ cup of water until relatively smooth. Add the oil, salt, parsley, and nutmeg and blend again. If the mixture seems too thick, add up to another ½ cup of water. It should be thicker than the consistency of hummus, but not by much.

Place in a covered bowl and chill for at least an hour.

Serving suggestions: Toast thin slices of vegan French bread. Spread with a few tablespoons of pâté, then place a slice of tomato on top. Sprinkle very lightly with salt and garnish with parsley.

CHESTNUT-LENTIL PÂTÉ

MAKES OVER 2 CUPS PÂTÉ /
TIME: 50 MIN, mostly inactive, plus chill time

1 pound whole chestnuts

½ cup dried French lentils, sorted, rinsed, and drained

2 cloves garlic, crushed

2½ cups water (for the lentils), plus ¾ to 1 cup (for blending)

¼ cup grapeseed oil

¾ teaspoon salt

2 tablespoons chopped fresh parsley leaves

¼ teaspoon freshly grated nutmeg (from about ½ whole nutmeg)

TIP

This dish is best made with fresh chestnuts when they are in prime season, between October and January. After that, the freshness of most nuts in stores is often dubious; all too often we've purchased a pound and found out after peeling them that many a chestnut was nasty, moldy, and shriveled. Instead, look for prepeeled, frozen, or jarred chestnuts available during the fall/winter months in many gourmet, natural, or specialty shops. Plus, they easily cut the prep time in half, giving you more time to procrastinate gift buying!

Chestnut-Lentil
Pâté, page 67

Sun-dried
Tomato Dip,
page 70

Asparagus-Spinach Dip,
page 72

Our longtime *Post Punk Kitchen* friend Paula Simone brought this classy pâté to a New Year's Eve party and we seriously couldn't stop freaking out due to its lush texture and complex, elegant flavor. For a moment in time we were transported out of our dollar-store leg warmers, huddled together in our freezing Brooklyn apartments, and fancied ourselves well-heeled society folk wearing cubic zirconia tiaras and elbow-length polyester satin gloves raising a glass of $30 champagne at the midnight ball.

Well, anyway, this pâté is stupid easy to make, delightfully rich and satisfying spread on crusty vegan-friendly breads and whole-grain crackers. Pile it high in a fancy dish for a party with nice drinks, or just tucked into pita with salad greens and cucumbers for a light dinner on a warm summer night.

Heat 2 tablespoons of the oil in a large skillet over medium heat. Add the onion and sauté for 3 to 5 minutes, or until translucent, then add the garlic, thyme, tarragon, salt, and pepper and cook for another minute. Next, add the mushrooms and cook for about 8 minutes, or until they are very soft, lowering the heat if necessary to prevent them from burning.

While the mushrooms are cooking, place the walnuts in a food processor or blender and pulse until fine (and a little like walnut butter is okay!).

Add the cooked mushroom mixture to the walnuts in the food processor, along with the balsamic vinegar, beans, and remaining tablespoon of oil. Process until smooth, adding the vegetable broth 1 tablespoon at a time, as needed. Continue to puree the ingredients until the pâté resembles a smooth, thick, and spreadable paste. Scrape the mixture into an airtight container and chill for at least an hour before serving to allow the flavors to meld.

WALNUT-MUSHROOM
PÂTÉ

MAKES OVER 2½ CUPS PÂTÉ /
TIME: 30 MIN, plus chill time

3 tablespoons olive oil

1 cup diced yellow onion

3 cloves garlic

1 teaspoon dried thyme

1 teaspoon dried tarragon

¾ teaspoon salt

Freshly ground black pepper

1 pound cremini mushrooms, chopped

1 cup lightly toasted walnuts

1 teaspoon balsamic vinegar

¾ cup cooked cannellini beans

Up to ¼ cup cold vegetable broth, purchased or homemade (page 223)

SWEET BASIL
PESTO TAPENADE

SERVES 6 TO 8 / TIME: 10 MIN

3 cups tightly packed fresh basil leaves

1½ cups walnut pieces or halves

2 cloves garlic (roasted garlic is great here!)

½ cup extra-virgin olive oil

3 tablespoons pure maple syrup

1 teaspoon freshly grated lemon zest

1½ teaspoons salt, or to taste

Freshly ground black pepper

Basil pesto is too good for just pasta. If you love it as much as we do, try this spreadable basil pesto that's thickened with extra walnuts and intriguingly sweetened with a hint of maple syrup. Instead of putting this on pasta—which can dilute the intense flavors—try this on hot, crusty bread, alongside hummus and olives on an appetizer tray. It's an absolute must on fresh tomato pizza or slathered on roasted squash.

Chop the basil, walnuts, and garlic together in a food processor until chunky, using a rubber spatula to scrape the sides of the processor bowl frequently. Add the oil, maple syrup, and lemon zest and process until thick and creamy. Season with salt and pepper to taste. Store in a glass jar with a thin layer of olive oil on the surface, and keep refrigerated until ready to serve.

SUN-DRIED TOMATO
DIP

MAKES ABOUT 3 CUPS DIP /
TIME: 25 MIN, plus chill time

2 cups sun-dried tomatoes (dried ones, not the kind packed in oil)

2 cups boiling water

½ cup slivered or sliced almonds

½ cup cooked white beans, drained (navy beans are good)

2 cloves garlic, chopped coarsely

¼ cup olive oil

2 tablespoons fresh lemon juice

⅛ teaspoon salt

Several pinches of freshly ground black pepper

A tangy, hummuslike dip that is great on a grilled veggie sandwich or on pita with a few cucumbers and sprouts.

Place the tomatoes in a bowl and pour the 2 cups of boiling water over them. Cover with a plate and let soak for about 15 minutes.

In a blender or food processor, grind the almonds to a powder. Use a slotted spoon or tongs to remove the tomatoes from the water (don't discard the water) and add them to the almonds. Add the remaining ingredients and puree, adding up to ¼ cup of the tomato water and scraping down the sides often until smooth.

Cover and chill for at least an hour.

VARIATIONS

SUN-DRIED TOMATO BASIL DIP: Add ½ cup of fresh basil leaves at the end and pulse a few times so that the leaves are chopped and dispersed but not pureed.

SUN-DRIED TOMATO & ROASTED GARLIC DIP: Use an entire roasted garlic bulb instead of the fresh garlic.

Vibrant yet thick and bursting with the refreshing flavors of cucumber and dill, this is a dairy-free variation of the classic Greek cucumber yogurt dip tzatziki. It's the perfect zippy companion to spicy, hearty foods (curries, absolutely!) and it created with Greek Zucchini Tomato Fritters (page 50) in mind, but there's nothing stopping you from serving it as a stand-alone appetizer with grilled, lightly olive-oiled pita bread.

Place the cashews in a small bowl, cover with 2 inches of warm water, and soak for 20 minutes; drain and discard the water. While the cashew are soaking, use a vegetable peeler to remove the skins from the cucumbers. Grate the cucumber with the large hole (coarse) side of a box grater into a mixing bowl.

Scoop up handfuls of grated cucumber and squeeze as thoroughly as you can to remove as much water as possible; do this over the mixing bowl to save some of the juice for later. Transfer the squeezed cucumber to a separate mixing bowl. While a little messy, we like this method as it just requires your hands, but you can do this by wrapping grated cucumber in a cheesecloth or heavy-duty paper towel to squeeze away the juices.

In a food processor, pulse together the drained cashews, lemon juice, half the squeezed grated cucumber, and the garlic, olive oil, oregano, salt, and pepper. Blend until creamy, scraping the sides of the processor bowl frequently. Add 1 to 3 tablespoons of reserved cucumber juice to the sauce to thin it out just slightly. The final consistency should resemble a loose, almost pourable hummus. Scrape the dip into a medium-size bowl and stir in the remaining grated cucumber and the chopped dill. Cover and chill until ready to use. If serving as a dip, swirl into a shallow serving bowl, top with a drizzle of quality olive oil, and garnish a few kalamata olives placed in the center. Serve immediately with warm pita bread. *Opa!*

MEDITERRANEAN-STYLE
CASHEW-CUCUMBER DIP

SERVES 6 TO 8 / TIME: 15 MIN

1 cup raw cashews (5 ounces)

1 pound seedless cucumbers, such as hothouse or English cucumbers

3 tablespoons fresh lemon juice

2 large cloves garlic

1 tablespoon best-quality extra-virgin olive oil

1½ teaspoons dried oregano

½ teaspoon salt

A few twists of freshly ground black pepper

¼ cup lightly packed chopped fresh dill

A few kalamata olives, for garnish

ASPARAGUS-SPINACH DIP

MAKES ABOUT 3 CUPS DIP /
TIME: 20 MIN, plus chill time

1 tablespoon olive oil

4 cloves garlic, chopped

1 pound asparagus, rough ends removed, cut into 2-inch lengths

⅓ cup water

1 pound spinach (about 2 bunches), washed well, stemmed, and chopped coarsely

1 cup raw cashews

3 tablespoons capers, with brine

Salt

Several pinches of freshly ground black pepper

1 tablespoon fresh lemon juice

A creamy, emerald dip that tickles your taste buds with the fresh tastes of springtime and a tangy kick from capers. Perfect for tank-top weather out on the porch, with a cold beer and some crackers. If only we had porches.

Preheat a large pan over medium heat. Sauté the garlic in the oil for about a minute, until fragrant, stirring to keep it from burning. Add the asparagus and water, cover, and bring to a boil. Let boil for about 5 minutes, until the asparagus is bright green. Lower the heat to medium. Add the spinach in batches, letting the leaves wilt so that there's room in the pan for more. Cover the pan to make the wilting go faster; it should take about 3 minutes. Once all the spinach has been added, cook, uncovered, for about 5 minutes.

Meanwhile, put the cashews, capers, salt to taste, and pepper in a food processor or blender and blend until the cashews are small, coarse crumbs. Scrape down the sides to make sure you get everything.

When the spinach is done cooking, add to the food processor and puree until relatively smooth. Try to get as much of the garlic from the pan as possible, and any remaining water. Add the lemon juice, adjust the salt and pepper if necessary, and transfer to a container. Cover and chill for at least an hour.

We used to feel silly putting a guacamole recipe in a cookbook, but every now and then you encounter something that claims to be guacamole. You stop what you're doing and wonder if there's something you could have done to change the course of events, and then it becomes clear we are not born with the recipe for a great guacamole encoded in our DNA. That's cool. So here's a recipe!

Terry is a guacamole purist and likes to keep it as simple as can be. Isa likes to put all kinds of junk in her guac, but the kids love it anyway. Like any guac, this should be made to order and served immediately. One avocado can make enough to serve two people or just one hungry avocado enthusiast, so just double, triple, or quadruple the ingredients to serve more. Make only as much as you need, though, because leftover guacamole (if there is such a thing) is a travesty.

The key to great guacamole is a great avocado. There's a sweet spot in the ripening cycle of this magical fruit that is ideal: the outside of the avocado should just start to give when very gently pressed. It should never be rock hard, but don't manhandle even unripe avocados or you'll be sorry. Bruised avocados may ripen into brownish, stringy fruits with a bitter aftertaste. And nobody likes that. Not that we've never made guacamole with these, but they don't make truly awesome guacamole.

Run a knife lengthwise all along the middle of the avocado. Firmly grasp each half and twist to separate the halves. Remove the pit by gently but firmly hacking the knife into the pit, gently twisting the knife, and pulling it away from the avocado. Separate the peel from the avocado halves and place the flesh in a medium-size bowl. Drizzle with the lime juice and sprinkle with the minced onion, salt, and black pepper. Mash it all up with a fork to the desired consistency. Mash in the cilantro. Add the other stuff if you really think you need it. Serve immediately!

GUACAMOLE

MAKES 1¼ CUPS GUACAMOLE /
TIME: 10 MIN OR LESS

2 ripe avocados; use Hass for best results

Juice of 1 lime (about 2 heaping tablespoons of juice)

1 small yellow or white onion, finely minced (about ¼ cup)

½ teaspoon kosher salt

A few twists of freshly ground black pepper

3 tablespoons chopped fresh cilantro

Optional—add one or more of the following:

1 ripe tomato, seeded and chopped

Pinch of ground cumin

1 jalapeño pepper, fresh or roasted, seeded and minced

1 clove garlic, minced

A HUMMUS RECIPE,

REMASTERED

**MAKES 3 CUPS HUMMUS /
TIME: 10 MIN, plus chill time**

- 2 (15-ounce) cans chickpeas, drained and rinsed
- ⅓ cup olive oil
- ¼ cup tahini
- 3 tablespoons fresh lemon juice
- 2 to 3 cloves garlic, crushed
- ½ teaspoon sea salt
- ¼ teaspoon ground cumin or ground coriander (optional)
- ¼ cup water, more or less for desired thickness

TIP

Would this hummus be even better with homemade chickpeas? Does pita bread have a pocket (well, not all do, but whatever)? Yes, once in your life please make homemade hummus with homemade cooked chickpeas; the flavors of your finished hummus will be clear, bright, nutty. For a guide to cooking beans, please see page 40.

It's 2017 and it's a well-established fact that hummus is to vegans what air is to the rest of humanity: we need it to live. And at least for most of us living in New York City, this ubiquitous chickpea puree can be found at most any party, appetizer spread, tucked in a sandwich, in a little plastic container (alongside some pretzels and carrot sticks) for a healthy hearty snack, or perhaps the vegan's best friend, as a healthy and protein-loaded schmear on a toasted everything bagel.

It's 2017 and admittedly the shelves of most any supermarket in the United States are buckling under the weight of tons of very good hummus brands. So, why bother making it yourself? We can't argue with the convenience, but you can't talk back when it comes to the satisfaction and lovely fresh flavor of homemade hummus.

And we now know the true secret to creamy hummus (we thought it was blenders, but nope): peel the chickpeas. Yes, really. Authentic and richly smooth Middle Eastern hummus is born of just that. Do not fear, though; you won't be cradling each bean by hand and removing the skin like a teeny orange: the process can be done in minutes while catching up on your Netflix queue. We promise the results are so worth it you'll never look at a fully jacketed chickpea again without longing to disrobe it!

Place the chickpeas in a large mixing bowl and cover with about 4 inches of warm water. With both of your hands, gently rub the chickpeas together in the water. Continue to agitate the chickpeas and you'll feel their skins start to loosen and slip off; you may find yourself carefully squeezing some of the beans to speed the process. Just take care not to premash everything. Occasionally set the bowl aside for a minute and the skins will rise to the top. Use your fingers or a small mesh strainer (or if you have it, a metal deep-frying skimmer) to skim away the skins; discard the skins. Continue like this while watching an episode of *It's Always Sunny in Philadelphia* and soon you'll have a bowl of naked chickpeas ready to party with Frank under a bridge (no, please don't let them party with Frank). Perfection is not required; a few random skins won't ruin your hummus party.

Transfer the chickpeas to a large blender or food processor and add the oil. Pulse several times, stopping to scrape down the sides with a rubber spatula. When the mixture is mostly smooth, add the tahini, lemon juice, garlic, salt, and cumin. Pulse, stopping to stir several times, until the mixture is creamy, thick, and smooth like a natural nut butter. If you want a looser, smoother hummus, drizzle in a tablespoon of water at a time until the desired consistency is reached. Taste and season with a little more salt, lemon juice, or olive oil if desired. If your food processor isn't big enough for the whole batch, divide the ingredients in half and process two separate batches of hummus.

Transfer the hummus to an airtight container and chill for 30 minutes before serving. If you're not going to eat it directly out of the container spread on everything in the house, be classy and spread hummus in an artful way into a shallow serving bowl and drizzle a tablespoon of olive oil on top. Serve with pita, crackers, crostini, vegetable crudités, pretzels, and so on.

VARIATIONS

FOLD IN AFTER PUREEING ½ TO 1 CUP OF THE FOLLOWING: caramelized onion or shallot, roasted garlic, roasted carrot, roasted beet, roasted red pepper (pages 28, 33).

HERBED HUMMUS: Add 2 to 3 tablespoons of the following: chopped fresh dill or fresh parsley.

ZA'ATAR HUMMUS: Sprinkle plenty of this delectable Middle Eastern spice blend on top of hummus before topping with olive oil.

OLIVE HUMMUS: Add ¼ cup of pitted black or green olives and pulse in after pureeing.

NOTE

Hummus for Bagels

Here in NYC we love our bagels, but a longtime dilemma for vegans has been what to put on them. Sometimes tofu cream cheese is just too heavy, too fake-tasting, or just not available. Hummus is a natural and typically on standby. Along with a thin slice of tomato and onion, a generous schmear of hummus is what a sesame or everything bagel really craves.

If making hummus just for bagels, a thicker, more spreadable consistency is helpful. Reduce the water to 1 to 2 tablespoons, or leave it out entirely.

CHAPTER TWO

BRUNCH

Why do we love brunch so much?

Maybe because the word is a most delicious-sounding portmanteau. It's a perfect feast of savory and sweet, hearty and fruity all possible on the same plate. Possibly because it's usually reserved for long, leisurely weekends so it has a holiday feel to it. Master brunch at your place and never leave the house before noon on the weekends to stand in line for hours for the one vegan muffin on the menu of the local brunch spot. Make it at home and you get to sip Bloody Marys and hang out with rollers in your hair.

We like our brunch fare hearty and savory. Our eggless Benedict (page 85) takes a vacation to the Greek islands with creamy dill-infused sauce, roasted red peppers (pages 28, 33), and plenty of kalamata olives. Try something different in the morning with a pretty baked strata (page 79), layered casserole of bread, herbed mushrooms, and fresh spinach held together with melt-in-your-mouth dairy-free custard. Or, for something quick and easy, a tasty, down-home hash of blue potatoes and tempeh (page 84) will have you ready for a day on the organic farm (or just sitting on the sofa watching interesting documentaries about people working on an organic farm).

And what would brunch be without something you can pour plenty of real maple syrup all over? We've expanded the selection to choose from: beyond the much loved chocolate or banana waffles and blue corn pancakes and crepes, there's classic vegan breakfast fare: versatile pancakes, tempeh bacon and maple seitan sausage, and an essential tofu scramble.

Eating a filling meal for brunch frees up your day from planning dinner so you can do fun stuff instead, like thrift store shopping, playing with the cats, or going back to bed. Just put off the dishes until Monday morning.

- - - - - - - - - - - - - - ◆ - - - - - - - - - - - - - - -

DINER
HOME FRIES

SERVES 4 TO 6 / TIME: 50 MIN

2 pounds Yukon gold potatoes, cut in half lengthwise, sliced ½ inch thick or so

3 tablespoons olive oil

1 green bell pepper, seeded and cut into ½ inch dice

1 medium-size onion, cut into ½-inch dice

Salt

½ teaspoon freshly ground black pepper

This is how we do it in Brooklyn: boiled and lightly fried potatoes with green peppers and onions. It's pretty bare bones, but no breakfast would be complete without them. We prefer not to spice these up because we're usually serving them with other flavorful foods and we don't want them to overpower the others. But for some Irish flair, drizzle a little malt vinegar over these spuds.

Place the sliced potatoes in a pot and submerge in cold water. Salt the water so it tastes not quite as salty as sea water. Cover the pot and bring to a boil. Once the potatoes are boiling, lower the heat to medium and cook for about 8 more minutes, until the potatoes are easily pierced with a fork but still firm. Drain and set aside.

Heat 2 tablespoons of the oil in a large, heavy-bottomed skillet (preferably cast iron) over medium-high heat. Add the potatoes and flip them around with a spatula to coat them in oil. Cook undisturbed for 5 to 7 minutes; they should be lightly browned. Cook for 10 more minutes, stirring and tossing occasionally to brown all sides. They won't all get browned and crispy; just do your best.

Add the pepper, onion, salt to taste, and pepper, and the last tablespoon of oil, and cook for 5 to 7 more minutes, stirring often, until the onion and pepper are lightly browned. Cover to keep warm until ready to serve.

TIPS

For nicely browned and evenly cooked home fries, use your biggest pan to avoid overcrowding.

To makes things faster: If you know in advance you are preparing these for breakfast, boil the potatoes the night before, drain them, and chill them in a sealed container overnight. Bring them to room temperature before cooking.

A strata is a layered bread casserole that traditionally is covered with an eggy custard and baked until puffy and golden. Our old friend tofu plays a starring role in this tasty veganized version, lavishly flavored with plenty of Italian herbs and shallots.

For simplicity, bake it in the same cast-iron skillet that you sauté the vegetables in. If you don't have an oven-safe skillet, a 9 x 13-inch pan should also work, although the strata will come out a bit thinner. Serve with Diner Home Fries (page 78) or a simple green salad. Cheezy Sauce (page 326) is great on this, too.

Preheat the oven to 350°F.

Sauté the shallots in 2 tablespoons of the oil in a large, oven-safe skillet, preferably cast iron, over medium heat for about 5 minutes. Add the mushrooms and sauté for 7 more minutes, until the mushrooms are tender.

Meanwhile, prepare the custard: Place all the custard ingredients in a blender or food processor, crumbling the tofu as you add it. Puree until completely smooth, scraping down the sides to make sure you get everything. Set aside until ready to use.

To the pan with the shallots and mushrooms, add the garlic, herbs, red and black pepper, and salt. Sauté for another minute. Add a handful of spinach and use tongs to mix with the mushrooms and shallots. Continue adding spinach by the handful as the previous bunch wilts and makes more room in the pan. This should take about 5 minutes.

Turn off the heat, move the vegetables to the side of the pan, and add the remaining tablespoon of oil. Just try to get as much oil as you can to cover the bottom of the pan to keep things from sticking. Toss in the sliced bread and mix to distribute.

Pour the tofu custard over everything. Use a spatula to smush the tofu into the veggies and bread. You want to get things as coated as you can without outright mixing it up.

Place in the preheated oven and bake for 55 to 60 minutes. The strata should be firmed and lightly browned. Let cool for 10 minutes, slice into eight pieces, and serve.

MUSHROOM & SPINACH
STRATA

SERVES 6 TO 8 / TIME: 1 HR 30 MIN,
lots of it inactive

1½ cups thinly sliced shallot (5 or 6 shallots)

3 tablespoons olive oil

8 ounces cremini mushrooms, sliced thinly (about 3½ cups)

3 cloves garlic, minced

2 teaspoons dried thyme

1 teaspoon dried rosemary

1 teaspoon dried oregano

½ teaspoon red pepper flakes

Several pinches of freshly ground black pepper

1 teaspoon salt

10 ounces spinach, well washed and chopped (about 8 cups)

6 slices stale or lightly toasted vegan bread, cut into 2-inch pieces

Custard:

1 pound firm tofu

2 tablespoons fresh lemon juice

2 teaspoons prepared yellow mustard

1 tablespoon cornstarch

¾ cup vegetable broth, purchased or homemade (page 223), or water

¼ teaspoon salt, or to taste

TIP

This recipe requires stale bread. If you are one of the few people in the world who doesn't have a sad-looking half-loaf of bread on your countertop, don't worry—just lightly toast your bread before proceeding with this recipe.

For me, a basic scramble should have nice big pieces in it. It's crumbled, yes, but not completely in crumbles. Just kind of torn apart and then broken up a bit when cooking in the pan. The flavor should be lip smacking and just a bit salty, but not overly so. Garlic, some cumin, a little thyme—that is the base. From there you can do countless variations using whatever is in your fridge that morning.

So, this is my basic recipe. When you want a trustworthy and easy to modify standard scramble, this makes a great go-to.

First, stir the spices and salt together in a small cup. Add the water and mix. Set aside.

Preheat a large, heavy-bottomed pan over medium-high heat. Sauté the garlic in the oil for about a minute. Break the tofu apart into bite-size pieces, add to the pan, and sauté for about 10 minutes, using a spatula to stir often. Get under the tofu when you are stirring: scrape the bottom and don't let it stick to the pan; that is where the good, crispy stuff is. Use a thin metal spatula to get the job done; a wooden or plastic one won't really cut it. The tofu should get browned on at least one side, but you don't need to be too precise about it. The water should cook out of it and not collect too much at the bottom of the pan. If that is happening, increase the heat and let the water evaporate.

Add the spice blend and mix to incorporate. Add the nutritional yeast and pepper. Cook for about 5 more minutes. Serve warm.

VARIATIONS

You can include these additions to your scramble by themselves or in combination with one another.

BROCCOLI: Cut about 1 cup into small florets and thinly slice the stems. Add along with the tofu.

ONION: Finely chop 1 small onion. Add along with the garlic and cook for about 5 minutes, until translucent. Proceed with the recipe.

RED PEPPER: Remove the stem and seeds, then finely chop one red bell pepper. Add along with the garlic and cook for about 5 minutes. Proceed with the recipe.

MUSHROOM: Thinly slice about a cup of mushrooms. Add along with the tofu.

OLIVES: Chop about ⅓ cup of pitted, sliced olives. Add toward the end of cooking, after mixing in the nutritional yeast.

SPINACH: Add about 1 cup of chopped spinach toward the end of cooking, after mixing in the nutritional yeast. Cook until completely wilted.

CARROT: Grate ½ average-size carrot into the scramble toward the end of cooking. This is a great way to add color to the scramble.

AVOCADO: I almost always have avocado with my scramble. Just peel, pit, and slice it and serve on top.

SCRAMBLED TOFU

SERVES 4 / TIME: 30 MIN

Spice blend:
2 teaspoons ground cumin
1 teaspoon dried thyme, crushed with your fingers
½ teaspoon ground turmeric
1 teaspoon salt
3 tablespoons water

2 tablespoons olive oil
3 cloves garlic, minced, or more, to taste
1 pound extra-firm tofu, drained
¼ cup nutritional yeast
Freshly ground black pepper

FLORENTINE

SERVES 4 / TIME: 1 HR

1 recipe Basic Broiled Tofu (page 192)

1 pound spinach (about 2 bunches), well washed, stems trimmed

1 recipe Diner Home Fries (page 78), or 4 vegan English muffins

Vegan butter, for English muffins (optional)

1 recipe Cheezy Sauce (page 326)

Chopped tomato, for garnish

Crispy on the outside, creamy in the inside, serve Tofu Florentine over a layer of Diner Home Fries (page 78) or, if you want to go all traditional, on a toasted, buttered English muffin. Smother it all in Cheezy Sauce (page 326) and be prepared to blow those sleepy taste buds away. Don't let the simple ingredients fool you; their combination and the cooking methods come together spectacularly (not to be conceited). If you crave a hearty, savory dish for brunch, this is the perfect recipe for you. And it wouldn't make a bad dinner, either.

While the tofu is broiling for the first 10 minutes, prepare the spinach: Preheat a large pan over medium-high heat. While the spinach is still wet from being washed, add half to the pan. The extra moisture helps to steam the spinach. Use tongs to toss it around. Once it is wilted, add another batch of spinach. After all the spinach is cooked, cover to keep warm.

To serve: If using home fries, put about 1 cup's worth in the middle of each plate. If using an English muffin, toast and butter it and place both pieces face up on the plate. Cover with a layer of spinach followed by four pieces of broiled tofu. Ladle Cheezy Sauce over everything and top with a little chopped tomato, just to give it some color. Serve immediately.

TIP

Tip for managing your time: Follow this guide and everything should be finished at about the same time.

1. Press your tofu and boil the potatoes first; meanwhile, prep all your other ingredients.
2. Prep the garlic for the Cheezy Sauce and for the Broiled Tofu at the same time.
3. Start cooking Cheezy Sauce and preheat the broiler; the potatoes should be boiled by this point.
4. Start cooking the home fries.
5. Broil the tofu.
6. Cook the spinach while the tofu is broiling (about 10 minutes in).

BLUE FLANNEL
HASH

SERVES 4 / TIME: 40 MIN

2 tablespoons olive oil

1½ pounds blue potatoes, cut into ½-inch dice

1 (8-ounce) package tempeh, cut into ½-inch dice

½ teaspoon red pepper flakes

1 medium-size onion, cut into ½-inch dice

2 tablespoons soy sauce

An all-American favorite gets a makeover with the unusual and earthy-tasting blue potato. Although blue potatoes have been cultivated in South America for hundreds of years, it's only in the past decade or so that they've become widely available in the United States. Simple seasoning and gentle cooking bring out the best flavors in these precious blue tubers. Craving a real sausage flavor? Toss in some crushed fennel seeds along with the tempeh. Sometimes purple potatoes are also called blue potatoes, but either kind will work here.

Preheat a large, heavy-bottomed pan (cast iron would be ideal) over medium-high heat.

Pour in the oil and let it heat up. Add the potatoes and tempeh and mix. Cover and let cook for about 15 minutes, stirring every now and again.

Add the red pepper flakes and onion and mix. Cover and cook for another 10 minutes, stirring whenever you feel like it.

Add the soy sauce and cook for another 3 minutes. Cover to keep warm until ready to serve.

This rustic, charming brunch specialty performs all kinds of feats. Roasted red peppers stand in for salmon and Dill-Tahini Sauce for the hollandaise in a luscious Mediterranean take on the classic Benedict. Serve over Diner Home Fries (page 78) or an English muffin. You can also opt to go Greek all the way and serve over sliced, toasted pita.

This is basically a conglomeration of other recipes, but don't be intimidated! Follow this list for time management and you'll be all set.

1. Press your tofu and boil the potatoes first; meanwhile, prep all your other ingredients.
2. Prepare the Dill-Tahini Sauce.
3. Start roasting the red peppers.
4. Cook the home fries.
5. Broil the tofu.

To assemble: Place the home fries, English muffin, pita, or other side dish on the plate. Layer with two pieces of roasted red pepper and four pieces of broiled tofu. If you are serving with extra vegetables, place those around your tofu stack. Ladle on the tahini sauce, scatter with kalamata olives, sprinkle the oregano hither and fro, and serve immediately.

NOTE The tofu method is the same as for the Tofu Florentine (page 82), but you can also use Marinated Italian Tofu (page 195), if you prefer.

GREEK
TOFU BENEDICT

MAKES 4 SERVINGS /
TIME: ABOUT AN HR

1 recipe Basic Broiled Tofu (page 192)
1 recipe Diner Home Fries (page 78),
    4 vegan English muffins, or pita
1 recipe Dill-Tahini Sauce (page 325)
2 roasted red peppers (pages 28, 33)
⅓ cup kalamata olives
Dried oregano, for garnish

OLD-FASHIONED
TEMPEH BACON STRIPS

SERVES 4 ALONGSIDE SCRAMBLE OR PANCAKES / TIME: LESS THAN 30 MIN

8 ounces tempeh

2 tablespoons pure maple syrup

2 tablespoons tamari

1 tablespoon natural ketchup

1 tablespoon olive oil or refined coconut oil, melted, plus more for frying

1 teaspoon hickory or mesquite liquid smoke

Nonstick cooking spray (optional)

Ten or more years ago when the world was still amazed and mystified by the idea of vegan bacon, a company called Lightlife made (and still does to this very day) a life-changing product, ready-to-cook bacon-flavored tempeh. It's so simple yet brilliant: douse strips of this nutty soy food in a salty-sweet-smoky marinade. Since then, we've made countless versions of the stuff at home, usually with favorite pantry staples, such as tamari, liquid smoke, and a touch of natural ketchup for a color and a bright tomato finish for a marinade. Fry it up and here it is, a crazy delicious old-school bacon-like thing that's equally at home tossed in a salad or served on a stack of waffles or pancakes.

Slice the tempeh into ¼-inch strips. For easiest frying, we recommend attacking the standard rectangle of tempeh from the short end for shorter, easier-to-handle pieces.

In a ceramic or metal baking dish, whisk together the maple syrup, tamari, ketchup, oil, and liquid smoke until smooth. Gently layer in the tempeh and gently toss to completely coat with the marinade, then let stand for 10 minutes or cover and chill overnight.

Place a lightly oiled cast-iron skillet over medium heat. Lay the tempeh pieces in the pan in a single layer, and, if desired, spritz with a little nonstick cooking spray. Cook for 2 to 3 minutes, until well browned on one side, flip, and cook the other side until browned. Serve hot, warm, or chilled.

A tasty and satisfying vegan breakfast sausage that's easy to make at home. You'll *want* to gather your loved ones around to see how the sausage is made: it's as easy as mixing the dough, shaping, and steaming into adorable little sweet and mellow spiced sausages. Keep a batch frozen (tightly wrap up the still foil-encased links) to fry up anytime to side with pancakes or waffles, or slice lengthwise and fry for sandwiches, too.

Set up your steaming setup of choice. An easy one to use is a stainless-steel pasta pot that comes with a shallow steaming basket that fits inside. Tear eight pieces of foil about 6 inches wide each.

Mash together the cooked brown rice or quinoa, navy beans, vegetable broth, maple syrup, tamari, and oil in a large mixing bowl until combined. In a separate bowl, stir together the remaining dry ingredients, except the flour. Pour the wet ingredients into the wet ingredients and use a rubber spatula or wooden spoon to fold everything together into a moist dough. Lightly dust both a clean work surface and your hands with a little whole wheat flour and knead the dough for about 2 minutes.

Fill the pasta pot with about 4 inches of water and bring the water to a boil over medium-high heat. Set the shallow steaming basket inside the pot and cover. Slice the sausage dough into four sections, and then each of those in four: you should have sixteen pieces in total. Shape each piece into a small sausage-shaped log about 4 inches long, then wrap each piece like candy in aluminum foil. Don't roll in foil too tightly; leave a little slack in the foil as the sausage will expand a bit as it steams (and you don't want exploding vegan sausages; trust us on this one). Steam for 10 minutes, or until the dough feels firm, has expanded a little, and pulls away easily from the foil. Transfer the sausages to a plate and allow them to cool completely before freezing or storing in the fridge.

To serve, fry freshly made (or thawed frozen) sausage in a little bit of olive oil in a cast-iron skillet over medium heat. Roll it around a bit to evenly brown the surface. As vegan sausages contain so little fat, add just enough to prevent sticking as they fry.

LITTLE MAPLE
BREAKFAST SAUSAGES

MAKES 16 LITTLE BREAKFAST
SAUSAGES / TIME: LESS THAN 30 MIN

½ cup cooked brown rice or cooked white quinoa

½ cup cooked navy beans or similar white bean

⅔ cup vegetable broth, purchased or homemade (page 223)

2 tablespoons pure maple syrup

3 tablespoons tamari

1 tablespoon extra-virgin olive oil

1 cup vital wheat gluten

½ cup garbanzo bean flour

1 teaspoon rubbed dried sage

½ teaspoon dried thyme

½ teaspoon garlic powder

½ teaspoon smoked sweet paprika

¼ teaspoon freshly ground black pepper

Whole wheat flour, for kneading and shaping sausages

WEDNESDAY
WAFFLES

MAKES 6 WAFFLES /
TOTAL TIME: 30 MIN

2 cups unsweetened nondairy milk

1 tablespoon organic cornstarch

1 tablespoon apple cider vinegar

2 cups all-purpose flour

3 tablespoons organic sugar

1 tablespoon baking powder

½ teaspoon salt

⅓ cup water

2 tablespoons canola oil

1 teaspoon pure vanilla extract

Oil or nonstick cooking spray, for waffle
   iron

You don't have to wait for Sunday to have a waffle! These can be yours any day of the week. Even Wednesday. They freeze just perfectly, so make a double batch, then pop one (or two) in your toaster and say, "Please, let go of my vegan waffle" when some ne'er-do-well tries to snatch yours.

In a 2-cup measuring cup, use a fork to vigorously mix about half of the milk with the cornstarch, until fully dissolved. Add the remaining milk and the vinegar and set aside.

In the meantime, combine the flour, sugar, baking powder, and salt in a large mixing bowl. Make a well in the center.

Add the milk mixture to the flour along with the water, oil, and vanilla. Mix until the batter is relatively smooth. A few lumps are A-OK.

Let the batter rest while you preheat a waffle iron according to the manufacturer's directions. Follow the manufacturer's directions regarding how much batter to use, spraying the waffle iron liberally with oil or nonstick cooking spray between each waffle as they are made.

Are they brownies or are they waffles? Anyone over the age of three won't mistake these fluffy chocolaty breakfast heroes for the former, but all the same they are irresistible. The perfect way to get more chocolate into your mornings, these shine for breakfast or brunch when served with maple syrup, fresh berries, chopped toasted almonds, and sliced bananas.

Or toss out the same old boring birthday cake and instead host a birthday waffle party: warm chocolate waffles make the ultimate plate for build-your-own ice-cream sundaes—top with scoops of your favorite vegan ice cream plus vegan chocolate syrup or melted peanut butter, crushed pineapple, walnuts, sliced bananas, and vegan candy sprinkles. You're welcome.

Preheat your waffle iron according to the manufacturer's directions. Have a heat-resistant silicone spatula on hand to help remove the hot waffles when ready.

Sift together the flour, cocoa powder, baking powder, baking soda, cinnamon, and salt into a large bowl. Form a well in the center of the sifted ingredients.

In a separate bowl, whisk together the milk, water, yogurt, oil, sugar, and vanilla.

Pour the wet ingredients into the well of the dry ingredients. Use a wire whisk to combine all the ingredients. Just before everything is fully blended, fold in the chopped chocolate chips and pecans. Combine until the ingredients are just moistened; do not overmix.

When the waffle maker is heated and ready to go, spray the cooking surfaces with nonstick cooking spray. Follow the manufacturer's directions regarding how much batter to use (for most square, Belgian-style waffle makers, about ½ cup batter per waffle works). Bake according to the waffle iron directions; the waffles should be lightly browned. Gently slide a spatula under finished waffles and transfer to a cutting board: if desired, cut the waffles in half or quarters and arrange on serving plates. Garnish with fruit and serve immediately with vegan butter and syrup.

TIP

Any waffle maker will work for these waffles, but we adore thick, round Belgian-style waffles for these. If you're using a regular waffle iron, you might need to use slightly less batter per waffle. Or don't just take our word for it; consult your waffle iron's user's manual for best baking results.

CHOCOLATE CHIP
BROWNIE WAFFLES

MAKES 12 WAFFLES / TIME: 30 MIN

2 cups all-purpose flour

⅔ cup unsweetened cocoa powder

1 tablespoon baking powder

½ teaspoon baking soda

½ teaspoon ground cinnamon

½ teaspoon salt

1¾ cups unsweetened almond, soy, or coconut-based milk

¼ cup water

½ cup vanilla or plain almond, soy, or coconut-based yogurt

⅓ cup canola oil or any mild-tasting vegetable oil

⅔ cup organic sugar

1½ teaspoons pure vanilla extract

1 cup vegan semisweet chocolate chips, chopped coarsely

⅔ cup coarsely chopped pecans

Nonstick cooking spray

Vegan butter, fresh strawberries or blackberries, and real maple syrup, for serving

With lots of bananas and walnuts, even the biggest morning-haters will roll out of bed for these. Sliced fresh strawberries and bananas on top make these bad boys really sing.

Preheat your waffle iron according to the manufacturer's directions.

Pour the milk, vinegar, and water into a measuring cup and set aside to curdle.

Mash the bananas very well in a large mixing bowl. Add the milk mixture, oil, syrup, and vanilla and stir.

Add the flour, baking powder, baking soda, salt, and nutmeg. Use a fork to combine. Don't overmix; just mix until there are minimal lumps left. Fold in the chopped walnuts.

Spray the cooking surfaces of your waffle iron with nonstick cooking spray and cook the waffles according to the manufacturer's directions. Serve with sliced strawberries and banana and plenty of maple syrup.

BANANA-NUT
WAFFLES

MAKES 12 WAFFLES / TIME: 30 MIN

1¾ cups unsweetened nondairy milk

2 teaspoons apple cider vinegar

¼ cup water

2 average-size bananas

3 tablespoons canola oil

3 tablespoons pure maple syrup or agave syrup

1 teaspoon pure vanilla extract

2¼ cups all-purpose flour

1 teaspoon baking powder

1 teaspoon baking soda

½ teaspoon salt

¼ teaspoon freshly grated nutmeg

1 cup walnuts, chopped finely

Nonstick cooking spray

Sliced fresh strawberries, sliced banana, and pure maple syrup, for serving

BLUEBERRY CORN
PANCAKES

MAKES 8 TO 10 PANCAKES /
TIME: 30 MIN

¾ cup all-purpose flour

½ cup cornmeal

2 teaspoons baking powder

½ teaspoon salt

2 tablespoons canola oil (any mild-tasting
    vegetable oil will do)

1¼ cups unsweetened nondairy milk

⅓ cup water

1 teaspoon pure vanilla extract

2 tablespoons pure maple syrup

2 teaspoons freshly grated lemon zest

1 cup fresh blueberries

Nonstick cooking spray or a little oil, for
    pan

The perfect summer pancake, with blueberries and a hint of lemon. Cornmeal gives the pancakes a little crunch and a bright sunny flavor.

Preheat a large, nonstick pan over medium-high heat.

Sift together the flour, cornmeal, baking powder, and salt in a medium-size bowl. In a separate bowl, combine the oil, milk, water, vanilla, maple syrup, and lemon zest, plus ⅓ cup of water. Add wet to dry, mix until just combined, then fold in the blueberries. Do not overmix or else the pancakes will be tough; a couple of lumps is okay.

Spray the pan with nonstick cooking spray. Use a ¼-cup measuring cup or an ice-cream scoop to measure the batter into the pan. Cook the pancakes until browned on the bottom and bubbles form on top, about 4 minutes. Flip the pancakes over, using a thin spatula, and cook until the bottom is brown and the pancakes are barely firm to touch. Transfer to plates. Repeat with the remaining batter, spraying the pan again as needed.

Blintzes are plump little packets, crepes folded around a sweet or savory filling. For your brunching pleasure, we present a hearty potato-mushroom filling. Serve with any sauce you'd use for crepes, such as Mushroom Gravy (page 322) or any natural applesauce. These blintzes are also an exceptional choice for dinner served alongside a basic green salad. Assemble the blintzes the day before and they'll sauté up crisp in mere minutes for a fun and filling meal.

First, prepare the crepes (see page 94): Stack the cooked crepes on a dinner plate, cover with plastic wrap, and set aside.

Next, prepare the filling: Peel and coarsely chop the potatoes. Place them in a medium-size pot, add enough cold water to cover by 1 inch, and boil for 20 to 25 minutes, or until easily pierced with a fork and tender. Drain, place the potatoes in a large bowl, and mash coarsely.

Heat the oil in a 10-inch skillet over medium heat and add the onion. Fry the onion, stirring, until it's golden-brown and very soft, about 15 minutes. Add the caraway seeds, thyme, and mushrooms. Sauté until the mushrooms are very tender and most of the liquid has been absorbed, about 5 minutes. Fold the cooked mushroom mixture into the mashed potatoes and season to taste with salt and plenty of pepper.

To assemble each blintz, place 3 rounded tablespoons of the filling in the center of a crepe. Pat the filling to shape it into an oblong. Fold two opposite sides of the crepe over the filling, then fold the remaining two sides over those. The resulting blintz should be a rectangular little bundle. Stack the assembled blintzes on a plate, seam side down.

Preheat a skillet or crepe pan over medium heat. The pan will be ready when a few droplets of water flicked onto its surface sizzle. Using a silicone brush, brush the bottom of the skillet with the vegan butter. Place two or three blintzes, seam side down, on the skillet and cook on each side for 3 to 4 minutes, until their pan-side surface is crisped and browned. Use a small, firm spatula to turn once. Serve the hot blintzes immediately with your sauce of choice.

VARIATION

POTATO-SPINACH BLINTZES: Substitute 1 pound of cooked, chopped fresh spinach for the mushrooms.

-45

POTATO-MUSHROOM
BLINTZES

MAKES 8 TO 10 BLINTZES /
TIME: 45 MIN, *not including making crepes*

1 recipe Savory Wheat or Buckwheat Crepes (page 94)

Vegan butter, at room temperature, for frying

Filling:

½ pound Yukon gold or other waxy potato (about 2 medium-size potatoes)

2 tablespoons olive oil

1 small yellow onion, diced finely

1 teaspoon caraway seeds

½ teaspoon dried thyme

½ pound mushrooms, any variety, sliced thinly

Plenty of freshly ground black pepper

Salt

Optional sauces for garnish:

Mushroom Gravy (page 322), Mustard Sauce (page 312), Dill-Tahini Sauce (page 325), all-natural unsweetened applesauce, store-bought vegan sour cream

-45

CREPES:

SAVORY & SWEET, BUCKWHEAT OR WHEAT

MAKES 8 TO 10 CREPES / TIME: 35 MIN,
plus chill time for batter

Savory wheat crepes:

1½ cups unsweetened almond, soy, or coconut-based milk

¼ cup water

¾ cup all-purpose flour

¼ cup chickpea flour

1 tablespoon arrowroot flour

½ teaspoon salt

Buckwheat crepes:

1½ cups plus 2 tablespoons unsweetened almond, soy or coconut-based milk

¼ cup water

½ cup buckwheat flour

¼ cup all-purpose flour

¼ cup chickpea flour

1 tablespoon arrowroot flour

½ teaspoon salt

To prepare the crepes:

Nonstick cooking spray, for pan

Refined coconut oil, softened, or vegan butter, at room temperature

Crepes: laughably flat pancakes or the most elegant carb to grace the brunch (or dinner) plate?

We love crepes, and want them as simple as can be with a touch of lemon juice and powdered sugar. We've included two versions of the batter to expand your crepe horizons: a basic but not boring wheat batter and a buckwheat batter, a hearty specialty of Brittany. We've enhanced both with a little starch to hold it all together plus a touch of chickpea flour for a delicate sweetness and golden "egg" texture.

Crepes are the perfect package for sweet or savory fillings, such as Mushroom Gravy (page 322), Mustard Sauce (page 312), or Cheezy Sauce (page 326), or top cooked vegetable fillings with a little White Bean Aioli (page 66) before rolling. Crepes require a little more skill than thicker American-style pancakes, but get that skill down pat and you'll appreciate how versatile and interesting they make most any meal.

Breakfast crepes are easy to make exciting: work wonders by dabbing a tablespoon of your favorite jam and rolling up each crepe. Expand on this with a smear of almond or cashew butter, slices of banana, strawberries, raspberries, sautéed apples, even curls of shaved dark chocolate dropped directly onto a hot, right-off-the-skillet crepe.

To make either the savory or buckwheat crepes, combine the milk, water, flour(s), arrowroot, and salt in a food processor or blender. If making sweet crepes or any of the variations, add the sugar and flavorings then, too. Blend for a few seconds, scraping the sides of the blender once, until everything is smooth. The batter will be very thin. Pour into an airtight container, cover, and chill in the refrigerator for at least an hour, or as long as overnight. Right before cooking the crepes, whisk the batter for a few seconds.

Preheat a 9- to 10-inch crepe pan or a heavy skillet over medium-high heat. The pan is ready when a few drops of water flicked into it sizzle. Spray with nonstick cooking spray, dab a silicone brush into coconut oil or vegan butter, and brush along the bottom and sides of the pan.

Ladle ⅓ to ½ cup (use the bigger amount for a bigger pan) into the center of the pan. The batter should sizzle when it hits the pan. Holding the pan firmly by the handle, use your wrist to tilt the pan in a circular motion so that the batter spreads in a thin layer across the bottom. Continue to tilt the pan until the batter is fully spread and then sets.

Cook until the top of the crepe is firm and dry and the edges are lightly browned, 1 to 2 minutes. Carefully run the spatula under the crepe to loosen it, then carefully flip and cook on the other side for 30 seconds. Slide the crepe onto a regular-size dinner plate.

Brush the crepe pan with a little more coconut oil or butter or a spray of oil for the next crepe; anytime the crepes start to stick, give the pan another spray of nonstick cooking spray. If bits of batter collect on the pan, or the pan gets just too oily, quickly swirl a crumpled paper towel across the surface of the pan to remove the crumbs. Cook the rest of the crepes, stacking one on top of another: simply slide the flipped crepe directly onto the stack. If not serving immediately, tightly cover the entire batch with plastic wrap and store in the refrigerator.

VARIATIONS

SWEET CREPES: Add 2 tablespoons of organic sugar.

SWEET ORANGE OR LEMON CREPES: Add 1 teaspoon of finely grated orange or lemon zest and 2 tablespoons of organic sugar.

WHOLE WHEAT CREPES: Substitute ½ cup of whole wheat pastry flour for ½ cup of the all-purpose flour to add extra fiber and nutrients.

NOTE

About Crepe Pans

Learn the ways of crepe making, and you may find it hard to imagine not making them all the time. If this is you, we highly recommend investing in a good crepe pan. The very best varieties are French made, usually of carbon steel or cast iron. Like steel woks and cast-iron skillets, these pans need to be seasoned (follow the manufacturer's directions), but will repay your efforts with a lifetime of perfectly cooked crepes made with minimal cooking fat.

We're not as fond of nonstick crepe pans, but if you must, go for a high-quality brand and never, ever use a metal utensil on its delicate surface. Avoid at all costs goofy plug-in "crepe machines" that require dipping some kind of contraption into crepe batter.

TIP

The fantastic four of tools for better crepes: a pastry brush, canola or olive oil cooking spray, a crumpled paper towel for wiping the crepe pan or skillet, and a long, thin spatula for flipping crepes (this doubles as a great tool to frost cakes).

A stack of tightly wrapped crepes can keep in the fridge for a little over a week for weekday breakfasts or comforting dinners. To reheat cooked crepes, simply heat your crepe pan, brush with a little vegan butter or a spray of nonstick cooking spray, and cook the crepes for about 30 seconds each side. Flip just once.

CHAPTER THREE

SALAD

&

DRESSINGS

Salads have become a way of life for us since the first edition of *Veganomicon* in 2007.

We used to feel a little defensive about presenting salads to vegans (or would-be vegans), as there's a strange misconception that salad is the ONLY thing vegans eat, and therefore must be pretty damned sick of it. Nothing could be further from the truth.

It's clear by now that there are so many healthy and delicious vegan options for entrées, it's tempting to overlook serving a hearty full-meal salad. Revisiting these salad recipes, along with gilding this chapter with a few essentials, shows that salad is one hell of a way to maximize your tasty quotient of daily vegetables. There's no excuse for the soggy limp bag of mixed greens and bottled dressing of yesteryear! Chop some veggies, whisk up some quality oils and vinegars, and filling salads are as straightforward as typing in your order on Seamless.

We still reach for substantial salads these days, so you'll notice lots of tender grains, beans, roasted vegetables, and mushrooms adding plenty of depth and flavor to the medley of traditional leafy greens.

Most of these salads are designed as entrées, but if all you want is something to liven up that bagged baby kale that's next to your casserole, there's a nice little selection of dressings that take mere minutes to make. Salads deserve to hang out all year round—not just during those steamy summer days—therefore, we proudly present a salad for most any occasion and season. So, dust off those salad tongs and rev up the salad spinner.

--------------- ◆ ---------------

SILKEN
CAESAR SALAD

with Roasted Garlic Croutons

SERVES 4 TO 6 AS A SIDE, 2 TO 3 AS
AN ENTRÉE / TIME: 30 MIN, plus chill time

Silken Caesar dressing:

½ cup slivered or sliced blanched almonds

4 cloves garlic, peeled and crushed

6 ounces silken tofu (preferably fresh, not
vacuum-packed) (about ¾ cup silken tofu;
crush tofu with a fork, then measure)

⅓ cup extra-virgin olive oil

3 tablespoons fresh lemon juice

1 heaping tablespoon capers

4 teaspoons caper brine

1 teaspoon organic sugar

½ teaspoon English mustard powder, or
1 teaspoon Dijon mustard

½ teaspoon sea salt

Croutons:

¼ cup olive oil

4 cloves roasted garlic (see page 34)

1 tablespoon fresh lemon juice

1 medium-size stale loaf vegan French or
Italian bread (a little less than 1 pound),
torn or sliced into bite-size pieces

½ teaspoon salt (optional)

Salad:

1 large head romaine lettuce, chopped

Handful or two of spinach and arugula, torn
into bite-size pieces

Freshly ground black pepper

- - - - - - - -
TIPS
- - - - - - - -

Completely chill dressing before serving to
allow the flavors to meld and use within 3 days.

For best results, use water-packed, refrigerated silken tofu (instead of shelf-stable boxed
tofu).

This is a gentle remastering of the original *Veganomicon* recipe, starring silken tofu as a basis for a thick and plentiful dressing. While these days we favor other ingredients as a basis for creamy dressings (see the Kale Tahini Caesar Salad, page 101), it's fun to time travel a bit and try silken tofu in a rare, savory usage.

Creamy, bold, garlicky—this is the classic salad that eats like a meal. In our version of a Caesar, ground almonds provide a texture similar to that of grated hard cheese, and capers bring on that essential briny flavor. Fresh, homemade croutons bathed in roasted garlic and olive oil really make this and are supereasy, so don't substitute lame store-bought ones if you can help it. (Be sure to roast a bulb of garlic in advance so that you can get on with the crouton recipe—see page 34.)

We like to add a little spinach and arugula to this Caesar salad—the rich dressing contrasts perfectly with these bitter greens—but it's not essential. Make an entrée out of it by tossing cubed, grilled tempeh or tofu (page 194) and grilled mushrooms, asparagus, or leeks. Other optional add-ins include roasted red peppers (see pages 28, 33), shredded red cabbage, shredded carrot, steamed or roasted green beans, or slivered toasted almonds. Really, you can make anything into a Caesar salad!

Prepare the dressing: Pulse the sliced almonds in a food processor or blender until crumbly. Empty the ground almonds into an airtight container that you'll be using to store the finished dressing. Blend the garlic, tofu, and oil in the food processor or blender until creamy. Add the lemon juice, capers, caper brine, sugar, and mustard powder and pulse until blended. Adjust the lemon juice and salt to taste. Pour into the container with the ground almonds and whisk to combine. Cover and allow the dressing to chill in the refrigerator for a minimum of 30 minutes, optimally 1 to 1½ hours.

Prepare the croutons: Preheat the oven to 400°F. Place the oil, roasted garlic, and lemon juice in a large bowl and use a fork to mash together. Add the torn bread and toss to coat each piece with the oil mixture. Spread on a rimmed baking sheet, sprinkle with salt, if desired, and bake for 12 to 14 minutes, or until golden brown, stirring the croutons twice during the baking process. Remove from the oven and let the croutons cool on the baking sheet.

Assemble the salad: Place 2 to 3 cups of lettuce, spinach, and arugula per individual serving (amount depending on whether it's a side or entrée) in a large bowl. If using, add vegetables, tempeh, and so on. Ladle on ⅓ cup of the dressing (or more or less to taste), and use kitchen tongs to toss the greens and coat them with dressing. Add the warm croutons, toss again, and transfer to a serving dish. Sprinkle with a little pepper. If not serving right away, warm the croutons in a 300°F oven for 5 to 8 minutes before adding to the salad.

Flipping through *Veganomicon*, it came as quite a shock to us that there were no kale salad recipes. Not a one! A decade ago we were only on the cusp of the kale revolution and had no idea how this chewy, leafy, cruciferous veg would rule everything around us.

Happily, vegan Caesar salad still, after all these years, reigns supreme as the most requested salad recipe. And it's arguably even better made with kale. Here's a simple and ridiculously flavorful variation on vegan kale Caesar, made all the richer and satisfying with plenty of tahini. While salad purists will want only some croutons in the mix, we love this creamy crunchy salad enhanced with bits of red onion, sun-dried tomato, or even the occasional artichoke heart.

Prepare the dressing: Pulse all the ingredients together in a blender until smooth. Taste and add another dab of miso or shot of lemon juice, if desired. Keep refrigerated for up to 2 days until ready to use.

Chilled dressing will thicken up just a little. If you prefer a thinner dressing, whisk in a tablespoon of hot water.

Assemble the salad: Wash and spin dry the kale. Tear away any thick stems, then tear the remaining kale with your hands into bite-size pieces. Transfer to a large salad serving bowl. Add the croutons, additional vegetables if using, and the dressing. Sprinkle with the nutritional yeast. With metal kitchen tongs, toss the salad to completely coat kale and croutons with dressing. Finish with another dusting of pepper and serve immediately.

◆ -45 ◆   ◆ SF ◆

KALE TAHINI
CAESAR SALAD

SERVES 2 TO 3 / TIME: 30 MIN OR LESS

Tahini Caesar dressing:

½ cup smooth tahini

½ cup hot water

2 tablespoons olive oil

1 tablespoon fresh lemon juice

2 teaspoons white or yellow miso

2 cloves garlic, peeled

2 teaspoons Dijon mustard

1 heaping tablespoon capers with brine

Freshly ground black pepper

Kale salad:

1 pound kale (ruffled, red, lacitano, etc.)

2 cups homemade croutons, from Caesar Salad with Roasted Garlic Croutons (page 98) or store-bought vegan croutons

2 tablespoons nutritional yeast

Optional veggies: paper-thin slices of red onion, shredded carrot, thinly sliced sun-dried tomato, sliced artichoke hearts

GRILLED
RANCH SALAD

SERVES 6 / TIME: 40 MIN

Shiitake bacon:

Olive oil cooking spray, for pan

1 pound shiitake mushrooms, tough stems trimmed, sliced a little over ¼ inch thick

¼ cup tamari or soy sauce

2 tablespoons nutritional yeast

1 tablespoon olive oil

2 teaspoons liquid smoke

Ranch dressing:

¾ cup Vegan Mayo (page 123) or commercially prepared vegan mayonnaise

2 tablespoons finely chopped fresh parsley

2 tablespoons finely chopped fresh dill

2 tablespoons finely chopped fresh chives

1½ teaspoons onion powder

½ teaspoon garlic powder

½ teaspoon lemon pepper

Romaine:

3 romaine hearts

Olive oil, for brushing

Salt

Freshly ground black pepper

Nonstick cooking spray, for pan

To serve:

2 cups halved cherry tomatoes

2 avocados, peeled, pitted, and diced

½ cup thinly sliced fresh chives

Freshly ground black pepper

Ranch salad is having a moment! Grilled salad is having a moment! Put them together and, oh man, this may count as a lifetime moment. Smoky shiitake bacon is a crunchy contrast to the rich, creamy, herby dressing. But the real fun part comes with grilling the romaine, making it a charred and warming salad that will make you want salad for dinner, even in the middle of winter.

Prepare the shiitake bacon: Preheat the oven to 425°F. Lightly spray a rimmed baking sheet with olive oil cooking spray.

Toss the sliced shiitakes in a bowl with the tamari, nutritional yeast, olive oil, and liquid smoke. Use your hands to coat.

Arrange the mushroom slices on the prepared baking sheet in a single layer. Bake until very crisp on the edges, 12 to 15 minutes. Remove from the oven and let them cool right on the baking sheet. They'll cook a little more from the heat of the baking sheet and become even crispier.

Prepare the ranch dressing: Just mix all the ingredients together in a little bowl!

Grill the romaine: Preheat a grill or grill pan over medium heat. Cut each romaine heart in half lengthwise. Brush with olive oil and sprinkle with salt and pepper.

Lightly coat the grill or grill pan with nonstick cooking spray. When hot, place the romaine, cut side down, on the grill or in the pan. Depending on the pan, it could take 2 to 3 minutes for grill marks to appear. You will probably have to do this in batches if using a grill pan on your stovetop.

To serve: For each serving, place a warm romaine heart, grilled side up, on a plate. Drizzle with the dressing. Scatter with the tomatoes and avocado. Finish with the chives and pepper to taste.

CORN & EDAMAME-
SESAME
SALAD

SERVES 4 TO 6 / TIME: 45 MIN

Dressing:

2 tablespoons toasted sesame oil

1 tablespoon rice vinegar (regular vinegar works, too)

2 teaspoons tamari or soy sauce

Salad:

2 cups frozen, shelled edamame

1 cup fresh corn kernels (1 or 2 ears, depending on the size) or partially thawed frozen corn

2 tablespoons toasted sesame seeds

Salt

This salad is ridiculously simple yet so satisfying—it's nutty, salty, fresh tasting, and crisp. We like to munch on it as a snack throughout the day. but it's also a perfect accompaniment to an Asian-inspired meal. Try it alongside Butternut Squash & Pumpkin Seed Rice Paper Rolls (page 49) for a delicious cold summer dinner. If you like, serve over a bed of baby greens. For an even heartier salad, add two thinly sliced avocado halves right before serving.

Prepare the dressing: Whisk all the dressing ingredients in a medium-size mixing bowl. Meanwhile, bring a big pot of water to a boil.

Prepare the salad: Boil the edamame for 3 minutes. Add the corn and boil for another 2 minutes. Drain into a colander and run under cold water until cool enough to touch. Add the edamame and corn to the dressing and toss to combine. Add the sesame seeds and toss again. Add salt to taste. Cover and chill for at least 15 minutes.

TIPS

If you don't have rice vinegar on hand, you can use a different kind, but nothing too strong (definitely not balsamic)—stick to something mild, such as red wine vinegar. If you have brown rice vinegar, not regular rice vinegar, that's fine, too. You can also use partially thawed frozen corn instead of fresh, but don't use canned.

Make a supercute hors d'oeuvre of this salad by placing it in radicchio cups. Just slice off the bottom of a head of radicchio, carefully peel off the leaves, and voilà! Cup!

Make a more dramatic-looking presentation by using black sesame seeds instead of regular toasted ones.

Jicama, sometimes referred to as the Mexican turnip, is like a dream come true; it's as if an apple decided to become a root vegetable. This salad is our attempt to re-create the Thai fusion that is so popular with the kids these days, using ingredients that aren't too difficult to find. The dressing has a spicy kick from the hot chile oil but the heat isn't intense, so don't let that scare you off. The avocado and peanuts make it a meal on its own, filling enough to serve as a refreshing summer lunch or dinner.

Prepare the dressing: Combine all the dressing ingredients and mix vigorously. If you have a small plastic bowl with a secure lid, you can mix it in there and shake it up. Let the dressing sit at room temperature for at least 10 minutes so that the sugar dissolves. Mix or shake again when you are ready to use it.

Assemble the salad: Place the shredded jicama in a large bowl. Reserve ⅓ cup of the dressing and pour the rest over the jicama; mix to coat.

Arrange a small bunch of watercress on an individual salad plate. It looks pretty if you keep it as bunched together as possible and if some of the leaves are hanging off the side, looking sort of like the long arm of a clock (stems in the middle and leaves facing outward). Drizzle a little reserved dressing over the leaves.

Place a pile of jicama (a cup or so) on the stems of the watercress to secure it. Sprinkle a little shredded carrot, if using, as well as a few half-moons of onion on top of the jicama. Add a few avocado slices either on top or along the sides. Sprinkle with peanuts. Drizzle with a little dressing and garnish with mint or cilantro, if using. Continue with the remaining plates.

JICAMA-WATERCRESS-
AVOCADO SALAD

with Spicy Citrus Vinaigrette

SERVES 6 TO 8 / TIME: 30 MIN,
if you have a food processor

Dressing:
¼ cup rice vinegar

½ cup fresh orange juice (juice of 1 navel orange)

2 tablespoons fresh lime juice

2 tablespoons peanut oil

2 tablespoons hot chile oil

2 tablespoons soy sauce

3 tablespoons organic sugar

1 teaspoon sesame oil

Salad:
1 medium-size jicama, peeled and shredded thinly (about 6 cups)

½ bunch watercress, roots removed

1 ripe avocado, peeled, cut in half, pitted, and sliced thinly

½ small red onion, sliced thinly

½ cup roasted unsalted peanuts, chopped coarsely

Optional garnishes:
Shredded carrot

Sprigs of mint or cilantro

TIP

Use a serrated peeler to peel the jicama, or alternatively, use a paring knife to slice off the skin in sheets. If you don't have a food processor to shred the jicama, just slice it matchstick thin.

Top secret: It isn't rocket science—you can make a salad like this with any leftover grains, beans, and fruit you have around. It is a really straightforward salad that uses simple, fresh ingredients. Each bite will bring new flavors to the table—mango, scallions, cilantro, red peppers . . . you never know what you're gonna get! Best of all, it takes practically no time if you have some leftover quinoa at hand.

Combine the mango, red bell pepper, scallion, and cilantro in a mixing bowl. Add the vinegar, oil, and salt, and stir to combine. Add the quinoa and stir until everything is well incorporated. Fold in the black beans. You can serve immediately or let it sit for a bit for the flavors to meld. To serve, place a few leaves of lettuce on a plate and scoop some salad on top. This tastes good chilled and is even better at room temperature.

TIP — If you don't have any leftover quinoa, don't sweat it; it's easy and fast to prepare. Bring 1 cup of rinsed quinoa and 2 cups of water to a boil in a small pot. Once the mixture is boiling, lower the heat to a simmer and cook for 15 minutes, until all the water has been absorbed. Then remove from the heat and fluff with a fork. Set aside to cool, and once it has cooled you can prepare this salad.

QUINOA SALAD

with Black Beans & Mango

SERVES 4 TO 6 / TIME: 35 MIN;
15 MIN if the quinoa is already cooked

1 mango, peeled, pitted, and cut into small dice

1 red bell pepper, seeded and diced as small as you can get it

1 cup chopped scallion

1 cup chopped fresh cilantro

2 tablespoons red wine vinegar

2 tablespoons grapeseed oil

¼ teaspoon salt

2 cups cooked quinoa, cooled

1 (15-ounce) can black beans, drained and rinsed

A few leaves of lettuce, for garnish

LENTIL SALAD
EVERYONE WANTS

SERVES 4 / TIME: 55 MIN,
mostly inactive

4 cups vegetable broth, purchased or homemade (page 223)

2 or 3 sprigs thyme

2 bay leaves

2 cloves garlic, crushed

½ teaspoon dried tarragon

¼ teaspoon salt

1 cup dried French lentils

1 small red onion, chopped very finely (about ⅓ cup)

1 small tomato, seeded and diced (about ½ cup)

2 radishes, grated (about ⅓ cup)

1 small carrot, grated

Several pinches of freshly ground black pepper

Dressing:

2 to 4 tablespoons olive oil

1 tablespoon balsamic vinegar

1 tablespoon Dijon mustard

1 tablespoon fresh lemon juice

1 clove garlic, minced

To serve:

8 cups fancy lettuce

This is that crowd-pleaser lentil salad that's just as at-home on weeknights as it is at a potluck. Thyme, tarragon, and garlic flavor this easy-to-prepare and hearty lentil salad. Serve over red leaf lettuce (or whatever kind of fancy-shmancy lettuce you can get your hands on) with oil and vinegar on the side. Having some warmed pita bread on hand wouldn't hurt, either. For a cute hors d'oeuvre idea, spoon small scoops of salad into endive leaves.

Bring the broth, thyme, bay leaves, garlic, tarragon, and salt to a boil in a medium-size saucepan. Add the lentils and bring again to a low boil. Cover the pot with the lid tilted, allowing a little room for steam to escape. Let cook for 20 to 25 minutes. The lentils should be soft enough to eat but still firm enough to not lose their shape.

Prepare the dressing: While the lentils cook, stir together all the dressing ingredients in a mixing bowl.

Drain the lentils in a mesh colander (so that the lentils don't fall out the holes). Let cool, giving the colander a few shakes every couple of minutes so that they drain and cool faster. Once the lentils are lukewarm (about 15 minutes), remove the bay leaves, chunks of garlic, and thyme sprigs. Add the lentils to the dressing along with the onion, tomato, and radishes, and toss to combine. Season with salt and pepper to taste, cover, and chill for at least half an hour.

When chilled, serve over lettuce with oil and vinegar on the side.

Peppery arugula adds a nice crisp bite to this rustic and wholesome salad. Bulgur is a great choice for a grain-based summer salad because it cooks quickly and you don't need to stand over the stove and tend to it. It's really delicious the way the bulgur, mushrooms, and beans get all tangy and succulent when they absorb the flavors of the dressing. A small amount of oregano adds fragrance, while paprika ties everything together and spices things up just a bit. You can use a different white bean, whatever is available, or even garbanzos or red kidney beans.

Steam the bulgur: Place the bulgur in a small pot or container that has a tightly fitting lid. Boil a pot of water and measure out 1⅓ cups. Pour the water over the bulgur and cover the pot. Let sit for 30 minutes. The bulgur should be tender but chewy.

Prepare the dressing: While the bulgur is steaming, mix all the dressing ingredients together in a large mixing bowl.

Stir the dressing well, add the mushrooms, beans, and onion, and let them marinate, stirring occasionally.

When the bulgur is ready, add it and any water remaining in the pot to the dressing while it's still warm. Toss to coat. Tear the arugula leaves into bite-size pieces and add them to the salad. Mix well. Cover and refrigerate until completely chilled, preferably overnight. Once the salad is chilled, you can adjust the salt and pepper to taste.

BULGUR, ARUGULA & CANNELLINI
SALAD

MAKES ABOUT 8 SERVINGS /
TIME: 35 MIN, plus an hr to chill

1 cup bulgur (cracked wheat)

2 cups thinly sliced cremini mushrooms

1½ cups cooked cannellini beans, drained and rinsed

1 small red onion, quartered and sliced thinly

2 cups lightly packed arugula leaves

Dressing:

¼ cup olive oil

¼ cup red wine vinegar

1 tablespoon balsamic vinegar

2 cloves garlic, minced really well or pressed

1 teaspoon paprika

½ teaspoon dried oregano

¾ teaspoon salt

Several pinches of freshly ground black pepper

TIP

It's a good idea to let this chill for as long as possible before digging in; it's one of those things that's even better the day after it's made and even better still the day after that.

PEAR & ENDIVE SALAD

with Maple Candied Pecans

SERVES 4 / TIME: 45 MIN

Maple candied pecans:

½ cup pecan halves

About 2 teaspoons vegetable oil

Scant ¼ teaspoon salt

¼ cup pure maple syrup

Salad:

3 Belgian endives, sliced widthwise into ½-inch slices

1 very ripe Anjou (or other soft) pear, thinly sliced into bite-size pieces

3 tablespoons grapeseed oil

2 teaspoons white balsamic vinegar

Candied pecans give this salad a yummy crunch, while the sweetness of the pear rounds out the delicate bitterness of the endive. It's a simple recipe but a smorgasbord of flavor and texture. We know grapeseed oil isn't a common oil to have around, but we insist you get it because it makes the best simple dressing for any salad. If you need to sub the vinegar, use red wine vinegar, not regular balsamic.

Prepare the pecans: Have ready a flat plate lined with baking parchment.

Preheat a heavy-bottomed pan (preferably cast iron) over medium-low heat. Toast the pecans in the dry pan for about 5 minutes, tossing them frequently after the first 2 minutes. Sprinkle the vegetable oil and salt over the pecans, and toss to coat. Add the maple syrup and toss to coat, heating until the maple syrup begins to bubble. Let bubble for about 30 seconds, tossing the entire time. Transfer to the parchment-lined plate and allow to cool completely. You can speed up the process by placing the pecans in the fridge once they've cooled down a bit. Once they have cooled, break apart the pieces and they are ready to serve.

Prepare the salad: Use tongs to toss together all the salad ingredients in a large bowl, making sure that the endive and pears are coated with the oil and vinegar. Divide among four plates and garnish with the candied pecans.

This salad is magical. At first blush, the ingredients look a little all over the place, but once it comes together it is out-of-control delicious, earthy, sweet, and fragrant. Oh, and it's raw! People like raw. You can serve it as a little accompaniment to a sammich, the same way you might serve coleslaw, or by itself as a dinner by placing it over a handful of mixed salad greens: drizzle the greens with some of the dressing and then plop a mound of the salad over that. If you would like to make it a meal, add Tangerine Baked Tofu (page 193) or tempeh.

You absolutely need a food processor to get the beets and parsnips to their desired uniform thinness. Sorry, non-food processor people.

Prepare the dressing: Whisk together all the dressing ingredients in a large mixing bowl.

Assemble the salad: Add the shredded beets and parsnips, using tongs to thoroughly mix them into the dressing. Let the veggies sit and macerate for about 15 minutes. Add the mint and mix again. Cover and refrigerate for at least 30 minutes until ready to eat.

SHREDDED
PARSNIP
& BEET SALAD
in Pineapple Vinaigrette

SERVES 6 / TIME: 50 MIN

Pineapple dressing:

2 cups pineapple juice

⅓ cup red wine vinegar

¼ cup grapeseed oil

2 tablespoons pure maple syrup or agave nectar (you can also dissolve 2 tablespoons organic sugar into it if you have neither ingredient)

1 clove garlic, grated with a Microplane grater or very well minced

¼ teaspoon salt

Salad:

1 pound beets, peeled and shredded (about 3 average-size)

1 pound parsnips, peeled and shredded (about 2 average-size)

½ cup coarsely chopped fresh mint

ROASTED
FENNEL & HAZELNUT SALAD

with Shallot Dressing

SERVES 4 / TIME: 1 HR 30 MIN, mostly inactive

Roasted vegetables:

2 heads fennel, sliced into ¼-inch-thick chunks

2 tablespoons olive oil

½ teaspoon salt

A few twists of freshly ground black pepper

3 large shallots, sliced in half

Dressing:

3 tablespoons olive oil

2 tablespoons hazelnut or walnut oil, or more olive oil

3 tablespoons champagne vinegar or white wine vinegar

2 tablespoons pure maple syrup

½ teaspoon dried tarragon

½ teaspoon dried thyme

Pinch of freshly grated nutmeg

1 teaspoon salt

Salad:

1 small head of chicory, washed and torn into bite-size pieces

¾ cup hazelnuts, roasted, skins removed (see tip) and chopped coarsely

¾ cup dried cranberries

Freshly ground black pepper

A gorgeous fall themed salad with an epic name but a relatively simple procedure. Roasting fennel lightly caramelizes and brings out the delicate licorice flavor. The crunch of roasted hazelnuts and chewy tang of dried cranberries makes this an ideal salad for winter holidays, but don't wait for Black Friday: make this lovely dish any blustery cold weekend and serve with your favorite fall soup. Allow the fennel and shallots adequate roasting time to ensure that their deep, sweet flavors really develop.

Roast the vegetables: Preheat the oven to 375°F. Place the sliced fennel on a large baking sheet, then rub with 2 tablespoons of the olive oil, a pinch of salt, and some pepper. Rub the shallots with a little extra oil and place in the corner of the baking sheet. Bake the vegetables for 20 to 25 minutes, or until the edges of the fennel are browned and the shallots are starting to caramelize. Remove from the oven and set aside to cool.

Prepare the dressing: In a food processor, combine the roasted shallots, olive oil, hazelnut oil, vinegar, maple syrup, tarragon, thyme, nutmeg, and salt. Blend until creamy, pour into a container, cover, and chill until ready to use.

Assemble the salad: Place the chicory, roasted fennel, hazelnuts, and cranberries in a large bowl. Pour in the dressing, add a twist of freshly ground black pepper, and toss with salad tongs until everything is completely coated. Serve immediately.

TIPS

Just like spinach, fresh chicory can be quite sandy. Wash thoroughly by soaking in cold water for a few minutes, swish around in the water, and drain. Repeat one or more times until no sand remains in the leaves or bottom of the bowl.

The easiest way to toast hazelnuts: Preheat the oven to 300°F. Place the raw hazelnuts on a baking sheet and roast for 8 to 10 minutes, until the skins are peeling and the nuts start to smell and appear toasted: be careful no to burn. Remove from the oven. Immediately pour the hot hazelnuts into the center of a large, rough kitchen towel. Twist the ends of the towel tightly around the nuts to form a sack. Agitate the sack vigorously for a few minutes to remove the skins. Some skin might still stick to the hazelnuts, but this is okay. Pick the hazelnuts out of the crumbled skins and set aside in a bowl to cool. The quickest way to clean the towel of hazelnut skins is to shake it outside.

This is a staple salad at Isa headquarters. It's got everything a vegan needs to feel healthy and happy: chickpeas, greens, avocado, and mushrooms. The mustard makes the dressing nice and creamy with just a little kick. The roasted portobello recipe is for two mushrooms, but as we say in those directions, you can make four for a more elegant presentation if you're trying to impress someone. You can also add other salad-y things to this; a few sprouts never hurt anyone . . . yet.

Prepare the dressing: Whisk all the dressing ingredients together in a small bowl. Done.

Prepare the salad: Throw together all the salad ingredients, except the portobellos, in a large mixing bowl. Pour on the dressing and use tongs to toss.

When ready to serve, place the dressed greens on a plate and add the sliced, warm portobellos. That's all there is to it!

PORTOBELLO
SALAD
with Spicy Mustard Dressing

SERVES 4 AS A MAIN OR 8
AS A SIDE / TIME: 45 MIN,
including mushroom cooking time

Dressing:

¼ cup prepared spicy, smooth mustard

3 tablespoons grapeseed oil

¼ cup red wine vinegar

2 tablespoons pure maple syrup

Salad:

8 cups mixed greens (whatever you like—we prefer crunchy things like radicchio and romaine; throw in some arugula scraps for good measure)

1 avocado, peeled, halved, pitted, and sliced thinly

1 small red onion, sliced into very thin half-moons

1 (15-ounce) can chickpeas, drained and rinsed

1 recipe Roasted Portobellos (2 mushrooms) (page 161)

AUTUMN ROOT
SALAD
with Warm Maple-Fig Dressing

SERVES 4 / TIME: 1 HR 30 MIN,
mostly inactive

Vegetables:

1 pound rutabaga, peeled and diced into
1-inch chunks

1 pound golden beets, peeled and diced into
1-inch chunks

1 pound parsnips, peeled and diced into
1-inch chunks

2 to 4 tablespoons olive oil

1 teaspoon salt

Freshly ground black pepper

About 6 cups field greens

Dressing:

1 tablespoon olive oil

2 cloves garlic, chopped

½ cup shallot, chopped coarsely

1 cup chopped dried Mission figs

¼ cup white cooking wine

¼ teaspoon salt

½ cup water

¼ cup pure maple syrup

1 tablespoon Dijon mustard

2 teaspoons white balsamic vinegar (regular
balsamic is okay, too, but try the white
stuff—you'll be hooked)

This is a classy start to an autumn dinner. You'll love the combination of earthy beets, rutabaga, and parsnip with the tart sweetness of Maple-Fig Dressing. The field greens add a fresh touch and we like the texture they get as they wilt from the dressing. Use golden beets instead of red so that the color doesn't dye all the other veggies.

Roast the veggies: Preheat the oven to 350°F. Line two large baking sheets with parchment paper.

In a large bowl, toss the veggies with the oil, salt, and pepper to coat. Transfer to the prepared baking sheets in a single layer.

Roast for about 40 minutes, tossing every 15 minutes and rotating the pans, until veggies are golden and tender.

Prepare the dressing: Preheat a small saucepan over medium-low heat. Sauté the garlic and shallot in the oil for about 3 minutes. Add the figs and wine, cover, and bring to a simmer. When the wine has mostly evaporated (about 3 minutes), add the salt, water, and maple syrup. Cover and simmer for another 3 minutes. Turn off the heat and mix in the mustard and vinegar. Let it sit for a few minutes, stirring occasionally, then transfer the dressing to a blender and puree until smooth. You may need to add a few tablespoons of water if it is too thick to puree; it depends on how much of the water evaporated. Serve warm, or refrigerate and reheat when ready to serve. To heat it, gently warm in a saucepan over low heat, adding a few splashes of water if necessary.

To serve: In a large bowl, use tongs to mix the greens with about half of the dressing. Reserve the rest to dollop on the vegetables after they have been arranged.

For individual servings, place the roasted veggies on a plate and place the greens on top in the center, leaving the beets, rutabaga, and parsnips peeking out from underneath. Drizzle the reserved dressing over the vegetables.

G-F

CREAMY
ASIAN PEAR & TEMPEH SALAD

with Wasabi Dressing

SERVES 4 / TIME: 35 MIN,
plus chill time

1 (8-ounce) package tempeh, diced into
½-inch cubes

½ cup frozen green peas or petits pois

2 scallions, sliced very thinly

1 Asian pear or other firm, crisp pear, pitted
and cut into ½-inch dice (about 2 cups)

⅔ cup Vegan Mayo (page 123) or
commercially prepared vegan mayonnaise

1½ to 2 teaspoons wasabi powder

1 tablespoon fresh lime juice

¼ teaspoon toasted sesame oil

½ teaspoon salt

Asian pears (also called Korean pears) are big, round, sand-colored pears with a unique, snappy crunch. And we love that contrast in this creamy, substantial tempeh salad that's cool and piquant thanks to wasabi. Great with rice crackers or daikon spears as a filling snack or as an alternative filling for Spicy Tempeh Nori Rolls (page 45) minus the green peas.

In a steamer basket, steam the tempeh for 8 minutes. Add the peas and steam for another 2 minutes, until the peas are bright green and tender. Remove from the steamer and toss into a large bowl with the scallions. Allow to cool for a few minutes. Crush the cubes of tempeh a little with your hands and toss in along with the diced pear.

In a small bowl, whisk together the vegan mayo, wasabi powder, lime juice, sesame oil, and salt. Taste and adjust the spice level with more wasabi, if necessary.

Pour the dressing over the tempeh mixture, stir to combine everything, and place in an airtight container. Chill for at least 30 minutes or overnight to allow the flavors to blend.

TIPS

To quickly thaw your peas, run them under hot water for about 30 seconds.

Not all wasabi powders are created equal. Some are more flavorful than others; use a reliable brand (ask your Asian grocer which brand he or she recommends) or you might have to add quite a bit to properly season the dressing. Purists might also want to avoid brands that contain green artificial coloring.

The perfect potato salad for any family reunion or general food fight. The mustard gives it a cool yellow color, with little bits of green dill. We love how the cucumbers taste like pickles when the salad has been sitting around for a while. This recipe really does make a lot, so if not taking to a picnic or family reunion, you might want to halve it. See the photo on page 120.

Slice the potatoes so that they are somewhere between ¼ and ½ inch thick. If very large potatoes, cut them into thirds lengthwise, then slice. If smaller ones, just cut them in half and slice. But it's nice to have different sizes because small bits fall apart and become part of the dressing, while most maintain their shape.

Place the potatoes in a very large pot and fill with water, about 4 inches or so above the tops of the potatoes. Boil for about 15 minutes, keeping an eye on them. Check that you can pierce one easily with a fork, but be careful not to overcook them; you want them to be tender but still firm and not falling apart.

Meanwhile, prepare the dressing: In a very large mixing bowl (big enough to add the potatoes later on), mix together the mayonnaise, mustard, oil, vinegar, sugar, dill, turmeric, salt, and pepper. Whisk briskly. Add the cucumber and place in the fridge until the potatoes are ready.

When the potatoes are done, drain them into a colander and give them a quick rinse under cold water. Shake the colander so that all the potatoes are rinsed. Let them cool for about 15 minutes.

Add the potatoes to the dressing and use a wooden spoon to mix and coat them. Grate the carrot directly into the salad and mix. Carrots are an essential ingredient because they add sweetness, so don't leave them out and don't chop them; they have to be grated. Taste for salt and pepper, and refrigerate until chilled.

Once good and cold, taste for seasoning one last time, and serve.

PROSPECT PARK
POTATO SALAD

MAKES A BOATLOAD /
TIME: 50 MIN, plus chill time

5 pounds white potatoes, peeled and washed

1 cup Vegan Mayo (page 123) or commercially prepared vegan mayonnaise

¼ cup Dijon mustard (whole-grain is best)

¼ cup olive oil

⅓ cup white vinegar

2 tablespoons organic sugar

1 tablespoon dried dill

1 teaspoon ground turmeric

1½ teaspoons salt, or to taste

1 teaspoon freshly ground black pepper, or to taste

1 seedless cucumber, sliced into small, thin pieces

1 large carrot, peeled

Prospect Park Potato Salad, page 119, and Brooklyn Deli Macaroni Salad, page 121

There are plenty of decadent and delicious vegan mayos on the market these days (and, yes, plenty of not-so-great ones, too). But there's just something so homey about making your own! A connection, I guess. To the land, to your kitchen, to life, and probably mostly to your blender. This homemade version is so fresh and delicious, it just levels up everything it touches. In life, so many things depend on mayo, so go ahead and experiment with making your own.

Combine the milk and ground flaxseeds in a blender. Blend on high speed until the flaxseeds are barely detectable and the mixture is frothy, about a minute.

Add the sugar, mustard powder, onion powder, salt, vinegar, and lemon juice, blending for a few seconds to combine.

Now, begin to add the oil. With the blender running, use the hole at the top to stream in a tablespoon of oil at a time, blending for about 30 seconds after each addition (if using a high-speed blender, such as Vitamix, 5 to 10 seconds should do it). Give your blender a break every now and again so that it doesn't heat up the mayo. You should notice it thickening by the halfway point. By the time you've used three quarters of the oil, it should be spreadable. And with the last addition, you should have a thick mayo. If it seems watery, keep blending.

It will probably taste saltier and tangier than you'd like straight out of the blender, but trust me, the flavors mellow and become perfect. Transfer to a glass storage container, seal tightly, and refrigerate for a few hours, and it will thicken even further. Use within a week.

NOTE

The kind of milk you use here is way important. Choose the most neutral-tasting milk you can find. Do not go for hemp or oat milk here. Select unsweetened, unflavored soy or almond milk for the best results.

Depending on the strength of your blender, your times may differ. The important thing is to pay attention to the consistency of the mayo through each step. No matter what your machine, you have to get the flaxseeds good and blended, so that the flecks are barely noticeable. That activates its gloopy properties and will also make your mayo prettier.

The other important thing to remember is that the oil needs to be added little by little. A lot of mayo recipes say to stream it in slowly but all at once, and I don't think that is quite necessary. Just add it a tablespoon or two at a time, blend for a while, then add more.

The taste of this mayo is very strong at first; the vinegar and salt mellow out over time, so don't adjust straight from the blender. Let it chill for at least a few hours before deciding on any tweaking you'd like to do for next time.

VEGAN MAYO

MAKES 1½ CUPS MAYO / TIME: 15 MIN,
plus chill time to set

½ cup cold unsweetened soy or almond milk (see note)

1½ tablespoons ground golden flaxseeds (sometimes called flax meal)

2 teaspoons organic sugar

1 teaspoon mustard powder

1 teaspoon onion powder

¼ teaspoon salt

1 tablespoon white wine vinegar

1 tablespoon fresh lemon juice

1 cup canola oil

SHALLOT 'N' HERB
DRESSING

MAKES ⅓ CUP DRESSING /
TIME: LESS THAN 10 MIN

2 tablespoons minced shallot
3 tablespoons olive oil
2 tablespoons apple cider vinegar
1 teaspoon dried thyme, oregano, or basil
Salt and freshly ground black pepper

A good, made to order vinaigrette that's great even just because you make only what you need and use right away. Got fresh herbs? Use 1 tablespoon of chopped-up fresh stuff in place of the dried.

Whisk the ingredients together in a cup and use immediately. Or, for a creamy dressing, pulse in a bullet blender until smooth.

MAPLE-MUSTARD
DRESSING

MAKES ⅓ CUP DRESSING /
TIME: LESS THAN 10 MIN

3 tablespoons Dijon or whole-grain mustard
3 tablespoons pure maple syrup
3 tablespoons olive or walnut oil
1 tablespoon apple cider vinegar
Salt and freshly ground black pepper

Sweet mustardy dressings are a no-brainer for instantly good-tasting salads. Once you make this a few times no recipe is required, just go for it and adjust to taste. Nice with salads featuring cooked grains or apples, too.

Whisk all the ingredients together in a cup and store in an airtight container. Keep refrigerated until ready to use.

How can just two ingredients and a little water taste so amazing? This dressing is based on an old standby that Terry used to whip up in her chef days long gone. It's perfect not just on fresh crisp greens but poured on steamed veggies, any grain, or simply seasoned and baked tofu.

It's really good as is, but if you're feeling experimental, a clove's worth of chopped garlic, a little fresh lemon juice, or a twist of freshly ground black pepper can jazz things up a bit.

Using a large spoon, blend the miso and tahini together in a medium-size bowl to form a creamy paste. Slowly pour in the warm water a little at a time, gently whisking until a creamy dressing forms. If a thinner dressing is desired, drizzle in a little more water. The dressing will thicken if allowed to sit awhile. Keep refrigerated until ready to use.

MISO TAHINI
DRESSING

MAKES ABOUT ¾ CUP DRESSING /
TIME: LESS THAN 10 MIN

¼ **cup white or yellow miso**
¼ **cup tahini**
⅓ **cup or more warm water**

As simple and yummy as it gets!

Whisk all the ingredients together in a cup and store in an airtight container. Keep refrigerated until ready to use.

MEDITERRANEAN
OLIVE OIL
& LEMON
VINAIGRETTE

MAKES ABOUT ⅔ CUP DRESSING /
TIME: 10 MIN

⅓ **cup olive oil**
¼ **cup fresh lemon juice**
3 cloves garlic, pressed or minced finely
1 teaspoon dried oregano
1 teaspoon dried thyme
1 teaspoon dried basil
½ **teaspoon salt**
Freshly ground black pepper

TOASTED SESAME

DRESSING

MAKES ABOUT ⅔ CUP DRESSING /
TIME: LESS THAN 10 MIN

¼ cup grapeseed or other light-flavored oil

3 tablespoons brown rice vinegar

2 tablespoons soy sauce

1 tablespoon agave nectar or pure maple syrup

2 teaspoons toasted sesame oil

1 rounded tablespoon roasted sesame seeds

Dress any greens with this sweet and nutty vinaigrette to serve alongside most any Asian dish. Also perfect for tossing with chilled soba noodles for a light summer side dish.

Whisk all the ingredients together in a cup and store in an airtight container. Keep refrigerated until ready to use.

A pretty, brilliant magenta dressing with a fresh and bold fruity flavor. Serve with the most tender, young salad greens you can find, or with chunks of ripe mango on a bed of arugula.

Use a large spoon to press the thawed raspberries in several batches through a large sieve into a medium-size bowl. Discard the seeds. Add the remaining ingredients, whisk to combine, and pour into an airtight container if not using immediately.

NOTE This dressing is still pretty good with the seeds left in. Or simply puree the whole thing in a blender: smooth dressing for lazy salad eaters.

RASPBERRY-LIME
VINAIGRETTE

MAKES ABOUT 1 CUP DRESSING /
TIME: 10 MIN

1 cup frozen raspberries, thawed

¼ cup grapeseed oil or mellow-tasting olive oil

Pinch of freshly grated lime zest

3 tablespoons fresh lime juice

2 teaspoons agave nectar or pure maple syrup

½ teaspoon salt

A few twists of freshly ground black pepper

CHAPTER FOUR

SAMMICHES

Sammiches, otherwise known by most people as "sandwiches," are the miracle of modern food technology.

They are simultaneously a finger food and a whole meal, loved by the young, old, and in between. We take them most seriously here in the *Veganomicon* and we're not afraid to pile on the good stuff, such as roasted vegetables, seared seitan, crunchy salads, and only the best bread we can get our hands on. These might take a little more work than your average PB&J, but they're no big cyclopean (huge, ancient, and made out of stone) effort.

---------------- ◆ ----------------

If we ever decided to drop out of cookbook-writing society completely and become surfer dudettes, we would eat these amazing tacos every single day, without even bothering to change out of our wet suits first. Beer and chile–marinated tempeh is first slapped onto the grill (or fried in a cast-iron pan) and then lovingly stuffed into steamy corn tortillas. Garnish those puppies with a bright mayo-free coleslaw, and drizzle with luscious lime crema dressing. It's the ultimate summertime dinner, or make whenever you wish you were on a tropical beach.

There are a few components to this recipe that need to marinate for about an hour each—half an hour if you're desperate—but it's easy enough to put together. Good news: the cabbage slaw tastes even better after resting overnight, so mix that up while you're marinating the tempeh.

Prepare the slaw first: Mix all the slaw ingredients well in a large glass or plastic bowl; don't use metal. Either leave in the bowl or transfer to a narrower, cylindrical nonreactive container, such as a 1-pint plastic takeout container. Cover the top of the container loosely with plastic wrap, press it down on top of the slaw, and put something heavy, such as a can of beans, on top. Marinate the slaw for at least an hour, or make it the night before; the flavor and texture develop with time. When ready to use, squeeze out handfuls to release any excess juice.

Make the lime crema: Blend all the crema ingredients together in a blender until creamy and smooth. Add more salt or lime juice to taste, if desired. Pour into an airtight container and chill until ready to use.

Marinate the tempeh: Whisk the marinade ingredients together in a glass pie plate or small casserole dish. Slice the tempeh into strips (parallel to the shorter end of the rectangle) about ¼ inch thick. Transfer to the dish and flip each piece a few times to coat in marinade. Set aside for at least 10 minutes, flipping them every now and again to cover every surface.

Preheat the oven to 200°F. Preheat a greased grill pan or cast-iron skillet (brush well with oil or use a high-heat grill spray) over medium-high heat. Working in two or three batches, grill each piece of the tempeh for 2 to 3 minutes, or until the edges are caramelized and the tempeh is hot. Occasionally brush each piece with plenty of marinade, and use metal tongs to flip the pieces halfway through the cooking. Transfer the cooked tempeh to a dinner plate and cover with foil to keep warm.

Recipe Continues

Taco slaw:

3 heaping cups finely shredded purple or white cabbage (10 to 12 ounces), or a mix of both

1 small carrot, shredded finely

3 tablespoons lime juice (see tip)

1 teaspoon organic sugar

1 to 2 fresh jalapeño peppers, sliced paper thin (remove seeds if you're freaked out by hot chiles)

1 teaspoon kosher salt

A few twists of freshly ground black pepper

Lime crema:

¾ cup plain, unsweetened nondairy yogurt

3 tablespoons lime juice

1 tablespoon olive or avocado oil

⅓ cup lightly packed fresh cilantro leaves

¼ teaspoon salt

Chile-beer marinade:

¾ cup pilsner- or ale-style beer (Mexican preferred)

3 cloves garlic, minced

3 tablespoons soy sauce

2 tablespoons olive oil

2 tablespoons lime juice

2½ teaspoons chili powder (premixed or mix your own with ancho, poblano, or chipotle powders)

½ teaspoon ground cumin

1 (8-ounce) package tempeh

High-heat-safe vegetable oil or high-heat grill spray, for grilling

12 to 16 soft, white corn tortillas (for double tortilla tacos, or use only 1 tortilla per taco)

Garnishes (use one or all of them!):
Red radishes, sliced paper thin
Fresh tomato, seeded and diced
Pickled jalapeño peppers, sliced
Your favorite Mexican-style hot sauce
Ripe avocado, peeled and sliced or diced

- - - - - - - -
TIPS
- - - - - - - -

Use Sour Cilantro Cream (page 319) in place of the lime crema. Thin it out slightly with additional lime juice or unsweetened nondairy milk so that it's the consistency of a thick salad dressing.

Leftover tempeh, lime crema, and garnishes make an amazing taco salad, served with salad greens and crunchy tortilla chip strips.

Bottled lime juice is just fine in the recipe, as you'll need some for each element of the tacos.

Serve these tacos with ice cold Mexican beer and Guacamole (page 73)

Create a taco assembly line: Line up the lime crema, slaw, sliced grilled tempeh, and garnishes, in that order, on the kitchen counter. Stack the tortillas on a plate right next to the stove, and heat a skillet over medium-high heat. Toast a tortilla on the skillet for 30 seconds, then flip the tortilla over and heat until it has become soft and pliable. Repeat with a second tortilla and arrange both, slightly overlapping, on a serving dish. We like to use two tortillas per taco (helps with piling on the fillings), but you can make smaller tacos by using just one tortilla.

Finish that taco: Spread a little lime crema down the center of the tortillas, add a few strips of tempeh, pile on some slaw, and top with any garnish you like. Drizzle with extra lime crema and hot sauce, if desired. Fold, eat, repeat!

Roasted cubes of butternut squash and black-eyed peas are great anytime, but are pure magic on top of crunchy tostadas and dressed with toasted pumpkin seed salsa. Sure, homemade salsa may seem like a time luxury, but make it once and you'll see it's worth a few minutes of extra dinner prep (or just use your favorite store-bought salsa; no judgments here). A fresh and feisty meal made with any winter squash, but even easier made with prepeeled chunks of squash from the refrigerated produce section.

If you'd rather make tacos instead of tostadas, simply warm up the tortillas on a hot griddle until soft, pile on the toppings, and eat pronto!

Roast the squash: Preheat the oven to 425°F and line a cookie sheet with foil or parchment paper. On the lined sheet, toss the cubes of squash with the oil, chili powder, paprika, and salt, and make sure each cube is coated with the spices and oil. Spread out into a single layer and roast for 25 to 30 minutes, stirring occasionally, or until the squash is golden and easily pierced with a fork. Remove from the oven but leave the oven on. Transfer the squash to a mixing bowl and cover with foil to keep warm.

Prepare the tortillas for the tostadas: Line a cookie sheet with foil or parchment paper. Generously oil each side of the tortillas, arrange on the baking sheet, and bake for 5 to 6 minutes, or until browned. Flip each tortilla over and bake for another 3 to 4 minutes, or until browned on the edges. Turn off the oven and crack open the door slightly to keep the tortillas warm but not overbrown them.

Prepare the black-eyed pea filling: Heat the oil in a heavy skillet over medium heat and sauté the garlic until fragrant, less than a minute. Add the onion and roasted jalapeño and continue to sauté until the onion is soft and translucent, about 2 minutes. Sprinkle with the cumin and add the broth or beer, black-eyed peas, and tomato. Continue to sauté, stirring occasionally, for 4 minutes. Remove from the heat and mash about a third of the peas with the back of a spoon. Pour the pea mixture into the roasted squash and stir to combine. Season with salt and black pepper to taste and keep the mixture warm until serving time.

Prepare the salsa: In a skillet or wok over medium heat, toast the pumpkin seeds. Stir frequently and, when they are golden and puffed, immediately transfer to a mixing bowl. When cool enough to handle, roughly chop on a cutting board with your handy chef's knife. Return the chopped seeds to the mixing bowl and combine with the remaining salsa ingredients. Add a little more salt and/or lime juice to taste, if desired.

Assemble the tostadas: Spread 3 to 4 tablespoons of filling mixture onto each warm fried tortilla. Top with the salsa, arugula, and avocado. Serve with lime wedges.

BLACK-EYED BUTTERNUT
TOSTADAS
with Chipotle Pumpkin Seed Salsa

MAKES 8 TOSTADAS, SERVING 4 / TIME: 45 MINUTES

Roasted squash:

10 ounces butternut squash, peeled, seeded, and cut into ½-inch dice

1 tablespoon olive oil

1 teaspoon chili powder (a blend or a single chile)

½ teaspoon ground smoked paprika

¼ teaspoon salt, or more to taste

Tostadas:

8 to 10 corn tortillas

Olive oil, for brushing tortillas

Black-eyed pea filling:

1 tablespoon olive oil

2 cloves garlic, chopped

½ cup diced white onion

1 to 2 jalapeño peppers, roasted (see page 33 for roasting tips)

½ teaspoon ground cumin

½ cup vegetable broth, purchased or homemade (page 223), or Mexican beer, such as Tecate

1 (15-ounce) can or 1½ cups cooked black-eyed peas, drained and rinsed

½ cup diced fresh or canned tomatoes (if using canned, drain)

2 tablespoons fresh lime juice

¼ teaspoon salt, or more to taste

Freshly ground black pepper

Chipotle–pumpkin seed salsa:

½ cup shelled pumpkin seeds (pepitas)

½ cup diced white onion

1 (15-ounce) can fire-roasted diced tomatoes

½ cup fresh cilantro, roughly chopped

2 tablespoons fresh lime juice

½ teaspoon salt

Toppings: arugula, avocado, lime wedges

BLACK BEAN
BURGERS

MAKES 6 BURGERS / TIME: 30 MIN

2 cups cooked or 1 (15-ounce) can black
  beans, drained and rinsed

½ cup vital wheat gluten

½ cup plain vegan whole wheat bread
  crumbs

1 teaspoon chili powder

½ teaspoon ground cumin

¼ cup water

1 tablespoon tomato paste or ketchup

¼ cup finely chopped fresh cilantro
  (optional)

2 cloves garlic

½ small onion

About 2 tablespoons olive oil, for pan

Olive oil spray

Vegan whole wheat buns

Here's a nice, wholesome Southwestern black bean burger. Everything's been kept fairly simple so that you can top it with all sorts of things—Sour Cilantro Cream (page 319), Tropical Avocado Salsa Fresca (page 322), Guacamole (page 78), or all of the above. Plain old ketchup is fine, too. Also include your good friends lettuce, tomato, and red onion. Did we mention that these freeze well, too? Once cooked, pack them in a resealable plastic bag with sheets of waxed paper to separate them, then reheat in a 350°F oven for 25 to 30 minutes.

Mash the beans with a fork in a mixing bowl. You don't want to puree them; just get them mashed so that no whole beans are left, but you should leave some half beans.

Add the wheat gluten, bread crumbs, chili powder, cumin, water, and tomato paste (and cilantro, if using), but don't mix yet. Use a Microplane grater to grate the garlic in. (A garlic press or very well minced garlic works, too.) Use the large holes on a box grater to grate in the onion.

Mix everything together with a fork and then proceed to knead with your hands, until the mixture is firm and uniformly mixed (about a minute).

Preheat a heavy-bottomed pan over medium heat.

Divide the burger mixture into six equal pieces. Roll each piece into a firm ball. Use your palm to press a ball down on a clean surface to form a patty that is about 1½ inches thick. Press so that the patty is flat on both sides. Make six patties.

Pour a thin layer of olive oil into the pan. Cook the patties, three at a time, for 5 minutes on each side, gently but firmly pressing down on them with a spatula. Spray with olive oil before turning over for uniform browning. Once cooked, the patties should be very firm when you press down on them.

Serve warm on burger buns.

This is a conglomeration of a few recipes from the cookbook that also would make great use of leftover Beanballs (page 289). We throw in a handful of spinach just for posterity; you need not be so healthy if you don't feel like it. Also, if you don't want to make the Cashew Tofu Cream (page 256) and just want to use vegan cheese, we won't judge you. These would be perfect for a Super Bowl party, or since you are vegan and hate football, a Nobel Prize party. Ooh, we can't wait to see who wins for physics this year!

Prepare the recipes of the first three components. Preheat the oven to 350°F. Place the Beanballs on a baking sheet and top with about 1 cup of marinara and all of the cashew tofu cream. Bake for 20 to 25 minutes, or until the cashew tofu cream is lightly browned. Spread more marinara sauce on one side of each roll and distribute the Beanballs evenly among the sammiches, layering the spinach leaves over them. Top liberally with more marinara sauce. Close your sammiches, slice in half on the diagonal, and serve.

BEANBALL SUB

MAKES 4 / TIME: 40 MIN

1 recipe Beanballs (page 289)

1 recipe (5 cups) Marinara Sauce, or any of the variations (page 314)

1 recipe Cashew Tofu Cream (page 256)

4 vegan hoagie rolls, split open

2 cups fresh spinach leaves, well washed

Every vegan cookbook needs a sloppy joe recipe with the name changed around a bit, right? Well, this is ours: those sloppy joes we loved as a child, but made with lentils. Snobby Joe thinks he's better than all the other Joes because he doesn't have any meat.

Place the lentils and water in a medium-size saucepan. Cover and bring to a boil. Once the mixture is boiling, lower the heat and simmer for about 20 minutes, until the lentils are soft. Drain and set aside.

About 10 minutes before the lentils are done, heat a separate medium-size saucepan over medium heat. Sauté the onion and bell pepper in the oil for about 7 minutes, until softened. Add the garlic and sauté for a minute more.

Stir in the cooked lentils, chili powder, oregano, and salt. Add the tomato sauce and tomato paste. Cook for about 10 minutes. Add the maple syrup to taste and the mustard, and heat through.

Turn off the heat and let the pot sit for about 10 minutes, so that the flavors can meld, or go ahead and eat immediately if you can't wait. We like to serve these open-faced, a scoop of Snobby Joe on each slice of bun.

SNOBBY JOES

SERVES 4 TO 6 / TIME: 60 MIN

1 cup dried lentils

4 cups water

1 tablespoon olive oil

1 medium-size yellow onion, cut into small dice

1 green bell pepper, seeded and cut into small dice

2 cloves garlic, minced

3 tablespoons chili powder

2 teaspoons dried oregano

1 teaspoon salt

1 (8-ounce) can tomato sauce

¼ cup tomato paste

2 to 3 tablespoons maple syrup

1 tablespoon prepared yellow mustard

4 to 6 vegan kaiser rolls or sesame buns, sliced in half horizontally

CHILE CORNMEAL-CRUSTED
TOFU
PO' BOY

SERVES 4 / TIME: 45 MIN

1 recipe Chile Cornmeal-Crusted Tofu
(page 191)

1 recipe Crispy Coleslaw (page 145)

Chipotle Mayo (see tip)

Bread-and-butter pickles

2 (12-inch) loaves vegan French bread,
sliced in half widthwise and split open
horizontally

This is another sammich that uses various recipes from this cookbook. Crusted tofu and creamy coleslaw meet a spicy chipotle mayo and a pickle. We know that po' boys usually don't have pickles, so save your e-mails! We just can't resist them.

Prepare the recipes of the components. Spread the mayo on the bottom halves of the bread and place the tofu, then the coleslaw, then the pickles on the bread. Spread some mayo onto the top half of the bread, close the sammiches, slice in half on the diagonal, and serve.

TIP *To make Chipotle Mayo,* add one canned chipotle along with a little of its sauce to ¼ cup of Vegan Mayo (page 123) or commercially prepared vegan mayonnaise and mash well with a fork.

Yes, you can have a to-die-for vegan version of this outrageously "meaty" creation: a toasty pressed loaf of a sandwich that's stuffed with juicy seitan roasted in a garlic citrus marinade, vegan cheese, ham, pickles and all the fixings.

This is the updated, vegan version of the Cuban lunchtime classic that was an instant hit with Terry's recipe testers for *Viva Vegan!* And sometimes classics require simple ingredients for the most authentic rendition. For the bread, seek out soft submarine-style vegan sandwich rolls or fresh vegan Italian bread loaves instead of hard, crusty peasant baguettes. In a world of elegant and flavorful vegan cheese, mellow slices of "American"-style cheese are perfect (we love basic Chao cheese here best), bread-and-butter pickle slices, and a healthy slather of old-fashioned bright yellow prepared mustard. Choose your favorite deli-sliced vegan ham here: Tofurky ham is our go-to favorite, but be on the lookout for other tasty new alternatives as they pop up. This is one of the few recipes where we've ever called for the addition of store-bought vegan meats, but sometimes nothing else will do!

The other essential for this hot sandwich is pressing it down firmly as it grills: it fuses all of the ingredients together for a dense yet sleek sandwich with a chewy interior and crisp, buttery exterior. A panini press is a fancy way to get the job done, but it's more fun to improvise: pressing the sandwich down with another cast-iron pan, or even better, a brick wrapped in a few layers of aluminum foil is the ideal shape and weight for sandwiches.

Prepare the seitan: Preheat the oven to 375°F. Whisk together all the mojo ingredients except the seitan in a ceramic or glass 7 x 11-inch baking pan. Add the seitan strips and toss to coat with the marinade. Roast for 10 minutes, then flip the slices over once, until the edges are lightly browned and some juicy marinade still remains (don't overbake!). Remove from the oven and set aside to cool.

Assemble the sandwiches: Slice each roll or piece of bread in half horizontally and generously spread both halves with the butter or brush with olive oil. On the bottom half of each roll, spread a thick layer of mustard, a few slices of pickle, two slices of the ham, and one-fourth of the seitan slices, and top with two slices of the cheese. Dab a little of the remaining marinade on the cut side of the other half of the roll, then place atop the lower half of the sandwich. Brush the outsides of the sandwich with a little more olive oil or spread with the butter.

Preheat a 10- to 12-inch cast-iron pan over medium heat. Gently transfer two sandwiches to the pan, then top with something heavy and heatproof, such as another cast-iron pan or a brick covered with several layers of heavy-duty aluminum foil. Grill the sandwich for 3 to 4 minutes, watching carefully to prevent the bread from burning; if necessary, lower the heat slightly as the sandwich cooks.

When the bread looks toasted, remove the pan/brick and use a wide spatula to carefully flip each sandwich. Press again with the weight and cook for another 3 minutes or so, until the cheese is hot and melty. Remove the weight, transfer each sandwich to a cutting board, and slice diagonally with a serrated knife. Serve hot!

CUBAN
SEITAN SANDWICHES

MAKES 4 BIG FAT SANDWICHES /
TIME: 45 MIN, not including making homemade seitan, if using

Mojo roasted seitan:

¾ cup fresh orange juice

3 tablespoons fresh lime juice

3 tablespoons olive oil

4 cloves garlic, minced

1 teaspoon dried oregano

½ teaspoon ground cumin

½ teaspoon salt

½ pound seitan, sliced into ¼-inch-thick slices

For assembly:

4 (6- to 8-inch-long) vegan submarine sandwich rolls, or 1 soft vegan Italian loaf, sliced widthwise into 4 pieces

Vegan butter, at room temperature, or olive oil

Prepared yellow mustard

1 cup bread-and-butter pickle slices

8 slices store-bought vegan ham

8 slices mild-tasting vegan cheese (American or yellow cheese flavor preferred)

- -
MAKE-AHEAD TIP
- -

Assemble each sandwich but do not brush outsides with vegan butter or oil; instead, wrap tightly with foil. Keep refrigerated for up to 3 days and grill as needed (which will be all the time)!

ROASTED EGGPLANT & SPINACH
MUFFULETTA SANDWICH

SERVES 4 / TIME: 45 MIN,
plus 3 hrs marinating time

Roasted eggplant:
1 smallish eggplant (less than 1 pound)
Kosher salt
3 tablespoons extra-virgin olive oil, for
roasting

Mixed olive salad relish:
1 cup pitted kalamata olives
1 cup pitted green olives
½ cup coarsely chopped flat-leaf parsley
4 cloves pickled garlic
½ cup sun-dried tomatoes, oil-packed
or dried and reconstituted (about
10 tomatoes)
4 teaspoons red wine vinegar or white
balsamic vinegar
1 teaspoon dried, crumbled rosemary
1 teaspoon dried, crumbled thyme
1 teaspoon celery seeds
1 teaspoon dried, crumbled oregano
1 teaspoon dried, crumbled basil
½ cup extra-virgin olive oil

3 cups fresh spinach leaves, washed and
spun dry
1 tablespoon red wine vinegar

Sandwiches:
1 (9- to 10-inch) round vegan peasant-style
loaf (1 to 1½ pounds)
2 roasted red or yellow peppers, from a jar
or homemade (pages 28, 33)

Only olive lovers need apply! This monster-size, New Orleans classic sandwich is drenched in a luscious multi-olive "salad" that—thanks to a long steep in the fridge—penetrates every succulent inch. The original is a medley of meat products; our version is stuffed to near bursting with roasted eggplant, sweet peppers, and fresh sweet spinach. Take this sturdy sandwich along to your next picnic or the beach, or drop (wrapped very tightly) into a backpack for a long bike ride. The longer it sits in a chilled environment, the better it will taste. It's really a meal in and of itself but would be really nice with a little sangria and veggie crudités.

Prepare the eggplant for roasting: Preheat the oven to 375°F. Line a baking sheet with parchment paper. Cut the eggplant widthwise into ¼-inch slices and rub each slice with kosher salt. Allow to drain in a colander for half an hour.

Meanwhile, prepare the relish: Place the olives, parsley, pickled garlic, and sun-dried tomatoes in a large bowl. Toss with the vinegar and dried herbs. With a food processor, chop the mixture in two or three batches, adding some of the oil to the mixture with each batch. Process only enough to chop up the olives and tomatoes; stop often and use a rubber spatula to move the stuff around. The idea is to create not a paste of olives but a chunky mixture. Scrape the relish, along with the remaining oil, into an airtight container.

Place the spinach leaves in a large bowl (you can use the one that once held the olives). Sprinkle with 1 tablespoon red wine vinegar.

Roast the eggplant slices: Rinse the salted slices with cold water, rub with the oil, and lay in a baking sheet (some overlapping is okay). Roast in the preheated oven for 20 to 22 minutes, flipping once, until the eggplant is browned and tender. Place the hot eggplant slices on top of the spinach and toss to combine (the hot eggplant will slightly wilt the spinach leaves).

Assemble the sandwich: Insert a thin, sharp knife into the side of the round loaf at a slightly downward angle. Cut the loaf in half, working the knife on the angle to create a shallow bread "bowl." Remove some of the bread from the bottom and top interior of the loaf to deepen the bowl (save the bread guts for crumbs or use it to nosh on leftover olive relish).

Spread the olive relish very thickly on each side of the loaf, making sure to get lots of the oil and juices onto the bread. Drizzle with a little extra olive oil if the relish looks a little dry. Layer the bottom with the eggplant, spinach, roasted red peppers, and more eggplant, then top with the last of the spinach. Replace the top of the loaf and press down very firmly with your body weight on the entire sandwich; don't be afraid to smush it down. Wrap tightly in foil, then wrap again in plastic wrap or a few resealable plastic bags. Refrigerate, putting a few heavy items on top of the sandwich to help press it down even further (one or two unopened cartons of nondairy milk work nicely). For maximum flavor, allow to sit at least 3 hours—or even better—overnight. To serve, hold the sandwich firmly and cut in half with a sharp serrated knife, then slice again into four wedges.

VIETNAMESE SEITAN BAGUETTE

with Savory Broth Dip

SERVES 4 / TIME: 30 MIN,
not including preparing seitan

Dipping broth:

2½ cups broth from the preparation of Simple Seitan (page 205)

4 cloves garlic, left whole and unpeeled but gently crushed

1 (1-inch piece) fresh ginger, peeled, sliced ⅛ inch thick, and gently crushed

½ teaspoon Chinese five-spice powder

1 teaspoon red pepper flakes

1½ teaspoons organic sugar

2 tablespoons fresh lime juice

Seitan:

1 pound Simple Seitan (page 205) or commercially prepared seitan, cut into thin slices

2 tablespoons canola or mild-flavored vegetable oil

2 tablespoons soy sauce or tamari

1 clove garlic, minced

High-heat-safe cooking oil (such as high-heat canola oil), for grilling

Sandwiches:

4 (6-inch) vegan French baguettes, or individual mini-baguettes

Vegan Mayo (page 123) or commercially prepared vegan mayonnaise, several tablespoons per sandwich or to taste

Red onion rings, sliced thinly

Cucumber (seedless is best), peeled and sliced into long, thin strips

Several sprigs fresh cilantro

We are proud to present this whimsical union of the traditional Vietnamese sandwich, bánh mì, and the American classic "French Dip" sandwich. While both sandwiches are traditionally a parade of meat products, our meatless version still delivers a savory bite with slices of grilled Simple Seitan (page 205). The sharp fresh flavors of cucumber and cilantro then team up with a spicy dipping broth that really satisfies. How to eat? Select a corner of your sandwich, dip in broth, bite, yum, repeat, yum.

Prepare the broth dip first: In a 2-quart saucepan, combine the broth, garlic, ginger, five-spice powder, and pepper flakes. Don't cover the pan. Bring to a boil and boil for 5 minutes, then lower the heat to medium-low and simmer for another 10 minutes. Turn off the heat, stir in the sugar and lime juice, and cover the broth to keep it warm until ready to serve. You may strain the broth before serving; it's easily done by ladling individual servings through a mesh strainer into serving bowls.

Grill the seitan: In a shallow baking dish, combine the sliced seitan, canola oil, soy sauce, and garlic. Cover with plastic wrap and set aside to marinate in the fridge for 20 minutes (or do this the night before). When ready to serve the sandwiches, heat a cast-iron grill pan over high heat. Generously oil with high-heat-safe cooking oil and grill the seitan strips in a single layer, flipping once, until the slices are hot and sizzling. Transfer the finished seitan to a plate and cover with foil to keep warm until ready to use.

Assemble the sandwiches: Slice each baguette in half horizontally. Keeping one long side intact, open up and lightly toast. Spread mayonnaise on each half of the baguette and layer one side with cucumber, onion rings, and seitan slices; top with the cilantro. Close the sandwiches and press down on top to smush down a little. Holding it firmly, slice each sandwich in half on the diagonal. Serve with a small cup of hot broth.

TIPS

Use a good-quality French bread for this sandwich, the kind with a crunchy, shiny crust and a chewy interior. Avoid the generic, soft, thin-crusted bread typically found in grocery store chains. It will disintegrate when the sandwich is dipped into the broth.

Preparing sandwiches for a crowd? Tuck the sliced seitan into split baguettes, wrap in foil, and keep warm in the oven until showtime.

Don't have any leftover broth from making seitan? Just use ready-made veggie broth plus 2 tablespoons of soy sauce. Proceed as directed for making dipping broth.

Nobody, and we mean not even the meatiest meat lover, can resist a sandwich piled high with thick cuts of saucy barbecued seitan and crunchy coleslaw. Inspired by the long gone S'nice café in Manhattan, we adore the summertime flavors of this sandwich all year round. The recipe is written for grilling seitan indoors on a cast-iron grill pan, but you can also use a regular cast-iron pan. Or try an outdoor grill; just be sure to use a high-heat grill spray, as the seitan has a tendency to stick on the grill. This BBQ sandwich is delightful served with thick-cut potato chips or crisp, chilled baby carrots.

First, prepare the slaw: Whisk together the mayo, dill, and mustard powder in a large mixing bowl. Add the shredded cabbage, carrot, and diced pickle. Toss to combine with dressing, cover tightly with plastic wrap, and refrigerate until ready to use.

Prepare the barbecued seitan: Pour the BBQ sauce in a pie plate or medium-size shallow bowl and keep near the stove. Heat a cast-iron grill pan over medium heat and brush generously with oil. Place a layer of sliced seitan on the grill, brush with more oil, and grill on each side for about 3 minutes, or until browned and sizzling. Use metal tongs to turn the seitan; grill in two batches. When cooked, toss the seitan in the BBQ sauce to coat.

Brush the grill with a little extra oil and grill the sauce-covered seitan in two batches, turning the strips once. The strips should be slightly browned and some of the edges just beginning to crisp when the seitan is ready to remove from the pan. Place the seitan back in the pie plate or bowl; if not serving right away, cover with aluminum foil and keep warm in a 275°F oven.

Assemble the sandwiches: Slice the rolls in half horizontally, spread with mayonnaise, and drizzle with a little extra BBQ sauce, if desired. Pile the slaw generously on the bottom half of the rolls, top with the seitan, and press down with the top half of rolls. Cut in half and serve.

-45

BBQ SEITAN
& CRISPY COLESLAW
SANDWICH

SERVES 4 / TIME: 45 MIN,
not including making seitan

Slaw:

⅓ cup Vegan Mayo (page 123) or commercially prepared vegan mayonnaise

½ teaspoon dried dill, or 1 tablespoon chopped fresh (hate dill? then replace with parsley or fresh basil!)

Pinch of English mustard powder or a dash of prepared Dijon mustard

3 cups finely shredded purple or white cabbage (or a combination of both)

1 carrot, peeled and shredded finely

½ cup finely diced bread-and butter-pickle (squeeze the slices first to remove excess brine)

Barbecued seitan:

1½ to 2 cups Backyard BBQ Sauce (page 316) or your favorite prepared BBQ sauce

High-heat-safe vegetable oil, for grilling

1 recipe Simple Seitan (page 205), sliced into ½-inch-thick strips

Sandwiches:

4 large, hearty vegan sandwich rolls or sliced baguettes

Vegan Mayo (page 123) or commercially prepared vegan mayonnaise (optional)

CHAPTER FIVE

MIX & MATCH

VEGETABLES · GRAINS · BEANS ·
TOFU · TEMPEH · SEITAN

In the beginning of nonmeeting eating time, Cro-Veganon men (and women) eschewed the meat at the center of their plate and subsisted almost entirely on discrete little mounds of side dishes:

potatoes, corn niblets, frozen peas, even a boiled Brussels sprout during festive times. This was called dinner. Then, they evolved. New taste buds and culinary skills blossomed, and even some of the Cro-Veganon's more carnivorous brethren started to get the drift that eating meat ain't cool. Increasingly palatable and interesting faux meat options appeared and continue to do so to this day. The former empty spot in the middle of that dinner dish once again was claimed by these wondrous, modern delights. Suddenly the great plains of the supermarket aisles and wilderness of the grocery store were flooded with herds of veggie burgers, tofu dogs, nondairy cheeses, and soy kielbasa (it exists). And all was good.

Well, sort of. We are happy that all of this stuff is there for newly minted vegetarians transitioning away from flesh eating. However, when we cook at home for ourselves and our nearest and dearest, we want to create meals from wholesome ingredients we can identify and in theory, make ourselves (someday we're gonna make tofu from scratch in our tiny New York City apartments). Our solution in 2007 and still today in 2017: make side dishes the main event! It's fun and completely delicious to make a nutritious meal out of balanced portions of grains, beans, and vegetables. Just add the "holy trinity" of tofu, tempeh, and homemade seitan for a supersatisfying plate every time.

--------------- ◆ ---------------

VEGETABLES

◆

No longer overboiled and pushed along the edges of the plate, vegetables have come of age in 2017.

The original recipes of 2007 were designed with the full plate in mind, a way to enrich any meal, even a vegan meal, with much needed plant life to balance out too many carbs or protein. We've added a substantial number of new recipes: for cauliflower, beets, and every vegan's beloved, kale.

These collards use up the leftover marinade from the Smoky Grilled Tempeh (page 201), so make them together. You can also just replace the marinade with vegetable broth (page 223) and a teaspoon each of liquid smoke and soy sauce. These greens are awesome because they aren't too oily and the marinade cooks them just right, tender enough to chew but not falling apart in your mouth. Well, that's how we like them, anyway. Use tongs to sauté everything; they are the best tool for throwing greens around in a skillet.

Preheat a large skillet over medium heat. Sauté the garlic in the oil for about a minute, being careful not to burn it. Add the collards and sauté for about 2 minutes. Add the marinade and cook for another 10 minutes, until the collards are tender and a deep green. Serve immediately!

TIP

This is our favorite way to prep collards: To get rid of the tough stem without having to sit there cutting it, you can actually easily tear the leaves from the stem with your hands. Fill the sink with water, pull off the leaves, rip them into large pieces (collards are tough; they can take it), and put the leaves into the water to rinse them. No need to drain; just give them a shake before adding to the pan.

SAUTÉED

COLLARDS

SERVES 4 / TIME: 15 MIN

4 cloves garlic, minced

1 tablespoon olive oil

1 pound collards, pulled off the stem (see tip)

½ cup leftover marinade from Smoky Grilled Tempeh (page 201)

This basic sautéed spinach recipe veers to the Asian side, thanks to the ginger; it's perfectly yummy with Samosa Stuffed Baked Potatoes (page 63). But you can also easily transform it for an Italian or Mediterranean side by omitting the ginger, doubling the garlic, adding toasted pine nuts, and using olive oil instead of coconut oil.

Preheat a large skillet over medium-high heat. Sauté the onion in the coconut oil for about 2 minutes. Add the garlic, ginger, red pepper flakes, and salt. Sauté for another 30 seconds or so. Add the tomatoes and sauté until moisture begins to release, about 2 minutes. Add the spinach and cook until the spinach is wilted. Add splashes of water to make the spinach cook faster without burning. Sprinkle with lemon juice and serve.

SAUTÉED

SPINACH & TOMATOES

SERVES 4 / TIME: 15 MIN

2 tablespoons coconut oil

1 small onion, chopped finely

3 cloves garlic, minced (or more if you like!)

2 teaspoons grated fresh ginger

½ teaspoon red pepper flakes

½ teaspoon salt, or more to taste

2 plum tomatoes, seeded and cut into a little less than ½-inch dice

1 bunch spinach, roots discarded, washed well (about 6 cups, loosely packed)

Juice of ½ lemon or lime

BABY BOK CHOY

with Crispy Shallots & Sesame Seeds

SERVES 4 / TIME: 20 MIN OR LESS

1 pound baby bok choy

2 small shallots, sliced into very thin rings

1 (½-inch) cube fresh ginger, peeled and minced

2 tablespoons peanut oil

1 tablespoon mirin or agave nectar

1 tablespoon tamari

1 tablespoon toasted sesame seeds

- - - - - - - -
TIPS
- - - - - - - -

If using regular "adult" bok choy: slice the white stems away from the leafy tops. Chop the stems into 2- to 3-inch chunks.

When ready to cook the bok choy, place the chunks in the pan first and sauté them for 2 to 3 minutes, then add the green leafy parts and continue as directed.

We can't deny that baby bok choy is our favorite Asian veggie. It looks like a cute little vase made of green leaves, and the flavor and texture is that of a very sweet, juicy white cabbage. Our favorite way is a rapid stir-fry, hearty enough for a multicourse meal but fast enough for a weeknight: lightly braised, topped with crispy brown shallots and a little bit of sesame. Perfect alongside a mound of Wasabi Mashed Potatoes (page 156).

Trim the tough ends from the base of the bok choy. If the bok choy is longer than about 4 inches, slice the stems once or twice into large chunks. Transfer to a large bowl, cover with 3 inches of cold water, slosh around in the water, and set aside for a minute to allow any sand to sink to the bottom of the bowl. Drain off water and grit and repeat a few times to remove any grit. Shake off any excess water.

Heat the peanut oil in a large skillet over medium heat. Add the sliced shallots, separating them in the pan with a slotted spatula. Fry for about 5 minutes, or until they're deep golden brown and crisp. It may take a while as the shallot soften first, but suddenly they will become crispy and brown: watch carefully to prevent burning. Remove the shallots from the pan with a spatula or spoon and set aside onto a plate. If no oil remains in the pan, drizzle in a little extra oil.

Add the ginger and stir-fry for 15 seconds. Add the bok choy and stir-fry for about 2 minutes, or until the green leaves start to wilt. Stir in the mirin and tamari and cover the pan. Steam for 2 minutes, then remove the lid. Transfer the bok choy to a serving plate, top with the fried shallots, sprinkle with toasted sesame seeds, and serve!

ESCAROLE

with Capers & White Beans

SERVES 4 AS A SIDE OR 2 AS A MAIN COURSE / TIME: 20 MIN

1 tablespoon olive oil

6 cloves garlic, chopped

¼ teaspoon red pepper flakes

1 head escarole, stem cut off, leaves left whole

Salt

⅓ cup capers with some brine

1 cup cooked small white beans (navy or great northern are A-OK)

Lemon wedges, for serving

Raw escarole looks more like a lettuce than the leafy dark greens you might usually prepare, but once sautéed it has a delicate flavor and a great texture that's a nice balance between soggy and crisp. And we use "soggy" in a positive way. Serve with grilled tofu and mashed potatoes or rice, but it's hearty enough to stand as a meal on its own. We also like to sprinkle it with nooch (nutritional yeast, to you), but that is top secret.

Preheat a large skillet over medium heat. Sauté the garlic in the oil for about 3 minutes, until just starting to brown. Add the red pepper flakes and cook just long enough to soften (a few seconds). Add the escarole and salt to taste, and use tongs to toss until it begins to wilt and release moisture. Add the capers and beans and cook just until heated through, about 3 more minutes. Serve with lemon wedges.

SWEET & SALTY
BRUSSELS SPROUTS

SERVES 3 TO 4 / TIME: 20 MIN

1 pound Brussels sprouts

2 tablespoons olive oil

2 tablespoons tamari

2 teaspoons pure maple syrup

3 tablespoons toasted pumpkin seeds, gently crushed or chopped (page 320)

A few twists of freshly ground black pepper

No longer does the world need convincing when it comes to Brussels sprouts: the perfect sweet-crunchy bite of hearty cruciferous veg. We eat oven-roasted sprouts by the boatload, but how about a simple stovetop treatment for seared sprouts with an irresistible sweet, salty finish?

Trim the ends of Brussels sprouts and slice each in half, horizontally. Transfer to a mixing bowl and drizzle with oil and tamari. Toss the sprouts to coat.

Preheat a large cast-iron pan over medium-high heat. Spread half the sprouts into the pan and arrange the sprouts so that each is cut side down on the pan. Sear the sprouts for 10 minutes. Drizzle with 1 teaspoon of maple syrup, then cook, stirring occasionally, for another 2 minutes. The sprouts are done when charred and blistered in spots, heated all the way through, but still have a little bit of crunch in the center. Transfer back to the mixing bowl and cook the remaining sprouts in the same way.

When both batches of sprouts are done, toss the pumpkin seeds over the hot sprouts. Top with a few twists of pepper and serve immediately!

TIP This recipe was developed with a standard 10-inch pan in mind, but if you have a great big 12-inch pan, go ahead and make one big batch instead of two. Basically, if you can fit all the sprouts at once in your pan, go for it!

It's no secret that roasting Brussels sprouts makes them irresistible: toss with oil, salt, roast, boom bam done. But if you want to go beyond basic, this streamlined version of the original 2007 recipe of "oven-fried" roasted sprouts gets a huge flavor boost by tossing them in an Indian-spiced crumbly cornmeal–chickpea flour coating. This rich and filling side can be a whole meal served with Spiced Yogurt Sauce (page 323), but also sings alongside a chickpea curry and basmati rice.

Preheat the oven to 400°F. Line a large baking sheet with parchment paper and spray the surface with a little nonstick cooking spray.

Trim and wash the Brussels sprouts, shake off any excess water, and pat dry lightly with a clean dish towel. Slice any really huge sprouts into two pieces. Place the sprouts in a large bowl, sprinkle with a little salt, and dust with 1 tablespoon of the chickpea flour, tossing to coat every sprout.

In a small bowl, mix together the cornmeal, remaining 3 tablespoons of chickpea flour, salt, garam masala, and cayenne. Pour in the oil and mix together with your fingers to form crumbs. Add the Brussels sprouts, toss to coat with the oiled crumbs, and press as much of the crumb mixture as possible onto them. It's okay if some of the coating doesn't stick to the sprouts. You'll still have plenty of crumb mixture left over that will toast up brown and crisp during the baking; try pressing some of this into some of the little leaves that will inevitably fall off the sprouts.

Pour the coated sprouts and crumbs onto the prepared baking sheet and spread them into a single layer. Bake for 25 to 30 minutes, or until the sprouts are browned and tender. Every 10 minutes or so while baking, stir the sprouts and crumbs with a wooden spoon or spatula, moving any overly browned crumbs on the edges of the pan toward the center to prevent burning.

To serve: Pile the sprouts on a plate, heap a spoonful or two of crumbles on top, and squeeze a lemon wedge over the sprouts.

MASALA
BRUSSELS SPROUTS

SERVES 4 TO 6 / TIME: 50 MIN

Nonstick cooking spray, for pan
1½ pounds Brussels sprouts
¼ cup chickpea flour
⅔ cup cornmeal
1 teaspoon salt
2 teaspoons garam masala
¼ teaspoon cayenne pepper
6 tablespoons olive oil
Lemon wedges, for garnish

VARIATION

MASALA ROASTED OKRA: Substitute whole, fresh okra pods for the Brussels sprouts. Proceed as directed, roasting the okra until golden and tender.

Garlic and herbs flavor these baked potato slices in a creamy sauce, perfect for serving with grilled tofu, tempeh, or seitan, or really anywhere mashed potatoes would fit in. If you absolutely hate nutritional yeast, use 3 tablespoons of flour in place of it. You can use any regular-size white potatoes, or even Yukon golds.

Preheat the oven to 400°F. Lightly grease a 9 x 13-inch glass baking dish or ceramic casserole pan. If you don't have one, a metal one lined with baking parchment is fine, too.

Layer the potatoes in the pan, allowing them to slightly overlap: lay them across the short way first, overlapping a little less than half of each potato slice; in each subsequent row, overlap the potatoes by about one quarter of each potato slice.

Pour most of the vegetable broth over the potatoes, reserving about 3 tablespoons (no need to be exact). Pour the milk and drizzle the oil over the potatoes, making sure to coat each one. If you need to use a little more than 1 tablespoon of oil, that is okay.

Scatter the minced garlic over everything, then sprinkle 2 tablespoons of the nutritional yeast over all the potatoes. Drizzle with the remaining vegetable broth—try not to wash all the nutritional yeast off the potatoes; you just want to get it moist, so drizzle slowly. Then, sprinkle with the last tablespoon of nutritional yeast, the herbs, and the salt and pepper.

Cover loosely with aluminum foil and bake for 35 minutes. Uncover and bake for an additional 15 minutes. Serve!

TIP   If you like your scalloped potatoes crispier, instead of baking in the oven for the last 15 minutes, turn on the broiler and broil them for 5 to 10 minutes, until the top is browned to your liking.

G-F

HERB-SCALLOPED
POTATOES

SERVES 4 / TIME: 60 MIN

2 pounds white potatoes (3 average-size), scrubbed, sliced into ⅛-inch-thick disks

¾ cup vegetable broth, purchased or homemade (page 223)

½ cup unsweetened nondairy milk

1 tablespoon olive oil

3 cloves garlic, minced

3 tablespoons nutritional yeast or all-purpose flour

½ teaspoon dried thyme

½ teaspoon dried basil

¼ teaspoon dried rosemary

¼ teaspoon paprika

½ teaspoon salt

Several pinches of freshly ground black pepper

LEMONY ROASTED POTATOES

SERVES 4 TO 6 /
TIME: ABOUT 50 MIN

2½ pounds russet potatoes (medium-size to small potatoes work best)

⅓ cup olive oil

6 cloves garlic, chopped finely

½ cup fresh lemon juice

1 cup vegetable broth, purchased or homemade (page 223)

2 teaspoons dried oregano

2 teaspoons salt

1 teaspoon tomato paste

Freshly ground black pepper

Chopped fresh parsley or dried oregano (optional)

The soul of every Greek restaurant in Queens, New York, is made of tender cuts of potato bathed in a bracing garlic-oregano-lemon sauce. Now you can bring this classic Mediterranean comfort dish to any potluck, or just make yourself a well-deserved batch. Serve alongside any Mediterranean-themed meal, Chickpea Cutlets (page 206), or seitan entrées. They're also excellent served with steamed greens laced with olive oil and lemon juice.

Preheat the oven to 375°F. Peel the potatoes, slice in half lengthwise, and slice each half into wedges no more than ¾ inch thick.

In a large rectangular casserole dish (at least 10 x 17 inches or bigger), combine the oil, garlic, lemon juice, vegetable broth, oregano, salt, and tomato paste. Add the peeled, sliced potatoes. Sprinkle with the pepper and toss the potatoes to cover with the sauce. Cover the pan tightly with foil (or use the lid of the casserole dish), place in the oven, and bake for 30 to 35 minutes, or until the potatoes are almost done. Several times during the baking process, remove the pan from the oven, uncover, stir the potatoes, place the cover back, and continue roasting.

Uncover the pan one last time, stir the potatoes, and bake, uncovered, for an additional 15 to 20 minutes. The potatoes are ready when most of the sauce has evaporated and the potatoes have just started to brown on their edges. Sprinkle with chopped fresh parsley and/or more dried oregano before serving.

MASHED POTATOES

& variations

SERVES 4 TO 6 / TIME: 30 MIN

2 pounds potatoes

3 tablespoons refined coconut oil

½ cup unsweetened nondairy milk

2 teaspoons salt

Ground white or freshly ground black pepper

TIP

Sure, use any potato you like, but different potatoes will yield different results. For light, fluffy mashed potatoes, use a starchy, pebbly skinned "baking" variety, such as Idaho. A dense, creamy mash can be obtained from waxy, thin-skinned potatoes, such as red or Yukon gold (which make awesome buttery-hued mashed potatoes). Sometimes we peel our potatoes, sometimes we leave the skins on for the ever-so-hip variation of "smashed" potatoes (mostly when using waxy potatoes).

A classic recipe that will never let you down, and only five ingredients! We've included tasty variations that happily mix and match with practically any cuisine you feel like cooking up tonight.

Wash your potatoes and peel them (or don't), cut them into 1-inch chunks, and place them in a 4-quart pot filled with salted water. Bring the whole thing to a boil, then lower the heat to simmer and cook until the potatoes are soft, 15 to 20 minutes. Drain.

Put the drained potatoes back in the pot or in a bowl, add the oil, and mash with a potato masher or heavy-duty fork. Add the milk and mash till desired consistency. Taste and add a little more oil or milk, if desired. Salt and pepper to taste. Serve!

VARIATIONS

Add 2 to 3 tablespoons of the following along with the oil: pesto, finely chopped chives, chopped parsley, roasted garlic.

Whisk 1 to 2 teaspoons WASABI POWDER OR CURRY POWDER into the nondairy milk (before adding to potatoes).

For the CREAMIEST CREAM DE LA CREAM of mashed potatoes, replace the milk with cashew cream.

Unwrapping a tinfoil beet is a lot like unwrapping a present. Well, maybe not really, because you know exactly what's going to be in there, but it's still somehow such an exciting surprise. Roasting brings out the beets' sweet flavor so they're like precious rubies in a candy box when ready to eat.

The cooking method and time really varies depending on the size of the beets you're using. If using small beets, say, golf ball–size, and they are very fresh, then slice in half, wrap, and roast. And remember to save the beet greens to sauté with some olive oil and garlic. But if using those big honkers of a beet that you're more likely to find come January and February, then it's a little different. Peel them and then slice, top down, into segments (like orange slices) that are about ¾ inch thick at their widest. Then, keeping all the slices together in a neat package, place on tinfoil and wrap so that it can be unfolded easily from the top.

Preheat the oven to 425°F, coat the beets with olive oil and salt, and wrap in tinfoil (see headnote).

Place the wrapped beets on a baking sheet and cook for about an hour, until easily pierced with a fork.

TINFOIL
BEETS

YIELD MAY VARY depending on beet size /
TIME: ABOUT 1 HR

1 pound beets, washed and scrubbed, sliced (see headnote)
1 tablespoon olive oil
¼ teaspoon salt

Rutabaga is the unsung hero of the root vegetable world, unless you live in Sweden (then you're probably like, "Enough with the rutabaga already!"). Fortunately, we're in NYC where the rutabaga is always a nice surprise. They taste like a slightly sweeter turnip, and in this recipe rutabaga is pureed with a little coconut milk, lime juice, and just a tiny hint of agave, for a li'l Thai twist. Also, try our variation, Cilantro-Pureed Rutabaga. It would go wonderfully with the Tamarind Lentils (page 186).

Place the rutabaga in a medium-size lidded saucepan and cover with water. Put on the lid and bring to a boil. Once the water is boiling, lower the heat to a simmer and cook for about 20 minutes, until the rutabaga is tender.

Drain and transfer to a food processor. Add the remaining ingredients and puree until smooth. Serve immediately, while still warm.

VARIATION

CILANTRO-PUREED RUTABAGA: Add 2 loosely packed cups of chopped fresh cilantro to the food processor and blend until the rutabaga is bright green.

RUTABAGA
PUREE

SERVES 4 TO 6 / TIME: 30 MIN

2½ pounds rutabaga, peeled and cut into ¾-inch chunks
2 tablespoons freshly squeezed lime juice
¼ cup canned full-fat coconut milk
2 teaspoons agave nectar
½ teaspoon salt

TIPS

Since you use very little coconut milk for this, make sure to cook some other recipe that calls for a full can. Most recipes won't miss the ¼ cup (you can just add ¼ cup of water to make up for it). Turnips work well with this recipe, too!

MASHED SPICED
SWEET POTATOES

SERVES 6 / TIME: 1 HR

3 pounds sweet potatoes
½ teaspoon salt
½ teaspoon ground cinnamon
⅛ teaspoon ground allspice
¼ teaspoon ground nutmeg
¼ teaspoon ground ginger
2 tablespoons pure maple syrup
1 tablespoon refined coconut oil

Everyone has a recipe like this, but this is the best one. Mashed sweet potatoes spiked with pumpkin pie–type spices are wonderful alongside collards (see page 149) and grilled tofu. You can also replace the spices with 1 teaspoon of pumpkin pie spice or apple pie spice.

Preheat the oven to 400°F.

Place the sweet potatoes directly on an oven rack (no tray is needed and no need to poke holes in them). Depending on the size of the sweet potatoes, the cooking time will vary. An average-size sweet potato takes about 45 minutes but large ones can take longer, sometimes up to 75 minutes if they are the giant kind.

Once you can easily poke through the potatoes in the center, they are done. Remove from the oven and split them lengthwise; leave them opened to speed up cooling.

When still warm but not too hot to handle, scoop out the sweet potatoes with a spoon and place in a large bowl. Discard the skins.

Add the remaining ingredients and mash everything with a strong fork. Serve warm.

CREAMED CORN

SERVES 4 / TIME: 45 MIN

½ cup plus ⅓ cup unsweetened nondairy milk, preferably almond
1 tablespoon cornstarch
1 tablespoon refined coconut oil
3 cups fresh corn kernels (from about 3 ears)
½ teaspoon salt

Creamed corn goes nicely with so many things: Latin dishes, Southern dishes, barbecue. Really, almost anything. Try with sautéed greens and Baked BBQ Tofu (page 196). Sautéing the corn before blending gives it a toasty depth of flavor. This recipe is best with fresh corn, but if using frozen, allow for 5 more minutes cooking time when you sauté the corn.

Mix ⅓ cup of the milk with the cornstarch in a cup to create a slurry and set aside.

Preheat a 4-quart, heavy-bottomed pan over medium-high heat. Sauté the corn in the coconut oil for about 5 minutes, or until tender and flecked brown.

Add the remaining ½ cup of milk (not the cornstarch slurry) and blend, using an immersion blender, until about three quarters of the corn is pureed and there are still some pieces left. If you don't have an immersion blender, transfer the mixture to a blender and pulse to your desired consistency, then transfer back to the pot. Increase the heat to medium.

Add the cornstarch slurry and salt and stir constantly until the corn mixture has thickened, 5 to 7 minutes. Serve immediately.

Here's a very simple way to serve butternut squash. Feel free to try it with different spices or even without any spices at all; the butternut will be able to stand on its own. To smash the coriander seeds easily, place them in a small plastic sandwich bag. Place a few layers of newspaper on top of the seeds and then have at it with a hammer or a mallet. You can also place them in a coffee grinder and pulse a few times (use caution; you don't want to reduce them to a powder).

Preheat the oven to 375°F.

Combine all the ingredients on a rimmed baking sheet (the "rimmed" part is essential, since you don't want the oil dripping off into the oven and causing a fire. Or do you?). Make sure that all the squash pieces are coated in oil and seeds, and spread into a single layer. Bake for about 35 minutes, tossing occasionally, until the squash is tender and slightly caramelized.

ROASTED
BUTTERNUT SQUASH
with Coriander Seeds

SERVES 6 TO 8 AS A SIDE /
TIME: 50 MIN

2 medium-size butternut squash, peeled, seeded, and cut into ¾-inch chunks

2 tablespoons olive oil

2 tablespoons coriander seeds, smashed

¼ teaspoon salt

These multipurpose succulent mushrooms are perfect for salads, in sammiches, or just as a veggie side for pretty much any type of savory meal, even brunch. You get enough marinade for four small caps or two huge ones, but your mileage may vary depending on the size of your caps. You can marinate and roast these in a glass pie plate or use a small casserole dish. Any pan greater than 8 inches across would spread the marinade too thinly. The ingredients are really simple, but you can add dried herbs, such as oregano, thyme, and basil, if you think it will go with whatever else you are eating. Using herbs is an especially good idea if you are going to make this into a portobello sammich.

Preheat the oven to 400°F.

Prepare the marinade: Combine all the ingredients for the marinade in a glass pie plate or small, nonreactive casserole.

Place the mushrooms upside down in the marinade and spoon a lot of the marinade into each cap to form a small pool. Marinate for about 20 minutes.

Cover with aluminum foil and bake for 30 minutes. Remove the foil, use tongs to flip the caps over, and cook, uncovered, for another 10 minutes. If you're using your portobello as a burger, just put that puppy between a bun with some lettuce, tomato, Vegan Mayo (page 123), and avocado, and call it a day. If using for a salad, let it cool a bit and then slice the mushrooms very thinly on the diagonal to make nice, meaty slices.

ROASTED
PORTOBELLOS

SERVES 2 AS A MAIN, 4 AS A SIDE /
TIME: 1 HR

Marinade:

½ cup cooking wine

1 tablespoon olive oil

2 tablespoons soy sauce

2 tablespoons balsamic vinegar

2 cloves garlic, minced

2 large or up to 4 small portobello caps

EASY
STIR-FRIED LEAFY GREENS

SERVES 4 TO 6 / TIME: 20 MIN

1 pound dark, leafy greens, such as mustard greens, Chinese broccoli, large bok choy, chard, water spinach, dandelion greens (use 2 pounds), watercress (use 2 pounds), green choy sum, etc.

2 tablespoons peanut oil

3 cloves garlic, minced finely

1 (½-inch) fresh cube ginger, grated

1 tablespoon rice cooking wine, cooking sherry, or mirin

2 teaspoons soy sauce

Pinch of organic sugar

1 teaspoon toasted sesame oil or chile-sesame oil (optional)

Eating enough green, leafy vegetables through the week can be a challenge for even the most dedicated vegan or vegetarian. While we're repeat customers when it comes to spinach, collards, and kale, there's a whole world of Asian and other greens that pack nutrition and flavor yet all too often don't get enough face time on our dinner plates.

Spicy mustard greens, crisp Chinese broccoli, sweet chard, and most any green sings with a touch of ginger, garlic, and soy sauce. There's no sticky, overly sweet sauce in this recipe. Only bright flavors and crunchy greens that cook in a flash, ready to dance with entrées of tofu, tempeh, beans, or grains.

Holding the greens together in bunches, slice into 1- or 2-inch-wide sections. If the greens have any thick stems or bottoms, remove and place the stems in a bowl separate from the leafy green tops. Wash and dry both bowls of greens, and shake off any excess water.

In a large, nonstick skillet or wok, heat the peanut oil over medium-high heat. Add the garlic and ginger; cook, stirring constantly, for 30 seconds. Add the thick stems and stir-fry for 1 to 2 minutes, or until the stems begin to soften.

Add the leafy tops and cook, stirring constantly, for another 2 to 3 minutes, until the tops begin to wilt and soften. Sprinkle with the wine, soy sauce, sugar, and chile–sesame oil. If the leaves are very large and piled high in the pan, cover the pan for 1 to 2 minutes to sweat and wilt them so that they can be easily stir-fried. Stir to combine all the ingredients. Stir-fry until the vegetables are bright green and the stems are tender but still slightly crisp. Remove from the heat and serve immediately.

TIPS

Any leafy green can be prepared this way, so if you see something new and interesting at the farmers' market, stir-fry it! Asparagus and green beans can be prepared in this manner. Just trim any overly tough stems and allow a slightly longer cooking time, depending on your desired degree of crispness.

We've included instructions on preparing greens with thick, juicy stems. This is not necessary when cooking thin-stemmed vegetables, such as water spinach, watercress, or dandelion, so skip the step of separating stems from leaves.

Long-handled metal kitchen tongs are the ideal tool for maneuvering leafy greens in a skillet or wok.

Keep it light and easy with a dressed up roasted cauliflower, ready to partner up with anything tofu, tempeh, or pasta. You can even skip the almonds entirely for the simplest of side veggies, but the nuts add hearty crunch.

Preheat oven to 400°F. Line a large baking sheet with parchment paper, and lightly oil the paper with olive oil.

Slice the cauliflower into ½-inch-thick slabs (crumbled bits are okay) and drizzle with 2 tablespoons of the oil. Sprinkle with the salt and pepper, then toss to coat the cauliflower with the oil. Spread the cauliflower into a single layer and roast for 20 minutes, remove from the oven, and use a spatula to flip pieces over and roast another 5 minutes until the edges of the cauliflower are well browned. Remove from the oven and transfer to a serving bowl.

Spread the chopped almonds in a single layer on a smaller, dry cookie sheet and roast for 4 to 6 minutes, or until the nuts are lightly toasted. Watch carefully and do not let them burn!

While the cauliflower is roasting, in a food processor or a mortar and pestle pulse (or pound) the remaining 2 tablespoons of oil, the mint leaves, and the lemon zest and juice into a chunky mixture similar to pesto.

To serve, spoon the pesto over the warm cauliflower and gently toss to lightly coat. Sprinkle with the warm toasted almonds and serve.

VARIATION

RAW CAULIFLOWER MINT & TOASTED ALMONDS SALAD: You can do this dish raw for a refreshing and zesty side! The key is slicing the cauliflower as thinly as possible: for best results, shave chunks off the cauliflower with a mandoline. Use a chef's knife to thinly slice any remaining pieces too small for the mandoline. Toss with the pesto, cover, and chill for 20 minutes before serving.

ROASTED
CAULIFLOWER
with Mint & Toasted Almonds

SERVES 4 / TIME: ABOUT 30 MIN

2 pounds cauliflower (about 1 large head, 8 inches across)

4 tablespoons olive oil, plus more for parchment paper

½ teaspoon salt, or more to taste

A few twists of freshly ground black pepper

1 cup whole raw almonds, roughly chopped

½ cup loosely packed fresh mint leaves

Grated zest of 1 lemon

2 tablespoons fresh lemon juice

GRAINS

◆

Carbs, glorious carbs!

We enjoy rice, quinoa, millet, polenta, and other grains incorporated into entrées, salads, and baked goods all the time, but this chapter is dedicated to savory dishes designed to partner up with veggies or beans.

This is mushy comfort food at its best: a simple, creamy polenta that goes great with strongly flavored savory dishes, such as Chickpea & Roasted Eggplant Stew (page 274). The poppy seeds make the usually humble polenta really aesthetically pleasing.

Bring the broth and salt to a boil in a medium-size saucepan. Add the polenta in a slow. steady stream, mixing as you pour it in. Add the poppy seeds and oil and lower the heat to a simmer. Cook for 12 minutes, stirring often. Turn off the heat and cover. Let sit for 10 more minutes, stirring occasionally.

SOFT
POPPY-SEED POLENTA

SERVES 4 TO 6 / TIME: 30 MIN

5 cups vegetable broth, purchased or homemade (page 223), or water

½ teaspoon salt

1 cup polenta corn grits (polenta)

2 teaspoons poppy seeds

2 tablespoons olive oil

Nothing fancy, just a nice basic and versatile pilaf with quinoa—the grain of the Aztecs. You can come up with all sorts of variations here—use different beans and different spices and what-not. We like to cook quinoa this way, rather than flavoring it after it's cooked, because it absorbs all the spices so well. Don't forget that cooking with quinoa at least once a week will elevate you to level 7 vegan in no time.

In a small stockpot over medium heat, sauté the onions in the oil for about 7 minutes. Add the garlic and sauté for 2 more minutes.

Add the tomato paste, coriander, cumin, pepper, and salt; sauté for another minute.

Add the quinoa and sauté for 2 minutes.

Add the chickpeas and broth; cover and bring to a boil. Once the mixture is boiling, lower the heat to very low, cover, and cook for about 18 minutes, or until the quinoa has absorbed all the water; stir occasionally. Fluff with a fork and serve.

CHICKPEA-QUINOA
PILAF

**SERVES 4 TO 6 AS A SIDE /
TIME: 40 MIN**

2 tablespoons olive oil

1 small yellow onion, chopped finely (about 1 cup)

2 cloves garlic, minced

1 tablespoon tomato paste

1 tablespoon coriander seeds, crushed (see page 161 for how to crush)

½ teaspoon ground cumin

Several pinches of freshly ground black pepper

½ teaspoon salt

1 cup quinoa, rinsed

2 cups cooked or 1 (15-ounce) can chickpeas, drained and rinsed

2 cups vegetable broth, purchased or homemade (page 223), or reconstituted bouillon

BROCCOLI
POLENTA

SERVES 4 TO 6 / TIME: 70 MIN

3½ cups vegetable broth, purchased or homemade (page 223), or water

½ teaspoon salt (you may need more depending on how salty your veggie broth is)

1 cup polenta corn grits (polenta)

4 cups very well-chopped broccoli stalks and tops (pieces should be no larger than ¼ inch)

2 tablespoons olive oil, plus more for greasing molds and cooking

Broccoli gives polenta a great texture. It just makes it, like, "RAR!" That's the only way we can describe it. We're giving you several options for molding and serving the polenta once it is prepped; try them all and see what you like best. You can serve this as a main dish with any of the marinara sauces or pesto, or serve it as a base for either the Braised Seitan with Brussels, Kale & Sun-dried Tomatoes (page 276) or the Sautéed Seitan with Mushrooms & Spinach (page 284). If you don't want to think about the various molding and cooking methods, then just do the muffin tin and broiling method, because it's cute. If you're short on time, you can even skip the molding step and just serve this as is after boiling.

Bring the broth and salt to a boil in a medium-size saucepan. Add the polenta in a slow, steady stream, mixing with a whisk as you pour it in. Add the broccoli and oil and lower the heat to low. Cover and let simmer for 15 minutes, stirring often. Turn off the heat, cover, and let sit for 10 more minutes, stirring occasionally.

Molding Methods

Tin Can: Grease two empty 20-ounce cans (tomato cans, for example) with olive oil. Spoon the polenta into the cans and place in the fridge for about 2 hours. Use a butter knife to help coax them out of the mold, slice into inch-wide pieces and proceed to Cooking Methods. This method of molding takes longer to chill because of the volume in each mold.

Muffin Tin: Grease 6-units of a muffin tin with olive oil. Spoon the polenta into the tin, almost all the way to the top of the compartments. Smooth the tops with the back of the spoon. Refrigerate for about an hour. Use a fork to pry the polenta out of the tin and proceed to Cooking Methods. This method works best when you broil the polenta.

Square Pan: Grease an 8-inch square (slightly bigger or smaller is okay) food storage container, casserole, or brownie pan. Spoon in the polenta and spread it out evenly. Refrigerate for about an hour. Cut into squares and proceed to Cooking Methods.

Cooking Methods

Broil: Preheat the broiler. Grease a rimmed baking sheet with olive oil. Place the polenta slices on the prepared baking sheet and broil 3 to 4 inches away from the heat, for about 7 minutes, or until lightly browned. If using the muffin tin molding method, place the polenta upside down on the baking sheet so that the rough tops are at the bottom.

Panfry: (Note: This doesn't really work with the muffin tin molding method.) Preheat a nonstick pan over medium heat. Pour a very thin layer of olive oil into the pan. Place the polenta slices in the pan and cook on both sides for about 5 minutes per side, until lightly browned.

Fresh spinach and dill paired with chickpeas and basmati rice make a complete meal. But we won't hold anything against you if you'd rather pair this alongside any vegetable side and Spiced Yogurt Sauce (page 323). It's best prepared in one of those serious Dutch ovens, but the dry rice plus the sautéed vegetables (and everything else) can be finished in a rice cooker (follow the manufacturer's instructions).

In a medium-size bowl, rinse the basmati rice with a few changes of water, then cover with at least 2 inches of water. Set aside while preparing the other ingredients, allowing the rice to soak in the water for at least 20 minutes. When ready to use, carefully drain the rice with a fine-mesh strainer.

Steam the chard either in a steamer or a large, covered pot filled with about 2 inches of boiling water. When the chard is limp and bright green, transfer it to a bowl to cool and squeeze as much water as possible from it. Roll tightly into bunches and chop finely.

Heat the peanut oil over medium heat in a Dutch oven. Add the cumin seeds, fry for 15 seconds, then add the shallots and onion. Sprinkle with the garam masala and sauté the mixture until the onion and shallots are soft, 6 to 8 minutes. Add the drained rice, folding to coat the grains with spiced oil mixture. Add the chopped dill, chard, chickpeas, water or veggie broth, salt, lemon zest, black pepper, and cayenne. Cover and increase the heat to bring to a boil, then quickly lower the heat to medium-low and tightly cover. Cook for 25 to 30 minutes, or until the liquid is absorbed and the rice is fluffy, watching carefully so as not to burn it.

Remove from the heat, sprinkle with the lemon juice, fluff the rice with a fork, and cover again. Allow to sit another 10 minutes before serving with lemon wedges.

FRESH DILL–
BASMATI RICE
with Chard & Chickpeas

SERVES 4 TO 6 /
TIME: ABOUT 65 MIN

2 cups white basmati rice

1 pound chard, cleaned, stems separated from leaves

2 tablespoons peanut oil

½ teaspoon cumin seeds

2 shallots, minced

1 small onion, finely chopped

1 teaspoon garam masala

1 bunch fresh dill, large stems removed, chopped finely (about ¾ cup)

1 (15-ounce) can chickpeas, drained and rinsed

2 cups water or vegetable broth, purchased or homemade (page 223)

1½ to 2 teaspoons salt (use less if using a salty vegetable broth)

1 teaspoon freshly grated lemon zest

Freshly ground black pepper

Pinch of cayenne pepper

Juice of 1 lemon

1 to 2 lemons, sliced into wedges (optional)

- - - - - -
TIP
- - - - - -

We like to soak the basmati rice before cooking because it makes the rice exceptionally fluffy. It's totally optional, so if you can't be bothered, skip this step—just rinse the rice and go!

ISRAELI COUSCOUS

with Pistachios & Apricots

SERVES 4 / TIME: 40 MIN

2 tablespoons vegetable oil

3 cloves garlic, minced

2 cups Israeli couscous

2½ cups water

1 cinnamon stick

1 teaspoon ground cumin

¼ teaspoon ground cardamom

Several pinches of freshly ground black pepper

½ teaspoon salt

Zest of 1 lime

¼ cup chopped fresh mint

½ cup chopped dried apricots, chopped to the size of raisins

½ cup shelled pistachios

Juice of ½ lime

Israeli couscous is bigger and more fun than your average couscous. You could say they are the beach balls of the couscous world. This is a Turkish-inspired dish, or at least we think it is; it's fragrantly spiced and would be perfect to serve with roasted or grilled veggies (pages 28–36)—try using it to complement sweet potatoes, Brussels sprouts, and/or red peppers.

Preheat a large, heavy-bottomed skillet over medium-low heat. Place the vegetable oil and garlic in the pan and sauté for 1 minute. Add the couscous, increase the heat to medium, and cook, stirring pretty constantly, for 4 or 5 minutes; the couscous should start to toast.

Add the water and the cinnamon stick, cumin, cardamom, pepper, salt, and lime zest. Increase the heat and bring to a boil. Once the mixture is boiling, lower the heat again to as low as possible and cover. (We know, lots of raising and lowering the heat, but that's cooking for you.) In about 10 minutes, most of the water should have been absorbed. Add 2 tablespoons of the mint and all of the apricots, pistachios, and lime juice. Stir, cover again, and cook for 5 more minutes. At this point, the water should be thoroughly absorbed.

Remove the cinnamon stick, fluff the couscous with a fork, garnish with the remaining mint, and serve.

TOMATO
COUSCOUS
with Capers

SERVES 4 TO 6 / TIME: 25 MIN

1 (28-ounce) can diced tomatoes

2 tablespoons olive oil

1 teaspoon dried oregano

1½ cups uncooked whole wheat or regular couscous

½ teaspoon salt

Generous pinch of cayenne pepper

¼ teaspoon ground cloves (optional)

2 tablespoons small capers, drained of brine (if using large capers, chop coarsely)

- - - - -
TIP
- - - - - -

Toasting the couscous before steaming it gives it a firmer texture and a deeper flavor.

With just a few more ingredients, regular old couscous transforms into a pretty pilaf that goes perfectly with any French, Spanish, or Italian main dish. Try it alongside Rustic White Beans with Mushrooms (page 179) or any kind of savory protein dish. After all of the ingredients have been measured and prepped, this side dish can be put together in less than 15 minutes.

In a medium-size bowl, strain the juice from the diced tomatoes to measure 1½ cups of juice, squeezing the diced tomatoes as much as possible to remove their excess liquid. Discard any remaining juice; if not enough juice is available to total 1½ cups, add either vegetable broth (page 223) or water. Gently crush any large chunks of diced tomatoes and set aside.

Combine the juice, oil, and oregano in a medium-size saucepan. Cover and heat to medium-high to bring to a boil. Stir continuously as you pour in the couscous in a steady stream. Quickly stir in the salt, cayenne, and cloves, if using. Stir to combine, turn off the heat, cover the pan, and allow it to sit for 5 minutes, or until the liquid is completely absorbed. Fold in the reserved diced tomatoes and capers, cover again, and allow to sit for 2 to 3 minutes to warm the tomatoes.

You might be tempted to call this recipe "Meximillet" or "Mexican Mullet," but just remember this tasty side is only a twist on lovely tomato-infused rice pilaf. Only here it's made with millet, providing a unique texture that's both a little soft and crunchy at the same time. Serve alongside any Mexican, Tex-Mex, or Latino-themed meal, or break all the rules and eat it for breakfast.

Heat the oil and garlic in a medium-size saucepan over medium heat. When the garlic begins to sizzle, add the onion and jalapeño, and fry, stirring occasionally, until the onion is soft and slightly golden, about 5 minutes. Add the millet and sauté for 4 minutes to gently toast until golden. Pour in the vegetable broth and whisk in the tomato paste, salt, cumin, and diced tomato.

Bring the mixture to a boil, stir once, and cover. Lower the heat to low and cook for 25 to 30 minutes, or until all liquid is absorbed.

Remove from the heat and let rest, covered, for 5 minutes. Fluff with a fork, sprinkle with the cilantro, and serve. Garnish each serving with a little lime juice and diced tomato, if you like.

S-F   G-F   LF   -45

MEXICAN
MILLET

SERVES 4 / TIME: 45 MIN

2 tablespoons peanut or vegetable oil

1 clove garlic, minced

1 small yellow onion, diced finely

1 jalapeño pepper, seeded and minced

1 cup uncooked millet

2 cups vegetable broth, purchased or homemade (page 223)

3 tablespoons tomato paste

½ teaspoon salt, or to taste

¼ teaspoon ground cumin

⅓ cup finely diced tomato (about 1 medium-size, firm, ripe tomato, seeded), plus more for garnish if desired

2 tablespoons finely chopped fresh cilantro

Fresh lime juice, for garnish

MESSY
RICE

SERVES 4 / TIME: 1 HR

1 tablespoon vegetable oil

¼ cup finely chopped yellow onion

2 teaspoons whole coriander seeds, crushed

2 cloves garlic, minced

2 tablespoons tomato paste

½ teaspoon salt

Several pinches of freshly ground black pepper

1 cup jasmine rice (plain old white rice works, too, but we love the flavor jasmine lends it)

1½ cups water

This is supposed to be like dirty rice, but the dirt is from crushed coriander seeds, not whatever gross stuff they traditionally put in dirty rice. The ingredients are simple but the rice is deceptively flavorful and scrumptious. Serve with Hot Sauce–Glazed Tempeh (page 202) and Creole Stuffed Peppers (page 64) for a down-home meal. Don't sub with commercially prepared coriander powder; it won't do this rice justice. See page 161 for how to crush coriander seeds.

Preheat a medium-size saucepan over medium heat. Sauté the onion in the vegetable oil for about 5 minutes, until softened and lightly browned. Add the crushed coriander and garlic and sauté for 2 more minutes. Add the tomato paste and stir it around for about a minute to get it well distributed. Add the salt, pepper, rice, and water, and stir. Cover and bring to a boil.

Once the mixture is boiling, give it another stir and lower the heat immediately to as low as it will go (to prevent sticking). Cover and cook for 35 to 40 minutes, until the rice is thoroughly cooked. Then, fluff with a fork and serve.

This bold and garlicky golden rice is easy to cook on a back burner while preparing a main-dish protein or vegetables, allowing you time to wonder why anyone should bother with rice pilaf mixes out of a cardboard box. Serve this aromatic side rice with any Spanish or Middle Eastern entrée or perfectly steamed asparagus paired with your favorite sauce. We like the full rich veggie bouillon flavor here, but if you're the CEO of a vegetable broth multinational and gotta keep your stockholders happy, then your top choice of vegetable broth it must be.

Place the water in a medium-size saucepan, bring to a boil, add the bouillon cube, and stir until the cube has dissolved. Turn off the heat, add the saffron threads, and stir. Cover and set aside until ready to use.

Preheat a medium-size pot over medium heat. Sauté the garlic in the oil until it has softened and is just starting to turn golden, 3 to 4 minutes. Add the onion and continue to sauté until the onion turns translucent, 5 to 6 minutes. Add the rice and stir to combine. Sauté the rice for about 1 minute. Pour in the warm vegetable broth and stir in the coriander. Cover and bring to a boil, stir the rice just once, and lower the heat to low. Cover and let the rice simmer for 20 to 25 minutes, until the liquid has been absorbed and the rice is tender.

Remove from the heat and allow the rice to stand for 10 minutes. Fluff with a fork, add the toasted almonds, and season with salt and ground white pepper, if desired.

TIP The saffron threads can be drained and used once more in another dish. The easiest way to do this is to place the threads in a small cup and pour in ¼ cup or less of the hot, prepared bouillon. Allow the threads to steep for at least 10 minutes. Using a small fine-mesh strainer (the kind used for straining tea leaves), pour the steeped broth back into the rest of the vegetable broth. Set the strainer aside, over the cup or on a dish, and allow the saffron to dry completely. Gently shake or tap the strainer to remove the dried saffron threads, and store in an airtight container.

SAFFRON-GARLIC
RICE

SERVES 4 / TIME: 45 MIN

1¾ cups water

1 vegetable bouillon cube

Pinch of saffron threads (3 to 4 threads)

2 tablespoons olive oil

5 cloves garlic, minced finely

1 small yellow onion, diced finely

1 cup long-grain white rice, such as jasmine or basmati, rinsed and drained

Pinch of ground coriander

⅓ cup toasted, sliced almonds (optional)

Salt and ground white pepper

Rich and cheesy tasting without a lick of cheese (and with plenty of nutritional yeast), this comforting and easy tomato and herb-drenched baked farro casserole may bump your favorite pasta bake down a notch or two. Farro is a rustic, chewy variety of whole-kernel wheat rich in protein and fiber, and usually stocked in nice groceries with other heirloom grains, such as quinoa, or look wherever Mediterranean pastas and rices are sold.

Preheat the oven to 350°F and lightly grease a 9 x 13-inch baking dish with 1 tablespoon of olive oil.

Sort through the farro to remove any broken grains and rinse in a colander. In a large saucepan over medium, sauté the garlic and shallot in 1 tablespoon of olive oil for 2 minutes to soften the shallot. Stir in the farro and the bay leaf and sauté for another minute, then pour in the vegetable broth and the tomatoes. Increase the heat to high and bring to a rapid simmer. Cook for about 2 minutes. Turn off the heat and add oregano, thyme, and salt. Remove bay leaf. Taste and season with a little more salt, if desired (if using water, you may want to), then stir in the parsley and nutritional yeast.

Pour the farro mixture into the prepared baking dish and smooth the top. Cover tightly with foil and bake for about 40 minutes, or until the farro has absorbed almost all of the liquid.

Pulse together the topping ingredients, except the olive oil, in a food processor (or pound with a mortar and pestle) into coarse crumbs. Take the casserole out of the oven, remove the foil, and cover the top evenly with the walnut topping. Drizzle those 2 tablespoons of olive oil on top and bake for 10 minutes to lightly brown the top of the casserole. For best results, allow the farro to sit for 10 minutes to cool slightly and firm up a bit. Serve warm; this casserole tastes even better the next day after the flavors have blended a bit more.

BAKED

FARRO

with Tomatoes & Herbs

SERVE 6 /
TIME: 1 HR, mostly baking time

2 tablespoons olive oil

2 cups uncooked farro

2 cloves garlic, minced

½ cup finely chopped shallot

1 bay leaf

2 cups vegetable broth, purchased or homemade (page 223), or water

1 (28-ounce) can diced tomatoes, with juices (do not drain)

2 teaspoons dried oregano

1 teaspoon dried thyme or basil

½ teaspoon salt, or more to taste

½ cup finely chopped flat-leaf parsley or fresh basil

2 tablespoons nutritional yeast

Topping:

¼ cup chopped walnuts

¼ cup nutritional yeast

½ teaspoon salt

½ teaspoon grated lemon zest

2 tablespoons olive oil

TIP

For a casserole with a more delicate texture, use pureed tomatoes in place of diced tomatoes.

BEANS

◆

**We've come a long way when it comes
to beans and lentils.**

Such a humble, protein- and fiber-loaded essential. For anyone looking to avoid soy products or fake meat, it's generally a good idea to
schedule in a bean-focused meal at least a few times a week. We
don't pick favorites when it comes to canned versus cooked from
scratch: both are great ways to get these nutrition and flavor pow-
erhouses into your life. While most of these recipes skew toward
made from scratch, we've provided instructions on how to adapt the
recipe with canned (or sometimes the other way around, for anyone
who knows and loves homemade beans).

Comforting and French-feeling, this pot of white beans is seasoned with aromatic herbs and vegetables and finished with the toothsome chew of sautéed mushrooms. In the original version we pleaded that you use only home-cooked beans, but on reflection it's obvious that few readers live like European farmers with long winter nights to simmer beans on the stove, so check out the newly expanded option for canned beans. For a real treat, prepare the casserole-style variation that follows: a delectable layer of buttery, herbed bread crumbs tops the beans and then the whole thing is baked to golden brown perfection. We love this dish paired with Tomato Couscous with Capers (page 172) and a side of shaved fennel dressed with olive oil and lemon juice.

If using dried beans: Sort through the beans and soak in plenty of cold water for 8 hours. Drain and rinse the beans and transfer them to a stockpot. Add 4 cups of cold water, cover, and bring to a boil. Boil for about 3 minutes. Skim off any white foam from the top. Cover the pot and lower the heat to medium; add the onion, celery, carrot, thyme, and tarragon.

Simmer for about 45 minutes, until the beans are very tender. Remove the onion, carrot, and celery (either discard or use in a broth). Lower the heat to low and continue to simmer while preparing the remaining vegetables. The beans should resemble a very thick stew, not a soup. If there's too much liquid, leave the pot uncovered and stir occasionally.

About 10 minutes before the beans are done, place 2 tablespoons of the oil and the garlic in a cold skillet. Heat the skillet over medium heat, allowing the garlic to sizzle for about 30 seconds. Add the chopped leek and sauté until soft, 1 to 2 minutes. Scrape the leek into beans. Add the remaining 2 tablespoons of oil to the pan, allow it to heat for about 30 seconds, and add the mushrooms. Sprinkle the mushrooms lightly with ½ teaspoon of the salt and sauté until most of the mushroom liquid has evaporated, anywhere from 8 to 12 minutes depending on the kind of mushroom. When most of the excess liquid is gone, add the mushrooms to the beans. Turn off the heat and season the beans with the remaining salt (or more, if desired) and pepper to taste. Allow the beans to stand for about 5 minutes before serving.

VARIATIONS

MADE WITH CANNED BEANS: This version is considerably faster and a little different but all tasty. Dice the onion, celery, and carrot and sauté with the herbs and garlic in half of the olive oil until slightly softened, about 3 minutes. Add the leek and sauté for another 2 minutes. Now, pour in the beans (undrained) along with 1 cup of water and simmer for 5 to 10 minutes to cook off some of the liquid and thicken. Cook the mushrooms in another skillet as directed and add just before serving. Or go the extra distance and make the bread crumb–topped casserole variation!

CRUMB-TOPPED CASSEROLE: Preheat the oven to 350°F. Spread the cooked bean mixture in a 2-quart casserole dish. Top with the Sage Bread Crumbs from the Pumpkin Baked Ziti (page 297), and bake for 20 to 25 minutes, until the bread crumbs are golden and the beans are bubbling.

RUSTIC
WHITE BEANS
with Mushrooms

SERVES 6 / TIME: ABOUT 1 HR, not
including bean soaking time

2 cups dried white beans, or 2 (15-ounce) cans white beans (such as butter or great northern) (see note)

1 small white onion, sliced in half

1 stalk celery, cut into 2 pieces

1 small carrot, sliced in half lengthwise

1 teaspoon dried thyme

2 teaspoons dried tarragon, or 2 tablespoons fresh

¼ cup olive oil

2 large cloves garlic, peeled and minced

1 large leek, well washed and sliced thinly

½ pound (about 2 generous cups) mushrooms (either cremini, shiitake, or oyster, or a combination), rinsed and sliced thinly

1½ teaspoons salt, or more to taste

Freshly ground black pepper

MEDITERRANEAN
BAKED LIMA BEANS

SERVES 6 TO 8 / TIME: 1 HR 30 MIN,
not including bean-soaking time

Beans:

1 pound dried, extra-large white lima beans,
soaked for at least 8 hours

2 bay leaves

Sauce:

¼ cup olive oil, plus more for Dutch oven

4 cloves garlic, minced

1 medium-size yellow onion, chopped finely

1 small carrot, shredded

1 (28-ounce) can diced or crushed tomatoes

2 teaspoons red wine vinegar

2 tablespoons tomato paste

1 tablespoon pure maple syrup or agave
nectar

1 tablespoon dried oregano

2 teaspoons dried thyme

1½ teaspoons salt

Pinch of freshly grated nutmeg

Freshly ground black pepper

¼ cup finely chopped fresh parsley

3 tablespoons finely chopped fresh mint

You may have childhood lima bean baggage, but this recipe will help you work through it. White kidney (cannellini) beans can be substituted, but "gigantes" is the Greek name for those extra-huge white lima beans and make this dish extra special. It's worth the trip to a market that stocks Mediterranean groceries: these sweet and pleasingly firm beans when baked have a mild starchy texture akin to potatoes that makes them so comforting smoothed in this light, zesty tomato sauce. This is a delightful riff on a traditional Greek home-style dish and is a hearty meal alongside rice, potatoes, and steamed greens.

Prepare the beans: Drain and rinse the soaked beans and place them in a large pot with 2 quarts of cold water and the bay leaves. Cover, bring to a boil, then lower the heat to medium. Simmer the beans for 30 minutes, until tender but not fully cooked (the interior of the beans will still be grainy). Skim off any foam that may collect while beans are cooking. Reserve 1 cup of the bean cooking liquid and drain the rest. Keep the bay leaves with the beans (don't discard just yet).

While the beans are cooking, preheat the oven to 375°F.

Prepare the sauce: Lightly oil a 4-quart Dutch oven or casserole dish (you can also prepare the beans in two batches in two 2-quart casseroles or Dutch ovens). In either the prepared Dutch oven, if using, or a separate large saucepan, heat the garlic and oil over medium heat until the garlic starts to sizzle. Add the onion and stir until translucent and softened, 3 to 4 minutes. Add the carrot, stir, and cook for another minute, and add the tomatoes, reserved bean cooking liquid, vinegar, tomato paste, maple syrup, oregano, thyme, salt, and nutmeg. Stir and bring to a boil, then lower the heat and cook for 10 to 12 minutes to reduce the sauce a little. Taste the sauce and season with pepper and more salt, if necessary. Stir in the beans, parsley, and mint.

Place in the prepared casserole dish (if not already using the Dutch oven), cover the dish, and bake the beans, stirring occasionally, for 30 minutes, until they are tender and the interior of the beans is creamy. Uncover and bake for an additional 10 to 15 minutes to reduce the sauce a little bit and give the beans a slightly dry finish. Remove from the oven, remove the bay leaves, and serve.

Feeling lazy, but not so lazy that you'll only open up that takeout menu? Then, you might like transforming ordinary canned black beans into a simple, savory side or main dish with just an onion and some time. A simple adobo sauce—featuring smoky chipotles—drizzled on top makes these beans special, but you can serve them without if you prefer. Pair it with Mexican Millet (page 173) or rice and a green salad.

Prepare the beans: Combine the beans, onion, bay leaf, and water in a large saucepan. Bring to a boil, then let boil for 1 minute. Lower the heat to medium and simmer, uncovered, for 40 minutes, until the beans are very tender and about half of the water has evaporated. Remove the bay leaf and onion before serving.

Meanwhile, prepare the sauce: In a heavy-bottomed skillet over medium heat, sauté the onion and garlic in the oil until the onion is very soft, 10 to 12 minutes. Stir in the chipotles and adobo sauce, cook for 30 seconds, and remove from the heat. Empty the sauce into a food processor bowl and briefly pulse until a chunky sauce forms. You may also use an immersion blender to do this. Serve the sauce drizzled over individual servings of beans.

S-F · G-F · LF · SF

BLACK BEANS
IN CHIPOTLE ADOBO SAUCE

SERVES 4 / TIME: ABOUT 50 MIN

Beans:
2 (15-ounce) cans black beans, drained and rinsed
1 large onion, peeled and halved
1 bay leaf
3 cups cold water
Salt and freshly ground black pepper

Chipotle adobo sauce:
3 tablespoons olive oil
1 large onion, cut into small dice
4 cloves garlic, minced
2 chipotle peppers in adobo, minced
2 tablespoons adobo sauce from the chipotles

CHEATER
BAKED BEANS

SERVES 6 / TIME: 75 MIN

2 tablespoons olive oil

1 medium-size yellow onion, diced as small as you can

3 cloves garlic, minced

1 (15-ounce) can tomato sauce

½ cup light molasses (not blackstrap)

2 teaspoons mustard powder

1 teaspoon salt

¼ teaspoon ground allspice

1 bay leaf

2 (15-ounce) cans small white beans (about 4 cups), drained and rinsed

These are "cheater" because the recipe uses canned beans—perfect for when you have some visitors from Boston drop by without any warning. We like these better than just using baked beans from a can because they aren't cloyingly sweet.

Serve with Smoky Grilled Tempeh (page 201) and collards (page 149). Or slice up tofu dogs and throw 'em in; see if we care. And while you're throwing around tofu hot dogs, for a proper New England kind of dinnuh, you must serve with slices of freshly steamed Boston Brown Bread (page 336) made right in the leftover bean cans.

Preheat the oven to 350°F.

Preheat a medium-size oven-safe pot over medium heat. Sauté the onion in the oil for about 10 minutes; you want the onion to be a little bit browned, but definitely not burnt, just a little caramelized. Add the garlic and sauté for 1 more minute. Add the tomato sauce, molasses, mustard powder, salt, allspice, and bay leaf and cook for about 5 minutes.

Add the beans, then cover the pot and transfer it to the oven. Bake for an hour, giving it a stir just once at about 30 minutes into the baking process. The sauce should thicken and sweeten. Keep warm until ready to serve.

Cheater Bakes Beans, page 184,
Boston Bread, page 336

TAMARIND LENTILS

SERVES 4 TO 6 / TIME: 45 MIN

3 tablespoons coconut or peanut oil

3 cloves garlic, minced

1 (½-inch) cube fresh ginger, peeled and minced

1 large onion, diced

1 teaspoon garam masala

½ teaspoon whole cumin seeds

Generous pinch of cayenne pepper

1 cup dried lentils, picked over and rinsed

2 cups vegetable broth, purchased or homemade (page 223), or water

2 teaspoons concentrated tamarind syrup or paste

1 tablespoon pure maple syrup or agave nectar

2 tablespoons tomato paste

½ teaspoon salt

Savory, tangy, and sweet, these Indian-inspired lentils are simple to prepare while cooking any basmati-type rice and vegetable side dish. We like them served over basmati rice with Poppy Seed–Cornmeal Roti (page 339).

In a heavy-bottomed medium-size pot with a lid, melt the oil over medium heat. Add the garlic and ginger and let sizzle for 30 seconds. Add the onion and fry until translucent and soft, 2 to 3 minutes. Stir in the garam masala, cumin seeds, and cayenne and stir for another 30 seconds, or until the spices smell fragrant. Add the lentils and vegetable broth, increase the heat to high, and bring the mixture to a boil. Stir and lower the heat to medium-low. Partially cover and simmer for 25 to 30 minutes, stirring occasionally, until the lentils have absorbed most of the liquid and are very tender. The lentils will be very thick; add a few tablespoons of water if a thinner consistency is desired.

In a small cup or bowl, combine the tamarind, maple syrup, tomato paste, and salt. Use a rubber spatula to scrape all of the mixture into the lentils; stir to completely dissolve the flavorings. Simmer the mixture for another 4 to 6 minutes, stirring occasionally. Adjust the salt to taste and serve immediately.

You can do this, make fantastic-tasting chana masala—sweet-and-sour Indian chickpea curry—at home that's infinitely healthier than takeout. It tastes even better heated up the next day after the flavors have mellowed out a little. It's so good with so many of the recipes in this book, our faves being Poppy Seed–Cornmeal Roti (page 339), puffy Naan Bread (page 338), Saffron-Garlic Rice (175), and Roasted Cauliflower with Mint & Toasted Almonds (page 163) or raw shaved cauliflower. The not-so-secret ingredient is pomegranate molasses, an outrageously tasty syrup made from pomegranates (see note). You can't substitute regular molasses, but markets that carry Middle Eastern or Mediterranean products should have little bottles of the pomegranate kind in stock.

In a large soup pot, melt the coconut oil over medium heat. Stir in the onion, ginger, garlic, and turmeric and fry for 3 minutes, or until softened and lightly browned. Stir in the garam masala, fry for 30 seconds, then stir in the diced tomatoes, chickpeas, pomegranate molasses, salt, and water.

Stir a few times, partially cover, and bring to an active simmer. Cook for 5 minutes. Lower the heat and simmer for another 5 to 10 minutes, or until slightly thickened. Taste and season, if desired, with a pinch more salt or an extra dash of the molasses. Turn off the heat and let the chana masala sit for a few minutes to cool slightly. When ready to serve, top with the fresh cilantro.

CAN DO

CHANA MASALA

SERVES 4 TO 6, with sides /
TIME: 45 MIN, not including time
to precook chickpeas

2 tablespoons unrefined coconut oil or mild olive oil

1 large red onion, minced

1 tablespoon finely chopped ginger

3 cloves garlic, minced

1 tablespoon finely chopped fresh turmeric, or 1 teaspoon ground

2 teaspoons garam masala

2 (15-ounce) cans diced tomatoes, undrained

4 cups cooked chickpeas, either made from scratch (see page 41) or 3 (15-ounce) cans, drained and rinsed

2 tablespoons pomegranate molasses (see note)

½ teaspoon salt, or more to taste

1 cup water

½ cup chopped fresh cilantro

NOTE

If you must make this without the pomegranate molasses, add 1 tablespoon each of tomato paste, fresh lime juice, and pure maple syrup. Not really at all like the flavor of pomegranates, but it will add that extra sweet/sour/fruity note to the masala.

A light coating of cornmeal, spices, and lime zest turns humble tofu into something we can get excited about. You can fry or bake these bad boys, so fry them up when you want to impress Paula Deen fans. Bake them when you're having a nice vegan night in, writing checks to Farm Sanctuary, and kicking back and leafing through vegan cookbooks. Be sure to check out the Po' Boys (page 138) that feature this tofu or serve with Southwestern Corn Pudding (page 238) and Green Pumpkin-Seed Mole (page 320).

Slice the tofu widthwise into eight slices, then cut each of those slices in half diagonally—from the upper left corner to the lower right corner—so that you have sixteen long triangles. Set aside.

Combine the milk and cornstarch in a wide, shallow bowl. Mix vigorously with a fork until the cornstarch is mostly dissolved.

In another shallow bowl, toss together the cornmeal, spices, lime zest, and salt.

For fried tofu: Heat about ¼ inch of oil in a large skillet, preferably cast iron, over medium heat. To test whether the oil is ready, sprinkle in a pinch of the milk mixture. When the mixture sizzles and bubbles form rapidly around it, you're good to go.

Dip each individual tofu slice in the milk mixture. Drop it into the cornmeal with your dry hand and use your other hand to dredge it in the mixture, so that it's coated on all sides. Transfer the tofu to the skillet in two batches so as not to crowd the pan. Fry the tofu for 3 minutes on one side, use tongs to flip over each piece, and fry for 2 more minutes. Drain the fried tofu on a clean paper bag or paper towels.

For baked tofu: Preheat the oven to 350°F. Line a baking sheet with baking parchment. Place the coated tofu on the baking sheet in a single layer. Spray with olive oil until lightly coated. Flip over and spray the other side. Bake for 12 minutes on each side.

TIPS You need a wet hand and a dry hand when dredging stuff in batter; otherwise the batter will clump up all over your hands and make you unhappy. So, use your left hand to soak the tofu and to drop it in the cornmeal. Then, use your right hand to do the rest of the dirty work.

For baking breaded things, ideally, you need a spray can of oil, and not the kind you buy in the supermarket (although that would work in a pinch). Use the kind that you fill yourself with oil. So, try to get one—if you are doing lots of low-fat cooking, it will be indispensable. If you don't have a spray bottle of oil, then just use a paper towel to spread a very thin coating of oil in the pan.

CHILE CORNMEAL-CRUSTED
TOFU

SERVES 4 / TIME: 20 MIN,
not including pressing tofu

1 pound extra-firm tofu, drained and pressed

1 cup unsweetened nondairy milk

2 tablespoons cornstarch

1 cup cornmeal

2 tablespoons chile powder

1 teaspoon ground cumin

¼ teaspoon cayenne pepper

1 tablespoon freshly grated lime zest

1½ teaspoons salt

Corn or vegetable oil for frying

A spray bottle of olive oil for baking (see tip)

BASIC BROILED
TOFU

SERVES 4 / TIME: 25 MIN

1 pound extra-firm tofu

Braising sauce:

¼ cup water

2 cloves garlic, minced

3 tablespoons fresh lemon juice

2 tablespoons soy sauce

A spray bottle of olive oil, or 1 scant
   teaspoon olive oil

Broiling tofu gives it a nice, dark, crusty skin. Intense heat concentrates and elevates the simple flavors of the ingredients—garlic, lemon juice, a little soy sauce. What we are saying is we like this method: it's fast, supereasy, and pretty hard to mess up. Using the broiler does require that you spend a few minutes at your oven on guard, making sure what you're cooking doesn't burn. But get to know your broiler and it's sure to be the beginning of a lasting relationship.

We use this tofu in several of our brunch recipes, including Tofu Florentine (page 82) and Greek Tofu Benedict (page 85), but you can also stuff it into a pita with lettuce, onion, and tomato and pour Dill-Tahini Sauce (page 325) over it, or just serve it as a simple dinner with some sautéed veggies.

Preheat the oven to broil.

Cut the tofu into triangles, like so: Slice widthwise into four equal slices. Cut each of those slices in half, widthwise, so that you have eight squares. Lastly, cut each of those squares in half diagonally to make sixteen triangles.

Prepare the braising sauce: Mix all the ingredients for the braising sauce in a small bowl.

When the broiler is good and hot, spray a thin layer of olive oil on the bottom of an oven-safe pan (cast iron works great) or small rimmed baking sheet. If you don't have a spray bottle of oil, then just use a paper towel to spread a very thin coating of oil in the pan.

Dip each piece of tofu in the braising liquid and place in the pan. Put the pan in the oven and cook for about 10 minutes, until the tofu is lightly browned. Remove the pan and pour a few spoonfuls of braising liquid over the tofu (no need to turn it). Put back in the oven for 3 more minutes, then repeat with the remaining braising liquid. Cook for about 3 more minutes—at this point the tofu should be golden brown. Remove from the oven and serve.

Tofu bakes up chewy and saucy when marinated in bright citrus juices and a healthy dash of rum. A nice 'fu that's ideal for Caribbean-themed meals, or anything Latin really. Try it topped on Quinoa Salad with Black Beans & Mango (page 107) or alongside Black Beans in Chipotle Adobo Sauce (page 183) and rice.

Preheat the oven to 425°F.

Prepare the marinade: In a shallow 7 x 11-inch glass baking dish, whisk together all the marinade ingredients.

Place the tofu cutlets in the marinade. Using a fork, carefully poke a few holes into the cutlets, flip them over, and do the same on the other side.

Bake the tofu for 45 minutes, flipping several times, about every 15 minutes or so. The tofu is ready when most of the marinade has reduced. Spoon any remaining marinade over the cutlets before serving.

TANGERINE
BAKED TOFU

SERVES 4 / TIME: 1 HR,
plus tofu pressing time

Marinade:

1 heaping teaspoon freshly grated tangerine zest

⅓ cup fresh tangerine juice (from 2 to 3 tangerines)

3 tablespoons fresh lime juice

2 tablespoons soy sauce

1 tablespoon agave nectar or pure maple syrup

1 tablespoon olive oil

¼ teaspoon ground cumin

⅛ teaspoon ground allspice

Freshly ground black pepper

2 tablespoons dark rum

1 pound extra-firm tofu, pressed and sliced widthwise into eighths

------
TIP

No tangerines? Substitute orange juice, or even tangelos or clementines.

CURRIED
TOFU

SERVES 2 TO 4 / TIME: TIME: 1 HR,
plus tofu-pressing time

Marinade:

½ cup vegetable broth, purchased or homemade (page 223)

3 tablespoons rice vinegar

2 tablespoons olive oil

2 tablespoons soy sauce

¼ cup curry powder

1 teaspoon cumin seeds

2 tablespoons mirin (optional)

1 pound extra-firm tofu, pressed and sliced into 8 equal pieces

Enjoy this flavorful tofu either baked or grilled. It's the perfect complement to any Indian meal or even on a sammich with curried mayo (just add 2 teaspoons of curry powder to ¼ cup of Vegan Mayo [page 123] or commercially prepared vegan mayonnaise). We love it with basmati rice and tamarind lentils. As always, reserve the marinade for the next time you make a stir-fry.

In a large mixing bowl, combine all the marinade ingredients and whisk together.

For grilled tofu: Cut the tofu widthwise into four equal pieces. Marinate for an hour, flipping every thirty minutes.

For baked tofu: Preheat the oven to 400°F.

Cut the tofu widthwise into eight equal pieces. Marinate for an hour, flipping after 30 minutes.

Place the tofu on a baking sheet and bake for 20 minutes. Flip over and bake for another 10 minutes. Switch to broil and cook for about 3 more minutes for extra chewiness.

TIP Since these cook so fast, a little advance planning will make your dinner a snap to prepare. Press your tofu the day before and prepare your marinades and refrigerate overnight. The next morning, slice up your tofu, drop into your marinade of choice, and refrigerate. When you get home, you should be able to have dinner on the table—or on your lap in front of the computer—in about 30 minutes.

Why mess with perfection? This recipe and the following one are two basic tofu marinades from *Vegan with a Vengeance*—simple recipes that go well with just about anything, either grilled or baked.

Prepare the marinade: Combine all the marinade ingredients in a wide, shallow bowl.

For grilled tofu: Cut the tofu widthwise into four equal pieces. Marinate for an hour, flipping over after 30 minutes.

Grease a stovetop grill pan (preferably cast iron) with vegetable oil. Preheat over high heat for about 3 minutes. Use tongs to distribute the tofu slabs evenly on the grill. Gently use the tongs to press the tofu into the grill ridges to get nice, dark lines. Cook for 3 minutes on one side without lifting, then turn the slabs 90 degrees to create a crosshatched pattern on the bottom of the tofu. Cook for 2 minutes, then flip over and cook for another 2 minutes. Transfer to a cutting board and use a sharp knife to cut each piece diagonally across into two triangles.

For baked tofu: Preheat the oven to 400°F.

Cut the tofu widthwise into eight equal pieces. Marinate for an hour, flipping after 30 minutes.

Place the tofu on a baking sheet and bake for 20 minutes. Flip over and bake for another 10 minutes. Switch to broil and cook for about 3 more minutes for extra chewiness.

MARINATED

ITALIAN TOFU

SERVES 4 / TIME: 1 HR 20 MIN, not including tofu-pressing time

Marinade:

½ cup white cooking wine

2 tablespoons olive oil

2 tablespoons balsamic vinegar

2 tablespoons Bragg Liquid Aminos or tamari

2 tablespoons fresh lemon juice

2 cloves garlic, smashed

A big pinch of dried basil

A big pinch of dried marjoram

A big pinch of dried thyme

1 pound extra-firm tofu, drained and pressed

Vegetable oil, for stovetop grill

BAKED
BBQ TOFU

SERVES 4 / TIME: 1 HR,
not including tofu-pressing time

1 pound tofu, drained and pressed, cut
widthwise into eighths

2 tablespoons peanut oil

1 tablespoon tamari

1 recipe Backyard BBQ Sauce (page 316) or
Apricot BBQ Sauce (page 317)

Forget digging a barbecue pit in your backyard. This chewy and succulent barbecue comes straight outta the oven. Serve with rice or mashed potatoes and steamed broccoli.

Preheat the oven to 350°F. In a 9 x 13-inch preferably glass or ceramic) baking pan, dredge the tofu in the peanut oil and tamari to coat. Bake for 15 minutes, then flip the slices and bake for 15 more minutes. Meanwhile, prepare whichever sauce you're using.

When the tofu is done baking, pour the sauce over it, smothering it all over. Return the pan to the oven and bake for 15 more minutes. Remove from the oven and serve.

This crispy fried tofu features the stunning flavor combination of red pepper, black pepper, and salt that's typically used for seafood in Chinese cuisine. Although the tofu may be fried, this recipe still uses less oil than anything you'll ever encounter in a restaurant, so rejoice. Serve it up with a mound of hot steamed jasmine rice and Baby Bok Choy with Crispy Shallots & Sesame Seeds (page 150), and you'll be in crispy, salty, and spicy tofu paradise.

Prepare the tofu: Combine sherry and soy sauce in a medium-size bowl. Add tofu cubes, gently stir, and marinate for 10 minutes, stirring occasionally. Use this downtime to set up your wok and any sides you'll be serving.

Heat the oil over medium-high in a large skillet or wok. Sift the cornstarch into a shallow bowl. Drain the tofu from the marinade, shake off any excess liquid, and dredge the tofu in the cornstarch. Using a slotted spatula, carefully lower half of the tofu into the oil to avoid splattering. Fry the tofu, occasionally moving each cube to lightly brown each side, for about a minute on each side. Transfer the browned tofu to a large dish or bowl. Repeat with the remaining batch. Remove the skillet from the heat and allow it to cool for 10 minutes. Drain or wipe away any excess oil or browned bits.

Stir-fry the tofu: Pour the tablespoon of oil into the skillet and heat over medium-high heat. Add the garlic and ginger and stir rapidly for 30 seconds until sizzling and fragrant. Add the red pepper flakes, black pepper, salt, and tofu and fry for 1 minute, stirring constantly and gently breaking up any chunks of tofu that stick together. Remove from the heat, sprinkle with the rice vinegar and scallion, and serve right away.

CRISPY

SALT & PEPPER TOFU

SERVES 4 / COOKING TIME: 40 MIN

Tofu:

1 tablespoon dry sherry or rice wine

1 pound firm tofu, drained, pressed, and cut into ½-inch cubes

2 teaspoons soy sauce

2 tablespoons canola or peanut oil, for frying

3 tablespoons cornstarch

Stir-fry:

1 tablespoon canola or peanut oil

2 cloves garlic, finely minced

1 (¼ inch) cube fresh ginger, peeled and minced

¼ teaspoon red pepper flakes, or to taste

½ teaspoon freshly ground black pepper

¼ teaspoon coarse salt, such as kosher salt

2 teaspoons rice vinegar

1 scallion, thinly sliced

MARINATED
ASIAN TOFU

SERVES 4 / TIME: 1 HR 20 MIN, not
including tofu-pressing time

Marinade:

½ cup mirin

3 tablespoons tamari

2 tablespoons rice vinegar

1 tablespoon sesame oil

2 teaspoons Asian chile sauce

1 (1-inch) chunk fresh ginger, peeled and
   chopped coarsely

2 cloves garlic, smashed

1 pound extra-firm tofu, drained and
   pressed

Vegetable oil, for stovetop grill

This tofu goes great with Wasabi Mashed Potatoes (page 158) and asparagus. It's also perfect to top off the Corn & Edamame–Sesame Salad (page 104).

Prepare the marinade: Combine all the marinade ingredients in a wide, shallow bowl.

For grilled tofu: Cut the tofu widthwise into four equal pieces. Marinate for an hour, flipping over after 30 minutes.

Grease a stovetop grill pan (preferably cast iron) with vegetable oil. Preheat over high heat for about 3 minutes. Use tongs to distribute the tofu slabs evenly onto the grill. Gently use the tongs to press the tofu into the grill ridges to get nice dark lines. Cook for 3 minutes on one side without lifting, then turn the slabs 90 degrees to create a crosshatched pattern on the bottom of the tofu. Cook for 2 minutes, then flip over and cook for another 2 minutes. Transfer to a cutting board and with a sharp knife cut each piece diagonally across into two triangles.

For baked tofu: Preheat the oven to 400°F.

Cut the tofu widthwise into eight equal pieces. Marinate for an hour, flipping after 30 minutes.

Place the tofu on a baking sheet and bake for 20 minutes. Flip over and bake for another 10 minutes. Switch to broil and cook for about 3 more minutes for extra chewiness.

This juicy tempeh is perfect alongside Sautéed Collards (page 149), which in turn make use of the tempeh marinade, so everyone is living in perfect harmony. It's equally delish with the Cheater Baked Beans (page 184), some greens, and a baked sweet potato.

Bring a medium-size pot of water to boil.

Prepare the marinade: Whisk all marinade ingredients together in a bowl large enough to fit the tempeh slices.

Cut the tempeh in half widthwise, then cut each of the resulting squares diagonally, to form four large triangles. When the water is boiling, lower the heat to a simmer, add the tempeh triangles, and cook for 10 minutes. This steams the tempeh and removes any bitterness, plus readies the tempeh to absorb the marinade.

Use tongs to immediately place the tempeh in the marinade bowl. Let marinate for 1 hour, flipping the tempeh every now and again to cover with the marinade.

To grill: Preheat a greased cast-iron grill pan over medium-high heat. To grease it, brush lightly with olive oil, or use a spray bottle of olive oil.

Grill each side of the tempeh for 5 minutes. When the second side is almost done, spoon some of the marinade over the tempeh and let cook for 30 more seconds.

To panfry: Preheat a heavy-bottomed pan over medium heat. Add about a tablespoon of oil to the pan. Cook the tempeh for about 10 minutes, turning often and spooning a bit more marinade over the tempeh as you turn it.

To broil: Preheat the oven to broil. Place the tempeh in an oven-safe pan (such as cast iron) or a rimmed baking pan. Spoon some of the marinade over the tempeh and broil for 5 minutes. Flip it and spoon some more marinade over it, and cook for another 5 minutes. When the second side is almost done, spoon some of the marinade over the tempeh and let it cook for 30 more seconds.

SMOKY
GRILLED TEMPEH

SERVES 4 AS A SIDE, 2 AS A MAIN /
TIME: 20 MIN, plus time for marinating

Marinade:

¾ cup vegetable broth, purchased or homemade (page 223)

2 tablespoons soy sauce

2 tablespoons apple cider vinegar

2 tablespoons liquid smoke

2 tablespoons olive oil

2 teaspoons pure maple syrup

2 cloves garlic, crushed

1 (8-ounce) package tempeh
Olive oil or a spray bottle of olive oil

NOTE

This recipe has the same basic directions as the Hot Sauce–Glazed Tempeh (page 202). Grilling is our preferred method, but we give you broiling and panfrying directions as well.

G-F

HOT SAUCE–GLAZED
TEMPEH

*SERVES 4 AS A SIDE, 2 AS A MAIN /
TIME: 20 MIN, plus time for marinating*

Marinade:

½ cup dry white wine

¼ cup hot sauce

2 tablespoons olive oil

2 tablespoons soy sauce

3 tablespoons fresh lemon juice

2 cloves garlic, crushed

1 teaspoon ground cumin

½ teaspoon dried oregano

⅛ teaspoon cayenne pepper (we know, with
    hot sauce? Yes.)

1 (8-ounce) package tempeh

Olive oil or a spray bottle of olive oil

There is no shortage of ways to serve this spicy and succulent tempeh. It goes well with mashed potatoes and Jalapeño-Corn Gravy (although, doesn't everything?) (page 329). Or try sautéed greens and baked sweet potatoes. If you wanna go all out, serve with Creole Stuffed Peppers (page 64) and Messy Rice (page 174).

Our preferred cooking method here is grilling, but we give you broiling and panfrying directions as well.

Bring a medium-size pot of water to a boil.

Prepare the marinade: Whisk all the marinade ingredients together in a bowl large enough to fit the tempeh slices.

Cut the tempeh in half, widthwise, then cut each of the resulting squares diagonally to form four large triangles. When the water is boiling, lower the heat to a simmer and cook the tempeh triangles for 10 minutes. This steams the tempeh and removes any bitterness, plus readies the tempeh to absorb the marinade.

Use tongs to immediately place the tempeh in the marinade bowl. Let marinate for 1 hour, flipping the tempeh every now and again to cover with the marinade.

To grill: Preheat a greased cast-iron grill pan over medium-high heat. To grease it, brush lightly with olive oil or, if you have a spray bottle of olive oil, that works, too. (Get a spray bottle of olive oil already!)

Grill each side of the tempeh for 5 minutes. When the second side is almost done, spoon some of the marinade over the tempeh and let it cook for 30 more seconds.

To panfry: Preheat a heavy-bottomed pan over medium heat. Add about a tablespoon of oil to the pan. Cook the tempeh for about 10 minutes, turning often and spooning a bit more marinade over the tempeh as you turn it.

To broil: Preheat the oven to broil. Place the tempeh in an oven-safe pan (such as cast iron) or a rimmed baking pan. Spoon some of the marinade over the tempeh and broil for 5 minutes. Flip it and spoon some more marinade over it, and cook for another 5 minutes. When the second side is almost done, spoon some of the marinade over the tempeh and let cook for 30 more seconds.

This is the *Vegan with a Vengeance* seitan recipe simplified. After publishing that book we got a lot of questions, often asking if one could substitute this, leave out that—sometimes just asking how we got to be so beautiful. While we won't reveal our beauty secrets, we will present you with this bare-bones boiled seitan recipe with clearer directions, simpler ingredients, and just the right amount of seitan for most recipes in this book.

Mix together the gluten flour and yeast in a large bowl. In a smaller bowl, mix together the veggie broth, soy sauce, oil, and garlic. Pour the wet into the dry and stir with a wooden spoon until most of the moisture has been absorbed and the wet ingredients are partially clumped up with the dry ingredients. Use your hands to knead the mixture for about 3 minutes, until the dough is elastic. Divide with a knife into three equal pieces and then knead those pieces in your hand just to stretch them out a bit.

Prepare the broth: Fill a stockpot with the water, bouillon cubes, and soy sauce and add the wheat gluten pieces. Cover and bring to a boil but watch carefully; you don't want it to boil for very long, or else the outside of the seitan will be spongy. Try to catch it as soon as it boils and then lower the heat as low as it will go so that it's at a low simmer.

Partially cover the pot so that steam can escape and let simmer for an hour, turning the seitan occasionally. Turn off the heat and take the lid off; let sit for 15 minutes.

Remove the seitan from the broth and place in a strainer until it is cool enough to handle. It is now ready to be sliced up and used. If you have extra seitan, store in the cooking liquid in a tightly covered container.

LF

SIMPLE
SEITAN

MAKES 1 POUND /
TIME: 1 HR 30 MIN

1 cup vital wheat gluten flour

3 tablespoons nutritional yeast

½ cup cold vegetable broth, purchased or homemade (page 223)

¼ cup soy sauce

1 tablespoon olive oil

2 cloves garlic, pressed or grated on a Microplane grater

Broth:

8 cups cold water plus 3 vegetable bouillon cubes, or 4 cups vegetable broth, purchased or homemade (page 223), plus 4 cups water

¼ cup soy sauce

CHICKPEA CUTLETS

MAKES 4 CUTLETS / TIME: 30 MIN

1 cup cooked chickpeas (page 41)

2 tablespoons olive oil, plus more for panfrying

½ cup vital wheat gluten

½ cup plain vegan bread crumbs

¼ cup vegetable broth, purchased or homemade (page 223), or water

2 tablespoons soy sauce

2 cloves garlic, pressed or grated with a Microplane grater

½ teaspoon freshly grated lemon zest

½ teaspoon dried thyme

½ teaspoon Hungarian paprika

¼ teaspoon rubbed dried sage

NOTE

In the decade that we've been making these, there've been countless instances of experimentation.

In the first edition, we predicted that these babies would take over blogs everywhere. And for once in our lives we were right! These have become a staple at many a vegan table, for weeknight meals or for a Thanksgiving centerpiece. A combination of chickpeas and vital wheat gluten formed into savory cutlets, it's perfect for when you want something "meaty" but don't want to go through the trouble of making seitan. We serve these cutlets in myriad ways, packed into sandwiches or smothered in mustard sauce, with a side of mashed potatoes and roasted asparagus. It's vegan food that you can eat with a steak knife and, best of all, it is fast and easy. You'll probably want to double the recipe if you're serving it to guests.

Mash the chickpeas together with the oil in a mixing bowl until no whole chickpeas are left. Add the remaining ingredients and knead for about 3 minutes, until strings of gluten have formed.

Preheat a large, heavy-bottomed nonstick or cast-iron skillet over medium heat. Meanwhile, divide the cutlet dough into four equal pieces. To form the cutlets, knead each piece in your hand for a few moments and then flatten and stretch each one into a roughly 6 x 4-inch rectangular cutlet shape. The easiest way to do this is to first form a rectangular shape in your hands and then place the cutlets on a clean surface to flatten and stretch them.

Add a moderately thin layer of olive oil to the bottom of the pan. Place the cutlets in the pan and cook on each side for 6 to 7 minutes. Add more oil, if needed, when you flip the cutlets. They're ready when lightly browned and firm to the touch.

Just in case you were wondering, you can bake these, too! Baking these patties gives them a toothsome chewy texture and firm bite. Preheat the oven to 375°F and lightly oil a baking sheet. Brush both sides of each patty with olive oil, place on the prepared baking sheet, and bake for 20 minutes. Flip the patties and bake for another 8 to 10 minutes, until firm and golden brown.

VARIATIONS

WHOLE CAN CUTLETS: Try using the whole 14- or 15-ounce can of chickpeas, which totals just under 2 cups. The patties hold up just fine and will be a little softer and with just a little extra chickpea flavor and texture.

SUN-DRIED TOMATO CUTLETS: Knead in ⅓ cup of finely chopped sun-dried tomatoes

BLACK OLIVE CUTLETS: Knead in ½ cup of pitted and chopped black olives. For fullest flavor, go for a real olive, such as kalamata or oil-cured black olives. A tablespoon of fresh rosemary (leave out the sage) ups the Mediterranean flavor game.

CHAPTER SIX

SOUPS

Soup is so basic that all too often it's totally ignored in cookbooks.

Everyone's always skipping past that section to check out the chocolate cake situation or the latest developments in lasagne. Don't be a follower like them; stop for a moment and really think about the abundance offered by soup and how it can change your life.

Soup can be smooth or chunky, creamy or clear, hearty or refreshing. The variations are really endless! Looking to drop a few pounds while eating fabulously? Make soup. Almost all of these recipes are modest in fat and absolutely loaded with tummy-filling fiber and nutrient-loaded veggies. Bean-based soups have the added benefit of plenty of protein. Eating a large bowl of soup for dinner is an easy way to avoid eating too many calories in the evening. And have you considered soup for breakfast: it's filling, warm, soothing, low in sugar, and big in flavor!

More important, soup can be serious food, not just the stuff you sip before an entrée. Take a wander in midtown New York on any weekday around lunchtime— what you'll most likely see are people standing in line for soup. And we're talking about the suit-and-tie, pumps-and-purses, no-nonsense, office-working crowd. They don't mess around when it comes to that precious lunch hour, and neither should you. Be a smart New Yorker (or Green Bayer, San Diegan, Portlander . . .) and write "making (really awesome) soup" into your weekly planner.

--------------- ◆ ---------------

BLACK BEAN—
VEGETABLE SOUP

SERVES 6 TO 8 / TIME: 1 HR 45 MIN,
not including soaking beans

Beans:

1 pound dried black beans, rinsed, soaked for 6 to 8 hours or overnight

6 cups water

2 bay leaves

Pinch of baking soda

Soup:

3 tablespoons olive oil

4 cloves garlic, minced

2 medium-size onions, diced finely

1 green bell pepper, seeded and diced finely

1 jalapeño pepper, seeded and minced

1 stalk celery, diced finely

1 carrot, peeled and diced finely

1½ teaspoons ground cumin

2 teaspoons dried oregano

1 teaspoon dried thyme

3 to 4 cups vegetable broth, purchased or homemade (page 223)

1 tablespoon white wine vinegar or sherry vinegar

2 teaspoons salt, or to taste

Freshly ground black pepper

For garnishing each serving of soup:

Chopped avocado, minced fresh cilantro, and lime wedges

Like that little black dress, a good black bean soup can really take you places and fit any occasion. The key to beautiful cooked black beans (black turtle beans, to be exact) is to cook until tender solo and then add the accompanying sautéed veggies afterward for a long, final simmer. Serve as is or topped with a swirl of Lime Crema (from the Baja-Style Grilled Tempeh Tacos recipe, page 131) or Sour Cilantro Cream (page 319), a twist of lime juice, or some diced avocado.

Prepare the beans: Drain the soaked beans, rinse again, and place the beans in a very large stockpot. Pour in the water and add the bay leaves and baking soda. Cover and bring to a boil, boil for about 3 minutes, and then lower the heat to medium-low. Allow to simmer for 1 to 1½ hours, until the beans are very tender and their skins are soft. Remove the bay leaves.

Begin to prepare the soup: About 20 minutes before the beans are done, preheat a large skillet over medium heat. Sauté the garlic in the oil for 30 seconds, then add the onions and bell pepper. Sauté for about 10 minutes, until the onions and peppers are very soft, then add the jalapeño, celery, and carrot. Cook for another 5 minutes, until the carrot has begun to soften, then remove from the heat.

When the beans are completely tender, stir in the sautéed vegetables and the cumin, oregano, thyme, and vegetable broth. Cover the pot, increase the heat to high, and bring to a boil. Lower the heat to medium-low, partially cover the pot, and simmer for 30 minutes, or until the carrot and celery are tender.

Remove from the heat, stir in the vinegar, and season to taste with salt and pepper. Like most soups, this soup will be richer and more flavorful the next day.

Garnish each serving of soup with chopped avocado and minced cilantro. Serve with lime wedges.

TIPS

We've added enough total liquid to create plenty of broth in this recipe; if you like your black bean soup more stewlike, add only two or three cups of veggie broth toward the end.

For a creamy-textured black bean soup, remove one or two cups of cooled soup and puree in a blender. Stir back into the soup and simmer for another 15 minutes. If you have leftover soup a few days down the road, try pureeing the whole thing and simmering until very hot. Season with a little more vinegar.

If you want to add a little heat, throw in a seeded jalapeño pepper or two.

Roasted garlic gives this pantry-staple tomato soup a little something special. Navy beans add protein and make it a complete meal. And since this recipe makes so much, it's a perfect contender for freezing and eating throughout the month. Or you can keep it in the fridge to eat throughout the week and forget that you ever ate anything else.

Preheat the oven to 425°F. Following the directions on page 34, roast the garlic for about 45 minutes, until soft. You should be able to feel if it's soft by pressing with a knife or your finger. Don't burn yourself, though.

Preheat a soup pot over medium heat. Sauté the onion in the oil for 5 to 7 minutes, until translucent.

Add the rice, bay leaves, thyme, marjoram, salt, and pepper and cook, stirring, for about 2 minutes. Add the crushed tomatoes, then fill up the can with water twice and add the water (so that's 56 ounces of water).

Bring to a boil, then lower the heat to medium-low, cover, and simmer for about 45 minutes.

Remove the garlic from the oven. When it is cool enough to handle, squeeze the roasted garlic out of its skin and into a small bowl. Use a fork to mash the garlic to a relatively smooth consistency, then add to the soup once the rice is nearly tender.

When the rice is completely cooked, add the beans and heat through. Then, it's ready to serve—just remove the bay leaves beforehand and thin with water or vegetable broth if it's thickened too much.

TOMATO-RICE SOUP

with Roasted Garlic & Navy Beans

SERVES 10 TO 12 / TIME: 45 MIN

2 bulbs garlic

1 tablespoon olive oil

1 medium-size yellow onion, diced as small as possible

1 cup long-grain brown rice

2 bay leaves

2 teaspoons dried thyme

1 teaspoon dried marjoram

2 teaspoons salt

Several pinches of freshly ground black pepper

2 (28-ounce) cans crushed tomatoes

1 (15-ounce) can navy beans, drained and rinsed (about 1½ cups)

- - - - - - - -
TIPS
- - - - - - - -

Use long-grain brown rice, not short-grain, because that kind doesn't like to cook in tomato broth.

If you don't have any roasted garlic hanging around and don't intend on making any, then mince and sauté six garlic cloves along with the onion.

ACORN SQUASH, PEAR & ADZUKI SOUP

with Sautéed Shiitakes

SERVES 6 / TIME: 1 HR

2 tablespoons peanut oil

1 large yellow onion, cut into ¼-inch slices

1 red bell pepper, seeded and cut into ¼-inch slices

2 teaspoons minced fresh ginger

2 cloves garlic, minced

½ teaspoon salt

½ teaspoon Chinese five-spice powder

2 acorn squashes, seeded, peeled, and cut into ¾-inch chunks

2 firm Bartlett pears, peeled, seeded, and sliced into thin (not paper-thin) slices roughly 1 inch long

4 cups vegetable broth, purchased or homemade (page 223)

1 (15-ounce) can adzuki beans, drained and rinsed (about 1½ cups)

About 1 tablespoon fresh lime juice

Mushrooms:

2 teaspoons peanut oil

½ teaspoon toasted sesame oil

4 ounces fresh shiitake mushrooms, sliced in half (about 1½ cups)

1 tablespoon soy sauce

This is a precious jewel of a soup studded with pretty, red adzuki beans along with just a hint of fragrant five-spice. We love the salty sesame shiitake mushrooms that adorn the soup and draw all the flavors together.

Preheat a large stockpot over medium heat. Sauté the onion and pepper in the peanut oil for about 10 minutes, or until the onion just begins to brown.

Add the ginger and garlic and sauté for 1 more minute. Add the salt, five-spice, acorn squash, and pear, and cook, stirring often, for another minute before adding the vegetable broth. Cover and bring to a boil. Once the soup is boiling, lower the heat to medium-low and simmer briskly for about 20 more minutes, or until the squash is tender.

Puree half of the soup, using either an immersion blender or by transferring half of the soup to a food processor or blender, processing, and pouring it back into the rest of the soup (don't forget, if using a blender or food processor, to let the soup cool a bit so that the steam does not compress in the processor and hurt you).

Add the adzuki beans and lime juice. Cover and simmer over low heat just until the beans are heated through, 7 to 10 minutes.

Meanwhile, prepare the mushrooms: Preheat a heavy-bottomed skillet over medium-high heat. Add the oils and sauté the mushrooms for about 7 minutes, until they are soft. Mix in the soy sauce and stir constantly until it is absorbed, about 1 minute.

Ladle the soup into bowls and top with the sautéed mushrooms.

TIPS

Acorn squash is a pain in the *tuchus* to peel. The best way we've found is to cut the squash in half and seed it, then cut into chunks (¾ inch, in this case). Use a paring knife to slice off the skin.

To remove the seeds from pears, peel and slice in half, then use a measuring teaspoon to scoop the seeds right out.

Okay, even though this recipe involves you making your own chile powder, we promise this is a fast soup that is even a little fancy. Not to mention yummy, warm, and comforting. The tart-sweet pineapple couples well with the deep, smoky chiles. Ancho chiles are fairly mild, so don't worry that this soup will be too spicy, unless you're a real big wimp. In fact, serve with hot sauce to prove your womanhood.

Prepare the chile powder: We're going to make our own ancho chile powder! Preheat a small, dry skillet over medium-low heat. Add the cumin seeds and ancho chile pieces and stir often, until fragrant and toasted, 3 to 5 minutes.

Transfer to a spice grinder (we use a clean coffee grinder) or small food processor and grind to a coarse powder. Some bigger pieces of chile are okay. Add the coriander seeds and pulse a few times to crush them—you don't want them completely ground to a powder, just broken up pretty well.

Prepare the soup: Preheat a big stockpot over medium heat. Sauté the onion in the oil until transparent, 5 to 7 minutes. Add the garlic and cook for another minute. Add the chile powder and mix into the onion mixture. Add the bay leaves, salt, lentils, and 7 cups of vegetable broth. Mix well. Increase the heat to high, cover, and bring to a boil. Once the soup is boiling, lower the heat to medium-low and let simmer for 30 minutes, stirring every now and again.

Meanwhile, heat your grill pan over high heat or preheat a broiler. Spray your grill pan with nonstick cooking spray and grill the pineapple slices for 4 minutes on each side, or until grill lines appear. If using a broiler, cook on one side for 3 minutes and on the other for about 2 minutes, until the pineapple begins to brown and slightly caramelize.

Once the lentils are tender, add an extra cup of broth if you think the soup needs thinning. Add the lime juice and stir.

Remove the bay leaves. Use an immersion blender to puree about half of the soup. If you don't have an immersion blender, use a potato masher to mash it up a bit, until the desired thickness is achieved. Taste and adjust the salt.

To serve, ladle into bowls and top with a pineapple ring, a slice of lime, and a few dots of hot sauce.

ANCHO-LENTIL SOUP

with Grilled Pineapple

SERVES 6 / TIME: 45 MIN

Chile powder:

1 tablespoon cumin seeds

2 dried ancho chiles, seeds removed, ripped into bite-size pieces

1 tablespoon coriander seeds

Soup:

2 tablespoons olive oil

1 large onion, cut into small dice

3 cloves garlic, minced

2 bay leaves

1 teaspoon salt

2 cups dried green lentils, washed

7 to 8 cups vegetable broth, purchased or homemade (page 223)

3 tablespoons fresh lime juice

Nonstick cooking spray, for pan 6 to 8 fresh pineapple rings

Lime slices, for serving

Hot sauce, for serving

BROCCOLI-POTATO SOUP

with Fresh Herbs

SERVES 6 TO 8 / TIME: 50 MIN

2 tablespoons olive oil

1 medium-size onion, cut into ¼-inch dice

3 cloves garlic, minced

½ teaspoon dried tarragon

Several pinches of freshly ground black pepper

1 teaspoon salt

6 cups vegetable broth, purchased or homemade (page 223), or 4 cups veggie broth plus 2 cups water, whatever

2 pounds potatoes, peeled and cut into ½-inch chunks

4 cups chopped broccoli (including the stalks: chop them into thin slices, and the tops into small florets)

¼ cup chopped fresh dill

¼ cup chopped fresh mint

This vibrant soup is a great start to a Mediterranean meal. Try it our way with fresh dill and mint, but keep in mind that it's also really versatile. So, if the day should come when all you've got is some potatoes, onions, and garlic, you can use this recipe as a guideline and add the herbs and spices of your choice. But if you mess it up with some crazy substitution, please don't go giving us two-star reviews on Amazon.

Preheat a soup pot over medium heat. Sauté the onion in the oil for 5 to 7 minutes, until softened. Add the garlic, tarragon, pepper, and salt, and cook for 1 more minute. Pour in the vegetable broth and add the potatoes. Cover and bring to a boil. Once the soup is boiling, lower the heat and let simmer for 15 minutes. Add the broccoli and cook for 15 more minutes.

Use an immersion blender to blend about one third of the soup; we like to keep it chunky with lots of whole potato chunks. If you don't have an immersion blender (get one!), transfer about one-third of the soup to a blender or food processor and puree, then add it back to the rest of the soup.

Add the fresh dill and mint, then let the soup sit for about 10 minutes to let the flavors meld. Serve!

TIPS
This soup tastes great with either homemade (page 223) or store-bought vegan bacon.

Don't know how to bake potatoes? Sigh. Preheat the oven to 350°F, poke the potatoes with a fork a few times, and wrap them in aluminum foil. Place in the oven and bake for about an hour, or until easily pierced with a fork.

Woodsy and earthy, this soup is rich with mushroom flavor. It is topped off with fresh chervil, which has a delicate, lemony taste that is not quite comparable to any herb, though if you can't find it, chopped fresh parsley works nicely. Go on a mission to find the chervil; if nothing else, it would make a great blog entry.

Garnished or not, this is an easy recipe for what tastes like a ten-dollar bowl of soup at a swanky Manhattan sidewalk café. Perfect for serving your yuppie friends.

Place the porcinis in a bowl. Measure 2 cups of boiling water and pour over the porcinis. Cover with a plate and set aside.

Preheat a stockpot over medium-high heat. Add the oil and sauté the onion for about 3 minutes. Add the garlic, thyme, salt, and pepper. Cook for about 10 minutes, or until browned, stirring frequently.

Add the sliced creminis and sauté for about 3 minutes. In the meantime, remove the porcinis from their broth (with tongs or a fork). Slice them thinly and add to the stockpot along with the porcini broth. Let the mixture cook for a few more minutes.

Add the wild rice and vegetable broth. Cover and bring to a boil. Once the soup is boiling, lower the heat to low and simmer for about 45 minutes.

When the rice is tender, grate in the carrot, turn off the heat, and let sit for 10 more minutes. If the soup is too thick, thin with water or broth. Ladle into bowls and garnish with sprigs of fresh chervil.

PORCINI-WILD RICE SOUP

SERVES 6 / TIME: A LITTLE OVER 1 HR,
most of it inactive

½ ounce dried porcini mushrooms

2 cups boiling water

2 tablespoons olive oil

1 large yellow onion, sliced thinly

4 cloves garlic, minced

2 tablespoons fresh thyme

1 teaspoon salt

Several pinches of freshly ground black pepper

8 ounces cremini mushrooms (about 3 cups), sliced thinly

1½ cups wild rice (try to find a wild rice blend with several kinds mixed together)

4 cups vegetable broth, purchased or homemade (page 223), plus more if needed

1 carrot, peeled

Several sprigs of fresh chervil, for garnish

CHICKPEA-NOODLE SOUP

SERVES 6 / TIME: 50 MIN

2 tablespoons olive oil

1 large yellow onion, sliced thinly

1 cup peeled, thinly sliced carrot (or chopped baby carrots)

2 cloves garlic, minced

2 cups sliced cremini mushrooms

½ teaspoon celery seeds

1 teaspoon dried thyme

½ teaspoon dried rosemary, crushed in your fingers

½ teaspoon freshly ground black pepper

2 tablespoons mirin (optional)

6 cups water or vegetable broth, purchased or homemade (page 223)

1½ cups cooked chickpeas (page 41), or 1 (15-ounce) can, drained and rinsed

6 ounces soba noodles

⅓ cup mellow white miso

Chickpea Soup for the Vegan Soul. A great soup for when you're feeling under the weather and need something tasty to slurp on while you watch TV and pity yourself. But don't let that dissuade you if you feel fine and just happen to want a nice, comforting bowl of soup.

Preheat a soup pot over medium-high heat. Sauté the onion and carrot in the oil for about 10 minutes. Add the garlic, mushrooms, celery seeds, and herbs, and sauté for another 5 minutes. Deglaze the pot with the mirin (or just a splash of water). Add the water or broth and the chickpeas. Cover and bring to a boil.

Once the broth is boiling, break the soba noodles into thirds and throw them in. Lower the heat to medium so that the soup is at a low boil. Cover and cook for 15 minutes, stirring occasionally.

Add the miso and stir until it's incorporated. Taste and adjust the salt and seasoning. Thin with a little water if needed.

TIPS

Some soba noodles come wrapped in 3-ounce serving sizes. If yours aren't wrapped, you can measure 'em this way: the circumference of one 3-ounce bundle is about the size of a quarter.

Soba noodles expand a lot when they're soaking, so this isn't the best soup to keep in the fridge overnight. If you don't plan on eating it all in one day, use instead regular pasta noodles broken in half or thirds.

Need a little green? Add some chopped greens toward the end of the cooking process. Spinach, kale, chard—whatever you've got. Let them wilt and then serve.

DOUBLE
PEA SOUP
with Roasted Red Peppers

SERVES 6 TO 8 / TIME: 1 HR 20 MIN

3 tablespoons olive oil

1 large onion, chopped finely

2 carrots, peeled and cut into small dice

2 stalks celery, chopped into ¼-inch pieces

2½ quarts water

1 pound dried split green peas

1 (1-inch) cube fresh ginger, peeled

1 bay leaf

2 teaspoons dried thyme

1 teaspoon dried tarragon

½ teaspoon ground coriander

½ teaspoon ground cumin

1 (16-ounce) bag frozen green peas

2 roasted red bell peppers (see pages 28, 33), cut into ½-inch pieces, diced

¾ teaspoons salt, or to taste

Freshly ground black pepper

Maybe because of that scene in *The Exorcist* or the common phrase comparing it to heavy fog, split pea soup is practically a pop-culture icon. Or at least we think so. Our contribution to the split pea soup canon is a little amped-up, featuring extra herbs, extra sweetness from fresh green peas, and smoky sweetness from roasted red peppers. A big bowl makes for a nourishing meal, especially when served alongside crusty bread and Hummus (page 74) for dipping.

Preheat a large stockpot over medium heat. Sauté the onion in the oil for 5 to 7 minutes, until softened. Add the carrots and celery and sauté for another 5 minutes, or until the veggies are soft and slightly golden.

Add the water, split peas, ginger, bay leaf, thyme, tarragon, coriander, and cumin. Cover, increase the heat to high to bring to a rolling boil, then lower the heat to medium-low and allow the soup to simmer, covered, for 45 to 50 minutes, or until the split peas turn soft and mushy.

Stir in the frozen green peas and diced roasted pepper. Season with ¾ teaspoon of salt and several dashes of black pepper. Cover, and increase the heat to bring to a boil again, then lower the heat and simmer for another 20 minutes, or until the green peas are tender.

Remove the ginger cube and bay leaf. Allow to sit for 15 minutes before serving.

This is the last lentil soup recipe you will ever need. Tarragon adds a wonderful peppery, licorice flavor that complements this soup like nobody's business. Just try to keep leftovers of this soup stored in the fridge—you will find yourself going back for more all night. After three helpings, keep the lid on it to retain some sense of dignity.

Preheat a large soup pot over medium heat. Sauté the onion and carrot in the oil for about 10 minutes, until the onion has browned a bit. Add the garlic, tarragon, thyme, and paprika, and sauté for 2 more minutes. Add the tomatoes and a little splash of water if necessary, and stir to deglaze the pot. Cover and cook for 5 minutes.

Add the water or broth, lentils, bay leaves, salt, and pepper, then cover and bring to a boil. Once the soup is boiling, lower the heat to a simmer and cook, covered, for about 45 minutes, or until the lentils are tender. If the soup looks too thin, uncover and simmer for a couple more minutes. If it looks too thick, add a little more water. Serve with good, crusty bread.

FRENCH LENTIL SOUP

with Tarragon & Thyme

SERVES 8 / TIME: 1 HR

1 tablespoon olive oil

1 large yellow onion, diced

1 large carrot, peeled and cut into fine dice

4 cloves garlic, minced

2 teaspoons dried tarragon

1 teaspoon dried thyme

1 teaspoon paprika (Hungarian if you've got it)

5 plum tomatoes, seeded and diced

6 cups water or vegetable broth, purchased or homemade (page 223)

2 cups dried French lentils

2 bay leaves

1½ teaspoons salt

Several pinches of freshly ground black pepper

ROASTED BEET
BORSCHT

SERVES 8 TO 10 / TOTAL TIME: 1½ HRS /
ACTIVE TIME: 20 MIN

3 pounds red beets, trimmed and scrubbed

4 tablespoons olive oil

1 cup thinly sliced shallot

¾ teaspoon salt, plus a pinch

3½ to 4 cups vegetable broth, purchased or homemade (page 223)

3 tablespoons sherry vinegar

So Very Sour Cream (page 318), for garnish

Chopped fresh dill, for garnish

Just like Grandma used to make! Prepare this dish in a housedress and slippers for maximum authenticity. Beets roast away in the oven while you watch your stories or stare out the window, and an hour or so later, blend everything up and you've got the most luxurious soup in the neighborhood.

Preheat the oven to 350°F.

Wrap the beets individually in aluminum foil and place them on a rimmed baking sheet. Bake, turning once about halfway through, until they are very easily pierced with a steak knife, about 1 hour. Transfer the beets to a cooling rack and let sit until cool enough to handle.

In the meantime, preheat a large pan over medium heat. Heat 2 tablespoons of the oil, then sauté the shallot with a pinch of salt until they become honey brown, about 10 minutes.

Once the beets are cooled, unwrap the foil, slide off the peels, and put the beets in a blender or food processor. Add the sautéed shallot, remaining 2 tablespoons of oil, 3½ cups of the vegetable broth, and the vinegar and remaining ¾ teaspoon salt and puree until completely smooth. Use up to ½ cup more vegetable broth, if needed, to achieve the desired consistency.

Transfer the soup to a 4-quart pot and heat over medium-low heat. When hot, ladle into soup bowls and serve garnished with a dollop of the vegan sour cream and a sprinkle of dill.

A rich vegetable broth for when you want to go the extra mile. This is a great way to use up the older veggies in your crisper; you can use different veggies, such as celery, squash, potatoes, or mushrooms, but make sure there is enough water to cover everything. Keep the skins on the onion for added color and flavor. Try other herbs, such as thyme, rosemary, or bay leaves, plus peppercorns, for a stronger broth.

Heat the oil in a large stockpot. Sauté the onion in the oil for about 5 minutes over medium heat. Add all the other ingredients and bring to a boil. Lower the heat and let simmer, uncovered, for an hour and a half.

Remove from the heat and let the broth cool until it's an okay temperature to handle. Strain into a large bowl through cheesecloth or a very fine mesh strainer. Press the vegetables with a gentle but firm pressure to get all the liquid out. This will keep in the fridge in a tightly sealed container for up to 3 days, or freeze for up to 3 months.

HOMEMADE
VEGETABLE BROTH

MAKES ABOUT 2 QUARTS / TIME: 2 HRS,
mostly inactive

1 tablespoon olive oil

1 large onion, skin included, roughly chopped

2 large carrots, peeled and roughly chopped

2 parsnips, peeled and roughly chopped

3 whole cloves garlic, crushed

2 leeks, cleaned well and roughly chopped

Handful (a loosely packed cup) of fresh parsley

9 cups water

1 teaspoon salt

HOT & SOUR SOUP

with Wood Ears & Napa Cabbage

SERVES 6 / TIME: 55 MIN

½ ounce dried wood ear mushrooms

2 cups boiling water

8 leaves napa cabbage

4 cups vegetable broth, purchased or homemade (page 223)

¼ cup soy sauce

¼ cup rice vinegar

1 tablespoon toasted sesame oil

1 teaspoon ground white pepper

1½ cups thickly sliced white mushrooms

1 heaping tablespoon arrowroot powder or cornstarch

1 cup cold water

1 tablespoon sriracha

½ cup shredded carrot

1 pound extra-firm tofu, pressed and cut into matchsticks (see tip)

1 cup chopped scallion

This is a totally inauthentic hot and sour soup, perfect for when you want to break out the cute Asian bowls and spoons. Wood ear mushrooms give the soup that traditional Chinese look and texture and they soak up all the flavors of the broth quite nicely. They can be a pain to find, so if you need to sub dried shiitakes, go ahead. We were able to track some down at a local Asian market, but ask at any natural foods or gourmet market; there's a good chance they have some.

Place the wood ear mushrooms in a bowl and pour the boiling water over them so that they are submerged by a few inches. Cover with a plate and let sit for 20 minutes.

To prepare the napa leaves, lay them on top of each other so that they're spooning. Thinly slice across them widthwise. Set aside.

Pour the vegetable broth, soy sauce, rice vinegar, sesame oil, and white pepper into a soup pot. Cover and bring to a boil. Once the broth is boiling, add the cabbage and the fresh mushrooms. Cook until the cabbage is completely wilted, about 5 minutes.

The wood ears should be ready at this point, so remove them from the bowl, cut into bite-size pieces, and add them to the soup as well.

Mix the arrowroot with the water until dissolved. Add to the soup and stir until just slightly thickened, a minute or two. This soup isn't going to be very thick, just more cloudy than anything else. But the starch gives the soup a little body.

Add the sriracha, shredded carrots, and tofu and cook just until heated through, about 5 more minutes. Ladle into bowls and garnish with scallion to serve.

TIPS Raw napa cabbage looks like very pale green romaine lettuce. It isn't as tough as European cabbage, so you can use your leftovers on sandwiches instead of lettuce to add a pleasant crunch.

The tofu slicing doesn't have to be perfect; basically, what you want are long, thin rectangles that are small but big enough that they won't fall apart. If you want to just make small cubes instead, that's fine, too. To make the matchsticks, cut the tofu into eight slices widthwise. Then slice those slices widthwise about ten times.

This soup just screams, "I just came back from the farmers' market! Look at my bulging canvas sack!" Go wild and try out different varieties of local corn in the peak of summer, purple or Thai basil, Yukon gold or Russian banana potatoes, and any heirloom tomatoes. Make this on a lazy summer evening when you don't need to be anywhere anytime soon, and use that extra time to prepare the Fresh Corn Stock (recipe follows), which gives this soup a rich, complex base. This chowder recipe rules because it doesn't rely on the addition of any soy dairy products to achieve a smooth, velvety texture (see photo on p 226).

On a large cutting surface or in a large bowl, hold an ear of corn by the thicker end and run a sharp knife carefully down the length of the ear, close to the cob, to slice off the kernels of corn. Repeat with the remaining ears. Set aside the kernels, and break each cob in half to use in the corn stock or add to the soup when simmering.

Preheat a large soup pot over medium-high heat. Sauté the garlic in the oil for 30 seconds, then add the onion, carrot, and celery and cook for another 2 minutes. Add the fennel and fry for 2 minutes. Add the chopped potato, thyme, and the corn and cook for 5 minutes.

Add the corn stock, stir, cover, and bring to a gentle boil. Lower the heat to low and simmer, partially covered, for 20 to 25 minutes, or until the potato pieces are very tender. Ladle 1½ cups of the soup into a blender and pulse until smooth (be careful; it's hot soup!) or pulse the soup with an immersion blender just enough to make it slightly creamy but still leaving plenty of texture.

Add the chopped tomatoes and basil, and simmer for an additional 2 minutes. Add salt and pepper to taste. Serve and, if you like, garnish each bowl with a little bit of chopped fresh basil, diced tomato, and a swig of olive oil.

Recipe Continues

MIDSUMMER

CORN CHOWDER

with Basil, Tomato & Fennel

SERVES 6 TO 8 / TIME: 1 HR

6 ears fresh corn, husks and silk removed

3 tablespoons olive oil

3 cloves garlic, minced finely

1 large onion, cut into fine dice

1 large carrot, diced

1 stalk celery, chopped finely

1 small bulb fennel (about ½ pound), diced

1 pound white, waxy potatoes (about 2 medium-size), peeled and diced

2 teaspoons dried thyme

2 quarts Fresh Corn Stock (see next page); vegetable broth, purchased or homemade (page 223); or water

1 pound tomatoes, seeded and chopped finely

⅓ cup fresh basil leaves, tightly rolled and chopped into thin strips

Salt and freshly ground pepper

FRESH CORN STOCK

This stock is very free form. Try tossing flavorful vegetable scraps (such as onion skins, carrot peelings, etc.) in with the rest of the ingredients.

8 cups water
6 corn cobs, broken in half
2 carrots, chopped coarsely
2 stalks celery, with leaves
1 leek, washed well and chopped coarsely
1 onion with skin, cut into chunks
Handful of fresh parsley, torn coarsely
1 teaspoon whole black or red peppercorns

Optional:
Carrot tops, additional celery leaves and stems, additional onion skins, lacy fronds from the fennel tops

In a large stockpot, combine the water, corn cobs, carrots, celery, leek, onion, parsley, and peppercorns. Add one or more of the optional vegetable trimmings. Cover and bring to a rolling boil. Remove the cover, lower the heat to medium-high, and allow to simmer for 1 to 1½ hours.

Remove from the heat and allow the stock to cool until tepid. Strain the stock with either a large metal strainer or cheesecloth. It can be refrigerated in a covered container for up to a week.

MAKES ABOUT 2 QUARTS / TIME: ABOUT 2 HOURS, mostly inactive

If there's no time for broth-making, Mr. or Ms. Jet-setter, and you absolutely insist on using just water, try simmering the soup with the corn cobs tossed in after adding the water, taking care to remove them before you add the tomatoes and basil.

ROASTED YELLOW PEPPER & CORN BISQUE

SERVES 6 TO 8 / TIME: 1 HR 20 MIN,
lots of it inactive

- **4 yellow bell peppers**
- **1 tablespoon vegetable oil**
- **1 medium-size Vidalia or Walla Walla onion, diced**
- **3 cloves garlic**
- **2 hot red chiles, seeded and sliced thinly**
- **3 cups fresh corn, cut from the cobs (you can use frozen, too, but fresh tastes better)**
- **1 yellow summer squash, cut in half lengthwise and sliced thinly (about 3 cups)**
- **3 to 4 cups vegetable broth, purchased or homemade (page 223)**
- **1½ teaspoons salt**
- **1 (14-ounce) can coconut milk (lite is fine)**
- **1 whole nutmeg**
- **1 tablespoon pure maple syrup**
- **Juice of 1 lime, or to taste**

TIP

To better manage your time, you can prep the roasted peppers up to a day ahead and leave them tightly sealed in the fridge overnight.

Yellow peppers, yellow corn, and yellow summer squash make for a bright and beautiful—you guessed it—yellow soup. Red chile peppers dot this soup and save it from a monochrome yellow, plus they add just a little spice. Partially pureeing everything makes this bisque really luscious and creamy, while nutmeg and lime tie the whole shebang together. Again, this is a great farmers' market soup, when everyone has yellow squash up the wazoo and you are sick at the thought of another night of yellow squash sauté.

Preheat the oven to 375°F. Cut the stems off the peppers and pull out the seeds. Place on a dry, rimmed baking sheet (cover with baking parchment to protect the sheet, or just ignore that if you don't care about your sheet) and bake for about 40 minutes, turning once. The peppers should be very soft and collapsed.

When the peppers are done, place them in a plastic bag and let them steam for about 30 minutes. This will make the skin very easy to peel away. Remove from the bag, peel away the skin, and roughly chop the peppers.

Preheat a soup pot over medium-high heat. Sauté the onion in the vegetable oil for 5 to 7 minutes, until softened and translucent. Add the garlic and chiles. Sauté for another minute or so. Add the corn and squash and cook for 3 to 5 minutes, or until moisture begins to release from the squash. Add the roasted peppers, vegetable broth, and salt. Cover and bring to a boil. Once the soup is boiling, lower the heat and simmer for about 20 minutes, covered.

Add the coconut milk and puree the soup, either by using an immersion blender or by slightly cooling and then transferring the soup to a food processor or blender in batches.

Let the soup heat through again and grate the nutmeg with a Microplane grater directly into the soup. Add the maple syrup and lime, stir, and serve!

Peanut butter soup is the real not-chicken soup for the soul. It's outrageously rich and savory, so go ahead and eat your feelings with a second helping. This peanutty thick concoction of meltingly tender eggplant and warming spices was a big hit with our recipe testers. It's a meal in itself, but would also pair nicely with a bowl of steamed jasmine rice and a simple green salad. True to soup form, tastes even better when heated up the next day.

Salt the eggplant if you wish (see tip on page 30).

In a large soup pot, sauté the shallots in 2 tablespoons of the peanut oil for about 8 to 10 minutes until very soft, browned, and slightly caramelized. Scoop the shallots out of the pot and set aside in a medium-size bowl.

Add 1 tablespoon of the peanut oil to the pot and add the eggplant, stirring to coat with the oil. Stir and cook the eggplant for about 10 minutes, until slightly tender. Transfer the eggplant to the same bowl as the shallots.

Add the remaining tablespoon of peanut oil to the pot and allow it to heat, add the ginger and chile, and fry for 30 seconds. Add the ground cumin, cayenne, if using, coriander, and turmeric, and fry for another 30 seconds, then add the onion. Stir-fry until the onion is just slightly soft and translucent, about 5 minutes. Add the tomato paste and stir-fry the mixture for another minute.

Stir in to the pot the diced tomatoes, water or broth, salt to taste, eggplant mixture, and string beans. Increase the heat to medium-high and bring to an active simmer. In a bowl, combine the peanut butter with a ladleful of hot soup. Stir until creamy; the peanut butter should be completely emulsified. Stir the peanut butter mixture into the rest of the simmering soup. Simmer the soup over medium-low heat, covered, for about 20 minutes, or until the eggplant is very tender. Turn off the heat and stir in the cilantro and lemon juice. Garnish each bowl and serve pronto!

SPICY

PEANUT & EGGPLANT SOUP

SERVES 6 TO 8 / TIME: 1 HR 20 MIN

1 pound eggplant, peeled and chopped in ½-inch cubes

1 teaspoon salt (optional, for eggplant; see tip on page 30)

5 large shallots, peeled and sliced very thinly

¼ cup peanut oil

1 (1-inch) cube fresh ginger, peeled and minced

1 hot chile, seeded and minced

1½ teaspoons ground cumin

⅛ to ¼ teaspoon ground cayenne pepper (optional)

2 teaspoons ground coriander

½ teaspoon ground turmeric

1 medium-size yellow onion, diced

⅓ cup tomato paste

1 (16-ounce) can roasted diced tomatoes with juice

5 cups water or vegetable broth, purchased or homemade (page 223)

½ teaspoon salt, or more to taste

½ pound fresh or frozen green beans, trimmed and cut into 2-inch pieces

½ cup creamy or chunky natural peanut butter

2 tablespoons fresh lemon juice

⅓ cup coarsely chopped fresh cilantro

Optional garnishes:
Whole cilantro leaves, and chopped roasted peanuts

BAKED POTATO

& GREENS

SOUP

with Potato-Wedge Croutons

SERVES 6 / TIME: 30 MIN,
not including baking the potatoes

6 to 8 baking potatoes (3½ pounds), baked and cooled

2 tablespoons olive oil

1 large yellow onion, sliced into short strips

3 cloves garlic, minced

½ teaspoon fennel seeds, crushed

1 teaspoon dried thyme

½ teaspoon rubbed dried sage

Plenty of freshly ground black pepper

1 teaspoon salt

¼ cup dry white wine (or just more broth if you prefer)

4 cups vegetable broth, purchased or homemade (page 223)

4 cups torn kale (bite-size pieces; about 6 leaves, rough stems removed)

¼ cup unsweetened nondairy milk

Potato wedges:

2 heaping tablespoons coarse cornmeal

¼ teaspoon dried thyme

½ teaspoon paprika

Generous pinch of salt

2 cloves garlic, minced

Olive oil in a spray bottle (or enough for light frying)

Kids really love this soup, as far as we can tell, so if your kids say they don't, please explain that we said yes, they do. There's a giant French fry in it, for heaven's sake—that is, a potato wedge that's been dredged in cornmeal and lightly fried. As for the healthy part, we use kale here, but escarole or spinach would be good, too. Make the baked potatoes the night before so that you can have this soup ready in thirty minutes. Or microwave them instead; just don't tell us about it. Sincerely, the Anti-Microwave Squad.

Once your potatoes are baked and cool enough to handle, preheat a soup pot and sauté the onion in the oil over medium-high heat until good and brown, about 12 minutes.

While the onion cooks, prep the potatoes: Slice the baked potatoes in half lengthwise. Reserve three of the halves to make the potato wedges. Slice the rest into ¾-inch chunks.

Once the onion is browned, add the garlic, fennel, thyme, sage, pepper, and salt. Cook for 2 more minutes, then add the wine to deglaze the pan. Add the chunks of potatoes and the broth, cover, and lower the heat a bit to bring to a low boil. Mix in the kale. Cover and cook for 15 to 20 more minutes.

Meanwhile, prepare the potato wedges: Slice the reserved potato halves in half lengthwise so you have six pieces. Preheat a heavy-bottomed skillet over medium-high heat. Combine all the ingredients for the wedges, except for the oil, on a plate. Wet the potato wedges with a little bit of water and dredge the two cut sides in the cornmeal mixture.

Lightly coat the skillet with oil. Cook the potatoes on each cut side for about 4 minutes, or until golden and crispy. Spray with oil as you alternate cooking sides.

The soup should be done by this point. Use a potato masher to mush up about half of the soup (for once, don't use an immersion blender; it will make the potatoes pasty and yucky), add the milk, and mix. If it's too thick, add a little water or vegetable broth.

Ladle into bowls and top with a potato wedge crouton.

CREAMY
TOMATO SOUP

SERVES 8 / TIME: 45 MIN

2 tablespoons olive oil

1 medium-size onion, chopped coarsely

3 cloves garlic, chopped

½ teaspoon dried rosemary, crushed
   between your fingers

½ teaspoon dried thyme

½ teaspoon dried oregano

1 teaspoon salt

Lots of freshly ground black pepper

1 pound waxy potatoes (2 to 4 average-size
   potatoes; weigh them to be sure), peeled
   and cut into 1-inch chunks

1 cup sun-dried tomatoes (not the kind
   packed in oil, just honest-to-goodness
   sun-dried tomatoes)

6 cups water or vegetable broth, purchased
   or homemade (page 223)

1 (28-ounce) can crushed tomatoes (the
   fire-roasted are especially worth it here)

Juice of ½ lemon, or to taste

VARIATION

TOMATO-BASIL SOUP: Add ½ cup of shredded fresh basil after pureeing.

This soup packs a double one-two punch of tomato. Just when you're thinking it's made from regular old tomato—BAM—a sun-dried tomato gets you in the jaw and you are out for the count.

Preheat a large soup pot over medium heat. Sauté the onion in the oil until translucent, 5 to 7 minutes. Add the garlic, herbs, salt, and pepper. Sauté for 1 more minute, until the garlic is fragrant.

Add the potatoes and sun-dried tomatoes. Pour in the water or broth. Cover and bring to a boil. Once the soup is boiling, lower the heat to medium, cover, and let simmer for about 20 minutes, until the potatoes are tender and the sun-dried tomatoes are soft.

Add the crushed tomatoes and heat through. If you have an immersion blender, you're in luck! Puree the living hell out of it until it is very smooth. If you don't have one, just transfer the whole shebang to a food processor or blender, in cooled batches, then transfer back to the pot. Add the lemon juice and adjust the salt if you need to.

Serve!

TIPS   The "creamy" comes from potatoes. Yukon golds work great here, but of course, you can use whatever you've got. Try to avoid a regular starchy russet, since waxy potatoes give a creamier texture.
This is a great soup to go along with panini or vegan grilled cheese.

A stick-to-your-ribs veggie gumbo that gets a kick of smokiness from roasted red peppers, smoked sweet paprika, and a little help from the magic of liquid smoke (and it's vegan, like a dream come true, so relax!). Traditionally, gumbos are served with a scoop of white rice in the middle, but this also pairs nicely with Skillet Corn Bread (page 341) or crusty French bread and a crisp green salad.

First we're going to make a roux: Heat the oil in a big soup pot over medium heat. Sprinkle in the flour and stir to dissolve it. Cook the flour mixture, stirring frequently, until it is a rich caramel color and smells toasty, anywhere from 10 to 12 minutes.

Add the chopped onions and bell peppers to the roux mixture, stirring to coat completely. Increase the heat to medium-high and cook until the vegetables are very soft, at least 12 minutes.

Add the celery, garlic, and okra, and cook for another 6 minutes. Add the tomatoes, roasted red peppers, kidney beans, and vegetable broth. Whisk together the beer and tomato paste and add that to the mixture, stirring to incorporate completely. Stir in the paprika, oregano, allspice, liquid smoke, cayenne, salt, and nutmeg, and lastly, tuck in the bay leaves and thyme sprigs.

Bring the mixture to a gentle boil and boil for 2 minutes, then lower the heat to low and partially cover. Allow the mixture to simmer for 35 to 40 minutes, stirring occasionally, until the okra is very tender. Allow to cool at least 5 minutes before serving, then season with black pepper to taste.

TIPS

Leftover Simple Seitan (page 205), diced small, makes a delicious addition. Add it to the vegetables when sautéing them in the roux.

Frozen okra makes this recipe a breeze; it slices up easily with little mess. If you've never used it before, you'll be blown away by that perfect rectangle of frozen okra, or at least marginally amused. Of course, sliced fresh okra (½ to ¾ pound) may be used instead.

SMOKY RED PEPPERS 'N' BEANS
GUMBO

SERVES 6 TO 8 / TIME: 1 HR 30 MIN

¼ cup olive oil

3 tablespoons all-purpose flour

2 medium-size onions, cut into small dice

2 green bell peppers, seeded and cut into small dice

1 stalk celery, sliced very thinly

4 cloves garlic, minced

1 (10-ounce) package frozen okra, slightly thawed and sliced thinly

1 (28-ounce) can diced tomatoes with juice, preferably fire-roasted tomatoes

3 roasted red peppers, jarred or homemade (see pages 28, 33, chopped into fine dice

1 (16-ounce) can kidney beans, drained and rinsed

3 cups vegetable broth, purchased or homemade (page 223)

1 cup ale-style beer

3 tablespoons tomato paste

2 teaspoons smoked sweet paprika

2 teaspoons dried oregano

¼ teaspoon dried allspice

½ teaspoon liquid smoke flavoring

Pinch of cayenne pepper

½ teaspoon salt, or to taste

Pinch of freshly grated nutmeg

2 bay leaves

4 to 5 sprigs of thyme

Several pinches of freshly ground black pepper

Everyone's Minestrone, page 235,
and Double Rosemary Focaccia,
page 337

Your basic amazing filling beany minestrone. It's always a crowd-pleaser. Or simply a you pleaser! You can, of course, customize to what you have on hand. Wilt some kale in at the end, add some zucchini, use a different pasta or bean. That's why it's everyone's minestrone, any day of the week.

Preheat a 4-quart soup pot over medium heat. Sauté the onion and celery in the oil with a pinch of salt until soft, about 5 minutes. Add the garlic and cook until fragrant, 30 seconds or so.

Add the carrot, potatoes, thyme, rosemary, red pepper flakes, vegetable broth, and remaining ½ teaspoon of salt. Cover and bring to a boil. Once boiling, lower the heat to a simmer, add the pasta and green beans, and cook until the pasta and vegetables are soft, about 10 more minutes.

Add the agave and tomatoes and bring to a boil. Simmer for 10 minutes. Remove from the heat. It tastes better the longer you let it sit, so give it 10 minutes or so before digging in, if you can. Taste for salt and seasoning, and serve.

EVERYONE'S
MINESTRONE

SERVES: 6 TO 8 / ACTIVE TIME: 20 MIN /
TOTAL TIME: 40 MIN

2 teaspoons olive oil

1 small yellow onion, diced small

2 stalks celery, sliced thinly

½ teaspoon salt, plus a pinch

4 cloves garlic, minced

1 cup diced carrot (½-inch dice)

¾ pound Yukon gold potatoes, cut into ½-inch dice

1 teaspoon dried thyme

1 teaspoon dried rosemary

½ teaspoon red pepper flakes

6 cups vegetable broth, purchased or homemade (page 223)

1 cup dried ditalini or macaroni pasta

2 cups green beans, cut into 1-inch pieces

1½ cups cooked navy beans or 1 (15-ounce) can, rinsed and drained

1 teaspoon agave nectar

1 (28-ounce) can crushed tomatoes with basil

CHAPTER SEVEN

CASSEROLES

**Perhaps at first the word *casserole*
evokes images of a '70s mom.**

You know, she's the not-quite-picture-perfect version of '50s mom: hair a bit messed up, mascara running, her apron slightly askew over her no-iron poly-blend twin set. But there she is, our hero, with her plaid oven mitts, getting dinner on the table even though she just returned from work an hour ago. And all she had to do was open a couple of cans, pour 'em into a ceramic, and throw it in the oven—patriarchy has never been easier!

Well, there's no canned mushroom soup here in our modern, newfangled kitchen, and we smudge our mascara on purpose. When we talk about casseroles, really what we mean are one-dish meals that are baked. They aren't necessarily faster than other dinners, but the oven time does give you downtime to do your nails, organize a "Take Back the Night" demo, or call your mom and apologize for being such an ingrate. So, don't let the longer cooking times for these recipes worry you.

These comfort meals—kugel, enchiladas, potpies of every description—come from all over the world. Some fall under the category of "side dish" and some are what laymen might call "main dishes," but if it goes into the oven in a baking dish, it's a casserole to us.

-------------- ◆ ---------------

CORN PUDDING

SERVES 6 / TIME: 1 HR 20 MIN

2 tablespoons corn oil

4 cups fresh corn kernels (about 6 ears)

1 red bell pepper, seeded and chopped finely

2 jalapeño peppers, chopped finely

¼ cup cornstarch

1 cup canned full-fat coconut milk

½ cup cornmeal

2 tablespoons pure maple syrup

1 cup finely chopped scallion

¼ cup finely chopped fresh cilantro

1 teaspoon salt

¼ teaspoon cayenne pepper

This insanely flavorful, velvety side dish is the perfect accompaniment to any Southwestern meal—that is, whatever else you're making with cilantro and scallions and jalapeños and stuff in it. Or serve with Green Pumpkin-Seed Mole (page 320) and Chile Cornmeal-Crusted Tofu (page 191).

Preheat the oven to 350°F and lightly grease an 8-inch square baking or casserole dish. A cast-iron pan would work here, too (in fact, to cut down on dishes, you can sauté the corn in a cast-iron pan and later use it to bake the batter).

Sauté the corn, bell pepper, and jalapeños in the oil in a large skillet for 10 to 12 minutes, stirring occasionally; the corn should be very lightly browned. Meanwhile, stir together the cornstarch and coconut milk in a small bowl until the cornstarch has mostly dissolved.

When the corn mixture is ready, transfer 2 cups of it to a blender or food processor. Add the coconut milk mixture and pulse about twenty times, until the mixture is mostly pureed but not completely smooth.

Transfer to a large mixing bowl and mix with the remaining corn, cornmeal, maple syrup, scallion, cilantro, salt, and cayenne.

Pour the batter into a baking dish (or your cast-iron pan) and bake for 40 minutes. Let cool for about 10 minutes before slicing and serving.

SPINACH-NOODLE
KUGEL

SERVES 8 / TIME: ABOUT AN HR

3 cups uncooked rombi pasta (or mafalde or any short, cut ribbon noodles, or broken-up lasagna noodles)

3 (10-ounce) packages frozen chopped spinach, thawed

1¼ cups matzo meal (from about 4 matzos) or plain vegan bread crumbs

1 cup vegetable broth, purchased or homemade (page 223)

2 tablespoons olive oil

12 ounces extra-firm silken tofu (the vacuum-packed kind)

1 small onion, finely chopped (about a cup)

¼ cup lightly packed, chopped fresh dill

2 tablespoons fresh lemon juice

¾ teaspoon salt (use ¼ teaspoon less if your matzo is salted)

½ teaspoon freshly ground black pepper

Nonstick cooking spray, for casserole dish

So, you've never made kugel before? If the word *kugel* scares you, just call this Spinach-Noodle Casserole. If matzo scares you, then use bread crumbs. See? There's no reason to be scared. This goes great alongside the lentil salad. And of course, serving with potato pancakes and applesauce would be awesome. Just a note: the frozen spinach needs to be completely thawed, so remember to leave it in the fridge overnight or well in advance.

Boil a pot of water and cook the noodles according to the package directions. Preheat the oven to 350°F. Meanwhile, place thawed spinach in a colander and leave it in the sink to drain. If making your own matzo meal, place the matzos in the food processor fitted with a metal blade and pulse until they are crumbs. Transfer to a medium-size mixing bowl.

Add the vegetable broth, oil, and tofu to the food processor and puree until smooth, scraping down the sides to make sure you get everything. Add the tofu mixture to the mixing bowl.

Press the spinach in the colander to get out as much water as you can, then add it to the mixing bowl. By this time, your pasta should be done, so drain it and run it under cold water.

Add the pasta along with the remaining ingredients (except, of course, for the cooking spray—cans don't taste good) to the mixing bowl and mix very well. Use your hands if you have to.

Coat a 9 x 13-inch glass casserole dish with nonstick cooking spray. Press the kugel into the casserole dish. Bake for 30 minutes. Remove from the oven and let sit for 5 to 10 minutes before slicing.

Holidays a pain in the butt? Nothing helps sooth holiday angst like comforting bread crumb–topped entrées, so why not make it the centerpiece of a meatless holiday spread? Hearty roasted chestnuts star in this hearty medley of tender butternut squash, white beans, and caramelized onions—it really is the parts of a holiday meal baked in a casserole dish. It's only natural to want to serve this with simply roasted Brussels sprouts (page 32) and Holiday Cranberry Sauce (page 324). We also love serving this after the holidays, January through early March, as a hearty cold weather entrée with a simple green salad.

P.S. We'll admit that peeling a pound of chestnuts could have you longing for a drive around the mall parking lot. So, if you'd rather not channel all your jolly, festive anxiety into peeling these little bastards, you can also grab a bag or jar of prepeeled chestnuts for this recipe. Look for peeled chestnuts (usually already lightly roasted and ready to eat) in specialty grocery stores or in markets around the holidays.

Prepare the casserole: Preheat the oven to 375°F. Toss together the onions and oil in a 9 x 13-inch casserole dish. Roast for 20 minutes, stirring occasionally with a wooden spatula until the onions are lightly browned. Remove from the oven and set aside.

While the onions are roasting, prepare the whole, unpeeled chestnuts according to the directions for the Chestnut-Lentil Pâté (page 67). If using prepeeled chestnuts, skip this step; thaw according to package directions if frozen, drain if using jarred chestnuts. Coarsely chop the peeled chestnuts and add to the roasted onions.

Fold the diced butternut squash, white beans, thyme, coriander, nutmeg, salt, pepper, and broth into the roasted onions. Tightly cover the baking pan with aluminum foil and bake for 35 to 45 minutes, or until the squash chunks can be easily pierced with a fork.

Prepare the crumb topping! Toss together the bread crumbs, oil, and sage in a bowl. Season to taste with salt, black pepper, and cayenne. Remove the foil from the casserole and sprinkle the crumb mixture evenly over the veggies. Bake for another 10 to 15 minutes to lightly brown the crumbs. Serve hot!

CARAMELIZED ONION–
BUTTERNUT
CASSEROLE
with Chestnuts

SERVES 6 TO 8 / TIME: 1 HR 30 MIN

Casserole:

1 pound yellow onions, peeled and sliced thinly

⅓ cup olive oil

1 pound chestnuts, fresh in the shell or frozen/jarred and prepeeled

2 pounds butternut squash (1 medium-size squash), peeled and cut into ½-inch cubes

1 (15-ounce) can white beans, such as cannellini or navy, drained and rinsed, or a (10-ounce) package prepared baby lima beans

2 teaspoons dried thyme

1½ teaspoons ground coriander

½ teaspoon freshly grated nutmeg

1½ teaspoons salt, or to taste

Freshly ground black pepper

½ cup vegetable broth, purchased or homemade (page 223)

Crumb topping:

½ cup dried white vegan bread crumbs

2 tablespoons olive oil

½ teaspoon rubbed dried sage

½ teaspoon salt, or to taste

Freshly ground black pepper

Pinch of ground cayenne pepper

ASPARAGUS QUICHE

with Tomatoes & Tarragon

SERVES 6 TO 8 / TIME: 1 HR 30 MIN,
plus cooling time

4 tablespoons olive oil

1 pound asparagus, rough ends discarded

1 cup walnuts

¼ cup loosely packed fresh tarragon, plus 2 tablespoons finely chopped

¼ teaspoon freshly grated nutmeg

¾ teaspoon salt

Several pinches of freshly ground black pepper

2 shallots, chopped coarsely

3 cloves garlic

1½ cups cooked navy beans, or 1 (15-ounce) can, drained and rinsed

2 tablespoons cornstarch

1 single Pastry Crust (page 409)

⅓ cup plain vegan whole wheat bread crumbs

4 slices beefsteak or Holland tomato, or any really big tomato

Real men are vegan, and they do eat vegan quiche. We really wanted to make a vegan quiche that didn't include tofu or nutritional yeast because every vegan cookbook in the world has one of those. So, instead, we created a blend of beans and walnuts, making this quiche tender and creamy with a crispy crumb top. It's a pleasure to sink your fork into during brunch, lunch, or dinner. Serve with a Caesar Salad (page 101) on the side.

Preheat a large skillet over medium-high heat. Cut the tips off four pieces of the asparagus and set aside for garnish. Slice the rest into ½-inch lengths.

Sauté the asparagus, except the reserved tips, in a tablespoon of the oil for about 7 minutes, stirring occasionally.

While the asparagus is cooking, place the walnuts, the ¼ cup of tarragon, and the nutmeg, salt, and pepper in a food processor. Pulse into crumbs, so that no whole walnuts are left.

Remove the asparagus from the pan and transfer to a shallow bowl to cool a bit. Sauté the shallots in another tablespoon of the oil for about 3 minutes. Add the garlic and sauté for 3 more minutes, being careful not to burn it. Transfer the shallot mixture to the asparagus and let cool for a few more minutes.

When the vegetables have stopped steaming, add them to the food processor. Pulse a few times and scrape down the sides. Add the beans and puree until relatively smooth, although the walnuts will still be grainy. Add the cornstarch (sift first, if very clumpy) and pulse until thoroughly combined. Transfer the mixture to a bowl (use the bowl the veggies were cooling in, to cut down on dish duties), cover, and refrigerate for about 45 minutes.

Preheat the oven to 350°F.

Roll out the pastry dough to fit an 8-inch glass pie plate. Cover with aluminum foil and bake for 15 minutes.

Remove the baked crust from the oven. Spoon the asparagus filling into the crust and smooth out evenly. Sprinkle the top with half the bread crumbs and drizzle with 1 tablespoon of the oil. Then, place the tomato slices on top of the bread crumbs with an asparagus tip tucked between each tomato. Sprinkle with the remaining bread crumbs, some pepper, a few pinches of salt, and the chopped tarragon. Drizzle again with the remaining tablespoon of oil.

Bake for 45 minutes. Let cool for about 20 minutes before serving. Serve warm or at room temperature.

In Brooklyn, people's worth is directly proportional to their ability to make an eggplant rollatini. If they can't perform, they are taken care of. While we're not going to kill you if you don't make this, we will be severely disappointed.

There are lots of little steps here but they are all pretty simple and this meal is worth it. It's not a weeknight dinner, more for company and special occasions when you want to be at the top of your vegan game. Since this can be a heavy meal if you are frying it, it's great to serve with steamed broccoli doused with the leftover marinara sauce. But if you wanna be real Brooklyn (and you do), make a double batch of sauce and serve with spaghetti. Two rollatini per person should get the job done.

Cut each eggplant lengthwise into twelve slices about ⅛ inch thick. You don't need to actually measure them, and it's okay if they are a little thicker or thinner in some areas. See the tip for help with this.

Generously sprinkle salt on both sides of the eggplant and rub it in (see "Eggplant: To Salt or Not to Salt? on page 30). Set in a colander to drain for 30 minutes. Meanwhile, you can make your sauce, make your Almesan, toast your pine nuts, and prep your other ingredients.

Make the dipping and breading mixtures: Mix the cornstarch with the water in a bowl that is large enough to fit your eggplant slices. Mix together all the breading ingredients on a large dinner plate.

Rinse the eggplant with cold water and set aside. Whether you are baking or frying the eggplant, have a 9 x 13-inch baking pan at the ready and preheat the oven to 350°F.

To fry: Preheat a large, heavy-bottomed skillet over medium-high heat. Let it heat for at least 3 minutes. Pour in and heat about ⅛ inch of oil. Let it get hot but not smoky; if it smokes, lower the heat just a bit. To test the oil for the correct temperature, sprinkle in a small amount of bread crumbs. If bubbles form rapidly around the crumbs, the oil is ready.

Dredge an eggplant slice in the dipping mixture. Sometimes the starch settles at the bottom of the bowl, so mix it with a fork if need be. Gently press the eggplant into the breading mixture on both sides so that the crumbs are firmly in place.

Prep a second slice the same way, then place both slices in the pan and cook on each side for 1½ to 2 minutes. Use tongs to flip the slices. The eggplant should be tender and golden brown on both sides. When done, transfer to paper towels to drain the oil and proceed with the remaining eggplant slices.

Recipe Continues

EGGPLANT ROLLATINI

with Spinach & Toasted Pine Nuts

MAKES 12 ROLLATINI, SERVES 4 TO 6 / TIME: 1 HR 30 MIN

3 large eggplants (a little over 3 pounds)

Salt

Oil, for frying (optional)

Spray bottle of olive oil or nonstick cooking spray, for baking (optional)

1 recipe (5 cups) Marinara Sauce or a variation of it (we love the olive variation here) (page 314)

1 recipe Tofu Ricotta (page 315)

12 large spinach leaves, washed very well and stemmed

¼ cup toasted pine nuts (optional)

1 recipe Almesan (page 316)

Chopped fresh basil, for garnish

Dipping mixture (before breading):

1 cup cold water

¼ cup cornstarch

Breading mixture:

2 cups vegan bread crumbs

1 teaspoon dried thyme

½ teaspoon dried oregano

½ teaspoon dried basil

To bake: Follow the same directions for breading as above. Spray two baking sheets with olive oil, place all the eggplant slices on the sheets, and spray the breaded slices with olive oil. If you don't have olive oil spray, nonstick cooking spray can be used, but it doesn't come out as well. Bake at 350°F for 20 to 25 minutes; no need to flip them. When ready, they should be tender and flexible. If you can't fit both sheets on one rack in your oven, then rotate them halfway through the baking process.

To assemble: Let the slices cool enough that you can handle them, usually 10 minutes. Pour 2 cups of the marinara sauce into a 9 x 13-inch casserole dish.

With the narrower end pointed toward you, place a leaf of spinach on the lower third of the eggplant slice. Place 2 heaping tablespoons of ricotta on the spinach, sprinkle a few pine nuts on top of that, if using, and then roll up. It should be easy! Place the rolled eggplant slices, seam side down, in the baking pan.

When everything is rolled, pour another cup or so of sauce over the rollatini. Bake for about 20 minutes; really, you just want to heat the ricotta through.

To serve: Sprinkle a little Almesan on top of each rollatini and garnish with chopped basil leaves. Serve with extra marinara on the side.

TIPS

Note that you aren't going to use all the eggplant. Since the skin can't be used here, you'll need to slice off two sides. Plus, there will likely be slices that are sacrificed because it is a little difficult to get them relatively uniformly thin. Save the scraps and use them in a soup or stew, or grill them and make a salad a day or two later.

Which brings us to the best way to evenly slice eggplant: First, use a large chef's knife to cut off the top and bottom. Stand up the eggplant on the cutting board. Next, slice off one side (that slice won't be used, since it has a lot of skin). Then, still holding the eggplant upright, begin to slice off ⅛-inch-thick pieces, going as slowly as you need to.

Should you salt eggplant? If the eggplant is very fresh and very firm, skip it! Not so fresh? Toss the eggplant slices or cubes with a teaspoon of salt in a large bowl or colander. Allow to sit 20 minutes to slightly soften, then gently rinse the eggplant with cold running water and drain.

SWEET POTATO–PEAR
TZIMMES

with Pecans & Raisins

SERVES 6 / TIME: 1 HR 15 MIN

2 pounds sweet potatoes, peeled and cut into ¾-inch chunks

3 firm Bartlett pears, seeded and cut into ¾-inch chunks

1 tablespoon vegetable oil, plus spray on a little more if it needs it

2 tablespoons mirin or any sweet cooking wine

1 tablespoon pure maple syrup

½ teaspoon ground cinnamon

¼ teaspoon salt

¾ cup pecan halves

¾ cup golden raisins

This can just as easily be called Roasted Sweet Potatoes and Pear, but tzimmes is what we Jews call it, isn't that adorable? The idea is actually to over-roast everything so it gets a bit chewy on the outside while still creamy on the inside. This would be a good side to round out a dinner with the Spinach-Noodle Kugel (page 240). But you can also just serve it with Tangerine Baked Tofu (page 193) and a green. Take this to your next Passover meal and please the whole *meshpuchah*!

Preheat the oven to 350°F.

Place the sweet potatoes and pears on a large, rimmed baking sheet. Sprinkle with the vegetable oil and mirin, and mix it all up to make sure everything is coated. Add the maple syrup, cinnamon, salt, and pecans, and toss to coat.

Cover with aluminum foil and bake for 30 minutes. Remove the foil and add the raisins. Using a thin, flexible spatula, carefully toss and mix, being careful not to break up the sweet potatoes. But tzimmes are a forgiving dish, so if some get mushed up, that's perfectly acceptable.

Return the pan to the oven, uncovered, and bake for 30 more minutes, tossing every now and again. Serve warm or at room temperature.

A cacophony of Tex-Mex good things that go "yum" in the belly. The Chile-Chocolate Mole (page 321) gets to work here and smothers tender greens and plump beans. Bake the top with a moist corn bread biscuit crust and see for yourself that cornbread makes everything better. You don't need a cast-iron skillet to enjoy this potpie; any deep casserole dish will do. Just as easily, any leftover cooked vegetables, our favorite being sweet potatoes, are just dreamy in this saucy skillet pie. It's a complete meal as is, but if you feel like partnering it up with a side chop up some kale and massage with a splash of Shallot 'n' Herb Dressing (page 124).

Prepare the filling: Heat the oil in a heavy cast-iron skillet over medium heat, then add the onion and sauté for 5 minutes. Add the carrot and continue to cook until the onion is tender and starts to turn golden, another 5 to 6 minutes.

Transfer to a large bowl and combine with the steamed greens, beans, and 1 cup of the mole sauce. Stir to coat everything with the sauce; if the mixture looks a little dry, add up to ½ cup more mole sauce. Place the mixture back in the skillet and smooth out the top. You should have a little over ½ inch of space between the veggies and the rim of the skillet; if it's filled to the top, remove a little, since the crust will require the extra room.

Prepare the crust: Preheat the oven to 400°F. Combine the milk and vinegar in a measuring cup. Place the oil in a large bowl, beat in the milk mixture, and sift in the flour, cornmeal, sugar, baking powder, baking soda, and salt. Mix until just moistened; small lumps in the batter are okay.

Pour over the vegetables in your skillet and smooth to cover. Sprinkle on some sesame seeds, if desired, and bake for 30 to 35 minutes, or until the crust is done and golden. Allow the pie to cool for 10 minutes (or until the filling stops bubbling), slice, and serve with extra mole sauce.

Filling:

3 tablespoons olive oil

1 yellow onion, diced

1 small carrot, diced

½ pound greens, such as collard, kale, spinach, or chard, chopped finely and steamed until tender

1 (15-ounce) can black, pinto, or white beans, rinsed and drained

1 to 1½ cups Chile-Chocolate Mole (page 321), plus more for serving

Corn bread crust:

1 cup unsweetened almond or soy milk

1 teaspoon apple cider vinegar or fresh lime juice

3 tablespoons canola or peanut oil

1 cup whole wheat pastry flour

½ cup cornmeal

1 tablespoon organic sugar

1¼ teaspoons baking powder

¼ teaspoon baking soda

¼ teaspoon salt

Sesame seeds (optional)

TIP

The mole sauce is a stand-alone recipe, so for best time management results, make the sauce up to 3 days in advance.

JAMAICAN YUCA SHEPHERD'S PIE

SERVES 8 / TIME: 1 HR

3 to 3½ pounds yuca, peeled and cut into 1½-inch chunks

1¾ teaspoons salt

3 tablespoons olive oil

1 yellow onion, diced

1 green bell pepper, seeded and diced

3 cloves garlic, chopped finely

1 tablespoon finely chopped fresh ginger

2 sweet potatoes, peeled and cut into ¾-inch chunks

2 Scotch bonnet peppers, scored down the sides (see tip)

2 bay leaves

2 sprigs fresh thyme

⅓ cup water

1 (15-ounce) can full-fat coconut milk

½ cup fresh corn kernels (from 1 ear of corn)

1 cup cooked kidney beans, or 1 (15-ounce) can, drained and rinsed

¾ cup cooked lima beans, or 1 (8-ounce) can, drained and rinsed

2 ripe yellow plantains that have just begun to blacken, sliced in half lengthwise and cut into ½-inch pieces

1 tablespoon Jamaican curry powder

Jamaican curries have a unique and irresistible blend of spices, typically including star anise, aniseeds, and coriander. This curry is one of our favorites—sweet potatoes, kidney beans, corn, and plantains (we also snuck some lima beans in there in hopes that you'll cultivate some love for the little guys) in creamy coconut milk. You can serve this as a curry over rice, but we've turned it into a shepherd's pie with a layer of yuca on top, because we are supercreative geniuses.

First, prepare your yuca: Place the yuca in a medium-size stockpot and cover with water until it's submerged. Cover and bring to a boil, add 1 teaspoon of the salt, and lower the heat to medium. Let the yuca boil for about 20 minutes, until tender enough to mash.

Meanwhile, prepare the filling: Preheat a medium-size stockpot over medium-high heat. Place the 2 tablespoons of the oil and the onion, bell pepper, garlic, and ginger in the pot. Sauté for about 5 minutes. Add the sweet potatoes, Scotch bonnets, bay leaves, thyme, remaining ¾ teaspoon of salt, and water. Cover and cook for about 15 minutes, stirring occasionally, until the sweet potatoes are easily pierced.

Set your oven to broil. Add the remaining ingredients to the filling mixture in the stockpot and lower the heat. Cook for about 5 more minutes, until everything is heated through. Remove and discard the thyme sprigs, bay leaves, and Scotch bonnets.

By this point, the yuca is probably done. Drain the yuca and then immediately place it back in the pot you boiled it in. Add the remaining tablespoon of oil to the yuca and mash with a potato masher. It usually takes about 15 mashes to get it to the right consistency, creamy but chunky.

Pour the curried filling into a 9 x 13-inch baking dish. Use a large wooden spoon or spatula to scoop the yuca over it in several mounds. Press the yuca mounds down to spread over the curry. It's okay if some of the filling is peeking through in places.

Place in the oven and bake for about 10 minutes, then transfer to the broiler for about 2 minutes. Keep a close eye; the top should be gently browned. Let sit for about 10 minutes before serving. Serve in rimmed plates or shallow bowls because it will be very saucy.

TIPS

Scotch bonnets are a really hot pepper, so instead of cutting them up, it's common in Jamaican cuisines to just score the sides in four places. To do this, use a paring knife to cut slivers up the sides. It releases all the peppery flavor without the searing hot heat, so it's spicy but not too spicy. Be careful not to crush the peppers when stirring; keep them intact and remove them when the curry is done cooking. If you can't find Scotch bonnets, you can use two serrano peppers instead.

The easiest way to peel yuca is to remove the rough ends and cut it widthwise into thirds. Place a piece vertically on the cutting board, secure with your nonwriting hand, and use a paring knife to slice the skin off.

SEITAN POTPIE

SERVES 6 TO 8 / TIME: 1 HR 20 MIN

Crust:

¼ cup olive oil

⅓ cup refined coconut oil, melted

2 cups all-purpose flour, or 1 cup each whole wheat and all-purpose, plus more for dusting

¼ cup cornmeal

2 teaspoons organic sugar

1 teaspoon salt

½ teaspoon baking powder

½ to ¾ cup cold water

2 teaspoons apple cider vinegar

Seitan filling:

5 tablespoons olive or peanut oil

1 recipe Simple Seitan (page 205), chopped into ½-inch cubes (about 3 cups)

¼ cup chickpea (garbanzo bean) flour

1 large onion, finely diced (about 2 cups)

1 large carrot, peeled and finely diced (about 1 cup diced)

2 stalks celery, finely chopped (about 1 cup diced)

⅔ cup light-colored ale, white wine, or more vegetable broth

½ pound white potato or celery root, scraped and cut into fine dice

1 cup frozen green peas or corn kernels

1½ cups vegetable broth, purchased or homemade (page 223)

1 tablespoon soy sauce

1 teaspoon dried thyme

1 teaspoon mustard powder

½ teaspoon ground sage

½ teaspoon freshly ground black pepper

½ teaspoon salt, or more to taste

Unsweetened nondairy milk, for brushing

Every time we've seen "potpie" on a vegan restaurant menu we feel the same rush of excitement and anticipation as when we were kids. It's as American as chickpea flour and seitan is now, and back then individual savory pies were a special weekend treat never to be fucked with, even if they were just reheated pies fresh from the supermarket freezer section. Years later we are adults (so it seems) and we can eat potpie anytime we damn well please, and make it ourselves a thousand times better than the frozen stuff: we do it with a silken gravy (spiked with beer and a little soy sauce for extra depth), tender chunks of seitan, root veggies, sweet peas, and a flaky crust that's sometimes whole wheat when we're feeling health conscious. And, of course, it's totally vegan and minus the freezer burn, so everybody's happy.

The steps involved in this recipe may look epic, but once you have the crust rolled out and chilled, you are more than halfway there. The filling, or even the entire pie, can be assembled a day or two ahead and popped in the oven a little less than an hour before dinner.

This IS a full meal in and of itself, but if you need something a little green to round out it out, steamed broccoli drizzled with Miso Tahini Dressing (page 125) or spinach salad with a simple dressing (see Dressings, page 122) will do the job.

Have a 3-quart square or oval deep-dish (9 x 13 x 2½-inch minimum) casserole ready.

Prepare the crust first: In a small plastic container, whisk together the oil and melted coconut oil, then freeze for about 20 minutes. Do not freeze the oil mixture rock solid; the oil is ready to use when it's solid and firm but still possible to scoop with a spoon, similar in consistency to sorbet. If the oil is too firm, allow it to warm up on a kitchen counter for a few minutes until ready to use.

Combine the flour, cornmeal, sugar, salt, and baking powder in a large mixing bowl. Add the firm oil mixture by the tablespoon, in small chunks, and cut it into the flour with a pastry cutter or two knives held together. Cut in the frozen oil until the mixture is crumbly.

Pour ¾ cup of the cold water into a small bowl and toss in a few ice cubes. Measure out ½ cup of ice water and stir the vinegar into it. Add the vinegar mixture to the dough in three batches, gently mixing it into the dough with a fork, until the dough holds together when pinched. If need be, add up to ¼ cup more water, a tablespoon at a time until all the dry ingredients are moistened and a firm dough is formed. In the work bowl, press the dough into a ball.

Tear two sheets of parchment paper slightly larger than the length of the casserole dish. Lay a sheet on your work surface and sprinkle generously with flour. Place the dough in the center, sprinkle with more flour, and lay the second piece of parchment paper on top. Pat the cover dough down into a thick rectangle, then use a rolling pin to roll and shape the dough until it's about 2 inches larger than the outline of the casserole dish.

Slide the dough (still sandwiched between parchment paper) onto a cookie sheet and keep chilled in the fridge until it's time to bake the pie.

Prepare the filling: Preheat the oven to 375°F (if you're going to bake the pie right after assembly). Preheat a soup pot over medium heat and add 2 tablespoons of the oil. Add the chopped seitan and sauté 3 minutes until the seitan is sizzling and lightly browned on the edges. Transfer the seitan to a dish and set aside for now.

Next, make a chickpea flour roux: Lower the heat to low, add the remaining 3 tablespoons of oil to the pot, and stir in the chickpea flour. Stir frequently and toast the flour for about 5 minutes, until the color of dark mustard. Take care not to overbrown or burn. Increase the heat back to medium and stir in the chopped onion, carrot, and celery. Cook for 5 minutes, or until the vegetables are slightly softened. Stir frequently!

Pour in the ale (wine, or broth), stirring to dissolve the browned bits of roux from the bottom of the pot. Cook for 2 minutes to reduce a little bit, then stir in the potato and frozen peas. Pour in the vegetable broth and add the soy sauce, thyme, mustard powder, sage, pepper, and salt. Simmer for about 8 minutes, until the broth has reduced slightly and a thin gravy has formed.

Ladle the filling into the casserole dish. Peel the top layer of parchment paper off the cold crust, slide your hand underneath the other side, and with one swift and steady movement flip and quickly center the crust on top of the casserole. Remove the remaining layer of parchment paper. Carefully pinch down the overhanging dough alongside the edge of the dish. Trim any excess dough beyond the 1½ inches with kitchen scissors or a sharp knife. Create a raised crust edge by rolling up the dough along the edges of the casserole dish, pinching along the way to seal the edges of the piecrust. Use the tines of your favorite fork to crimp the edges. Lastly, poke a few holes with that fork on top of the crust: this allows steam to escape while baking, and it just looks cool.

Bake for 40 to 45 minutes. The pie is ready when the filling is bubbling and the crust is golden brown and slightly puffy. It's a good idea to slide a large, rimmed baking sheet (or big swaths of aluminum foil) on the rack under the pie to catch any bubbling gravy bits that love burning the bottom of your oven. As the pie bakes, brush the top with unsweetened nondairy milk once or twice during baking, for a light sheen on the crust.

The insides of the pie will be volcano-level hot straight out of the oven, so be careful! For best results, carefully make a few slits in the top crust and if you can stand it, allow it to cool 10 minutes before serving.

For individual pies: We recommend about four deep, ovenproof bowls or substantial mini pie tins for this recipe. For the crust, divide the dough into the appropriate number of sections, one per bowl. Form the sections into balls and roll out to the shape of the bowls/tins, plus an inch or two for shaping the edges of the crust. Proceed as directed for the crust, stacking the individual crusts between sheets of waxed paper before chilling.

Prepare the filling as directed, dividing among the bowls. Top with the crust, seal, and crimp as for a large pie, and bake for 30 to 35 minutes at 375°F or until the top is golden and the filling is bubbling.

As this is a chapter about casseroles, the main instructions are for one big pie made in a deep-dish casserole. For individual pies, you will need four ovenproof bowls or extra-large ramekins that can hold at least 2 cups of filling. If you don't have those, you can make several smaller pies in smaller dishes or cups. Instructions for individual pies follow the main instructions.

If you're feeling particularly industrious, double the crust recipe and prepare a bottom crust. It doesn't need to be chilled before fitting into the casserole dish; just roll out, fit, and trim, then cover the entire crust with plastic wrap and keep in the refrigerator while preparing the top crust and filling. Rip off the plastic wrap before filling and you're good to go!

You'll (almost) look forward to the next chilly night with this ultrahearty cauliflower and mushroom potpie with a velvety leek gravy. Serve with Sautéed Collards (page 149) or shaved fennel and chopped parsley tossed with Mediterranean Olive Oil & Lemon Vinaigrette (page 125).

Preheat the oven to 375°F. Have handy a 3-quart oven-to-table Dutch oven or 9 x 13-inch casserole dish to bake the finished potpie.

Prepare the sauce: In a heavy-bottomed saucepan (not the Dutch oven) over medium heat, warm the oil and sprinkle in the flour. Stir to form a thick paste. Cook the mixture until slightly golden, about 3 minutes. Stir in the leek and continue to fry until the leek has softened, another 4 to 6 minutes.

Slowly pour in the milk and broth, constantly stirring with a wire whisk until smooth. Whisk in the dried herbs, mustard powder, and salt and add the bay leaf. Continue to cook, stirring constantly with a whisk, for 8 minutes, or until the sauce has thickened slightly. Turn off the heat, remove the bay leaf, and adjust the salt and pepper to taste.

Heat the oil in the Dutch oven over medium heat. Add the carrot and sauté for 2 minutes, then stir in the mushrooms and vinegar and cook another 6 minutes until most of the excess liquid from the mushrooms has evaporated. Stir in the cauliflower, partially cover the pot, and sweat the cauliflower for about 8 minutes to soften it up slightly. Remove the lid and turn off the heat.

While the cauliflower is cooking, prepare the biscuit crust: Sift together the flour, baking powder, salt, and thyme in a small bowl. With a pastry cutter or two knives held together, cut in the cold coconut oil until crumbs form, then drizzle in 3 tablespoons of the cold milk and mix. Drizzle in additional tablespoons of cold milk, one at a time, until a soft dough forms (but be careful not to overwork it). Fold in the olives.

Tear a piece of parchment paper the size of the top of the Dutch oven or casserole. Dust with flour, then transfer the biscuit dough to the center. Pat out the dough on a lightly floured surface into a circle or appropriate shape slightly smaller than the edge of the Dutch oven.

To assemble: Give the sauce a good whisking (no worries if a skin has formed over it), pour into the cauliflower mixture, and stir completely to blend the veggie juices and sauce.

Slide your hand under the parchment paper (with the dough on top), then with one movement flip it onto the top of the Dutch oven. Hurray, the crust is now on the pie! Now take a sharp knife and cut the crust into diamond shapes about 2 inches apart. Brush the top of the crust with additional milk.

Bake for 35 to 40 minutes, or until the cauliflower is tender and the biscuits are cooked.

Allow to cool at least 10 minutes before serving, as the filling will be hot as hell straight out of the oven. Scoop into serving bowls and enjoy!

CAULIFLOWER & MUSHROOM
POTPIE
with Black Olive Crust

SERVES 4 TO 6 / TIME: 1 HR

Sauce:

3 tablespoons olive oil

2 tablespoons all-purpose flour

1 leek, green part removed and cleaned, minced

1 cup unsweetened almond or soy milk

1 cup vegetable broth, purchased or homemade (page 223)

2 teaspoons dried tarragon

½ teaspoon dried thyme

½ teaspoon dried marjoram

¼ teaspoon mustard powder

1 teaspoon salt

1 bay leaf

Freshly ground black pepper

Vegetables:

2 tablespoons olive oil

1 small carrot, cut into small dice

½ pound cremini mushrooms, washed, trimmed, and sliced into large chunks

1 teaspoon apple cider vinegar or freshly squeezed lemon juice

1 pound cauliflower, trimmed, washed, and cut into bite-size pieces

Black olive biscuit crust:

1¼ cups all-purpose flour or a combination of whole wheat pastry and all-purpose, plus more for dusting

1 teaspoon baking powder

1 teaspoon salt

Pinch of dried thyme leaves

3 tablespoons refined coconut oil, cold enough to be firm

4 to 5 tablespoons cold unsweetened almond or soy milk, plus more for brushing

⅓ cup pitted black olives (kalamata recommended), chopped coarsely

POTATO & KALE
ENCHILADAS
with Roasted Fresh Chile Sauce

SERVES 4 TO 6 / TIME: 1 HR

Enchilada chile sauce:

2 tablespoons olive oil

1 yellow onion, cut into small dice

3 large green chiles (such as poblano, Anaheim, or Italian-style long green peppers), roasted, seeded, peeled (see page 35), and chopped coarsely

2 teaspoons chile powder, preferably ancho

1½ teaspoons ground cumin

1 teaspoon ground oregano, marjoram, or Mexican oregano (epazote)

1 (28-ounce) can diced tomatoes with juice (roasted preferred)

1 teaspoon organic sugar

1½ teaspoons salt, or to taste

Potato kale filling:

1 pound waxy potatoes (Yukon gold or red)

3 tablespoons olive oil

4 cloves garlic, minced

½ pound kale, washed, trimmed, and chopped finely

½ teaspoon ground cumin

¼ cup vegetable broth, purchased or homemade (page 223), or water

3 tablespoons freshly squeezed lime juice

¼ cup toasted pepitas (pumpkin seeds, see page 320), chopped coarsely, plus additional for garnish

1½ teaspoons salt, or to taste

12 corn tortillas

Just like tamales, enchiladas are a precious gift from Mexican cuisine that requires just a little extra work than most casseroles do. Making the sauce and the filling can be stretched out over a day or two, which makes assembly of the final dish relatively snappy. Enchiladas taste even better the next day, so be bold and double the recipe for intentional leftovers.

In this alternative to traditional fillings, garlicky potatoes and braised kale are spiked with lime, chile, and toasted pepitas, all wrapped in corn tortillas and a homemade green chile sauce. Accompany individual servings with diced ripe avocado, a dollop of Sour Cilantro Cream (page 319) and a side of Mexican Millet (page 173) for a Sunday supper in your finest yoga pants, or on weeknights serve with store-bought corn and black bean salad for streaming video and chill and laundry-day leggings.

Preheat the oven to 375°F and have ready a 3-quart shallow casserole dish.

Prepare the enchilada sauce first: In a large, heavy-bottomed saucepan over medium heat, sauté the onion in the oil for 2 minutes, until softened. Add the remaining sauce ingredients, bring to a gentle simmer, and cook for 10 minutes. Turn off the heat and set aside to cool enough to safely handle. Taste and season with a little salt, if necessary. Puree with an immersion or regular blender until the mixture is smooth.

Prepare the filling: Peel and dice the potatoes. Place in a large pot and cover with a few inches of cold water. Bring to a boil over high heat and simmer until easily pierced with a fork but not completely mushy, about 12 minutes. Drain well.

In a large saucepan over low heat, heat the oil, then stir in the garlic and cook for 30 seconds. Add the kale, sprinkle with a little salt, and increase the heat to medium, stirring constantly to cover the kale with the oil and garlic. Partially cover the pot to steam the kale until it has wilted, about 4 minutes.

Remove the lid and add the potatoes, vegetable broth, lime juice, pumpkin seeds, and salt. Use the back of a wooden spoon to partially crush the potatoes. Cook for another 3 minutes, or until most of the broth is absorbed. Add more salt or lime juice to taste.

Create an enchilada assembly line: Line up, left to right (or vice versa if you're a southpaw): a stack of corn tortillas, a pie plate, a casserole dish, and the filling. Preheat a griddle or cast-iron pan over medium heat (for softening the tortillas).

Ladle about ¾ cup of the enchilada sauce into the pie plate, then spread about ½ cup of the sauce on the bottom of the casserole dish. Warm a tortilla on the griddle for about 30 seconds, until softened. Drop the warm tortilla into the pie plate filled with sauce and quickly flip it over, coating it completely with sauce.

Immediately transfer the tortilla to the casserole dish. Spread about ¼ cup of the filling down the center and carefully roll it up. Move it to one side of the dish. Continue coating and filling the remaining tortillas, tightly packing the enchiladas next to each other in the dish.

Pour 1 cup of the sauce over the top (reserving some for later), cover the dish tightly with aluminum foil, and bake for 25 minutes. Remove the foil and bake for another 10 to 15 minutes, until the edges of the tortillas poking out of the sauce are golden. Use a large spatula to lift the hot, delicate enchiladas onto serving plates. Warm the remaining enchilada sauce and pass around!

TIPS

There are a dozen different ways to assemble enchiladas, but we prefer intersecting two gently warmed, sauce-soaked tortillas like a spicy Venn diagram to form one big tortilla so that we can get as much filling as possible into each enchilada.

Do you live in New Mexico and/or have an abundance of Hatch chiles? Yes to one or both of those questions, then go right ahead and use Hatch chiles in this recipe!

EGGPLANT-POTATO
MOUSSAKA
with Cashew Tofu Cream

SERVES 6 TO 8 / TIME: 1 HR 20 MIN

Vegetable layer:

3 tablespoons olive oil or more, for brushing, plus more for pans

1 pound eggplant

1 pound zucchini

1½ pounds russet or large baking potatoes (large, long potatoes work perfectly in this recipe)

Sea salt

Sauce:

2 tablespoons olive oil

3 cloves garlic, minced

½ cup finely chopped shallot

⅓ cup dry red wine

3 (15-ounce) cans diced fire-roasted tomatoes

2 teaspoons dried oregano

½ teaspoon ground cinnamon

2 bay leaves

1½ teaspoons salt

Cashew tofu cream (Béchamel):

½ cup unroasted cashews, soaked in cold water until softened (about 20 minutes)

2 tablespoons olive oil

12 ounces soft silken tofu

1 tablespoon fresh lemon juice

1 teaspoon arrowroot powder

2 cloves garlic, peeled and chopped

1 teaspoon dried oregano

¼ teaspoon freshly grated nutmeg

1 teaspoon salt

For assembly:

Olive oil

½ cup fine dried vegan bread crumbs

¼ cup pine nuts

Dried oregano

Freshly grated nutmeg

This vegan rendition of the Greek casserole tastes like it was made in a fabulous vegan restaurant nestled in a majestic olive grove at the base of Mount Olympus.

Taste what moussaka could really be and warm up to this idyllic dish of roasted eggplant, potatoes, and zucchini layered under cinnamon-spiked tomato sauce and silky cashew and tofu Béchamel sauce (a recipetester favorite!). This refined recipe has more tomato sauce and cashew cream for an extra substantial dish perfect for potlucks or nibbling on all week long, as the flavors deepen the next day. Serve with a simple salad of diced tomatoes and cucumbers.

Prepare the vegetables: Preheat the oven to 400°F. Line three large baking sheets with parchment paper and generously oil the sheets with olive oil. Wash the eggplant and zucchini, and trim the stems. Scrub and peel the potatoes. Slice the eggplant, zucchini, and potatoes lengthwise into approximately ¼-inch-thick slices.

Arrange the vegetable slices by kind on separate baking sheets in a single layer; do not overlap the slices. Brush the slices with olive oil and sprinkle the vegetables with little bit of sea salt. Roast the pans of zucchini and eggplant for 15 minutes, or until tender. The potatoes may take longer, 20 to 22 minutes, or until the slices can be easily pierced with a fork. Remove from the oven.

Meanwhile, prepare the tomato sauce: Place the oil and minced garlic in a large, heavy-bottomed saucepan over medium heat. Fry the garlic for about 30 seconds, then add the shallot and cook until soft and translucent, 3 to 4 minutes. Add the wine and simmer to reduce slightly, about 2 minutes. Add the crushed tomatoes, oregano, cinnamon, bay leaves, and salt. Partially cover and simmer over medium-low heat for 12 minutes, stirring occasionally. The sauce should reduce slightly. Turn off the heat and remove the bay leaves.

Make the cashew tofu cream: In a food processor, blend the cashews (remember to drain the soaking liquid) and oil, scraping the sides of the bowl with a rubber spatula, until a creamy paste forms. Add the remaining cashew tofu cream ingredients. Blend until completely creamy and smooth.

Assemble the moussaka, opa! Generously rub a 9 x 13-inch casserole with olive oil and preheat the oven again to 400°F. Spread ¼ cup of the sauce on the pan, then add successive layers in order of eggplant, potatoes, sauce, and half the bread crumbs. Spread all the zucchini on top of this. Top with a final layer each of eggplant, potatoes, sauce, and bread crumbs. Use a rubber spatula to evenly spread the cashew tofu cream over the entire top layer. Decorate the top by scattering with pine nuts and healthy drizzles of olive oil. Dust the top generously with oregano and a tiny pinch of nutmeg.

Bake, covered with foil, for 45 minutes, uncover and bake for another fifteen, then broil the top for 2 to 4 minutes until browned spots appear (for that authentic Greek homemade casserole touch). For easier slicing, cool 10 minutes to allow the topping to firm up.

TIP

Very fresh zucchini may be watery after roasting. If so, when cool enough to handle, gently squeeze the slices by the handful to remove any excess water. See our tips for roasting summer squash (page 35), for further suggestions.

KASHA
PHYLLO PIE

SERVES 8 / TIME: ABOUT AN HR

Filling:

3 tablespoons olive oil

1 medium-size onion, cut into small dice

1 stalk celery, cut into small dice

½ pound cremini mushrooms, sliced thinly

1 small carrot, grated

1 teaspoon caraway seeds

1 teaspoon ground coriander

½ teaspoon salt

Freshly ground black pepper

1¼ cups uncooked kasha

2¼ cups vegetable broth, preferable mushroom-flavored, heated to almost boiling

1 cup sauerkraut, well drained of excess liquid

Phyllo:

1 (16-ounce package) frozen phyllo dough, thawed according to package directions

½ cup olive oil, or more, for brushing

TIPS

Kasha is roasted buckwheat, our favorite protein-packed grain! It has a distinctive, "earthy" taste that might take some getting used to for the uninitiated.

Look for fresh, water-packed sauerkraut in the refrigerated section of the grocery store.

Working with temperamental phyllo can sometimes make you curse the Greek gods, but with a little practice and these tips, you'll fly through it. Keep the phyllo right next to the casserole dish, covered with either plastic wrap or a lightly damp, clean dish towel, so that it doesn't dry out. Make sure the phyllo stays covered when not using, even between adding layers.

This filling wintertime pie is a little like a great big mushroom and kasha knish, with a secret sauerkraut filling and wrapped up in layers of flaky phyllo dough. The filling can be made two days in advance, but to prevent soggy phyllo, assemble when you're ready to bake and serve. We love it served straight up with a big dollop of spicy brown mustard, but if you want to show off do it up with a side of Horseradish-Dill Sour Cream (page 318) or douse everything with Mustard Sauce (page 312).

Prepare the filling: Heat the oil in a 3-quart saucepan over medium heat and add the onion and celery. Fry until slightly soft, 2 minutes, then add the mushrooms and cook until most of the mushroom liquid has evaporated, another 6 to 8 minutes. Add the grated carrot, caraway seeds, coriander, salt, pepper, and kasha. Stir to coat the kasha with the oil and pour in the hot vegetable broth. Bring the mixture to a boil, lower the heat to a low simmer, and cover.

Cook for 12 minutes, or until the liquid is absorbed and the kasha is tender. Remove from the heat, fluff with a fork, and partially cover. Allow the mixture to sit for 10 minutes so that the kasha is cool to the touch before you proceed with assembling the pie.

Preheat the oven to 375°F. Lightly oil a medium-size casserole dish. Set up your work area to work with phyllo dough. We like to spread out a clean, damp tea towel on a cutting board, and keep nearby the stack of phyllo covered in plastic wrap and draped with another damp towel. Set your oil and brush next to the dough. Consult the phyllo package directions if you're looking for additional support.

Lay a sheet of phyllo dough on your work area. Brush it with olive oil and layer with another sheet. Repeat four or five more times, then fold the entire thing in half and press into the bottom of the casserole dish to form a bottom crust. Work steadily: hustle only enough to keep the dough from drying but not so fast you tear the fragile phyllo. Push up the edges of the dough along the sides to form the sides of the pie.

Press half of the kasha mixture onto the dough. Spread the drained sauerkraut over the kasha and sprinkle with a little pepper. Top with the remaining kasha and press the mixture to the edges of the pie to even out. Repeat the process of layering and folding the phyllo dough (as for the bottom crust) to form the top crust of the pie, then press this top crust onto the kasha filling and fold any hanging edges into the sides of the pie.

With a sharp, serrated knife, slice the pie into eight pieces: cut all the way through the top and bottom layers of phyllo. Brush the top with plenty of olive oil and bake for 30 to 35 minutes, or until the phyllo is puffed and golden. Remove from the oven and let cool for 10 minutes before serving, carefully score the pieces again with a knife, and use a spatula to serve 'em up.

As we were developing this recipe we found ourselves wondering why every vegan cookbook has a shepherd's pie recipe when sheep herding is so not vegan? Our answer to this riddle is the winning combo of tempeh, peas, and corn in a zesty mushroom gravy.

Prepare the tempeh layer: In a large skillet, crumble the tempeh into small, bite-size pieces. Add the water, tamari, and 1 teaspoon of the oil. Cover and let boil for about 10 minutes. Start boiling the potatoes in the meantime (directions follow).

Remove the lid from the tempeh and continue to boil until most of the water has evaporated, about 5 more minutes. Drain the tempeh in a colander and return the pan to the stove top over medium-high heat (you don't need to wash it).

Sauté the onion in the remaining oil for 5 minutes. Add the garlic and sauté for 1 more minute. Stir in the tempeh, along with the sliced mushrooms and the spices. Cook for about 10 more minutes over medium heat, until the mushrooms are juicy and the tempeh is slightly browned. While this cooks, your potatoes should be ready for mashing and you can go ahead and preheat the oven to 375°F.

Add the corn and peas, and cook until heated through. You may need to add a little extra oil here; if you have a spray bottle of it, you should use it.

Mix together the flour and vegetable broth until pretty much dissolved (a few lumps is okay). Add to the tempeh, along with the parsley, and stir. Let thicken for about 3 minutes, stirring occasionally. It will thicken more as it bakes.

Prepare the potatoes: Place the potatoes in a soup pot and cover with water (the water should be about 1 inch above the potatoes). Cover and bring to a boil. Let boil for 20 minutes, or until they easily cut with a fork. Drain and return to the pot. Use a potato masher to mash them up a bit, then add the milk, oil, salt, and pepper. Mash very well, until creamy. Cover to keep warm until ready to use.

Assemble the pie: Place the tempeh filling in a 9 x 13-inch casserole dish. Spoon the potatoes over the filling (although, truth be told, we use our hands for this because it's just easier).

Place in the preheated oven and bake for 20 minutes; the potatoes should be slightly browned on top. If they are not, place under a broiler for 2 to 3 minutes.

Remove from the oven, garnish with chopped parsley, use a spatula to cut into eight squares, and serve.

TEMPEH
SHEPHERDESS PIE

SERVES 8 / TIME: 1 HR 20 MIN

Tempeh layer:

2 (8-ounce) packages tempeh

⅓ cup tamari or soy sauce

2 cups water

2 tablespoons plus 1 teaspoon olive oil

1 large onion, cut into ½-inch dice

3 cloves garlic, minced

8 ounces cremini mushrooms, sliced (about 3 cups)

1 teaspoon dried thyme

1 teaspoon ground coriander

Lots of freshly ground black pepper

1 cup fresh or frozen corn kernels

1 cup frozen peas

¼ cup all-purpose flour

2 cups vegetable broth, purchased or homemade (page 223)

¼ cup finely chopped fresh parsley, plus a little more for garnish

Potato layer:

3 pounds Yukon gold potatoes, peeled and cut into 1-inch chunks

⅓ cup unsweetened nondairy milk, warmed or at room temperature

¼ cup refined coconut oil

¾ teaspoon salt, or to taste

Plenty of freshly ground black pepper

TIP

For a fun and colorful variation, use mashed sweet potatoes (peeled and boiled), instead of regular mashed potatoes, as the topping.

CHAPTER EIGHT

ONE-POT MEALS & STOVETOP SPECIALTIES

**This chapter is very much a two-part biopic—
"a tale of two recipes," one might say—but even better
because you won't be tested on any of the material.**

It centers on the secret life of food that's cooked on top of the stove. Some meals use but one pot, some use a few more. Both end happily with the tummy full of joy and, well, fullness.

Part I. We like the sound of "One-Pot Meals." It makes us feel like we're hanging out in a *Little House on the Prairie* remake, chopping wood, building barns, sewing quilts, and at the end of the day getting ready for a big dinner scooped out of a big, cast-iron pot.

"And what do those city girls know about cast-iron pots?" you ask? Enough that somehow stews and casseroles just taste better cooked in them. Good one-pots also include enameled cookware and stoneware, which are pricey but worth trading a few blankets for. We'll often recommend starting a recipe on top of the stove, then moving it to the oven to finish cooking. We're not being fickle; it's just the best way to give dumpling biscuits the perfect toasted top or to ensure that a steaming vat of jambalaya rice cooks up tender instead of burned. But if you haven't traveled down to the general store yet for a stove-to-table pot, fear not. You can just as easily transfer the recipe from a pot on the stove and into an oven-safe dish to complete the cooking process.

Part II. Let us turn our attention for a moment to "Stovetop Specialties," shall we? This is just a catch-all name for meals that require you to use those pots (and pans) you thought might never see some action. If you're scared you'll have to pull out all the stops like some kind of TV chef, be assured we'll keep your budding career in check—these recipes simply require an extra sauté pan or small saucepan. As you'll see, stovetop meals include flavorful and thrilling sautés of vegetables, seitan, and tofu. Normal people (read: not the authors of the *Veganomicon*) would probably call these dishes "entrées."

---◆---

SEITANIC RED & WHITE BEAN
JAMBALAYA

SERVES 6 / TIME: 1 HR 25 TO 35 MIN,
depending on the rice

6 tablespoons olive oil

1 recipe Simple Seitan (page 205), or
16 ounces store-bought seitan, diced or
pulled apart into small bite-size pieces

1 large yellow onion, cut into ½-inch dice

2 stalks celery, cut into small dice

1 green bell pepper, seeded and cut into
½-inch dice

4 cloves garlic, minced

3 heaping tablespoons tomato paste

½ cup cooking sherry or more vegetable
broth

2 cups long-grain white rice

1 (28-ounce) can diced tomatoes

1 (15-ounce) can white kidney (cannellini)
beans, drained and rinsed

1 (15-ounce) can red kidney beans, drained
and rinsed

1 bay leaf

4 to 6 sprigs fresh thyme (optional but
really great here)

1 teaspoon dried thyme

1 teaspoon dried marjoram

1 teaspoon dried paprika

½ teaspoon celery seeds

½ teaspoon onion powder

¼ teaspoon cayenne, or to taste

1 teaspoon salt

Several pinches of freshly ground black
pepper

2 cups vegetable broth, purchased or
homemade (page 223)

Chopped, fresh flat-leaf parsley for garnish

Warning: Just a taste of this luscious, tomato-laced concoction of rice, vegetables, and seitan, and you just might feel like shouting at the devil. But please, make sure you do it with teased metal-band hair or while wearing skin-tight black pleather pants, lest you scare the kids. Perfectly sinful for hardcore meat-eaters and vegans alike, seitanic jambalaya is a favorite at parties, potlucks, or wherever a hungry, Cajun-spice lovin' crowd may be. Serve with French bread rolls, Sautéed Collards (page 149), and your favorite Louisiana-style hot sauce.

Preheat the oven to 375°F. Heat 2 tablespoons of the oil in a large oven-to-table Dutch oven or heavy soup pot over medium-heat. Sauté the seitan for 4 to 6 minutes, until lightly browned. Remove from the pot and set aside. Add the remaining 4 tablespoons of oil to the pot, then stir in the onion, celery, green pepper, and garlic. Sauté for 10 minutes, or until the vegetables are soft and a tad mushy. Stir in the tomato paste and cook, stirring frequently, for another 2 minutes.

Stir in the cooking sherry to deglaze the vegetables, cook for 30 seconds, then add the rice. Stir the rice for about 4 minutes, then stir in the diced tomatoes, seitan, beans, bay leaf, all of the herbs, and the salt and black pepper. Bring to a simmer, pour in the vegetable broth, and return to a simmer. Taste the broth and adjust the salt and pepper to taste.

If using a Dutch oven, cover and place in oven. Bake for 30 to 35 minutes, until the rice is tender. If using a pot, transfer to a deep casserole dish, cover tightly with aluminum foil, and bake for 30 to 35 minutes.

Remove from the oven, stir the jambalaya, then cover and allow to sit for about 10 minutes before serving. Garnish with chopped parsley, if desired.

VARIATION

BROWN RICE JAMBALAYA: Replace the white rice with long-grain brown rice and increase the broth to 3½ cups. You'll also need to roughly double the final baking time in the oven to about 1 hour. Test the rice about 40 minutes into cooking: pluck a few grains from the center; if the rice still has crunchy centers, cover and continue to bake for another 10 to 15 minutes, or until all the rice is tender.

TIPS

If you haven't used the technique of deglazing (page 27) yet, here is the place to give it a shot. If bits of seitan stick to the bottom of the pot and start to burn while you're sautéing, deglaze the pot with a few tablespoons of cooking sherry. Then, remove the seitan from the pot and continue as directed. The browned bits add lots of flavor, while the deglazing prevents them from sticking around and burning when cooking the vegetables.

If using fresh thyme, just poke the sprigs into the rice before baking. The leaves will fall off the stems while it's cooking. Just remove the stems before serving.

Have a favorite Cajun-style seasoning mix? Use 3 or more teaspoons in place of the dried herbs and spices, but still add the fresh thyme.

This mild green chili has a secret weapon! Okay, it isn't so secret if you speak Spanish—it's apples. They give this chili mellow notes of sweet and tart. Tomatillos, poblano peppers, jalapeños, and cilantro add flavorful verdeness; little white beans and cubes of tender white potatoes give it heartiness. Perfect with the Jalapeño-Onion Skillet Corn Bread (page 341). The next time your family or loved ones complain that all you vegans ever make is chili, serve this one and graciously accept their apology.

Place the chopped potatoes in a small saucepan, cover with water, and bring to a boil. Let boil, covered, for a little less than 20 minutes, until the potatoes are easily pierced with a fork. Drain and set aside. Of course, you should be preparing everything else while they are boiling.

Preheat a soup pot over medium-high heat. Sauté the onion, jalapeños, and poblanos in the vegetable oil for about 10 minutes, until everything is softened and the onion is slightly browned.

Add the garlic, cumin, oregano, and salt. Sauté for 1 more minute, or until the garlic is fragrant. Add the white wine and tomatillos and increase the heat a bit to let the wine reduce and the tomatillos release their juices, about 5 minutes.

Add the apples, vegetable broth, scallion, and ½ cup of cilantro. Lower the heat to a simmer (medium-low), cover, and cook for 20 minutes.

Use an immersion blender to partially puree everything. If you don't have one, then let the mixture cool slightly and transfer to a blender or food processor; pulse until just slightly chunky. Don't forget that if you are using a blender, you need to be careful not to have a steam explosion, so pulse quickly and then lift the lid to let steam escape, then pulse again and repeat. Or just go get yourself an immersion blender; it will save your life! If using a blender or food processor, transfer the mixture back to the pot.

Taste for sweetness/tartness. Tomatillos are sometimes bitter; if that is the case, add a teaspoon or two of sugar and that should level things out. Add the cooked potatoes and the beans, and simmer for a few more minutes, until everything is heated through.

Add the remaining ½ cup of cilantro and the lime juice. Ladle into bowls, garnish with avocado and scallion, and serve.

MANZANA CHILI VERDE

SERVES 4 TO 6 / TIME: 1 HR

1 pound baby Yukon gold potatoes, cut into ½-inch pieces

2 tablespoons olive oil

1 large yellow onion, cut into small dice

3 jalapeño peppers, seeded and sliced thinly

2 poblano peppers, seeded and chopped into 1-inch pieces

4 cloves garlic, minced

1 tablespoon ground cumin

1 teaspoon dried oregano (preferably Mexican oregano)

1 teaspoon salt

⅓ cup dry white wine

1 pound tomatillos (about 10 small to medium-size ones), papery skin removed, washed, chopped into ½- to ¾-inch pieces

2 Granny Smith apples, cored, quartered, and sliced thinly

2 cups vegetable broth, purchased or homemade (page 223)

¼ cup chopped scallion, plus more for garnish

1 cup loosely packed fresh cilantro

1 (15-ounce) can small white beans, such as navy or cannellini, drained and rinsed (1½ cups)

Organic sugar, if needed

Juice of 1 lime

Avocado slices, for garnish

This is home-cooked comfort food to the max. Leeks, potatoes, carrots, peas, and white beans in a savory stew, with biscuits that are baked right on top of it. The perfect dinner for a rainy day, so make sure you instruct loved ones to have it ready and waiting for you.

Prepare the stew: Preheat the oven to 425°F. Place the potatoes in a small pot and add salted water to submerge them. Cover and bring to a boil. Once boiling, lower heat and simmer for about 10 minutes, until the potatoes are just tender enough to be pierced with a fork. Drain immediately so that they do not over-cook. While they are boiling, you can prep the rest of the veggies and start preparing the biscuits—the potatoes should definitely be done by the time you are.

Now, prepare everything for the biscuits: You're not going to make them yet, but it's good to have everything ready when it comes time to top the stew. Add the vinegar to the milk in a measuring cup and set aside to curdle. Mix together the flour, baking powder, and salt in a medium-size mixing bowl.

Now leave that alone and cook the other veggies for the stew: Mix the cornstarch into the vegetable broth in a small cup, until dissolved. Preheat an oven-safe skillet, preferably cast iron, over medium heat. Sauté the leeks, onions, and carrots in the oil until very soft and just beginning to brown, about 10 minutes. Keep the heat moderate so that they don't burn.

Add the garlic, thyme, pepper, and salt, and cook for 1 more minute. Add the cooked potatoes and frozen peas, then pour in the vegetable broth mixture. Increase the heat just a bit; it will take a few minutes but the liquid will start simmering. Once it does, lower the heat again. Let it simmer for about 7 minutes, stirring occasionally, but no longer than that. If you need more time for the biscuits, then turn off the heat under the stew.

Back to the biscuits: Add the coconut oil to the flour in clumps and work it into the dough with a fork or with your fingers until large crumbs form. You don't want to cream it in; there should be clumps. Drizzle in the milk and mix with a fork until everything is moistened (some dry parts are okay).

Wash and dry your hands, then lightly flour them and get them dirty again. Gently knead the dough about ten times right in the bowl, just so that it is holding together and not very sticky. If it seems sticky, as in sticking to your fingers, then gently work in a little more flour. Set that aside and check on your stew.

The stew should be simmering and slightly thickened. Mix in the beans. Now, let's add the biscuits. Pull off chunks of dough that are slightly larger than golf balls. Gently roll them into balls and flatten a bit; they do not have to be perfectly round. Add them to the top of the stew, placed an inch or so apart.

Transfer the whole megillah to the preheated oven. Bake for about 15 minutes. The biscuits should be just slightly browned and firm to the touch. Remove from the oven and use a large serving spoon to place some of the stew and a biscuit in each shallow, individual bowl. Sprinkle with a little chopped fresh thyme. This is especially yummy when you break up your biscuit and mix it in a bit with your stew.

LEEK & BEAN
CASSOULET
with Biscuits

SERVES 6 / TIME: 1 HR 20 MIN

Stew:

2 Yukon gold potatoes, cut into ½-inch dice

3 cups vegetable broth, purchased or homemade (page 223)

3 tablespoons cornstarch

2 tablespoons olive oil

2 leeks, washed and sliced thinly (about 2 cups)

1 small onion, cut into medium-size dice

1½ cups carrot, peeled and cut into ½-inch dice

2 cloves garlic, minced

1 heaping tablespoon chopped fresh thyme, plus more for garnish

Several pinches of freshly ground black pepper

½ teaspoon salt

¾ cup frozen peas

1 (15-ounce) can navy beans, drained and rinsed (about 1½ cups)

Biscuits:

¾ cup unsweetened nondairy milk

1 teaspoon apple cider vinegar

1½ cups all-purpose flour

2 teaspoons baking powder

¼ teaspoon salt

¼ cup refined coconut oil, softened

TIP

We've never had this problem but if you're worried about spillover when baking the stew for 15 minutes, place it on a rimmed baking sheet.

SEITAN PICCATA

with Olives & Green Beans

SERVES 4 / TIME: 40 MIN

1 pound Simple Seitan (page 205)

Olive oil

⅓ cup all-purpose flour

1 cup thinly sliced shallots

4 cloves garlic, chopped

⅓ cup dry white wine

2 cups vegetable broth, purchased or homemade (page 223)

¼ teaspoon salt

Several pinches of freshly ground black pepper

Small pinch of dried thyme

¼ cup capers with a little brine

½ cup pitted kalamata or black olives, cut in half

½ pound green beans, ends trimmed

3 tablespoons finely chopped fresh parsley

Juice of 1 lemon (2 to 3 tablespoons)

Mashed potatoes, to serve

Okay, enough messing around with everything else we call "recipes"; piccata is where it's at. If you've ever wanted to impress someone with something other than your ability to touch your tongue to your nose, then serve them piccata. Never heard of it? It's capers and white wine and garlic and shallots and lemon and breaded seitan, and despite its fanciness, it's easy to make. We serve it with olives and crunchy string beans over a big pile of mashed potatoes, and we serve it often. The seitan is the star of the show here, so we suggest using homemade for this.

Preheat a large heavy-bottomed skillet over medium-high heat.

Cut the seitan into long, thin pieces, slicing off any rounded ends so that they will lay flat. Ideally, the slices should be a little over ¼ inch thick, 3 inches long, and 2 inches across, but who is counting?

Coat the bottom of the skillet with the oil and let it get hot. Dredge half the seitan slices in flour to coat. Add to the pan and cook until lightly browned, about 2 minutes on each side. Proceed to coat the other slices and repeat. Place the cooked seitan slices on a tray or plate covered with aluminum foil, to keep warm. Do not rinse out the skillet or turn the heat off, as you're going to make the sauce in it.

Bring a pot of water to a boil for the green beans, but don't boil them just yet. You just want to have the water at the ready.

If there is enough oil left in the seitan pan to sauté the shallots and garlic, then do so; if not, add a little oil and sauté them for about 5 minutes, stirring often so as not to burn.

Add the white wine to the sauce and increase the heat to bring to a rolling boil. Add the vegetable broth, salt, pepper, and thyme. Again, bring to a rolling boil and let the sauce reduce by half; this should take about 7 to 10 minutes.

Add the capers and olives to heat through, about 3 minutes. At this point, add the beans to the boiling water and let them cook for 2 minutes, then strain.

Add the parsley and lemon juice to the sauce and turn off the heat.

To serve: Make a pile of mashed potatoes. Place the seitan over the mashed potatoes and place the green beans around the seitan. Use a ladle to douse everything in plenty of sauce. Serve immediately.

BBQ BLACK-EYED PEA—
COLLARD ROLLS

MAKES 12 ROLLS, SERVES 3 TO 4 /
TIME: 40 MIN

12 large collard leaves

1 tablespoon vegetable oil

8 ounces cremini mushrooms, sliced thickly

4 cups chopped collards

1 (15-ounce) can black-eyed peas, drained and rinsed (1½ cups)

3 cups Backyard BBQ Sauce (page 316)

Black-eyed peas love BBQ sauce and everyone loves rolling things. The combination makes this meal extra special. One bunch of collards should give you enough to prepare this recipe. It's yummy with mashed potatoes and Jalapeño-Corn Gravy (page 329) or any gravy, really. Prepare the BBQ sauce first and boil water for the collard leaves, then when the BBQ sauce is almost finished, begin cooking the mushrooms and beans. For a really quick and easy meal, prepare the sauce a day in advance.

Bring a large pot of water to a boil.

When the water is boiling, submerge the collard leaves and cover for 6 minutes. When done, use tongs to transfer them to a strainer and let cool. Handle them gently so that they don't rip.

Preheat a large skillet over medium heat. Sauté the mushrooms in the vegetable oil for about 5 minutes, until softened. Add the chopped collards. Cook for 7 to 10 minutes, or until most of the moisture has cooked off. Add the black-eyed peas and cook through. Add 2 cups of the BBQ sauce and cook for about 5 more minutes. If it looks watery, increase the heat a bit and cook for a few more minutes.

Let cool just a bit so that you can make the rolls without burning yourself.

Place a collard on a flat work surface with the side that has not been sliced facing you. Place about 2 tablespoons of the black-eyed peas and company in the lower third of the collard. Fold the bottom up over the mixture, then fold in the sides. Roll up the collard, gently but firmly. If the filling is spilling out, remove some of the black-eyed peas and try again.

Continue to roll the remaining collards. When ready to serve, spoon extra BBQ sauce over the rolls.

If you throw the word Mexicana on something it automatically connotes that there's black beans and corn in it, right? Okay, good. This is baked spaghetti squash tossed with mildly spicy black beans and corn, topped off with a fruity salsa fresca. We used pineapple, but you can use mango or papaya, if you prefer. Spaghetti squash gets its name because, when cooked, the flesh divides into pretty strings that resemble, you guessed it, spaghetti. It's a good idea to make the roasted squash a day in advance; that way you can have this dish on the table in under half an hour.

First, bake the squash: Preheat the oven to 375°F. Cut the squash in half across its waist (widthwise). Scoop out the seeds. Prick the squash halves with a fork five or six times. Fill a baking dish with about an inch of water and place the squash cut side down in the dish. Bake for about 45 minutes, or until the skin is easily pierced with a fork.

Meanwhile, prepare the salsa: In a small mixing bowl, toss all those ingredients together. Cover and refrigerate until ready to use.

Then, prepare the bean mixture: Preheat a large, heavy-bottomed skillet over medium-high heat and sauté the onion and jalapeño in the oil for about 5 minutes. Add the garlic and coriander seeds and sauté 2 more minutes. Add the remaining spices, salt, and wine, increase the heat, and boil for about 2 minutes, stirring often.

Lower the heat and add the corn, black beans, and hot sauce. Cook for 5 to 7 more minutes, or until the corn is heated through and the wine has reduced.

If the squash is not done by this point, cover the bean mixture. If the beans cool by the time the squash is ready, then gently reheat. The bean mixture should be hot when served.

When your squash is ready, remove it from the oven and let cool for about 10 minutes until you can handle it without burning yourself. Cut the squash halves in half lengthwise. Shred and scoop out the flesh with a spoon, add to the bean mixture, and toss with tongs to separate the strings and mix.

Divide among individual plates and top with salsa fresca. Serve immediately.

SPAGHETTI SQUASH

MEXICANA

with Tropical Avocado Salsa

SERVES 4 TO 6 / TIME: 1 HR 15 MIN

1 spaghetti squash (use one in the 3-pound range)

Tropical salsa:

1 cup chopped tomato (½-inch chunks)

1 cup chopped pineapple, mango, or papaya (½-inch chunks)

1 avocado, peeled, pitted, and cut into ½-inch chunks

¼ cup lightly packed chopped fresh cilantro

Juice of 1 lime

Bean mixture:

1 tablespoon vegetable oil

1 medium-size yellow onion, cut into small dice

2 jalapeño peppers, seeded and chopped small

3 cloves garlic, minced

2 teaspoons coriander seeds, crushed (see page 161 for how to crush)

1½ teaspoons chile powder

½ teaspoon ground cumin

¼ teaspoon ground cinnamon

½ teaspoon salt

½ cup red cooking wine

1 cup fresh or frozen corn kernels (if frozen, partially thawed)

1 (15-ounce) can black beans, drained and rinsed (1½ cups)

2 teaspoons hot sauce, or to taste

Pineapple fans, welcome to your pineapple heaven; it's all here in this South Asian–inspired dish. Quinoa, the high-protein South American grain, gets an extra splash of flavor cooked with a little pineapple juice, then stir-fried with colorful veggies, fresh ginger, and crunchy cashews. Make the quinoa a day or two in advance, store it in the fridge, and you'll be able to put this stir-fry in a snap. It's a meal in itself, or serve alongside any marinated and grilled tempeh (pages 201–206) or tofu (pages 191–199). Try it with red or a multicolored blend of white, red, and black quinoa for gorgeous confetti-like stir-fry!

Prepare the quinoa first: Place the pineapple juice, cold water, and soy sauce in a large saucepan and bring to a boil over high heat. Stir in the quinoa, lower the heat to low, and simmer for about 20 minutes, or until all the liquid has been absorbed and the quinoa grains are tender. Fluff with a fork and set aside to cool for at least 10 minutes or chill in the fridge until cold, if possible.

For best results, transfer the quinoa to an airtight container and refrigerate overnight. When ready to use, break up any chunks of cold quinoa with a fork.

Prepare the stir-fry: Use the largest nonstick skillet you have (at least 10 inches in diameter) or a wok. Have all of your ingredients chopped and easily within reach. Toast the cashews in the dry pan over low heat for about 4 minutes, or until lightly toasted. Dump them into a small bowl and soldier on with the rest of the stir-fry.

Increase the heat to medium-high and stir in the peanut oil, scallions, and garlic. As soon as the garlic starts to sizzle, add the sliced chile pepper and ginger. 1 minute later, toss in the bell pepper and peas. Stir-fry for another 2 minutes, or until the bell pepper is softened and the peas are bright green. Add the basil and mint and stir for another minute before adding the pineapple and quinoa. Add most of the cashews, saving a handful to garnish each serving.

In a measuring cup, combine the soy sauce, vegetable broth, and mirin. Pour over the quinoa mixture. Vigorously fold the quinoa and continue to stir-fry for 5 minutes, or until the quinoa is very hot. Scoop into serving bowls, top each serving with a few reserved cashews and a lime wedge, and please do pass around additional soy sauce and sriracha!

PINEAPPLE-CASHEW-
QUINOA STIR-FRY

SERVES 4 / TIME: ABOUT 30 MIN,
not including cooling the cooked quinoa

Quinoa:
1 cup pineapple juice
¾ cup cold water
¼ teaspoon soy sauce
1 cup quinoa, well rinsed and drained

Stir-fry:
4 ounces cashews, raw and unsalted
3 tablespoons peanut oil
2 scallions, sliced thinly
2 cloves garlic, minced
1 red chile, sliced into very thin rounds
1 (½-inch) piece fresh ginger, peeled and minced
1 red bell pepper, seeded and diced
1 cup frozen green peas or cooked edamame
½ cup fresh basil leaves, rolled and sliced into thin shreds (just like slicing collard greens)
2 tablespoons finely chopped fresh mint
10 ounces fresh pineapple, cut into bite-size chunks (about 2 cups)
3 tablespoons soy sauce
3 tablespoons vegetable broth, purchased or homemade (page 223)
1 tablespoon mirin or pure maple syrup
Lime wedges, for garnish
Additional soy sauce and sriracha sauce, for serving

TIP

Don't feel like butchering a fresh pineapple? Hit the grocery store salad bar (or produce section) for peeled, ready-to-eat fresh pineapple.

LENTILS & RICE

with Caramelized Onions & Spiced Pita Crisps

SERVES 4 TO 6 / TIME: 1 HR 20 MIN

3 large yellow onions, peeled and sliced into thin rings (about 2 pounds)

¾ cup olive oil

4 cups water

1 cup long-grain brown basmati rice

1 (1-inch piece) cinnamon stick

1½ teaspoons ground cumin

½ teaspoon ground allspice

½ teaspoon salt, or to taste

1 cup dried red lentils, rinsed

A few twists of freshly ground black pepper

VARIATION

SUBSTITUTE BROWN, GREEN OR BLACK LENTILS for the red lentils. Unlike red lentils, these varieties hold their shape. So, this dish will have more of a pilaf-like consistency, but still be delicious.

Add this to your comfort food rotation: spiced red lentils and caramelized onions melt into aromatic rice for a supremely comforting creamy golden mash. Terry says she could live for months (and be assured she has damn well tried) on this spin of classic Middle Eastern *mujadarah*. Try it yourself and be amazed how just a few cheap and wholesome ingredients can make something so yum. Serve alongside steamed chard, roasted cauliflower, or a kale salad.

Preheat the oven to 400°F. In a large baking pan, toss the onion rings with the oil to coat. Be sure to separate the rings and spread them out in the pan. Roast in the oven for 25 to 30 minutes, stirring often. The idea is to get most of the onion rings deep brown, crisp, and even burned on the edges. The deeper they roast, the sweeter they'll taste. When done, remove from the oven and set aside.

Bring the water to a boil in a large, heavy-bottomed pot. Add the rice, cinnamon stick, cumin, allspice, and salt. Bring back to a boil, then lower the heat, cover, and simmer for 15 minutes.

Uncover and add the lentils, stir gently only a few times (too much stirring can break the rice grains), cover, bring to a boil again, lower the heat to low, and cook for an additional 45 minutes, or until the liquid is completely absorbed. Remove from the heat and set aside the covered pot for 10 minutes.

Sprinkle the top of the rice with black pepper to taste. Use a fork to gently fluff the lentils and rice. Remove the cinnamon stick. Gently fold the caramelized onions into the lentils and rice, making sure to drizzle on any remaining olive oil from the roasting pan. Stir thoroughly. Serve warm or at room temperature.

SPICED PITA CRISPS

Crunchy, easy to make, and great with any dip or spread, too. A nice way to use up pita that's just a little past its prime.

4 white or whole wheat pitas

Olive oil, for brushing

1 teaspoon or more per pita of the following spices;
   pick just one and stick with it, or be like a crazy
   spice person and experiment with these mixtures:

   Garam masala

   Garlic powder, ground cumin, cayenne pepper,
      and salt or

   Lemon pepper, garlic powder, and salt

Preheat the oven to 350°F.

Slice open a pita along the edges and carefully open and separate each half. Brush with olive oil, then sprinkle with your seasoning(s) of choice. Spread the pitas on ungreased cookie sheets (a little overlapping is okay) and bake for 8 to 10 minutes, until golden brown and crisp. Watch and be careful not to burn.

Remove from the oven, let cool on the cookie sheets, and store in plastic bags.

SERVES 4 / TIME: 15 MIN

CHICKPEA & ROASTED EGGPLANT
STEW

SERVES 6 / TIME: 1 HR 10 MIN

2 large eggplants (3 pounds)

Olive oil

1 bulb garlic

2 red bell peppers, seeds removed, sliced in half

1 white onion, sliced into thin half-moons

Salt

2 teaspoons dried tarragon

1 teaspoon dried thyme

1 teaspoon ground coriander

1 teaspoon red pepper flakes

½ teaspoon smoked paprika

2 bay leaves

½ cup white wine

Several pinches of freshly ground black pepper

1 (28-ounce) can whole peeled tomatoes, with juice

1 (15-ounce) can chickpeas, drained and rinsed, or 1½ cups cooked chickpeas (page 41)

1 cup fresh flat-leaf parsley, roughly chopped

Roasted eggplant, garlic, and red bell peppers team up with chickpeas and tomatoes in this Mediterranean-inspired dish. This deeply satisfying stew also doubles as a sauce; go ahead and serve with Soft Poppy-Seed Polenta (page 165) by scooping the polenta into the center of a wide bowl and ladling the stew around it. Or serve atop penne pasta or big chunks of crusty bread.

This recipe looks really long but it's mostly our detailed notes on how to time everything right. Most of the cooking time isn't active; it's the veggies roasting and the soup simmering. Granted, there's a lot of steps and chopping of veggies, but it's worth it for the eggplant lover in your life.

Preheat the oven to 450°F. Quarter the eggplant lengthwise and slice across into ¾-inch slices.

Line two large baking sheets with parchment paper and brush with olive oil. Arrange eggplant slices on the baking sheets and brush tops with 3 tablespoons of olive oil.

Break the garlic apart and remove the skin from the cloves. Rub the cloves with a little olive oil and arrange on the baking sheet with the eggplant slices. On the other sheet, wherever there's a little room, place the bell peppers and rub them with oil. We're going to roast everything together at once! Sprinkle the veggies with a little salt. Roast for 25 to 30 minutes.

Halfway through, flip the eggplant and red pepper pieces and brush a little oil on any pieces that look dry. Remove when the eggplant can be easily pierced with a fork. The garlic cloves are ready when soft and golden. Let the veggies cool to the touch, then roughly chop eggplant and peppers, and mash the garlic slices with a fork until similar to a puree.

In a 3-quart Dutch oven, heat 1 tablespoon of olive oil, add the onion, and sauté for 5 minutes, or until very soft. Stir in the herbs and spices, fry for 30 seconds, and stir in the wine. Simmer for 1 minute and stir in the eggplant, bell peppers, and garlic. Add the tomatoes, tearing up each tomato with your hands before adding to the pot, and add the remaining tomato juice from the can. Add the chickpeas. Lower the heat and simmer for 10 minutes, stirring occasionally.

Turn off the heat, stir in the parsley, sprinkle with black pepper, and serve!

TIPS

You are going to need two large, rimmed baking sheets to get the job done and baking parchment to make sure that you don't ruin the baking sheets—unless they're already ruined and you don't care.

If you don't have a pastry brush for applying the oil, a spray bottle of olive oil will work, too. Otherwise just drizzle it on.

It's freezing outside in late February and your body wants fries, but your brain knows spring is right around the corner and vegetables are the right thing to do. Feel healthy or fake feeling healthy today with a mellow broth loaded with shiitake mushrooms, sweet kabocha squash, and newly improved with more sea vegetables. If you haven't guessed already, you'll need a few Japanese specialty items for this stew. We recommend making this if you've ever stepped into a huge, well-stocked Asian market, got really excited, brought home a big bag of groceries, then asked yourself, "What the hell am I going to make with all this stuff?" Now you can go shopping with purpose!

Prepare the broth: Place the mushrooms in a bowl and soak in about 1 cup of cold water for 30 minutes, or until soft and plump. Remove the mushrooms and gently squeeze into the water, then slice into ¼-inch thick strips. If the mushrooms contained any grit, it will settle at the bottom of the bowl. Carefully drain this mushroom soaking liquid into the soup pot you'll be using, making sure to leave grit at the bottom of the bowl (discard this; it's only grit!). Add the remaining 7 cups of cold water to the soup pot along with the kombu, shoyu, sliced shiitakes, and ginger. Bring the kombu broth to a boil, then lower to a gentle simmer.

Prepare the noodles and veggies: While the broth is simmering, prepare the udon noodles according to the package directions. Rinse the cooked noodles in cold water to stop the cooking, and divide the noodles among serving bowls.

Simmer the broth for 20 minutes, then remove and discard the kombu (it's gonna be slippery, so use tongs to grab it). Add the leek, carrot, parsnip, kabocha, tofu, and wakame seaweed to the broth. Simmer over medium-low heat for another 20 minutes or until the squash is tender and can be pierced easily with a fork. Stir in the sake, mirin, and toasted sesame oil. Use a slotted spoon to add the vegetable chunks to the bowls, then a ladle to spoon on the broth. Top each serving with a mound of grated daikon and sprinkle with chopped scallions and hot pepper, and scatter a few bits of pickled ginger on top. Eat with a large spoon and chopsticks.

TIPS

Kabocha squash is an Asian pumpkin with deep orange flesh that's sweeter and slightly drier than regular pumpkin. A bonus for lazy cooks: the thin deep green skin of kabocha squash cooks up tender and edible, so no need to peel. We have no problem finding it in supermarkets but, if you can't find it, use peeled sugar pumpkin, acorn, delicata, or butternut. You'll probably need to extend the cooking time for these squash, cooking for an additional 10 to 15 minutes until the squash is tender.

Kombu, dried giant kelp, is a standard ingredient in Japanese soups and condiments. When cooked in a broth, it will unfold into a big sheet. Don't freak out; just let the broth cook as directed and then remove and discard the kelp when it's done.

KABOCHA UDON
WINTER STEW

SERVES 4 / TIME: ABOUT 35 MIN

Shiitake dashi broth:

2 quarts cold water

½ ounce dried shiitake mushrooms (about 5 large dried mushroom caps)

2 (4-inch) pieces kombu (kelp)

¼ cup shoyu (Japanese soy sauce)

2 (¼-inch-thick) slices fresh ginger, lightly crushed with the side of a knife

Noodles and veggies:

½ pound dried udon noodles

1 large leek, washed well and sliced into ½-inch lengths

1 large carrot, peeled and sliced into ½-inch-thick pieces

1 parsnip, peeled and sliced into ½-inch-thick pieces

1½ to 2 pounds kabocha (about 1 small squash), unpeeled, sliced into 1-inch chunks

6 ounces fried tofu pouches (aburage), or firm silken tofu, sliced into strips or cubes

¼ cup dried wakame seaweed

⅓ cup sake (the cheap stuff is ideal for soup!)

2 tablespoons mirin, or 1 tablespoon pure maple syrup

2 teaspoons toasted sesame oil

Garnishes:

1 (4-inch) piece daikon, peeled and grated

2 scallions, sliced very thinly

Japanese hot pepper powder

Pickled sliced ginger

BRAISED SEITAN

with Brussels, Kale & Sun-dried Tomatoes

SERVES 4 / TIME: 30 MIN

2 tablespoons olive oil, plus a little more if
  needed

6 average-size shallots, sliced thinly

2 cups seitan, sliced on the diagonal into
  bite-size pieces

½ pound Brussels sprouts, quartered (about
  2 cups sliced)

4 cloves garlic, minced

½ teaspoon dried thyme

½ teaspoon dried basil

¼ teaspoon dried tarragon

½ teaspoon salt

Several pinches of freshly ground black
  pepper

½ cup sun-dried tomatoes, chopped into
  bite-size pieces

2 cups vegetable broth, purchased or
  homemade (page 223)

¼ cup red wine (any wine will do, really)

4 cups chopped kale

If you make this recipe once, the cooking lesson will last a lifetime. It's the base for a hearty, delicious thirty-minute meal! Sauté some aromatics, brown some protein and veggies, and make a pan sauce—all with one vehicle. This makes an easy weeknight meal served over mashed potatoes, pasta, or rice. Make it a little fancier with either Soft Poppy-Seed Polenta (page 165) or Broccoli Polenta (page 166). The sun-dried tomatoes should be the actual dried ones, not the ones from oil in a jar.

Preheat a large, heavy-bottomed pan over medium-high heat. Sauté the shallots and seitan in 2 tablespoons of the oil for about 7 minutes, until they have both browned. Add the Brussels sprouts and sauté for 3 more minutes, adding a little extra olive oil if need be. Add the garlic, herbs, salt, and pepper and sauté for another minute. Mix in the sun-dried tomatoes.

Add the vegetable broth and wine. Once the liquid is boiling and the tomatoes are tender, which should be pretty quick if the heat is right, add the chopped kale. Stir the kale until it is wilted. Cover the pan, leaving a little room for steam to escape, and lower the heat. Simmer for 3 more minutes or so. Taste and adjust the salt, and serve immediately.

Cholent is a Jewish beef stew that's typically served on the Sabbath. Here, we use seitan, kidney beans, and lentils to create a thick, full-bodied pot of stick-to-your-ribs yumminess. Caraway seeds give it the Eastern European flavor that sets it apart from your run-of-the-mill stew, so now would be a great time to add them to your spice rack arsenal. We like to just crush crackers over the top and serve, but rice would be good, too. Or serve with bread for scooping. Warning: You might start inexplicably calling people *meshugenahs* and *putzes* after you've eaten this.

This is one of those stews that really benefits from a night in the fridge, but don't let that deter you from eating it right away (or any day of the week).

Preheat a large soup pot over medium heat. Sauté the onion in the oil until translucent, 5 to 7 minutes. Add the garlic, tarragon, caraway seeds, salt, and pepper. Sauté until the garlic is fragrant, about a minute more.

Deglaze the pot with the red wine. Add the water, bay leaves, lentils, carrots, potatoes, tomato sauce, and seitan. Mix together. Cover and simmer for about 30 minutes, until the lentils are fully cooked and stewy, and the potatoes and carrots are tender.

Add the lima and kidney beans and cook until heated through. Serve like crazy. *Ess gezunterhait.*

LENTIL & SEITAN
CHOLENT

SERVES 6 / TIME: 45 MIN

2 tablespoons olive oil

1 large onion, cut into medium-size dice

3 cloves garlic, minced

½ teaspoon dried tarragon

1 teaspoon caraway seeds

1 teaspoon salt

Several pinches of freshly ground black pepper

½ cup red cooking wine, water, or vegetable broth, purchased or homemade (page 223)

3 cups water

2 bay leaves

½ cup French lentils, rinsed

1 cup peeled, sliced carrot (sliced about ½ inch thick)

4 medium-size potatoes (about 1¼ pounds), peeled and cut into ¾-inch chunks)

1 (15-ounce can) tomato sauce

2 cups bite-size seitan

1 cup frozen lima beans

1 (15-ounce) can kidney beans, drained and rinsed (1½ cups)

PLANTAIN & PINTO
STEW
with Parsnip Chips

SERVES 4 / TIME: 45 MIN (STEW),
1½ HRS TOTAL

1 tablespoon vegetable oil

1 large white onion, chopped finely

1 yellow bell pepper, chopped finely

3 jalapeño peppers, seeded and chopped finely

3 cloves garlic, minced

8 plum tomatoes, diced

¼ cup dry white wine or vegetable broth, purchased or homemade (page 223)

1 teaspoon salt

2 teaspoons ground cumin

1 (15-ounce) can pinto beans, drained and rinsed

2 ripe plantains, peeled, sliced in half lengthwise, and sliced into ½-inch pieces

1 cup chopped fresh cilantro

1 recipe Parsnip Chips (recipe follows)

In NYC, plantains abound in the supermarkets and we're always looking for new ways to use them. This is a spicy and flavorful yet delicate stew. Use fresh tomatoes instead of canned so that you don't get a concentrated flavor that overpowers the plantains. Choose plantains that are ripe yellow and flecked with black yet not completely blackened. The parsnip chips are optional but yummy!

In a soup pot over medium heat, sauté the onion, bell pepper, jalapeño, and garlic in the vegetable oil for 5 to 7 minutes, until softened. Add the tomatoes, sherry, salt, and cumin. Cover and bring to a simmer; let simmer for 15 minutes, stirring occasionally, or until the tomatoes are cooked and broken down.

Add the pinto beans and plantains. Cover and simmer for another 20 to 25 minutes. The plantains should be soft and sweet. Add the cilantro and mix in so that it wilts.

Ladle into bowls and stick a few plantain chips into each bowl, like spears.

PARSNIP CHIPS

If you like sweet potato fries, you will like these. There are only two ingredients here, but sprinkling them with ground cumin is yummy, too. For parsnip fries, just cut them into ¼-inch-thick slices instead of ⅛ inch and bake for an additional 5 to 10 minutes.

1 pound parsnips (2 medium-size)

2 teaspoons or so peanut oil

Salt

Preheat the oven to 400°F.

Peel the parsnips and slice them lengthwise. Place them cut side down and slice into ⅛-inch-thick strips, or as close to that as you can get them.

Line them in a single layer on a baking sheet and drizzle with peanut oil. Toss them around and try to get the oil over all of them, adding a little more oil if necessary.

Bake for 15 minutes, then flip them (use tongs for this). Bake for an additional 10 to 15 minutes. The parsnips should be flecked with black and dark brown. If some are thinner than others, they will cook faster, obviously; remove the skinny ones from the baking sheet as they finish baking.

Sprinkle with salt and serve.

SERVES 4 / TIME: 45 MIN

Saag is Hindi for a curry that's made of greens—in this case, we use spinach. Baked pumpkin works as a flavorful backdrop to make this a healthier-than-usual saag (it's typically loaded with lots of ghee and cream or coconut cream). Garam masala complements the pumpkin nicely because of its autumnal blend of cinnamon, cloves, and cardamom. What we're going for here is mushy in a good way, with just a little bit of chunky pumpkin bites thrown in. Serve with basmati rice and some sort of chutney (page 323) and flatbread (page 324).

Preheat the oven to 350° F.

First, bake the pumpkin: Carve out the top of the pumpkin to remove the stem. Use your strongest knife to cut the pumpkin in half along the vertical. Remove the seeds (reserve them to toast sometime) and scrape out the stringy stuff with a spoon. Place the pumpkin halves, cut side down, on a lightly oiled baking sheet. Bake for about 45 minutes, until a fork can easily pierce the flesh.

Remove from the oven and let the pumpkin cool completely. Peel away the skin and then chop the pumpkin up into 1-inch chunks.

Preheat a soup pot over medium-high heat. Sauté the onion in the peanut oil for about 5 minutes. Add the garlic and sauté for 2 to 3 minutes more, or until everything is honey brown.

Add the pumpkin and cook until heated through, about 3 minutes. Add the spices and salt, and grate the ginger directly into the pot (use a Microplane grater, if possible). Add the water and cook for about 5 minutes, mixing often. Use your mixing spatula to mush the pumpkin up a bit, but leave some pieces chunky.

Add the spinach in batches (three or four should do it), mixing well after each addition.

Cook for about 10 more minutes, stirring often. Add the lime juice; taste and adjust the salt.

This is best if it's had time to sit for a while, but if you want to eat it immediately, we understand.

PUMPKIN
SAAG

SERVES 4 TO 6 / TIME: 1½ HRS

3 pounds sugar pumpkin

3 tablespoons peanut oil, plus more for pan

1 large white onion, diced finely

4 cloves garlic, minced

1½ teaspoons garam masala

¼ teaspoon ground cinnamon

½ teaspoon salt

⅛ teaspoon cayenne pepper

1 (1-inch) cube fresh ginger, peeled

1 cup water

10 ounces fresh spinach (this is about 2 bunches), washed well and chopped coarsely

Juice of ½ lime

TIP

Roast the pumpkin a day in advance so that you can throw this together the next day. Just wrap the cooled, baked pumpkin in plastic wrap, refrigerate, and you'll be good to go.

VEGETABLES OR SEITAN SIMMERED IN MOLE SAUCE

Who doesn't want chocolate for dinner? Presenting two variations on the same concept; tender vegetables or seitan, simmered in a not-quite-authentic but rich and comforting homemade chocolate mole sauce for a simple and very saucy meal. Change the vegetables to suit the season, if you please. Serve with a starchy side, such as Mexican Millet (page 173), plain steamed brown rice, cooked quinoa, or soft, warmed corn tortillas to sop up any remaining bits of mole sauce.

SEITAN IN MOLE SAUCE

Seared, succulent chunks of seitan and spicy-sweet mole sauce will warm you up. Serve with a lightly steamed green, such as chard or collards, to offset some of the richness of the mole and seitan.

2 tablespoons olive oil
1 recipe Simple Seitan (page 205), cut into 1-inch chunks
1 large onion, diced
2 large carrots, peeled and sliced diagonal into ½-inch pieces
½ cup vegetable broth, purchased or homemade (page 223)
2 cups Chile-Chocolate Mole (page 321)
2 tablespoons toasted sesame seeds or slivered almonds
Warm corn tortillas, for serving
Mexican hot sauce, for serving

Preheat a big cast-iron skillet over medium heat. Add 1 tablespoon of the oil and sauté the seitan for 4 to 5 minutes, until it is lightly browned.

Remove the seitan from the pot, set aside, and heat the remaining tablespoon of oil in a pot. Add the onion, sauté for 5 minutes, or until soft, add the carrots plus the vegetable broth, and cover. Steam the carrots for 8 minutes, until partially tender, remove the cover, and stir in the seitan and mole sauce. Mix completely and allow everything to simmer over medium-low heat for 10 to 12 minutes, until the carrots are tender. Remove from the heat, sprinkle with the toasted sesame seeds, and serve directly from the skillet on the table (use a trivet so as to not burn a hole in the dining room table) and pass around the tortillas and favorite Mexican hot sauce.

SERVES 4 TO 6 / TIME: 50 MIN, not including preparing mole sauce

SWEET SQUASH IN MOLE SAUCE

This is a delectable stew of sublime mole sauce and a fresh-tasting blend of summer squash and tropical calabaza pumpkin. Calabaza can be found in most any grocery that carries Latino groceries; it's usually conveniently precut into manageable-size chunks and can be easily peeled with a vegetable peeler. We love it so because it's the pumpkin that's commonly available year-round (note our pumpkin fetish). Sugar pumpkin or butternut squash in season can be substituted instead.

1 pound zucchini, yellow summer, or pattypan squash

Kosher salt

2 tablespoons peanut oil

1 large yellow onion, diced

1 pound calabaza or butternut squash, peeled, seeded, and diced in 1-inch cubes

2 tablespoons water

2 cups Chile-Chocolate Mole (page 321)

2 tablespoons toasted sesame seeds or slivered almonds

Warm corn tortillas, for serving

Mexican hot sauce, for serving

Trim and slice the zucchini into ½-inch-thick rounds and place in a large colander. Sprinkle a few large pinches of kosher salt onto the zucchini and rub to coat each piece. Allow the colander to remain in the kitchen sink or over a bowl for at least 30 minutes to allow the excess moisture to drain from the squash. If you haven't prepared the mole sauce already, this is a good time to do so. Rinse and allow the zucchini to drain before using.

Heat the peanut oil in a cast-iron skillet over medium heat. Add the onion and sauté until slightly softened and translucent, 5 minutes. Add the diced calabaza squash and water and partially cover. Steam for 8 to 10 minutes, or until the squash is partially tender but not completely cooked.

Remove the cover, add the drained zucchini, and sauté for 5 minutes. Add the mole sauce, lower the heat slightly, and stir to completely combine the squash juices with the sauce. Simmer for 10 to 12 minutes, or until both kinds of squash are tender. Remove from the heat, sprinkle with the toasted sesame seeds, and serve directly from the skillet on the table (use a trivet so as to not burn a hole in the dining room table) and pass around the tortillas and favorite Mexican hot sauce.

SERVES 4 TO 6 / TIME: 50 MIN, not including preparing mole sauce

TIP

Don't skip the salting-the-zucchini step; it really helps the zucchini slices keep their shape and fully develop their flavor. Salting does this by removing the excess water that usually makes sautéed summer squash fall apart. Cutting the squash into ½-inch-thick cuts will also help retain its shape.

STIR-FRIED
CHICKPEA & CAULIFLOWER CURRY

SERVES 4 / TIME: ABOUT 30 MIN

2 tablespoons virgin coconut oil, softened

1 (14-ounce) can chickpeas, drained and rinsed

3 cups cauliflower, cut into bite-size pieces

2 star anise

1 teaspoon cumin seeds

1 teaspoon nigella seeds (optional but awesome)

2 teaspoons garam masala

1 to 2 fresh red chiles, minced

1 (1-inch) piece fresh ginger

1 (1-inch) piece fresh turmeric, or ½ teaspoon ground turmeric

2 cloves garlic, minced

1 cup diced yellow onion (1-inch chunks)

1 red bell pepper, seeded and diced into 1-inch chunks

1 (15-ounce) can diced tomatoes (preferable fire-roasted)

½ teaspoon salt, or to taste

1 to 2 tablespoons fresh lime juice, or to taste

½ cup roughly chopped fresh cilantro

A chunky, spicy stir-fried curry that's fast enough for weeknights and has big fresh flavors that no takeout can come close to. This recipe is inspired by the Indian-British *jalfrezi* curries, using typically Indian seasonings and ingredients with Chinese cooking techniques: what we really have here is a great way to use your favorite vegetables, beans, even tofu in a fast-cooking stir-fry loaded with bold Indian flavors. As this is a "dry" curry, moist but not too soupy, it's ideal for scooping up with Yogurt Naan Bread (page 338) or basmati rice that's cool enough to handle.

Make this curry twice, and you'll be ready to experiment by preparing the following batches with different proteins and vegetables in place of the chickpeas and cauliflower. Seared extra firm tofu in place of chickpeas or eggplant in place of cauliflower will make this feel a little more Chinese, but you can sway it toward a more Indian feel by using pumpkin or okra.

Heat about 2 teaspoons of the coconut oil in a wok or large deep skillet over medium-high heat, add the chickpeas, and fry for 3 minutes, or until golden. Add the cauliflower and fry for another 5 minutes, or until it browns a little on the outside. Transfer the chickpea mixture to a bowl and place the remaining 4 teaspoons of coconut oil in the wok.

Heat the wok over high heat and stir in the star anise, cumin seeds, nigella seeds (if you have them), garam masala, minced chile, ginger, turmeric, and garlic and fry for less than a minute, stirring constantly to prevent burning. Stir in the onion immediately (this will cool down the pan to prevent burning), add the bell pepper, and fry for 2 minutes to soften up the veggies. Stir in the chickpea mixture, add the tomatoes and salt, and simmer for 10 to 12 minutes: the cauliflower will release moisture and the vegetables will simmer. The curry is done when the cauliflower is tender but still firm and the curry has thickened; the curry should be a little saucy but not overly soupy like stew.

Turn off the heat, sprinkle with lime juice and cilantro, and serve hot with naan bread!

VARIATIONS

REPLACE THE CHICKPEAS with extra-firm tofu sliced into ½-inch cubes; make sure to brown them well before adding vegetables.

REPLACE THE CAULIFLOWER with peeled, seeded, and diced winter squash (butternut, acorn, Hubbard, etc.); okra, sliced into 1-inch pieces; or Chinese eggplant, diced into 1-inch cubes.

IF USING WINTER SQUASH, the cooking process may take a little longer and require a few additional tablespoons of water to help soften up the squash. Just allow it to simmer to reduce the total liquid volume for a nice thick curry!

SAUTÉED
SEITAN
with Mushrooms & Spinach

SERVES 4 / TIME: 35 MIN

1 tablespoon olive oil

2 cups seitan, sliced on the diagonal into bite-size pieces

1 small onion, sliced into thick half-moons

2 cups sliced white or cremini mushrooms

3 cloves garlic, minced

1 teaspoon dried thyme

½ teaspoon dried basil

1 teaspoon salt

Several pinches of freshly ground black pepper

¼ cup white wine

¼ cup vegetable broth, purchased or homemade (page 223), or water

6 cups spinach, washed well

Lemon slices (optional)

One of our testers remarked that this is how Julia Child would have cooked if she had been vegan. Simple, fast preparation makes this a great choice for a weeknight date or for any time when you want something a little fancy but don't have much time. Serve over quinoa or mashed potatoes or rice or . . . you get the picture.

Preheat a large, lidded skillet over medium-high heat. Sauté the seitan in the oil for about 2 minutes. Add the onion and sauté for another 5 minutes, or until softened, covering the pan but lifting the lid to stir occasionally to make the onion and seitan cook faster.

Add the mushrooms, garlic, thyme, basil, salt, and pepper and sauté for another 8 minutes, again covering but occasionally stirring. Once the mushrooms are cooked and soft, add the wine and broth. Add the spinach in batches and use tongs to incorporate it with everything else. Cook for about 5 more minutes.

Serve immediately, with slices of lemon, if desired.

CHAPTER NINE

PASTA, NOODLES & RISOTTO

Sometimes pasta just seems too good to be true.

What did we ever do to deserve to be on the same planet with a food so easy to make, (usually) inexpensive, and always fun to eat? The world needs more pasta-like miracles.

Not only that, but pasta and noodles are a vegan godsend when it comes to making a quick, substantial weeknight dinner. A bag of whole wheat spirals is transformed by the addition of vegetables, a little olive oil, and garlic. We're especially in love with how a can of crushed tomatoes and a little time on the stove can make a homemade sauce that rivals anything you'll pour out of a jar. And although pasta is sometimes thought of as void of nutrition, we've been digging the fiber-ific whole wheat, brown rice, and quinoa varieties, as well as gluten-free brown rice pasta.

Even if you're an old hand at whipping up spaghetti, you'll find something to love in this collection of old-time favorites and exciting new combinations. You want lasagne? We got your lasagne layered with creamy basil–tofu ricotta and homemade sauce right here! Too lazy to make eggplant Parm? We have roasted eggplant, garlicky bread crumbs, and fettuccine to soothe your soul. Go east with a lively, rich Japanese-style curry stir-fry of udon with seitan. Or head to the coast and savor California-inspired spinach linguine, spiked with fresh lime juice and wrapped around delicately sautéed chunks of avocado.

Last but never the least, a duo of risottos will get you excited about standing over a hot stove in ways you never dreamed possible. Take your pick from lively lemon and fresh peas or tender asparagus scented with exotic lemongrass. Impress your guests or just even yourself with how a bag of rice and a little elbow grease can become the creamiest, comforting food in existence.

-------------- ◆ ---------------

We usually don't eat spaghetti, opting instead for more interestingly shaped pastas, but we absolutely have to have spaghetti with meatball-type comfort meals or the world just feels off kilter. These "meatballs" can be baked or panfried, depending on your mood. Begin your sauce right before preparing the beanballs because you will need some of it for this recipe.

Prepare the beanball mixture: We're going to use the food processor fit with a metal S blade for most of the work here, so it should come together pretty quickly. First, toss in the garlic and pulse until finely chopped. Now, add the onion and pulse until minced. You don't want any big pieces, or else they will ruin the texture of the meatball.

With a plastic spatula, transfer the onion mixture to a mixing bowl and set aside. It's okay if some remnants are left; just try to get most of it.

Now, in the food processor, pulse the lentils, nutritional yeast, wheat gluten, soy sauce, tomato paste, oil, and water. Once everything gets mixed well, puree until totally smooth, scraping down the sides to make sure you get everything.

Combine this mixture with the onion mixture and add the herbs and bread crumbs. Mix really well with your hands for about 2 minutes.

Preheat the oven to 350°F.

Roll the meatballs into golf ball–size balls. This goes very fast if you keep your hands clean and dry. You should get around sixteen balls. Preheat a large skillet over medium heat and pour in a thin layer of olive oil. You don't want to crowd the pan, so panfry in two batches. You should be able to tilt the pan and have all the meatballs roll around and get coated in oil, cooking until browned (no more than 5 minutes).

Transfer the first batch to a baking pan, cook the second batch, and transfer those to the baking pan as well. Bake for 18 to 20 minutes, shaking the pan every once in a while to toss the balls so that they cook evenly.

Bring a large pot of salted water to a boil, for the spaghetti. Boil the pasta according to the package directions, starting right about now, for perfect timing.

When the beanballs are browned on all sides, add ⅓ cup of marinara sauce to them, and toss to coat. Cook for an additional 15 minutes.

To assemble: Drain your spaghetti and put it back in the pot. Pour your remaining marinara sauce over the pasta and mix. Use a pasta spoon to transfer the spaghetti to plates, then top with three or four beanballs.

SPAGHETTI & BEANBALLS

SERVES 4 / TIME: 40 MIN

Beanballs:

1 clove garlic

1 small onion, peeled

1½ cups cooked green or brown lentils, rinsed and drained (a 15-ounce can is fine)

3 tablespoons nutritional yeast

2 tablespoons vital wheat gluten flour

2 tablespoons soy sauce

1 tablespoon tomato paste

1 teaspoon olive oil, plus more for panfrying

2 tablespoons water

½ teaspoon dried thyme

½ teaspoon dried oregano

½ cup plain vegan bread crumbs

1 recipe (5 cups) Marinara Sauce, any variation (page 314)

½ pound spaghetti

-45

SPICY
TEMPEH & BROCCOLI RABE

with Rotelle

SERVES 4 / TIME: 40 MIN

½ pound whole wheat or bean-based rotelle or other spiral-shaped pasta

1 to 2 teaspoons olive oil

Spicy fennel tempeh:

1 (15-ounce) package tempeh, cubed

½ cup plus 2 tablespoons vegetable broth, purchased or homemade (page 223)

2 tablespoons tomato paste

2 tablespoons soy sauce

1 clove garlic, pressed

1 tablespoon fennel seeds

1½ teaspoons red pepper flakes, or more to taste

1½ teaspoons dried oregano

½ teaspoon red wine vinegar

2 tablespoons olive oil

Broccoli rabe:

2 tablespoons olive oil

5 cloves garlic, sliced thinly

1 bunch broccoli rabe (½ to ¾ pound), tough stems trimmed, chopped coarsely

Salt

2 tablespoons white wine, water, or vegetable broth, purchased or homemade (page 223)

2 teaspoons red wine vinegar or balsamic vinegar

Freshly ground black pepper

TIP

If you don't like the bitter edge of broccoli rabe, simply substitute regular broccoli, trimming it into bite-size pieces.

We still adore the bittersweet flavor of broccoli rabe (also called broccoli rape, rapini, or rabini) matched with whole wheat pasta and peppery braised tempeh. Spiral-shaped pasta nicely captures the tiny bits of tempeh, red pepper, and olive oil, but substitute any shape you like, or use one of the new and hearty bean-based pastas out there, made with chickpeas, edamame, or lentils of all kinds. Our recipes testers loved how it was a perfect balance of pasta, protein, and greens; we love that it's fast, fun to make, and pleases even the most die-hard Italian sausage 'n' pasta fan.

Bring a large pot of salted water to a boil, add the pasta, and cook according to the package directions, usually about 10 minutes. Drain the pasta, toss with a teaspoon or two of the oil, and keep covered either in a large, covered serving bowl or the cooking pot. While your pasta is boiling, prepare the other ingredients.

Prepare the tempeh: First, we'll steam the tempeh in a spicy marinade. In a measuring cup, whisk together the vegetable broth, tomato paste, soy sauce, garlic, fennel seeds, red pepper flakes, oregano, and vinegar. Combine the marinade with the tempeh in a large, nonstick skillet. Bring the mixture to a boil over high heat. Then, lower the heat to medium, cover the pan, and steam the tempeh for about 8 minutes, or until the liquid is absorbed, stirring occasionally. Transfer the tempeh to a bowl and crush about half of the cubes with the back of a spoon.

Wipe down the skillet to remove any leftover tempeh sauce, return the skillet to medium heat, then add the oil. To test the heat, drop a bit of tempeh into the oil—when it sizzles, the oil is hot enough. Add the tempeh and stir-fry for 4 to 5 minutes, until it begins to brown. Remove from the heat, add to the pasta, and keep covered.

Prepare the broccoli rabe: Heat the oil over medium heat and add the sliced garlic. When the garlic begins to sizzle, cook it, stirring, for about a minute. Add the broccoli rabe, stir to coat it with the oil, sprinkle with a little salt, and cover the pan. Steam for 2 minutes. Sprinkle with 2 tablespoons of the white wine and steam for about 4 to 6 minutes, until the broccoli rabe is bright green and its stems are tender. Depending on the size of your skillet, you may need to do this in two batches; just add the second batch of broccoli rabe as soon as the first batch has softened slightly and there's a little extra room in your pan.

Remove the cover, sprinkle with a little salt to taste, and continue to sauté for an additional minute or two, until any excess liquid is evaporated. Transfer the cooked broccoli rabe to the bowl with the tempeh and pasta and toss with the vinegar and pepper. Use a pasta spoon to divvy up onto plates, or place everything in a big pasta bowl and serve family style.

LINGUINE

with Basil-Cilantro Pesto & Artichokes

SERVES 4 / TIME: 35 MIN

½ pound spinach linguine

2 tablespoons olive oil

1 medium-size red onion, sliced into thin half-moons

4 cloves garlic, thinly sliced

2 tablespoons white cooking wine, vegetable broth, purchased or homemade (page 223), or water, whatever

½ teaspoon salt

Several pinches of freshly ground black pepper

1 recipe Basil-Cilantro Pesto (page 325)

1 (15-ounce) can artichoke hearts, drained and sliced in half (don't use the jarred kind in oil, it's expensive and too oily for this; get the kind that comes in brine)

TIP

Make your pesto while the water for the linguine is boiling, so that you can time this right.

You will be craving this from now on, mark our words. Spinach linguine is sautéed with fragrant pesto, while red onions add just a hint of sweetness, color, and texture. Don't replace the red onions with regular ones unless you really can't find a red onion within miles. Artichokes round everything out and give a great bite. This also makes a great fast and fancy meal if your in-laws or the IRS decides to drop by for a surprise visit.

Bring a large pot of salted water to a boil and cook the linguine according to the package directions, usually about 10 minutes. Once you've added the pasta to the water, proceed with the recipe.

Preheat a large skillet over medium-high heat and sauté the onion in the oil until softened, 5 to 7 minutes. Add the garlic and sauté for a minute more. Add the white wine, salt, and pepper, and cook for another minute or two. Lower the heat to low. At this point, the linguine should be done.

When the linguine is ready, don't drain it. Use a pasta spoon to transfer it to the pan in batches. This is a good method because you can use the pasta water to thin out the pesto and make sure that everything gets evenly coated. When you add one batch, add a bit of the pesto, too, and using the pasta spoon, sauté to coat. Proceed with the rest of the pasta and pesto until you've added all of it. If it seems dry, add extra splashes of pasta water.

Add the artichoke hearts and toss to coat. Cook gently over low heat just until the artichokes are heated through, about 3 minutes. Serve immediately!

If we said in the title that this was pasta with avocados, no one would take us seriously, so instead we call it Pasta Della California. Anything with avocado in it can be called "California," right? Anyway, this is so damn good. The pasta is sautéed in lots of garlic and lime along with broccoli and peppery arugula. Then the avocados are gently tossed in just until they are warm. So, if the idea of "cooked" avocados scares you, don't worry. This is especially astounding with the Smoky Grilled Tempeh (page 201).

Bring a large pot of water to a boil and prep all your ingredients while the water boils, because this dish comes together in no time. Once the water is boiling, add the pasta and cook according to the package directions, usually about 10 minutes. In the last minute of cooking you will be adding the broccoli, so keep that in mind.

Meanwhile, heat a large nonstick skillet over medium heat. Add the oil, garlic, lime zest, and red pepper flakes and gently heat, stirring often, for about 2 minutes, being careful not to burn the garlic. Pour in the wine and increase the heat to bring to a boil, to reduce the wine, about 2 minutes. Add the vegetable broth, lime juice, salt, and pepper, and bring again to a boil. Once the sauce is boiling, lower the heat to a simmer. Add the arugula.

By this point the pasta should be almost done, so add the broccoli to the boiling pasta and cook for 1 more minute. Drain all into a colander.

When the arugula is wilted, add the pasta mixture to the pan and use a pasta spoon to toss it around, making sure to get everything coated in garlic. Cook for about 3 more minutes. Add the avocado and turn off the heat. Gently toss the pasta for another minute to incorporate the avocado without smushing it, just until it is warmed through.

Serve with generous grinds of black pepper. There is usually a lot of garlic left in the pan, so be sure to spoon that over your bowls of pasta.

PASTA
DELLA CALIFORNIA

SERVES 4 / TIME: 35 MIN

½ **pound linguine**

2 **tablespoons olive oil**

8 **cloves garlic, minced (yes, 8, that's not a typo!)**

¼ **teaspoon freshly grated lime zest**

½ **teaspoon red pepper flakes**

¼ **cup white wine**

1 **cup vegetable broth, purchased or homemade (page 223)**

2 **tablespoons fresh lime juice**

½ **teaspoon salt**

Several pinches of freshly ground black pepper

4 **cups loosely packed arugula leaves**

3 **cups sliced broccoli (tops cut into small florets, stalks sliced thinly)**

2 **avocados, peeled, pitted, and sliced into 1-inch chunks (see tip)**

TIP

Choose avocados that are ripe but still firm. An avocado that is too mushy and has brown spots will not work here. If it's warm in your house, once the avocado is ripe you should refrigerate it for several hours—this way, it will hold its shape when peeled and sliced. For this recipe, slice the avocado in half and remove the pit. Peel off the skin, then slice each half lengthwise down the middle. Next, slice across into chunks.

PENNE VODKA

SERVES 4 / TIME: 35 MIN

½ cup unroasted whole cashews, soaked for 2 hours

½ cup water

1 (28-ounce) can crushed tomatoes

2 teaspoons olive oil

4 cloves minced garlic

¼ teaspoon red pepper flakes

¼ cup vodka

¼ teaspoon dried thyme

¼ teaspoon dried oregano

½ teaspoon salt

A few pinches of freshly ground black pepper

½ pound penne pasta

¼ cup finely chopped fresh basil, plus a little more for garnish

No Brooklyn Italian restaurant is complete without this classic creamy tomato dish. We blend cashews into the sauce to get that expected creaminess and a little fresh basil to bring it home.

In a blender, combine cashews with the water and half of the crushed tomatoes. Blend until completely smooth. Set aside.

Bring a pot of water to boil for the pasta. Preheat a saucepan over medium-low heat. Add the oil, garlic, and red pepper flakes to the saucepan and sauté for about a minute, until fragrant, being careful not to burn. Add the remaining crushed tomatoes, vodka, thyme, oregano, salt, and black pepper. Cook for about 5 minutes over high heat, then add the cashew mixture, cover, and bring to a simmer. Cook for about 15 minutes, stirring occasionally. Meanwhile, add the pasta to the boiling water and cook according to the package directions.

When the pasta is cooked, drain and set aside in the pot. Add the basil to the sauce, then mix the sauce and pasta together in the pot. Serve, garnished with a little extra chopped basil.

Sometimes pronounced pasta fazool by real New Yorkers, fagioli is beans to you, bub. This is a simple but filling dish that is made from fresh plum tomatoes that are cooked down with garlic and herbs. The light fresh taste and texture go well with the heartiness of the beans. We suggest white beans—cannellini, navy, or great northern—but use kidney or garbanzos if that floats your legume boat.

Bring a pot of water to boil for the pasta and heat another large pan over medium heat.

Prepare the sauce: Place the oil and garlic in the large pan and sauté for about 1 minute, until the garlic is fragrant. Add the tomatoes, wine, thyme, oregano, pepper, and salt. Bring to a boil, then lower the heat to medium and cook until the tomatoes are broken down and the sauce is reduced and thickened, about 20 minutes.

Meanwhile, add pasta to the water and cook according to the package directions.

Once the sauce is thickened, simmer over low heat to keep warm. Drain the pasta and set aside. When the sauce is finished, add the beans and pasta and use a pasta spoon to mix. Serve when pasta and beans are heated through, about 3 minutes.

PASTA E FAGIOLI

SERVES 4 / TIME: 35 MIN

Sauce:

2 tablespoons olive oil

6 cloves garlic, minced

2 pounds plum tomatoes, cut into ½-inch dice

¼ cup dry white wine or vegetable broth, purchased or homemade (page 223)

½ teaspoon dried thyme

½ teaspoon dried oregano

A few pinches of freshly ground black pepper

1 teaspoon salt

½ pound small tube-shaped pasta, such as penette or tubetti, or even small shells

1 (16-ounce) can white beans, drained and rinsed

Can't get enough pumpkin in your life? Then this creamy baked pasta casserole will get you into a fall-leaves-and-crisp-cool-days state of mind with pumpkin-laced tofu-cashew ricotta, caramelized onions, sage, and a hint of nutmeg. Serve alongside lightly braised chard or an arugula salad tossed with a little shaved fennel.

Over the years we have updated this fan favorite, crowd-pleasing recipe to include a zestier pumpkin filling, easier caramelized onions, and improved herb crumb topping. And if you're looking for something stunning to bring to your next vegan Thanksgiving table, this dish makes a kick-butt centerpiece and feeds the crowd.

Prepare the ziti according to the package directions but cook only until al dente (do not overcook). Drain into a colander and rinse with plenty of cold water.

While the pasta is cooking, make the caramelized onion: Preheat a large, heavy-bottomed pan, preferably cast iron, over medium heat. Add the onions, oil, and just a tiny pinch of baking soda (this will help speed up the caramelization process) and sauté. Continue to fry the onions, stirring occasionally, until very soft and deeply caramelized, about 15 minutes. Turn off the heat.

Meanwhile, preheat the oven to 375°F. Rub a 9 x 13-inch casserole dish with olive oil.

Combine the cashew ricotta, maple syrup, paprika, thyme, salt, nutmeg, cayenne, pumpkin puree, milk, and black pepper in a large mixing bowl. Add the caramelized onions. Shake any excess water from the cooked pasta and stir into the pumpkin mixture. Pour into the oiled casserole dish and smooth the top.

Prepare the bread crumbs: Clean and dry the mixing bowl you just used for the pasta layer and use it to combine the bread crumbs, walnuts, nutritional yeast, sage, rosemary, and salt. Drizzle with the oil and rub the oil into the crumbs. Sprinkle the crumbs evenly over the top of the casserole. Bake the casserole, uncovered, for 30 minutes, or until the crumb topping is golden brown. Remove from the oven and let cool for 10 minutes. Scoop servings with a big spoon or wide spatula.

TIP If you've never made homemade bread crumbs before, try it today, as store-bought crumbs won't have the same crunchy texture. It really makes a difference in this recipe—the top layer of crumbs contrasts wonderfully with the chewy, rich bottom layer of pasta. Simply tear up your old bread and process in a food processor until you get coarse crumbs.

SERVES 6 TO 8 / TIME: 1 HR

¾ pound uncooked ziti or penne pasta

1 pound yellow onions, sliced very thinly

3 tablespoons olive oil, plus more for baking dish

Pinch of baking soda

1 recipe Cashew Ricotta (page 315)

1 tablespoon pure maple syrup

1 teaspoon sweet paprika

1 teaspoon dried thyme

½ teaspoon salt

¼ teaspoon freshly grated nutmeg

¼ teaspoon cayenne pepper

2 cups pureed pumpkin, or 1 (15-ounce) can pure pumpkin puree (don't use pumpkin pie mix)

½ cup unsweetened almond or coconut-based milk

A few big twists of freshly ground black pepper

Sage bread crumbs:

1½ cups white bread crumbs, preferably homemade from ciabatta bread

⅓ cup walnut pieces, chopped in a food processor into coarse crumbs

3 tablespoons nutritional yeast

1 tablespoon finely chopped fresh sage, or 1 teaspoon dried

1 teaspoon dried rosemary

½ teaspoon salt

¼ cup olive oil

MAC DADDY

SERVES 8 TO 10 / TIME: 1 HR 10 MIN

2 recipes Cheezy Sauce (page 326)
¾ pound elbow macaroni
1 pound extra-firm tofu
1 teaspoon salt
1 tablespoon olive oil
2 tablespoons fresh lemon juice

Here she is, the ultimate in comfort food: our version of mac and cheese. We use mashed tofu to give this dish body and douse it in Cheezy Sauce (page 326) for creaminess. Serve with a very simple salad of baby greens or arugula with oil and red wine vinegar. This is the perfect thing to use up all your vegetable odds and ends, so see our variations. Any vegan potluck would be incomplete without Mac Daddy, but since omnivores tend to be sketchy about nutritional yeast, save this for appreciative vegans and vegetarians.

Bring a large pot of salted water to a boil. Add the macaroni and cook according to the package directions, about 10 minutes. Meanwhile, prepare your Cheezy Sauce.

Preheat the oven to 325°F. When the pasta is ready, drain and set aside. When the sauce is ready, begin assembling.

To assemble: Crumble the tofu into an 11 x 13-inch glass or ceramic baking dish. Mash the tofu with your hands until it resembles ricotta cheese. Add the salt, oil, and lemon juice, then stir.

Add ½ cup of Cheezy Sauce to the tofu and stir. Use a dry measuring cup with a handle so that you can just dip it into the sauce and pour—you don't need to be very precise. Add the macaroni to the tofu, along with 3 more cups of sauce, and stir well.

Smooth the top of the pasta mixture and press it down with a spatula to level it. Then, pour the remaining sauce over the pasta and smooth again.

Bake for 30 minutes; the top of the macaroni should be slightly browned. It's a good idea to wait about 20 minutes before serving, so that it can cool down and firm up a bit, but if you can't wait, more power to you.

VARIATIONS

MAC & PEAS: Add 2 cups of frozen peas when you add the macaroni to the casserole.

BROC MAC DADDY: Add 3 cups of small broccoli florets when you add the macaroni.

AUTUMN MAC DADDY: Add 3 cups of roasted or boiled butternut squash when you add the macaroni. Omit the thyme from the nutritional yeasty sauce and add 1 teaspoon of freshly grated nutmeg.

SPICY MAC DADDY: Add ¾ teaspoon of red pepper flakes to the nutritional yeasty sauce when you add the pepper.

MAC & GREENS: Add 4 cups of finely chopped kale, spinach, or chard when you add the macaroni.

MAC & CHICKS: Instead of tofu, use 2 cups of mashed chickpeas.

Lasagne is a great way to showcase how delicious vegan cooking can be. It's endlessly versatile, depending on what flavor you feel like making the Marinara Sauce (page 314), what fresh vegetables are found at the market that day, which Tofu Ricotta (page 315) is used, and whether the Cashew Tofu Cream (page 256) is featured on top. Lasagne can be served alone or with a sprinkling of Almesan (page 316), breadsticks, and a crisp green salad.

As this recipe is made of other recipes, divide the prep work over a few days: make the marinara and filling the day before (that's plenty of cooking for one day!), then the next day you'll be bright eyed and ready to build a lasagne. If you have a favorite way of assembling lasagne, go right ahead and use that instead. We've included directions for the traditional boiled noodle and the "controversial" no-cook pasta method. Both methods work great here.

Prepare the Marinara Sauce, the Tofu Ricotta, the Almesan, and if using, the Cashew Tofu Cream. When you've achieved all of that, preheat the oven to 375°F. Have ready to go a 9 x 13-inch casserole pan and a double layer of aluminum foil that can tightly cover the pan.

Wash the spinach well, drain, and place in a steamer basket in a large pot. Cover and steam for 8 minutes, until the spinach is wilted. Remove from the heat, uncover, and let cool. Squeeze handfuls of the spinach to remove the excess water and finely chop. Fold the spinach into the Tofu Ricotta and season with salt and pepper to taste.

Ladle about ½ cup of sauce into the bottom of the lasagne pan and layer with five or six noodles, either precooked or raw. Add about half of the tofu ricotta and about one third of the sauce. Add another layer of noodles (four or five), the rest of the ricotta, and another third of the sauce. Top with the remaining noodles, then top the noodles with the remaining sauce.

If using uncooked noodles, gently pour 1 cup of warm water over the top of the assembled casserole, being careful to pour into the gaps between noodles and the edges of the pan as well. Skip this step if using cooked noodles. Generously sprinkle Almesan on top of the lasagne before baking.

Tightly crimp two overlapping layers of foil over the top of the pan. Bake for 30 to 35 minutes, or until the pasta is tender, then remove the foil and bake for another 20 minutes, or until the edges of the noodles are slightly browned and the sauce is bubbling. Allow to cool for 10 minutes before slicing. Best if served with additional marinara sauce (see tip).

VARIATIONS

MUSHROOM-SPINACH LASAGNE: In addition to the spinach layers, add 1 pound of white button or cremini mushrooms, sliced thinly and sautéed in 2 tablespoons of olive oil. Cook until all of the water has evaporated and the mushrooms are browned and tender.

WHITE & RED LASAGNE: After removing the foil for the final baking step, top the lasagne with Cashew Tofu Cream. Bake for an additional 20 to 24 minutes, until the topping is lightly browned and cracked.

LASAGNE MARINARA
with Spinach

SERVES 6 TO 8 / TIME: 1½ HRS

2 recipes Marinara Sauce (page 314), plain or any variation (roasted garlic is particularly good here)

2 recipes Tofu Ricotta (page 315) or Cashew Ricotta (page 315)

1 recipe Almesan (page 316)

1 recipe Cashew Tofu Cream from Moussaka recipe (page 256; optional)

2 pounds spinach or a mix of spinach and other greens (kale, chard, dandelion, etc.)

Salt and freshly ground black pepper

1 (1-pound) package lasagna noodles, cooked according to the package directions or left uncooked

TIPS

The recipe calls for a double batch of Marinara Sauce, which makes an evenly moist but not overly saucy casserole. For deliciously saucy lasagne, triple the sauce and reserve one third for ladling over individual servings.

You can prepare the noodles either by the traditional "boiling first" method or by layering the uncooked noodles into the casserole and pouring a scant 1 cup of water over the entire assembled casserole before baking. The precooking method is more work but results in a "neater" layered lasagne. The uncooked method is very easy and less messy but the noodles tend to curl up a bit during the baking, which doesn't matter much if additional sauce will be poured on top of individual servings.

SAVORY
BUTTERNUT RISOTTO

SERVES 4 / TIME: 2 HRS

½ cup raw cashews, soaked for at least 2 hours, or boiled for 20 minutes

3 pounds butternut squash

2 tablespoons olive oil, plus more for baking sheet

1 cup thinly sliced shallot

10 cloves garlic, sliced thinly

2 tablespoons chopped fresh thyme

1 tablespoon chopped fresh rosemary

½ teaspoon red pepper flakes

1½ cups Arborio rice

⅓ cup dry white cooking wine

½ teaspoon salt

6 to 7 cups warm vegetable broth, purchased or homemade (page 223)

½ teaspoon freshly grated nutmeg

2 tablespoons fresh lemon juice

TIP

If you'd like to add some crunch (and protein) to this risotto, roasted pumpkin seeds, toasted walnuts, or pine nuts would all be good choices. For some green, how about roasted Brussels sprouts or broccoli? You can roast them in the oven with the squash for about 15 minutes.

This is creaminess three ways. First, the natural starches in Arborio rice, locking in all of the amazing flavors of shallot and garlic. Then, the squash itself, a little sweet, delicate, and earthy. And lastly, the cashew cream, rich and decadent. The wine and thyme bring out the savory nuance of the butternut, and you know what, risotto doesn't have to be difficult. Everything is pretty simple, but still really special. Like you.

First prepare the squash: Preheat the oven to 425°F. Cut the long part off of the round part and slice in half lengthwise. Now, cut the round part in half lengthwise and remove the seeds with a tablespoon. Line a rimmed baking sheet, lightly oil, and place the squash on it, cut side down. Bake for about 35 minutes, or until easily pierced with a fork, but not completely mushy. Remove from the oven and let cool to the touch. Once cooled, peel off the skin and chop the pumpkin into bite-sized pieces.

While the squash is cooking, make the cashew cream: Drain the cashews and place in a blender with 1 cup of the vegetable broth. Puree until smooth.

In the meantime, start the risotto: Preheat a heavy-bottomed pot over medium heat. Sauté the shallot, garlic, thyme, rosemary, and red pepper flakes in the oil for about 7 minutes, stirring often so that it doesn't burn. A slanted wooden spoon is the perfect tool for stirring. Add the rice and stir to coat with the oil. Add the wine to deglaze the pot, then add the first cup of warm vegetable broth along with the salt. Stir until most of the water is absorbed. You don't have to stir the entire time, just as frequently as you can.

Continue adding veggie broth by the cupful, then stirring a few more times, until only a cup of broth is left. It should take about 45 minutes, and by this point your squash should be ready to add. When you're at the last cup, add the prepared squash. When most of the liquid has absorbed, add the nutmeg and lemon juice. Stir in the cashew cream. Cook for about 5 more minutes, stirring occasionally. Taste and adjust the salt.

It's now ready to serve!

ASPARAGUS & LEMONGRASS
RISOTTO

SERVES 4 TO 6 / TIME: 1 HR 20 MIN

Lemongrass broth:

1 small stalk lemongrass, or 1 tablespoon dried, chopped

3 cloves garlic, whole and unpeeled

1 teaspoon black peppercorns

1 large yellow onion, unpeeled, sliced in half

1 (1-inch) piece fresh ginger

6 cups vegetable broth, purchased or homemade (page 223)

½ teaspoon salt, or more to taste

Risotto:

1 pound asparagus, tough ends trimmed

¼ cup peanut oil or refined coconut oil

6 large shallots, sliced thinly

2 cloves garlic, unpeeled

⅓ cup inexpensive sake or white wine

1 serrano red chile, sliced very thinly, or ½ to 1 teaspoon red pepper flakes

1½ cups Arborio rice

2 tablespoons fresh lime juice

1 cup fresh basil leaves (Thai basil preferred), rolled and sliced into very thin strips

2 tablespoons chopped fresh mint

Chopped roasted peanuts, for garnish

Lime wedges, for garnish

TIP

You'll need to make a mini bouquet garni when preparing the broth: it sounds intense but we promise this makes the whole broth-making process easier. Tuck the lemongrass into a small, porous pouch along with the peppercorns and garlic. Tie the top tightly; it should hold together during the simmer. Long, empty tea bags sold for use with loose-leaf tea are ideal for this. You can also use cheesecloth and tie it into a little bundle, but double- or triple-layer it to make sure none of the lemongrass bits leak into the broth.

Find your purpose in life with this unusual risotto. You begin by pondering your existence while stirring aromatic vegetables in Arborio rice. Gradually add a steaming broth (updated with traditional pho broth flavoring techniques) scented with lemongrass, shallots, and ginger. After stirring for a few years this luscious, creamy asparagus risotto with a decidedly Thai twist will burst deliciously into life. It's delightful served garnished with chopped roasted peanuts and a twist of lime, or serve alongside grilled Tangerine Baked Tofu (page 193) for a complete meal. Existential crisis over.

Prepare the lemongrass broth: If using fresh lemongrass, peel away and discard any brown stems from the stalk. Slice the stalk in half lengthwise, cut those sections into 3- to 4-inch lengths, and then slice into thin matchstick pieces.

Lightly flatten the ginger by gently pounding it with the side of your knife. Crush the garlic cloves with the side of your knife as well, but keep whole; just lay the flat part of the blade over a clove of garlic and give it a good whack. Prepare a bouquet garni with the lemongrass, garlic, and peppercorns as described in the tip.

Arrange the sliced onion and the ginger in a cast-iron skillet. Sear over high heat for about 10 minutes, or until the cut side of the onion is blackened, then turn off the heat. Transfer the blackened stuff to a large stockpot, add the peppercorns, veggie broth, salt, and lemongrass bouquet garni, and bring to a boil, then lower the heat to medium-low. Simmer for 10 minutes, then lower the heat to low.

Prepare the risotto: Slice the asparagus into ½-inch pieces, removing any tough parts from the bottom of the stem. Separate tips from the stems and place each in separate small bowls. In a medium-size, heavy-bottomed pot, sauté the asparagus tips in 1 tablespoon of the oil over medium heat until the tips are bright green and crisp-tender, 3 to 4 minutes. Return them to their small bowl. Add 1 more tablespoon of oil to the pot and sauté the sliced asparagus pieces until crisp-tender, 5 minutes.

Add the remaining 2 tablespoons of oil to the pot. Sauté the shallots and garlic, stirring occasionally, until the shallots are very soft and just starting to brown, 6 to 8 minutes. Deglaze the shallots by pouring in the sake and simmer for a minute. Stir in the chile pepper and rice and sauté for about 8 minutes, until the rice smells slightly toasted.

Now meditation time begins. Ladle about ½ cup of the lemongrass broth at a time into the rice, stirring constantly until each addition is absorbed. Cook, stirring, until the rice is creamy but still somewhat firm in the center. When the broth is almost gone, stir the lime juice into the last of the broth before adding to the risotto. You may add more water or additional regular vegetable broth in ¼-cup increments if the broth runs out and the rice isn't cooked enough yet. This will take about 35 minutes.

Stir the asparagus stems (not tips) into the risotto and cook for another 5 minutes, until the asparagus has reached the desired tenderness. Stir in the basil and mint. Garnish individual servings with the sautéed asparagus tips, chopped roasted peanuts, and lime wedges.

This bright-tasting risotto features summer's vivid bounty. Use vegetable broth that isn't too strongly flavored so that the lemon, snap peas, and parsley really shine through. You can gently sauté the snap peas if you don't have a grill pan, nbd.

Toss the snap peas in a bowl with a little olive oil and a pinch of salt. Set aside.

Warm the vegetable broth in a saucepan. Keep it warm on the lowest setting possible as you prepare the risotto. Preheat a heavy-bottomed soup pot over medium heat. Sauté the shallot in 1 tablespoon of oil for about 5 minutes. Add the garlic, thyme, rosemary, and pepper, and sauté for 2 more minutes.

Add the white wine and ½ teaspoon of salt, and increase the heat so that the wine boils and reduces for about 2 minutes. Lower the heat back to medium.

Add the rice and stir for about 3 minutes. The rice should soak up the liquid from the pot and have turned light brown. Add the broth by the cupful, stirring the risotto after each addition, until the broth is mostly absorbed, 6 to 8 minutes. If the broth isn't absorbing, increase the heat a bit. It absorbs faster as the rice gets more and more tender.

During your last addition of broth, preheat a grill pan over medium heat for the snap peas. Meanwhile, add the lemon zest and juice and chopped parsley to the rice and stir until the broth is completely absorbed.

Grill the snap peas for about 2 minutes on each side, just until grill marks appear.

Spoon the risotto into a wide bowl or plate and scatter with the snap peas. Garnish with fresh parsley and serve.

LEMON & GRILLED SNAP PEA
RISOTTO

SERVES 4 / TIME: 45 MIN

2 cups snap peas, trimmed

Olive oil

Salt

6 cups vegetable broth, purchased or homemade (page 223)

1 cup finely chopped shallot

4 cloves garlic, minced

½ teaspoon dried thyme

½ teaspoon dried rosemary

Several pinches of freshly ground black pepper

½ cup dry white wine

1½ cups Arborio rice

2 teaspoons freshly grated lemon zest

2 tablespoons fresh lemon juice

½ cup loosely packed chopped fresh parsley, plus more for garnish

This saucy noodle dish is inspired by the mellow comforting curries that are hugely popular in Japan for lunch and dinner. Or so we hear; we've still never been but when we get there, we expect a whole lot of curry, just like this. While there are plenty of instant curry mixes out there, we love making this from scratch with a flour-based roux and our all-time hero of curry powders, S&B golden curry powder. These are often on the sweet side, but you can leave out the sugar and it's still fabulous. Once the sauce is ready it's as easy as adding cooked udon, bits of sautéed seitan, and crisp veggies. Experiment—change the vegetables, use tofu in place of seitan, try different brands of curry powder (but why mess with the best?)—the variations are endless.

Prepare the udon first: Cook the udon according to the package directions, about 5 minutes. Drain and rinse well with cold water.

Prepare the curry roux sauce: Combine the flour and oil in a small saucepan. Cook over medium-low heat, stirring constantly with a wooden spoon, until the mixture browns to the color of rich caramel and smells toasty, about 8 minutes or less. Stir in the curry powder and garam masala and cook for another minute while stirring constantly. Switch to using a wire whisk, then pour in the vegetable broth in a steady stream. Whisk in the sugar, if using, and cook the roux, stirring constantly, until a thick sauce forms, about 2 minutes. Remove from the heat and set aside.

Proceed to stir-fry: Heat 1 tablespoon of peanut oil in a large nonstick skillet over high heat. Add the seitan and stir-fry until lightly browned, about 5 minutes. Transfer to a plate and wipe the pan clean. Add the onion, ginger, and hot chile, if using, and fry for 2 minutes, or until the onion is slightly softened. Add the bell pepper and stir-fry for 2 minutes, or until it starts to soften. Add the broccoli and stir-fry for 5 minutes, until it looks bright green. Now add the seitan strips!

Return to the udon noodles—if they're sticking together, rinse with warm water and drain. Add the udon to the stir-fried vegetables, sprinkle with soy sauce, and stir-fry for 2 to 3 minutes. It may help to use two large spatulas or extra-large chopsticks (the ones that come with some wok kits) while doing this.

Whisk ¼ cup of the vegetable broth into the curry roux sauce in the saucepan. Pour the sauce over the udon stir-fry and stir to coat everything completely with the sauce. Stir and cook for 2 to 3 minutes, until the sauce is simmering and the noodles are warm. Remove from the heat and serve.

TIPS

You can use either dried or fresh udon noodles for any recipe calling for them. Dried noodles are sold packaged like spaghetti and can be prepared the same way. Cook the noodles according to the package directions till just tender and rinse in cold water. Keep them handy in a colander until ready to use. Give them a brief rinsing in cold water before adding to a soup or stir-fry.

Fresh udon noodles require only a brief cooking time in boiling water (follow the package directions), about 3 to 4 minutes. Drain and rinse with cold water. Rinse again in warm water to unstick any noodles before using.

-45-

CURRIED
UDON NOODLE STIR-FRY

SERVES 4 / TIME: 35 MIN

½ pound fresh or dried udon noodles

Curry roux sauce:
2 tablespoons peanut or vegetable oil
2 tablespoons all-purpose flour
2 teaspoons curry powder
½ teaspoon garam masala
½ cup vegetable broth, purchased or homemade (page 223)
2 teaspoons organic sugar (optional)

Udon stir-fry:
3 tablespoons peanut oil
1 recipe Simple Seitan (page 205), sliced into thin strips, or about 2 cups of thinly sliced seitan
1 large yellow onion, sliced into thin strips
1 teaspoon grated fresh ginger
1 hot red chile pepper, sliced very thinly (optional)
1 red bell pepper, seeded and sliced into thin strips
½ pound broccoli florets, sliced into bite-size chunks
2 to 3 tablespoons soy sauce, preferably shoyu (Japanese soy sauce)
¼ cup vegetable broth, purchased or homemade (page 223)

UDON

WITH SHIITAKE MUSHROOMS
& KALE

in Miso Broth

SERVES 4 / TIME: 35 MIN

½ pound fresh or dried udon noodles

2 tablespoons vegetable oil

1 medium-size red onion, sliced into thin half-moons

4 ounces shiitake mushrooms, stems trimmed, sliced

3 cloves garlic, minced

2 teaspoons minced fresh ginger

2 cups water

2 tablespoons mirin (optional)

3 tablespoons miso (see tip)

2 tablespoons soy sauce, or to taste

4 cups chopped kale

Supersimple ingredients result in superflavorful returns. That sounds a little like a fortune cookie. This is a great weeknight meal that's healthy and hearty. Make it even heartier by adding sautéed seitan to each serving.

Bring a pot of water to a boil. Cook the udon according to the package directions, about 10 minutes. When done, drain and rinse with cool water until ready to use.

Meanwhile, heat a large skillet over medium heat. Sauté the onion and mushrooms in the vegetable oil for 5 to 7 minutes, until the mushrooms are tender and the onion is softened but still has some crunch. Add the garlic and ginger and sauté for another minute.

Add the water, the mirin, if using, the miso, and the soy sauce, and bring to a gentle boil. Lower the heat to a simmer and add the kale. Toss the mixture around with tongs until the kale has wilted. Add the noodles and use a pasta spoon to stir them into the broth for about 2 minutes.

Divide the udon and vegetables among bowls and spoon some broth over each serving.

TIPS

In this recipe, we use a strong, dark miso. If you are using a light, mellow miso, you may want to add another tablespoon or so.

See the Curried Udon Noodle Stir-fry recipe (page 307) for tips on using dried or fresh udon noodles.

For when you want something like eggplant Parmesan but don't want to go through the trouble of breading and frying, this is lazy gourmet at its best. Making a quick, fresh, garlicky tomato sauce is a great way to let the taste of the toasted bread crumbs shine through, but you can replace it with a 20-ounce can of crushed tomatoes if you're pressed for time.

First, prepare your eggplant: Coat the slices generously with salt and set them in a colander to drain for half an hour. In the meantime, prep all your other ingredients.

Rinse the salt off the eggplant and pat dry. Stack your eggplant slices into two piles and cut them in half to form semicircles.

Preheat a large, nonstick or cast-iron pan over medium heat. Add the oil to coat the bottom, then add the eggplant in as much of a single layer as you can. Flip pieces occasionally until the eggplant is softened and lightly browned, 15 to 20 minutes. As it's cooking, keep spraying or drizzling more oil in to keep the eggplant moist.

Meanwhile, bring a pot of water to boil for the pasta and heat another large pan over medium heat.

Prepare the sauce: Place the oil and garlic in the heated large pan and sauté for about 1 minute, until the garlic is fragrant. Add the tomatoes, wine, oregano, pepper, and salt. (Don't add too much salt because the eggplant may be a little salty; you can adjust later if need be.) Bring to a boil and then lower the heat to medium. Cook until the tomatoes are broken down and the sauce is reduced and thickened, about 20 minutes. If using canned crushed tomatoes, 10 minutes will be fine. Once the sauce is thickened, simmer over low heat to keep warm.

In the meantime, add your pasta to the boiling water and cook for about 12 minutes (or according to package directions.)

When the eggplant is done cooking, add the bread crumbs and thyme to the eggplant and stir to coat. The crumbs should toast and become a few shades darker in about 2 minutes. Once toasty, turn the heat off completely.

Drain the pasta. Alternate adding batches of pasta and eggplant to the sauce and stir with a pasta spoon to incorporate. Add any leftover bread crumbs from the pan into the sauce as well. Mix well and serve.

EGGPLANT & BREAD CRUMBS
FETTUCCINE

SERVES 4 / TIME: ABOUT AN HR

Eggplant:

1 medium-size eggplant, sliced into ¼-inch disks

Salt

2 tablespoons olive oil, plus more in a spray bottle or for drizzling

½ cup plain vegan bread crumbs

½ teaspoon dried thyme

Sauce:

2 tablespoons olive oil

6 cloves garlic, minced

2 pounds tomatoes, cut into small dice

¼ cup dry white wine or vegetable broth, purchased or homemade (page 223)

A big pinch of dried oregano

A few pinches of freshly ground black pepper

Pinch of salt

8 ounces fettuccine

CHAPTER TEN

SAUCES
&
FILLINGS

**Here you'll find toppings and fillings
we use throughout the book, but more important,
you'll find sauces.**

We are going to go out on a limb and say that the sauce can make or break your cooking. Watch as you transform mere mortal vegetables into the foods of gods and goddesses! Marvel as your pasta goes from "Pasta again?" to "Pasta again!"

Consider this chapter a master class in sauce making. In fact, go ahead and call yourself a saucier just because you've glanced at it. Every culture in the world has its trademark sauce, making this section truly transcontinental. Not only is the perfect marinara now within your reach, but you'll learn to make a roux, the toasted fat- and flour-based sauce that is the mama of French cooking; our spin on pesto, the classic Italian paste of herbs, nuts, and garlic; two kinds of mole, the classic Mexican blend of chiles and chocolate as well as a green one that uses pumpkin seeds; and barbecue sauce that is sure to get the kids lickin' their fingers.

Most of these sauces take less than twenty minutes to prepare and require minimum equipment for prepping, and you can keep them refrigerated in an airtight container until ready to use. So stop pushing your food around on your plate barren, lonely, unsauced, and unloved. It's time to get saucy!

--------------- ◆ ---------------

MUSTARD SAUCE

**MAKES ABOUT 1½ CUPS SAUCE /
TIME: 20 MIN**

2 tablespoons cornstarch

¾ cup vegetable broth, purchased or
homemade (page 223)

3 cloves garlic, minced

½ teaspoon dried thyme

1 tablespoon olive oil

½ cup sherry cooking wine

1 tablespoon soy sauce

¼ cup whole-grain Dijon mustard

1 tablespoon fresh lemon juice

2 tablespoons capers (with brine)

For mustard lovers only! Add a little elegance to your meal with this thick, tangy and savory sauce that's great over Chickpea Cutlets (page 206), baked or broiled tofu, and roasted vegetables—especially asparagus.

Mix the cornstarch with the vegetable broth in a measuring cup and set aside.

In a small saucepan over medium heat, sauté the garlic and thyme in the oil for about a minute.

Add the wine and soy sauce, and increase the heat to high. Once the mixture is boiling, lower the heat to medium and simmer to reduce for about 4 minutes. Add the vegetable broth mixture, mustard, lemon juice, and capers. Stir often, using a whisk. Once the sauce is bubbling, lower the heat to low, and simmer for about 3 minutes. The sauce should be on the thick side.

Let cool a bit before serving; this sauce tastes great just above room temperature.

This luscious, French-inspired sauce packs a rich bouquet of flavors. Serve on anything seitan, tempeh, roasted cauliflower, or mashed potatoes. Our favorite way by far is served on Chickpea Cutlets (page 206) and a side of French Bakes (page 34) for a real un-meat and potatoes meal with just a touch of class.

In a small saucepan, dissolve the bouillon cube in boiling water. Keep the bouillon warm over the lowest heat possible.

Heat the oil and the flour together in saucepan over medium heat. Stir with a wooden spoon until the mixture is deep golden brown and smells toasty, about 5 minutes. Add the shallots and garlic and continue to cook for another 5 minutes. Stir in the celery and cook for another 3 minutes, until the celery has softened.

Switch to a wire whisk and add the hot veggie bouillon, whisking until smooth. Add the bay leaf, marjoram, thyme, and rosemary. Keep whisking, increase the heat, and bring to a rapid simmer. Gradually pour in the wine and bring to a rapid simmer one more time. Lower the heat and simmer for 5 minutes, or until slightly reduced. The sauce is ready when it's thickened just enough to easily cling to the back of a metal spoon.

Remove from the heat, stir in the chopped chives, and either ladle directly over food or serve alongside in a gravy boat.

This sauce will become very thick if refrigerated, but it reheats easily. Place the sauce in a small saucepan, heat over medium-low heat while stirring occasionally, and whisk in a little vegetable broth until the desired consistency is reached.

RED WINE &
HERB SAUCE

MAKES 2 CUPS SAUCE / TIME: 15 MIN

1¼ cups boiling water

1 vegetable bouillon cube

2 tablespoons olive oil

3 tablespoons all-purpose flour

3 large shallots, minced finely

1 clove garlic, minced

¼ cup finely minced celery

1 bay leaf

1 teaspoon dried marjoram

½ teaspoon dried thyme

½ teaspoon dried rosemary, crumbed between your fingers

¾ cup dry red wine

2 tablespoons minced fresh chives

- - - - - - - -
TIPS
- - - - - - - -

This sauce will thicken considerably as it cools and may form a skin on top. Don't worry, just give it a good whisk and reheat over low flame.

For best results, try to mince the vegetables as small as possible. Also, very dry wines taste best in this sauce.

MARINARA SAUCE

& variations

MAKES ABOUT 5 CUPS SAUCE,
enough for 4 servings of pasta /
TIME: 20 MIN

2 teaspoons olive oil

4 cloves garlic, minced

1 (28-ounce) can crushed tomatoes

¼ teaspoon dried thyme

¼ teaspoon dried oregano

½ teaspoon salt

Several pinches of freshly ground black
   pepper

The secret to a great marinara sauce is KISS—keep it simple, stupid! Oh yes, and a hell of a lotta garlic. Store-bought sauce tends to be too sweet and tastes, well, store-bought. We use this in all of our tomato-based Italian dishes from pasta to eggplant rollatini, and it doesn't take much time, so go ahead and pour some love onto your spaghetti. Go crazy with the variations that follow.

Preheat a saucepan over medium-low heat. Add the oil and garlic and sauté for about a minute, until fragrant, being careful not to let it burn. Add the remaining ingredients, cover, and increase the heat a bit to bring to a simmer. Simmer for about 15 minutes, stirring occasionally.

VARIATIONS

ROASTED RED PEPPER MARINARA SAUCE: Add a chopped roasted red pepper (pages 28, 33) along with the tomatoes. Blend the sauce when done cooking, if you like.

MUSHROOM MARINARA SAUCE: Increase the oil to 1 tablespoon, and sauté 1 cup of thinly sliced mushrooms before adding the garlic.

ROASTED GARLIC MARINARA SAUCE: Decrease the minced garlic to 2 teaspoons. Add a whole bulb of peeled, roasted garlic to the sauce halfway through the cooking process. Blend the sauce when done cooking.

OLIVE MARINARA SAUCE: Add ½ cup of chopped black olives to the sauce about halfway through the cooking process.

CARAMELIZED ONION MARINARA SAUCE: Increase the oil to 1 tablespoon. Sweat 1 cup of finely chopped white or yellow onion for about 15 minutes. (To sweat, keep the heat low and cover, stirring every few minutes; the onions should not brown.) Uncover and cook for 15 more minutes at higher heat, until browned and caramelized. Proceed with the rest of the recipe.

WE ALSO LIKE TO MIX AND MATCH SOME OF THESE VARIATIONS: Caramelized Onion and Roasted Red Pepper, Mushroom and Olive, you get the idea.

Straight outta *Vegan with a Vengeance*, we've included the recipe in this book, too, because, well, tofu ricotta doesn't get better than this! We use it in Eggplant Rollatini (page 243) but feel free to use it anywhere that ricotta might be found; stuffed shells, as a pizza topping, you name it.

In a large bowl, mush the tofu up with your hands until it's crumbly.

Add the lemon juice, garlic, salt, pepper, and basil. Mush with hands again; this time you want it to get very mushy, so squeeze through your fingers and mush until it reaches the consistency of ricotta cheese, 2 to 5 minutes.

Add the oil and stir with a fork. Add the nutritional yeast and mix all the ingredients well. Use a fork now, because the oil will make it sticky. Cover and refrigerate until ready to use.

TOFU RICOTTA

MAKES 3½ CUPS RICOTTA /
TIME: 10 MIN

1 pound extra-firm tofu

2 teaspoons fresh lemon juice

1 clove garlic, minced

¼ teaspoon salt

Pinch of freshly ground black pepper

Handful of fresh basil leaves, chopped finely (10 leaves or so) (optional)

2 teaspoons olive oil

¼ cup nutritional yeast

Before we lived in a post–cashew cheese revolution, there was this upgrade on tofu ricotta! Cashews add a creamy sweetness to homemade dairyless ricotta for extra-special lasagne, on pizza, or dynamite in Pumpkin Baked Ziti with Caramelized Onions (page 297). This recipe also makes a smooth, savory sandwich spread paired with crusty herbed vegan peasant bread.

Cover the cashews with 3 inches of warm water in a small bowl. Soak for 20 minutes, or until softened, then drain off the water. In a food processor, blend together the cashews, lemon juice, oil, garlic, basil, and salt until a thick creamy paste forms. Add the crumbled tofu to the food processor, working in two or more batches if necessary. Pulse into a smooth mixture that looks like . . . ricotta!

CASHEW RICOTTA

MAKES 2 CUPS RICOTTA /
TIME: 15 MIN

½ cup raw cashews (approximately 4 ounces)

¼ cup fresh lemon juice

2 tablespoons olive oil

2 cloves fresh or roasted garlic (see page 34)

1½ teaspoons dried basil

1½ teaspoons salt

1 pound firm tofu, drained and crumbled

ALMESAN

MAKES ⅓ CUP ALMESAN /
TIME: 5 MIN OR LESS

¼ cup slivered or sliced almonds
1 tablespoon toasted sesame seeds
⅛ teaspoon salt
¼ teaspoon freshly grated lemon zest

This is our vegan version of Parmesan, made with almonds, sesame seeds, and a little lemon zest. It's great for when your pasta needs a sprinkle of a little somethin' somethin'. If you have a mini processor, there is no better time to use it.

Combine all the ingredients in a blender or food processor. Pulse until everything turns to tiny crumbs. That's it!

BACKYARD
BBQ SAUCE

MAKES ABOUT 4 CUPS SAUCE /
TIME: 40 MIN

1 tablespoon vegetable oil
1 medium-size yellow onion, chopped as finely as you can
4 cloves garlic, minced
¼ teaspoon salt
1 teaspoon red pepper flakes
1 (28-ounce) can crushed tomatoes
⅓ cup molasses
⅓ cup white vinegar
2 tablespoons organic sugar
1 tablespoon prepared yellow mustard (Dijon is fine, too)
2 teaspoons liquid smoke

The basic components of a BBQ sauce are something sweet, something sour, and something tomato-y. This sauce is superversatile—you can replace the molasses with maple syrup or just plain sugar, you can replace the crushed tomatoes with tomato sauce or diced tomatoes (but you should puree it at the end if you use crushed tomatoes). Red pepper flakes add a little heat, but you can use a bit of cayenne or hot sauce instead. The longer you cook this sauce, the thicker and more delicious it gets, but if all's you got is half an hour, it's still yummy!

Preheat a saucepan over medium heat. Place the onion in the pan and sauté in the vegetable oil until browned, about 7 minutes. Add the garlic and sauté for another minute. Add all the other ingredients, except the mustard and liquid smoke, and cook, uncovered, for at least 30 minutes and up to 1 hour, stirring occasionally. Lower the heat if the sauce begins to splatter everywhere. Add the mustard and liquid smoke, and taste for sweetness/sourness. Adjust the flavors if you think it's necessary, and cook for 5 more minutes. If you like a smooth BBQ sauce, then puree it, but that's not entirely necessary.

This is a fruity, kid-friendly BBQ sauce that isn't too sweet. It's wonderful on any of the holy trinity (tofu, tempeh, or seitan). See the recipe for Baked BBQ Tofu (page 196). It's also wonderful on steamed veggies, especially broccoli. As with all recipes where you cook with fruit, the sweetness will need to be adjusted depending on how sweet your fruit is.

In a small saucepan over medium-high heat, sauté the onion in the peanut oil for 7 to 10 minutes, until browned. Add the garlic and sauté for 2 more minutes. Add the vegetable broth to deglaze the pan. Add the apricots, pepper, ginger, and coriander. Cover and bring to a boil. Once the sauce is boiling, lower the heat to medium-low and let cook for about 10 minutes, until the apricots are mushy.

Uncover and add the remaining ingredients. Cook for about 10 more minutes, stirring often and mashing the apricot as you stir. Taste the sauce and adjust the sweetness, if necessary.

Remove from the heat and let cool until it's not steaming, stirring occasionally to speed up the cooling. Transfer to a blender or food processor and puree until completely smooth.

APRICOT
BBQ SAUCE

MAKES ABOUT 4 CUPS SAUCE /
TIME: 40 MIN

1 tablespoon peanut oil

1 small yellow onion, diced

2 cloves garlic, chopped

½ cup vegetable broth, purchased or homemade (page 223), or water

1½ pounds apricots (6 to 8, depending on their size), pitted and sliced about ½ inch thick

Several pinches of freshly ground black pepper

¼ teaspoon ground ginger

¼ teaspoon ground coriander

¼ cup molasses

2 tablespoons pure maple syrup

2 tablespoons tomato paste

3 tablespoons soy sauce

1 teaspoon liquid smoke

SO VERY SOUR
CREAM

MAKES 1 QUART SOUR CREAM /
ACTIVE TIME: 10 MIN /
TOTAL TIME: 3 HRS BUT PREFERABLY AT
LEAST A DAY (TO SET)

1 cup raw cashews, soaked in water for at
least 2 hours and drained

1 (14-ounce) can full-fat coconut milk

½ cup fresh lemon juice

¼ cup refined coconut oil, melted

½ teaspoon onion powder

A big pinch of salt

Coconut and cashews join forces to create the richest, coolest, creamiest sour cream ever! Use it on everything from latkes to chili, it will never disappoint.

In a blender, puree all the ingredients until completely smooth; this can take up to 5 minutes, depending on the strength of your machine. Periodically stop the machine to keep it from overheating, and scrape down the sides of the blender jar with a rubber spatula to make sure you get everything.

Transfer the sour cream to a quart-size container, cover, and let set for at least a day. Dollop away!

HORSERADISH-DILL
SOUR CREAM

MAKES ABOUT 3 CUPS SOUR CREAM /
TIME: 15 MIN, plus chill time

1 pound soft tofu

2 tablespoons freshly grated horseradish

1 tablespoon apple cider vinegar

1 tablespoon agave nectar or real maple
syrup

¾ teaspoon salt

3 cloves garlic, crushed

¼ cup grapeseed oil

1 cup loosely packed fresh dill

This is our cream of choice for latkes both of the potato persuasion and the beet kind (see Autumn Latkes, page 53). It also makes a wonderful dressing, especially for cucumbers. We used fresh horseradish, but if you can only find the jarred kind, go ahead and use it. Since it's stronger than fresh, add a tablespoon at first and taste from there.

Remove the tofu from the package and shake off any excess water. Place in a blender or food processor (a food processor works better) along with the horseradish, vinegar, agave, and salt. Blend until smooth.

Preheat a small saucepan over medium-low heat. Place the crushed garlic and grapeseed oil in the pan. Cook gently, stirring occasionally, for about 2 minutes. The garlic should "blond" (that means "lightly brown" in French) but not burn. Remove the garlic from the oil and discard. Add the oil to the tofu mixture and blend again until smooth. Add the dill, and blend until smooth—the cream will be light green with some flecks of dill. Scrape down the sides to make sure you get everything.

Taste and adjust the salt and vinegar, if necessary. Transfer to a bowl and seal tightly with plastic wrap and refrigerate for at least 30 minutes.

Here's a nice replacement for sour cream on anything where cilantro would fit in: burritos, tacos, black bean soup, you name it. It's also a yummy salad dressing and great on a Black Bean Burger (page 134).

Remove the tofu from the package and shake off any excess water. Place in a blender or food processor (a food processor works better) along with the lime juice, agave, and salt. Blend until smooth.

Preheat a small saucepan over medium-low heat. Place the crushed garlic and grapeseed oil in the pan. Cook gently, stirring occasionally, for about 3 minutes. The garlic should blond (that means "to lightly brown") but not burn. Add to the tofu mixture and blend again until smooth. Add the cilantro and, guess what? Yep, blend until smooth and light green with some flecks of dark green. Scrape down the sides to make sure you get everything.

Taste and adjust the salt and lime, if necessary. Transfer to a bowl, seal tightly with plastic wrap, and refrigerate for at least 30 minutes. It will get a little bit firmer but will still have a pourable consistency.

SOUR CILANTRO CREAM

MAKES ABOUT 3 CUPS SOUR CREAM / TIME: 15 MIN, plus chill time

1 pound silken tofu (not the vacuum-packed kind)

2 tablespoons fresh lime juice

1 tablespoon agave nectar

¾ teaspoon salt

3 cloves garlic, crushed

¼ cup grapeseed oil

2 cups loosely packed fresh cilantro (stems and leaves)

What Mexican meal is complete without a little salsa verde? Maybe a Mexican meal using some other Mexican sauce, but that's neither here nor there. Salsa verde (green sauce to you, bub) is made with those mysterious tomato-like wonders, tomatillos. Serve chilled with chips and Guacamole (page 73), or hot over enchiladas and burritos. This is a mild version, so add more jalapeños if you like it hot. Wear gloves to avoid touching the seeds, or your hands will burn all day. (If you're like us and don't have gloves, just be careful!)

In a small saucepan over low heat, sauté the garlic and jalapeño in the oil until fragrant, about 3 minutes.

Add the tomatillos and salt, and sauté until the tomatillos begin to soften and release moisture, about 5 minutes. Add the vegetable broth, bring to a slow boil, and cook for about 20 minutes, stirring occasionally.

Remove from the heat, let cool until it is not steaming, then add the cilantro and lime juice. Pour into a blender and blend until relatively smooth, about 30 seconds.

SALSA VERDE

MAKES ABOUT 2 CUPS SALSA / TIME: 40 MIN

1 teaspoon olive oil

3 cloves garlic, minced

1 jalapeño pepper, seeded and minced

10 tomatillos (husks removed), cleaned and diced

¼ teaspoon sea salt

1½ cups vegetable broth, purchased or homemade (page 223)

1 cup loosely packed fresh cilantro

Juice of 1 lime

GREEN PUMPKIN-SEED
MOLE

**MAKES A LITTLE OVER 2 CUPS MOLE /
TIME: 20 MIN**

1 cup hulled raw pumpkin seeds

4 whole black peppercorns

1 cup lightly packed fresh cilantro

1 cup lightly packed fresh parsley

1 (7- to 8-ounce) can tomatillos

1 serrano chile, stemmed, seeded, coarsely
chopped

2 scallions, white part discarded, coarsely
chopped

2 lettuce leaves (such as romaine or green
leaf), torn into pieces

2 cloves garlic, coarsely chopped

¼ cup olive oil

TIP

If you can't find tomatillos, you can use salsa
verde; just check that the ingredients list contains nothing more than tomatillos, garlic, and
cilantro.

A thick diplike sauce made from pumpkin seeds, herbs, tomatillos and peppers, this mole will turn any Mexican type of meal into a revolutionary upris-
ing. Canned tomatillos makes this thick sauce a snap to prepare; the only
cooking required is the toasting of the pumpkin seeds (also called pepitas).
It's wonderful with rice and beans, and especially delish with Southwestern
Corn Pudding (page 238).

Preheat a large skillet over medium-low heat. Toast the pumpkin seeds, turning
occasionally, for 3 to 4 minutes. Transfer the seeds to a food processor or blender
(a food processor works better). Add the peppercorns and pulse into a coarse
powder.

Add everything else, except the olive oil, and grind into a thick paste. Add the
oil and blend for about 30 seconds. Scrape down the sides of the processor to
incorporate all the ingredients. Add salt to taste (it may not even be necessary).

Not authentic by any means, this spin-off of traditional mole poblano takes a few modern shortcuts to whip up a thick, rich sauce with a complex blend of hot, sweet, bitter, and nutty flavors. Highly versatile, this mole can be used for any number of Mexican specialties, such as enchiladas, tamales, or tostadas, or just scooped up with big, crunchy tortilla chips. The simplest way to enjoy it as a hearty entrée is to simmer vegetables and other foods on the stovetop, as in Vegetables or Seitan in Mole Sauce (page 280).

Prepare the spice mixture: In a skillet over medium heat, toast together the almonds, tortilla chip crumbs, sesame seeds, and aniseeds. Toast for about 2 minutes, taking care not to let it burn. Remove from the heat and pour the toasted ingredients in a food processor, add the chile powder, cinnamon, marjoram, allspice, and cumin, and grind into a coarse powder.

Prepare the mole base: In a 2-quart pot or saucepan over medium heat, sauté the garlic in the peanut oil for 30 seconds. Add the onion and fry until soft and golden, about 3 minutes. Meanwhile, combine the peanut butter and a few tablespoons of hot vegetable broth, stirring until the peanut butter is emulsified and easy to pour.

Add the remaining vegetable broth, peanut butter mixture, spice mixture, and diced tomatoes to the onions. Bring to a rapid simmer, then lower the heat slightly and continue to simmer for 10 minutes, or until the sauce has reduced slightly.

Remove from the heat and use an immersion blender to puree until smooth. Return the pot to the stove over medium heat, and add the chopped chocolate. Stir until the chocolate has completely melted. Taste and season with salt, if desired.

Some ideas for using this mole: Prepare Potato & Kale Enchiladas (page 254), substituting the mole for the enchilada sauce. Thin the mole with ½ cup of vegetable broth before using.

Drizzle onto tostadas, nachos, and tacos. Tuck into black bean burritos.

Serve the mole (warmed, thinned slightly with vegetable broth) over freshly steamed winter squash, green beans, or asparagus.

Mole makes an interesting dip alongside salsas and Guacamole (page 73) with tortilla chips (don't thin the mole with broth).

CHILE-CHOCOLATE
MOLE

MAKES 3 CUPS MOLE / TIME: 30 MIN

Spice mixture:
- ⅓ cup sliced almonds
- ⅓ cup crushed tortilla chips
- 2 tablespoons sesame seeds
- 1 teaspoon aniseeds
- 3 to 4 teaspoons chile powder, preferably a mix of ground ancho and chipotle
- 1¼ teaspoons ground cinnamon
- 1 teaspoon dried marjoram
- ¼ teaspoon ground allspice
- ½ teaspoon ground cumin

Mole base:
- 3 tablespoons peanut oil
- 4 garlic cloves, chopped
- 1 small onion, peeled and diced
- 2 tablespoons creamy, all-natural peanut butter
- 2 cups hot vegetable broth, purchased or homemade (page 223), kept warm on the stovetop
- 1 (15-ounce) can diced fire-roasted tomatoes
- 3 ounces chopped vegan semisweet baking chocolate (60% cacao is best)

TIP

An immersion blender is your friend for this recipe, in particular if it has a mini food-processor cup attachment. It makes grinding up the spice mixture ridiculously easy.

MUSHROOM GRAVY

**MAKES ABOUT 4 CUPS GRAVY /
TIME: 30 MIN**

2 cups vegetable broth, purchased or
homemade (page 223)

¼ cup all-purpose flour (use ⅓ cup for a
thicker gravy)

2 tablespoons olive oil

1 medium-size onion, thinly sliced

10 ounces cremini mushrooms, thinly sliced
(about 4 cups)

3 cloves garlic, minced

1 teaspoon dried thyme

½ teaspoon dried sage

¼ teaspoon salt

Several pinches of freshly ground black
pepper

¼ cup dry white wine

We don't need to tell you what to do with it, do we? Smother it on absolutely
everything!

Mix the flour into the vegetable broth until dissolved and set aside.

Preheat a large, nonstick pan over medium heat. Sauté the onion in the oil for
about 5 minutes, until translucent. Add the mushrooms and sauté for 5 more
minutes, until they are tender.

Add the garlic, thyme, sage, salt, and pepper. Sauté for another minute. Add the
wine and increase the heat to bring to a simmer. Let simmer for about a minute,
then lower the heat and add the flour mixture. Stir constantly until thickened,
about 5 minutes. If not serving immediately, gently reheat when you are ready
to serve.

TROPICAL AVOCADO
SALSA
FRESCA

**MAKES A LITTLE UNDER 3 CUPS SALSA /
TIME: 15 MIN**

1 cup chopped tomato (½-inch chunks)

1 cup chopped pineapple, mango, or papaya
(½-inch chunks)

1 avocado, peeled, pitted, and cut into ½-
inch chunks

¼ cup lightly packed chopped fresh cilantro

Juice of 1 lime

This little fruit and avocado combo is culinary magic. It will turn plain old rice
and beans into "I've never had such kick-ass rice and beans!" It's especially
yummy with the Spaghetti Squash Mexicana on page 269.

Mix all the ingredients together in a mixing bowl. Refrigerate until ready to use.

This is totally inauthentic, but so what; it's really yummy! And after you've prepped everything, you only need to cook it for five minutes. Serve with any Indian meal, on a curry, or on Samosa Stuffed Baked Potatoes (page 63). I like the sourness of the asafetida, but you can use any Indian-y sort of spice instead—such as curry powder or garam masala.

Preheat a small saucepan over medium-low heat. Place the peanut oil, garlic, ginger, and jalapeño in the pan. Sauté for about 1 minute. Add the mango, sugar, and 2 tablespoons of water. Increase the heat to medium, cover, and cook for 3 minutes, until it's boiling. Add the vinegar and asafetida, and cook, uncovered, for another minute.

Chill until ready to use.

TIP Asafetida is a pungent spice (a resin from sap, if you want to be technical about it) that hasn't quite caught on in the American kitchen just yet. You can find it in a fancy-shmancy gourmet store or in Indian markets. Definitely seek it out; one great bonus is that the tin it comes in is usually very cool looking and colorfully decorated.

5-MINUTE
MANGO CHUTNEY

**MAKES ABOUT 2 CUPS CHUTNEY /
TIME: 15 MIN, plus chill time**

2 teaspoons peanut oil

2 cloves garlic, minced

2 teaspoons grated fresh ginger

1 jalapeño pepper, seeded and chopped

1 large mango, peeled and cut into bite-size pieces (you should get a little under 2 cups of fruit)

2 tablespoons organic sugar

2 tablespoons red wine vinegar

½ teaspoon asafetida

This easy, quick sauce is the perfect companion to any Indian meal, authentic or otherwise. Cool and refreshing, it contrasts nicely against warm and spicy foods. There are so many great vegan yogurt options now; try it with almond, coconut, hemp, or whatever new soy yogurt comes your way.

In a small bowl, combine the yogurt, garam masala, salt, lemon juice, and cilantro.

In a small skillet, toast the cumin seeds over medium-low heat for 30 to 45 seconds, stirring constantly and taking care not to burn them. Pour the seeds immediately into the yogurt mixture. Whisk to combine. Cover and chill until ready to use.

SPICED
YOGURT SAUCE

**SERVES 2 TO 4 / TIME: 10 MIN,
plus chill time**

1½ cups plain, preferably unsweetened, almond, coconut, hemp, or soy yogurt

1 teaspoon garam masala

¼ teaspoon salt

1 teaspoon fresh lemon or lime juice, or to taste

1 tablespoon finely chopped fresh cilantro

1 teaspoon cumin seeds

CRANBERRY-CHILE
DIPPING SAUCE

MAKES 2 CUPS SAUCE / TIME: 25 MIN

1 cup whole, fresh cranberries

1½ cups cold water

½ cup organic sugar

2 large serrano chiles, seeded and finely minced

2 tablespoons fresh lime juice

Pretty, red, sweet, tart, and hot. This lovely sauce is a nice low-sodium alternative to the soy-based dipping sauces that are typically served alongside steamed or fried Asian appetizers. It's also the ideal dipping sauce to serve with Butternut Squash & Pumpkin Seed Rice Paper Rolls (page 49).

Combine the cranberries, water, and sugar in a medium-size saucepan. Cover and bring to a boil. When the cranberries begin to pop, lower the heat to medium and simmer, partially covered, for about 5 minutes. Add the minced chiles and lime juice, bring to a boil again, and then lower the heat to medium-low. Stir the sauce occasionally, using the back of a wooden spoon to mash some of the cranberries against the sides of the pot. Simmer the sauce, uncovered, for an additional 10 to 12 minutes, until it has reduced by about less than one fourth and looks syrupy.

Remove from the heat. The sauce will thicken up more as it cools. Store in an airtight container in the refrigerator.

TIP For a more intensely hot sauce, don't remove the seeds from the chile. Conversely, if you want a less spicy sauce, use just one chile.

HOLIDAY
CRANBERRY SAUCE

**MAKES ABOUT 5 CUPS SAUCE /
TIME: 35 MIN, plus chill time**

1½ cups apple cider

2 tablespoons agar flakes (if you have agar powder, 2 teaspoons would be the equivalent)

12 ounces fresh cranberries (a little over 3 cups)

¾ cup organic sugar

Does cranberry sauce really need an introduction? You know what to do with it! We use agar to make this a little firm and the ingredients are kept simple— no orange rind or sneaky flavorings. But apple cider is the secret ingredient that keeps things interesting.

Pour the apple cider into a small pot and stir in the agar. Let soak for 10 minutes to soften up the agar and make it easier to dissolve. Skip the soaking step if using agar powder.

Cover and bring to a boil. Once the cider is boiling, add the cranberries and sugar. Lower the heat to medium; the mixture should be at a steady simmer. Cover, leaving a little gap for the steam to escape, and cook for about 10 minutes. At this point, the cranberries should be popping and the juice should be red. Use your mixing utensil to crush some of the cranberries and help them along. Cook, uncovered, for about 5 more minutes. The cranberries should be mostly popped and crushed, and the juice should be thick and red.

Transfer to a container and refrigerate. Let cool until it mostly stops steaming, then cover tightly with plastic wrap and place in the refrigerator until completely cooled and slightly jelled, about 3 hours.

This is our cheapskate pesto that uses almonds, which also have the benefit of making the pesto very bright and creamy.

Place the basil, cilantro, almonds, garlic, lemon juice, and salt in a food processor and blend until pasty, scraping down the sides occasionally. With the food processor on, slowly drizzle in the olive oil. Blend until relatively smooth and no large chunks of almonds are left. If you don't have a food processor and are using a blender, then just add the oil at the end, since many blenders aren't equipped with an opening to drizzle into.

BASIL-CILANTRO
PESTO

MAKES ABOUT 1 CUP PESTO /
TIME: 10 MIN

2 cups loosely packed fresh basil leaves

1 cup loosely packed fresh cilantro

⅓ cup slivered or sliced almonds

2 cloves garlic, crushed

2 tablespoons fresh lemon juice

½ teaspoon salt

¼ cup olive oil

A great dressing for a Mediterranean salad or just to serve with steamed veggies, greens, sautéed veggies, roasted veggies . . . you get the idea. It has a vibrant and tangy flavor, so it isn't recommended for anything that is already strongly flavored. It's definitely one of those things that will have you licking the spoon after you ladle it out.

Combine all the ingredients, except the dill, in a blender or food processor. Blend until smooth. Add the dill and pulse a few times until the herb is just small green flecks. You can serve immediately or refrigerate until ready to use, then bring back to room temperature because it will thicken a lot when cold.

DILL-TAHINI
SAUCE

MAKES 1½ CUPS SAUCE / TIME: 5 MIN

½ cup tahini, at room temperature

½ cup water, at room temperature

1 clove garlic, chopped coarsely

¼ cup fresh lemon juice

2 tablespoons olive oil

1 tablespoon balsamic vinegar

½ teaspoon paprika (Hungarian, if you've got it)

¼ teaspoon salt

1 cup lightly packed fresh dill

CHEEZY SAUCE

**MAKES ABOUT 3 CUPS SAUCE /
TIME: 15 MIN**

2 cups vegetable broth, purchased or
    homemade (page 223), or water

¼ cup all-purpose flour

1 tablespoon olive oil

3 cloves garlic, minced

Pinch of dried thyme (crumbled in your
    fingers)

¼ teaspoon salt

Several pinches of freshly ground black
    pepper

⅛ teaspoon ground turmeric

¾ cup nutritional yeast flakes

1 tablespoon fresh lemon juice

1 teaspoon prepared yellow mustard

This is the nooch sauce that we use whenever we need a melty cheesy topping for a meal. It's quick, tangy, and flavorful. So many sauces like this call for a stick (gasp) of margarine—this recipe needs a measly tablespoon of olive oil, which makes you wonder whether some cookbook authors are just being hateful. We use this on nachos, pastas, brunch things (see Tofu Florentine, page 82), or just to dip raw veggies in.

Combine the broth and flour in a measuring cup and whisk with a fork until dissolved (a couple of lumps are okay).

Preheat a small saucepan over medium-low heat. Place the oil and garlic in the pan and gently cook for about 2 minutes, stirring often and being careful not to burn the garlic.

Add the thyme, salt, and pepper and cook for about 15 seconds. Add the flour mixture, turmeric, and nutritional yeast, and increase the heat to medium. Use a whisk to stir constantly. The mixture should start bubbling and thickening in about 3 minutes; if it doesn't, increase the heat a bit more.

Once the mixture is bubbling and thickening, cook, stirring, for about 2 more minutes. Add the lemon juice and mustard. The mixture should resemble a thick, melty cheese. Taste for salt (you may need more, depending on how salty your vegetable broth is), turn off the heat, and cover the pan to keep it warm until ready to use. The top might thicken a bit while it sits, but you can just stir it and it will be fine. Serve warm.

This sweet, tangy, complex sauce pairs perfectly with kale, collards, and other bitter greens. And it's made with tahini, too, so you know it's on trend. Serve either at room temperature, or cold in warmer weather. Try it also on roasted green beans or steamed, sliced kabocha squash.

Soak the dates in the orange juice in the refrigerator for a minimum of 2 hours or overnight. Transfer to a food processor or blender, add the remaining ingredients, except the salt and pepper, and blend until smooth and creamy. Taste the sauce, then season with salt and pepper to taste. Serve over steamed greens or vegetables. Sprinkle the top of the sauce with additional sesame seeds for garnish, if desired.

TIPS The sauce will thicken when refrigerated. Feel free to thin it slightly with additional teaspoons of juice or water until the desired consistency is reached.

For a tangier dressing, substitute ¼ cup of fresh lemon juice for ¼ cup of the orange juice. Try substituting other sweet citrus for oranges, such as Minneolas, tangerines, or clementines.

CITRUS-DATE
SESAME SAUCE

MAKES 2 CUPS SAUCE / TIME: 10 MIN,
plus 2 hrs for soaking dates

1¼ cups fresh orange juice
½ cup chopped and pitted soft dates
½ cup tahini
2 tablespoons sesame seeds, plus more for garnish (optional)
2 tablespoons yellow miso
1 teaspoon toasted sesame oil
Salt and freshly ground black pepper

SWEET
VIDALIA ONION SAUCE

**MAKES A LITTLE LESS THAN 2 CUPS
SAUCE / TIME: 40 MIN**

2 tablespoons olive oil

2 large Vidalia onions, quartered and sliced thinly (about 2 cups once sliced)

¼ cup mirin or white wine

2 tablespoons pure maple syrup

1 teaspoon white balsamic or red wine vinegar

1 teaspoon Dijon mustard (not the whole-grain kind)

Pinch of salt

Perfect over Roasted Portobellos (page 161) or Chickpea Cutlets (page 206) or even just to dress up your veggie burger. You want the onions to caramelize, not crisp up, so it's important that you keep a close eye on them and keep the heat low.

Preheat a large, nonstick pan over medium-low heat. Sauté the onions in the oil for about 20 minutes, turning often so that they don't burn. If it looks as if they are getting crisp, lower the heat. They should be very soft and honey brown. Add the remaining ingredients and stir for about 30 seconds. Turn off the heat and cover to keep warm until you're ready to serve.

Kids these days, they'll make a gravy outta anything. We like this gravy on mashed potatoes for a change of pace. It's yummy and corn-y with a little kick for ya.

Preheat a saucepan over medium-high heat. In a measuring cup, mix the cornstarch with the vegetable broth and set aside.

Sauté the onion and jalapeños in the oil for about 5 minutes, until the onion is translucent. Add the garlic and sage and sauté for 1 more minute.

Add the corn and cook for about 5 minutes, until it is slightly browned.

Add the vegetable broth mixture, milk, and salt. Stirring often, let thicken for 3 or 4 minutes. Remove from the heat and let cool a bit, just so that it's not steaming very much. Transfer to a blender or food processor and puree. Add the lemon juice to taste and puree again, then taste for salt. Gently heat before serving if not serving immediately.

JALAPEÑO-CORN
GRAVY

MAKES ABOUT 3 CUPS GRAVY /
TIME: 20 MIN

1 tablespoon cornstarch

1 cup vegetable broth, purchased or homemade (page 223)

1 tablespoon olive oil

1 medium-size onion, chopped coarsely

2 jalapeño peppers, seeded and chopped

3 cloves garlic, chopped

Generous pinch of rubbed dried sage

2 cups fresh or frozen corn kernels (thaw partially if frozen)

¼ cup unsweetened nondairy milk

¼ teaspoon salt

Juice of ½ lemon

CHAPTER ELEVEN

BREADS, MUFFINS & SCONES

Baking is different enough from cooking that it's tempting to divide the world into "bakers" and "cookers."

Tempting indeed, but don't go labeling yourself just yet . . . we believe that knowing how to do both well is not only possible but essential to being the best vegan home chef you can be.

True, baking takes a slightly different mind-set: it's somewhat scientific and takes a little more practice, even a little more intuition, than does boiling pasta or simmering a soup. But at least a baking disaster is interesting and messy in a fun way, like a ninth grade chemistry project. And no matter how much you may try to get people (as in those people sitting on your couch and hogging the remote) excited about tempeh burgers, a loaf of warm banana bread will always get their attention.

Muffins and scones are still regularly on baking rotation for us—a must on weekend mornings or for spontaneous late-night treats. They can (sometimes almost) be made with one bowl, use ingredients that any decently stocked pantry should have, and require thirty minutes or less from mixing bowl to cooling rack. They also take readily to healthy additions, such as whole grains, fruits, spices, and nuts. Bake a batch of scones or muffins on Sunday morning and enjoy them toasted the next morning, or as a high-energy snack that afternoon.

If you're hungry to flex more baking muscles, don't miss out on the recipes for everyday yeasted breads and quick breads. Hearty whole-grain soda bread makes an ideal treat at breakfast, and a moist cranberry-nut bread is seriously awesome when paired with (organic, fair-trade) coffee. Cinnamon pinwheels thrill guests at any brunch, and an easy herbed focaccia makes a bowl of soup a complete meal. Make sure to try your hand at one of the unleavened flatbreads: flatbreads can be mixed, shaped, and baked on a hot griddle—without additional oil—for an exciting and fast alternative to rice that's ready to go in about the same time it takes a curry or stew to simmer on the stovetop.

-------------- ◆ ---------------

HOME-STYLE
POTATO ROLLS

MAKES 24 ROLLS /
TIME: ABOUT 45 MIN,
not including rising time

1 (¼-ounce) package active dry yeast

1½ cups warm water

1 cup plain, unsweetened almond, coconut-
based, or soy milk

2 tablespoons refined coconut oil or olive
oil

5 cups all-purpose flour, plus up to ½ cup
more

2 tablespoons organic dark brown sugar

2¼ teaspoons salt

1¼ cups cold mashed potatoes, preferably
Yukon gold

Glaze:

⅓ cup plain, unsweetened, plain almond,
coconut-based, or soy milk

2 teaspoons cornstarch or potato starch

3 tablespoons poppy seeds

These tender, puffy rolls dotted with poppy seeds are just like soft, homey hugs from the oven. They are prototypical dinner rolls, but you may just find yourself toasting leftover rolls for breakfast or for after-school snacks, even if you haven't been to school for decades. For a lovely pale yellow hue, use yellow waxy potatoes, such as Yukon gold.

In a measuring cup, mix together the warm water and the yeast. Set aside for a few minutes, or until the yeast is foamy. Meanwhile, warm the milk in a small saucepan over low heat for about 2 minutes, or in a glass or ceramic bowl in the microwave on low for about 45 seconds. Stir in the oil.

In a large mixing bowl, sift together the flour, brown sugar, and salt. Using your hands, mix the mashed potatoes into the flour to create a crumbly mixture, as if you were making pie crust. Form a well in the center and pour in both the yeast mixture and the milk mixture. Use a large silicone spatula to stir the mixture into a damp, soft dough: when it's ready, it should pull away from the sides of the bowl. If the dough is very sticky, add a little more flour, a few tablespoons at a time, until the dough does indeed pull away from the sides of the bowl. It's okay if there's bits of potato poking out of the dough, just push them back in.

Lightly flour a work surface and turn out the dough onto a lightly floured board and knead until smooth and stretchy, about 5 minutes. Rub a little coconut or olive oil around the inside of the mixing bowl, then return the dough to the bowl. Cover with a kitchen towel and set it in a warm, draft-free place to rise for 2 hours, or until doubled in size. A general rule of thumb for testing whether a bread dough has risen enough: press a finger into risen dough and the dough should spring back slowly.

While the dough is rising, prepare the glaze: In a small saucepan whisk together the milk and cornstarch. Simmer over medium-low heat for about 3 minutes, or until slightly thickened. Remove from the heat and set aside to cool.

Lightly grease two 12-cup muffin tins. Punch down the dough, knead briefly on a floured board, and divide the dough in half. Roll each half into a long rope about 16 inches long. Use kitchen shears or a sharp knife to slice the ropes into pieces slightly less than 2 inches long. Lightly flour your hands and roll each piece into a ball. Into each greased muffin cup, push together three balls. This is how to shape classic "cloverleaf" dinner rolls! Brush the top of each roll with cooled glaze, sprinkle with poppy seeds, and very loosely cover each tin with plastic wrap and drape with kitchen towels. Set aside for 25 to 35 minutes, until the rolls have doubled in bulk.

Preheat the oven to 400°F. Bake for about 20 minutes, or until the tops are shiny and browned. When the rolls are cool enough to touch, transfer from the pans to wire racks to complete cooling.

VARIATION

ALL NEW SUPERSHINY AQUAFABA-GLAZED ROLLS: Ten years ago we could have never foreseen how recycling the goo from a can of chickpeas could change everything about vegan cuisine. In this instance, we invite you to try an easy alternative for a shiny eggless "egg wash" using the liquid from draining a can of chickpeas, otherwise known as aquafaba! Prepare by whisking together ¼ cup of canned chickpea liquid (you may want to strain it to eliminate any bits of chickpea skin) with 1 teaspoon of cornstarch. Simmer as directed for the milk glaze, let cool, and use as directed. Try this glaze on other baked goods in this chapter!

TIPS

If you're wondering "can I use leftover mashed potatoes here?" yes, you can! Additional flavorings (roasted garlic or rosemary, for example) in your mashed potatoes will influence the flavor of the final rolls, but it will likely be delicious.

No leftover mashed potatoes? Grab about ½ pound of potatoes, peel if desired, and dice into ½-inch cubes. In a large pot cover with cold water and bring to a rapid boil over high heat. Lower the heat and simmer for 10 to 12 minutes, or until the potatoes can be easily pierced with a fork. Drain and mash until creamy; a splash of unsweetened nondairy milk or even warm potato cooking water will help move things along nicely. There's no need to be a perfectionist about it. A few little flecks of potato never hurt anyone!

WHOLE WHEAT
SODA BREAD
with Millet & Currants

MAKES 1 LARGE LOAF /
TIME: 1 HR 30 MIN

Cold refined coconut oil, for pan

Millet:

1 teaspoon canola oil

½ cup uncooked millet

1 cup boiling water

1½ cups Zante currants or dark raisins

Dough:

2 cups whole wheat flour or white whole
    wheat flour

1½ cups unbleached all-purpose flour

⅓ cup organic sugar

1 heaping tablespoon caraway seeds

1 tablespoon baking powder

2 teaspoons baking soda

¾ teaspoon salt

⅓ cup cold refined coconut oil

1¼ cups plain unsweetened almond,
    coconut-based, or soy milk, plus more
    for brushing top of loaf

1 tablespoon apple cider vinegar

Our whole-grain soda bread is more like a giant old-school hippie bakery scone—not too sweet, with a toothsome, hearty, whole-grain texture and slight crunch with the addition of cooked millet worked into the dough. Simmering the Zante currants with the millet plumps them up nicely in one amazing feat of culinary dexterity. Even with the addition of caraway seeds, this is not a traditional soda bread in the slightest, but whatever! It's Terry's most favorite thing in the whole world, thinly sliced, toasted, and served with strong black tea.

Preheat the oven to 375°F for at least 20 minutes. Grease a 9-inch round cake pan with coconut oil.

Prepare the millet: In a saucepan, heat the canola oil over medium heat and add the millet. Toast the millet for 2 to 3 minutes, stirring constantly, until golden and fragrant. Pour in the boiling water and stir in the currants. Cover the pan and cook for 20 minutes, or until the liquid is absorbed. Remove from the heat and fluff with a fork. Set aside the millet to cool while preparing the rest of the dough.

Prepare the dough: In a large mixing bowl, sift together the whole wheat flour, all-purpose flour, sugar, caraway seeds, baking powder, baking soda, and salt. Cut in the cold coconut oil with either a pastry cutter or two knives held together until well blended into the flour. It should resemble fine crumbs.

Combine the milk and the vinegar in a measuring cup: it will curdle to create a kind of homemade vegan buttermilk. Stir the curdled milk and the cooled millet mixture into the flour mixture. When the dough starts to pull away from the sides of the bowl, fold the dough a few times and shape into a ball (if the dough is too sticky, knead in more flour, 1 tablespoon at a time). Resist the urge to overknead the dough.

Drop the ball of dough into the prepared cake pan. Pat down the dough a little but keep a ½-inch space all around from the edge of the pan. Use a knife to score a crisscross into the top of the loaf. Brush the top with extra milk to glaze. Bake, brushing the top of the loaf a few more times with the glaze, for 35 minutes, or until it is well browned and a knife inserted into the center comes out clean. Let cool on a wire rack for 10 minutes before slicing, and allow it to cool completely before storing. This bread keeps fresh for days longer than the average quick bread. Loosely wrap it in foil or store in a resealable plastic bag.

TIPS

Zante currants are little seedless grapes, completely different from black currants. Still referred to as currants, zantes are commonly used as such, and are typically much cheaper and easier to find in North America. Look for them in your supermarket, right next to the raisins. But if you have the real-deal black dried currants, use them!

Bake this bread the old-fashioned way, in cast iron. Preheat a seasoned 3-quart Dutch oven for 20 minutes. Generously dust the bottom of the round of dough with whole wheat flour. Now, with great care (careful not to burn your fingers), lower the dough into the pot. Score the top of the loaf twice and bake (uncovered) as directed.

BROWN BREAD

MAKES 4 SMALL (15-OUNCE) LOAVES /
TIME: 1½ HRS

Coconut oil, for greasing cans

1 cup whole-grain rye flour

1 cup whole wheat flour

1 cup yellow cornmeal

1 teaspoon baking powder

½ teaspoon baking soda

1 teaspoon salt

½ teaspoon ground cinnamon

¼ teaspoon freshly grated nutmeg

1 cup dark raisins, pitted and chopped dates, or finely diced Mission figs (or a mix of all three)

2 cups plain, unsweetened almond, coconut-based, or soy milk

2 tablespoons apple cider vinegar

¾ cup light molasses

TIP

Traditionally, brown bread is steamed for hours in leftover 1-pound tins from ground Maxwell House coffee. Nowadays Maxwell House coffee comes in 1-pound plastic tubs, so scratch that idea. And if you live in New England and want a big regular coffee, you hit up the Dunkin Donuts drive-through anyway. With 1-pound cans in short supply, you'll find it much easier to prepare this delicacy with four standard 15-ounce cans and steam for about 45 minutes.

Bread in a can . . . what sorcery is this? Nope, it's just old-fashioned New England thrift, a dark quick bread batter rich with molasses, hearty whole wheat, rye, and cornmeal that's poured into recycled bean (or tomato sauce or soup) cans and steamed to perfection. And when you're a vegan New Englander, the ideal reason to still keep that big old lobstah pot. The result is a springy, dense quick bread that's tender, slightly sweet, and moist, just like a no-nonsense bran muffin but without a drop of added fat.

The idea of steaming bread may seem awkward, but once you locate the right big pot (or two slightly smaller ones) and the right mix of trivet/wire rack/ramekins to balance the cans on, you'll discover your own DIY custom system that works like a charm every time. And you'll want to make this bread again and again. It's the natural companion to Cheater Baked Beans (page 184), of course, but also makes a wicked good breakfast toasted and spread with your favorite vegan cream cheese or with a dab of good vegan buttah.

Have ready four 15-ounce clean, dry, and if you can find them, BPA-free aluminum cans, labels removed.

Prepare the bread steaming setup first: Use one large steamer pot (or two smaller pots) that can hold either all four or two aluminum cans each. Inside the bottom of the pot(s), arrange either a wire rack or turn upside down four ramekins, one for each can to sit on. Pour in about 4 inches of water, cover the pot, and bring to a gentle boil over medium-high heat.

Grease the interior of the cans with coconut oil. Tear off four squares of foil large enough to wrap on top of each can, then grease one side of each foil square.

In a large mixing bowl, combine the rye flour, whole wheat flour, cornmeal, baking powder, baking soda, salt, cinnamon, and nutmeg. Add the dried fruit and gently toss to coat in the flour. In a separate bowl, combine the milk and vinegar and leave it alone for 2 minutes to curdle. Stir in the molasses, then fold the liquid ingredients into the dry. Stir just enough to moisten everything, then divide the batter equally among the four greased tins.

Crimp the foil, greased side down, over each tin. Gently place each tin inside the steaming pot on top of each ramekin (or whatever steaming set up you've devised). Steam for 45 minutes to 1 hour, or until a toothpick inserted into the center of each bread comes out clean. Transfer the cans to a cooling rack and allow the breads to cool for at least 15 minutes before removing from their can. The easiest way to do so is just use a can opener to remove the bottom from a can, then gently push the bread out. Wrap any leftover bread tightly in foil and store chilled, or freeze for up to 2 months.

This fluffy and yeasty flatbread is exactly what any soup needs to be a complete meal. Focaccia is the ideal fresh homemade bread that doesn't require much planning in advance. We've updated the recipe considerably, now featuring both fresh and dried rosemary for a rosemary one-two punch! Once you get the hang of making focaccia, try experimenting with different fresh herbs and chopped olives.

We also love thin strips of focaccia with dip, so obviously you must make and serve this with Hummus (page 74), or any spread in the appetizers chapter, to go along with everything. And while you're at it, if you want to be the most annoying person at the focaccia-soup-dip party you are going to host, always remind your guests that the plural of *focaccia* is *focacce*.

In a large mixing bowl, sprinkle the yeast over the warm water and set aside for 2 minutes to allow the yeast to foam up a bit. Stir in the flour, olive oil, chopped rosemary, and salt. When the dough pulls away from the sides of the bowl, turn out the dough onto a lightly floured surface and knead for 2 to 3 minutes, or until smooth. If the dough is sticky, work in a little flour, 1 tablespoon at a time. Splash a little olive oil in the original bowl, return the dough to the bowl, and turn a few times to completely coat the surface with oil. Cover the top of the bowl with plastic wrap and set the bowl in a warm, draft-free place for 1½ to 2 hours, or until the dough has doubled in size.

Generously oil a 9 x 13-inch jelly-roll pan with olive oil. Punch down the dough and flip it to a floured surface. Use your hands to shape the dough into a rectangle roughly the size of the oiled pan. Lift and drop the dough into the pan and gently press it into the edges of the pan. Cover with a kitchen towel and leave the dough to rise for 30 minutes.

Get your toppings ready: When the dough is ready to bake, preheat the oven to 425°F. Use your knuckles (the secondary ones of your fingers are best) to poke a series of dents all over the surface of the dough. Press the fresh rosemary leaves onto the top of the dough, drizzle with the extra-virgin olive oil, and finish with a flourish of salt. Bake for about 20 minutes, or until the top is golden brown. Remove from the oven and let cool for 10 minutes before slicing.

VARIATIONS

THE EASIEST WAY TO VARY UP FOCACCIA IS TO THROW IN A HANDFUL OF THE FOLLOWING BEFORE BAKING: chopped kalamata olives, sautéed shallots, caramelized onions, squeezed and mashed cloves of roasted garlic, freshly ground black pepper, or chopped fresh sage, parsley, oregano, or basil. The variations are endless!

APPLE ROSEMARY FOCACCIA: A daring combination that's beautiful in the fall! Remove the core from a small red cooking apple (Cortland, Macoun, or Winesap are great) and don't peel. Slice as thinly as possible and press into the top of the dough after the second rise, before baking. Drizzle the top with olive oil, sprinkle with salt and fresh rosemary, and add a drizzle of fresh lemon juice. Bake as directed! For an extra sizzle, broil the top of the focaccia on high for 1 or 2 minutes, to brown the apples.

DOUBLE
ROSEMARY FOCACCIA

MAKES 1 LARGE, FLAT LOAF /
TIME: 2 HRS, including rising time

1 (¼-ounce) package active dry yeast

1¼ cups warm water

3 cups all-purpose flour, or 1½ cups each all-purpose and whole wheat flour, plus more for dusting

3 tablespoons olive oil, plus more for bowl and pan

1 teaspoon chopped dried rosemary

1 teaspoon salt

Toppings:

3 tablespoons whole fresh rosemary leaves

3 tablespoons high-quality extra-virgin olive oil

1 teaspoon flake sea salt (e.g., Maldon)

TIPS

Sammiches (a.k.a. sandwiches) loaded with lots of fresh or grilled veggies are even better if stuffed into sliced, fresh focaccia. Try toasting or even grilling them, maybe with a slap of Sweet Basil Pesto Tapenade (page 70) or Sundried Tomato Dip (page 70), used as a spread. You are welcome.

Live in cold, drafty bat cave and looking for a cozy place to let sleeping dough rise? Preheat the oven to 250°F for about 10 minutes, turn the oven off, and ta-da, you have a warm place for your dough to rise.

YOGURT
NAAN BREAD

MAKES 8 LARGE FLATBREADS / TIME:
ABOUT 2 HRS, mostly dough rising time

¾ cup warm water

1 tablespoon organic sugar

1 (¼-ounce) packet (or 2¼ teaspoons)
active dry yeast

1 cup plain, unsweetened soy, coconut,
almond, or cashew yogurt

3 tablespoons melted coconut oil (your
choice, virgin or refined)

1½ teaspoons salt

2 cups all-purpose flour

1½ cups whole wheat flour, plus more for
kneading

3 tablespoons melted vegan butter or
melted coconut oil

VARIATIONS

*Plain naan are excellent, but have some fun
by kneading into the dough one or more of the
following:*

3 tablespoons chopped garlic

½ cup finely minced red onion

1 cup roughly chopped scallion

½ cup roughly chopped fresh mint or
cilantro

*Or try pressing into the top of each naan
(after brushing with vegan butter)*

1 tablespoon cumin seeds

1 tablespoon kalonji seeds (also called
nigella or black cumin)

1 tablespoon dried rosemary

1 tablespoon sesame seeds

Rice is nice, but the excitement of eating and also making naan—the tender, puffy raised Indian flatbread—makes any curry feel like a party. The addition of your favorite vegan plain yogurt adds tangy depth and a wholesome moist texture to these rip-able, dip-able, foldable, and totally delicious naan. Why not double or triple the recipe and stock the freezer for naan-stop action anytime?

Combine the water and sugar in a large mixing bowl. Sprinkle in the yeast and set aside for 5 minutes to proof; the yeast will start to foam. Stir in the yogurt, only 2 tablespoons of the coconut oil, and the salt with a wooden spoon. Add the all-purpose flour and stir, then sprinkle in a little bit of the whole wheat flour (about ½ cup at a time) to form a soft dough. If the dough is very sticky, sprinkle in a few more tablespoons of whole wheat flour.

Lightly flour a clean work surface with whole wheat flour and knead the dough for 2 to 3 minutes, or until smooth. Clean the mixing bowl and grease the inside of the bowl with the remaining tablespoon of coconut oil. Add the dough, turn it a few times to coat with oil, and cover the bowl with a clean dish towel. Set the bowl in a warm, draft-free place for about an hour, or until the dough has doubled in size.

Punch down the dough and spread out a little on a lightly floured work surface. If you're adding herbs, seeds, or garlic (see variations), sprinkle it on the dough and fold a few times to mix it in. Roll the dough into a log about 12 inches long, then cut into eight equal pieces and gently shape the pieces into rounds. Cover the rounds with plastic wrap and set aside for about 20 minutes to rise a bit and relax the dough.

It's baking time! Lightly flour the work surface (and continue to flour as you work if the dough gets sticky), flour a rolling pin, and roll out each dough round into a circle less than ½ inch thick. It's okay if your circles are not perfect; naan should look carefree and handmade!

Preheat the largest skillet or griddle you have (a 10- to 12-inch cast-iron skillet or griddle is great) over high heat. Have ready nearby the melted vegan butter or coconut oil, a pastry brush, and any toppings you may be using (see variations). Ideally the hot surface should keep your naan from sticking, but also make sure the bottom of the dough is well-floured. Gently lower a dough circle into the hot pan, brush the top with some melted butter, and sprinkle with goodies, if desired. Cook for 2 to 3 minutes, or until the bread is puffy and feels firm; then carefully lift a corner of the naan and check to see whether the bottom has toasted to a nice golden brown color. If so, it's ready to flip: slide a spatula under the naan and flip over. Cook on the other side for 1 to 2 minutes to brown the tops of any large bubbles that have formed.

Promptly remove the finished naan and wrap it in a big, clean dish towel to keep warm and soft. Repeat with the remaining naan, wrapping together in the towel to keep the bread warm and tender. Serve hot, either ripping it with your fingers or cutting it into quarters for dipping and scooping curries! Save any remaining naan by wrapping up tightly in foil and freezing for up to 2 months, reheating in the oven or on a griddle as needed.

These soft little roti (West Indian–style flatbreads) are not exactly meant for wrapping around fillings; rather, they're the ideal size for shaping, grilling, and scooping up that curry simmering on the stovetop. The addition of poppy seeds makes them crunchy, munchy good and the breads themselves are cleverly stuffed with a crumbly poppy seed mixture. Leftovers are fabulous toasted for breakfast, great with coffee and jam. Rolling and folding the dough (with new, improved instructions!) may be something new to get the hang of, but with practice you can have flaky, tender flatbread in under thirty minutes.

Prepare the roti dough: In a large bowl, combine the whole wheat flour, cornmeal, poppy and cumin seeds, and salt. Stir in the water and mix to form a soft dough. Knead the dough in the bowl for 5 minutes, or until smooth. If the dough is very sticky, knead in a little extra flour, 1 tablespoon at a time. Coat the dough in a little oil by pouring a teaspoon of oil onto the dough and turning it several times in the bowl. Cover with a damp, clean dish towel and let it rest for 10 minutes.

Make the crumbs: In a small bowl, combine the flour, cornmeal, oil, and salt. Mix with fingers or a fork until a dry, crumbly mixture forms.

After the dough has rested, divide it into eight balls on a surface dusted with flour. Use a rolling pin, lightly dusted with flour, to roll a ball into a circle as thin as possible and brush with oil. Roll the dough into a tube, then tightly coil the tube into a circle. Flatten and roll the coil into a thin circle. Brush with oil and repeat the rolling and coiling, and roll into a circle again. This time, brush with oil and sprinkle on some of the crumbs. Roll, coil, and roll out into a circle about 8 inches wide.

Repeat with the remaining dough. Be sure to sprinkle extra flour on top of the dough circles when stacking, or use pieces of waxed paper to separate.

Preheat a cast-iron pan or heavy-bottomed, nonstick skillet over medium heat. Gently place a dough circle on the hot pan and bake on each side for 3 to 4 minutes, using tongs or a large wooden spatula to turn it. The dough will bubble and brown spots will form; pressing down on cooked parts of the roti can cause bubbles to grow. Stack the cooked roti on top of one another and keep warm and soft by wrapping in a clean, damp dish towel until ready to serve.

To reheat, wrap tightly in foil for conventional ovens or wrap in damp paper towels for a microwave.

VARIATION

WHOLE WHEAT PUMPKIN SEED ROTI: Use 1½ cups whole wheat pastry flour and 1½ cups of regular whole wheat flour for the dough. Add ½ cup of pepitas (shelled pumpkin seeds) to the dough while kneading.

POPPY SEED–
CORNMEAL ROTI

**MAKES 8 (8-INCH-WIDE) FLATBREADS /
TIME: 30 MIN**

Roti dough:

3 cups whole wheat flour, plus more if needed

½ cup cornmeal

2 tablespoons poppy seeds

1 teaspoon cumin seeds

1¼ teaspoons salt

1½ cups warm water

Olive or sunflower seed oil, for bowl

Crumbs:

¼ cup whole wheat pastry flour

¼ cup cornmeal

2 tablespoons olive or sunflower seed oil, plus more oil for brushing

¼ teaspoon salt

This tender and moist bread is packed with corn-y goodness to maximum capacity. It's yummy plain, but even better with a savory topping or sautéed corn in the batter; see variations. Chili, beans, and barbecued things seem a little naked when not accessorized with this corn bread. We bake it in a cast-iron skillet, but if you don't have an oven-safe skillet, use a 9 x 13-inch baking pan.

Preheat the oven to 350°F. If making plain corn bread, lightly oil the bottom and sides of the cast-iron pan and place it in the oven to warm while the oven preheats, then proceed to prepare the corn bread. If using a variation, follow its directions first before proceeding further.

If preparing the jalapeño-onion variation: Preheat a cast-iron skillet over medium heat. Sauté the onion and jalapeño in the oil for about 5 minutes, or until the onion is softened. Add the salt and mix well. Transfer to a bowl. Don't wash the pan; you'll pour the batter right into it in a bit.

If preparing the double corn variation: Preheat a cast-iron skillet over medium heat. Sauté the corn kernels in the oil for about 7 minutes, until the corn is slightly browned. Transfer to a bowl. Don't wash the pan; you'll pour the batter right into it in a bit.

Prepare the corn bread: Combine the milk and vinegar in a measuring cup and set aside to curdle as you prepare everything else.

In a large mixing bowl, sift together the cornmeal, flour, sugar, baking powder, and salt. Create a well in the center and add the milk mixture and oil. Use a wooden spoon to mix together until just combined; some lumps are okay. If using the double-corn variation, fold the corn into the batter.

Pour the batter into the cast-iron skillet. If using the jalapeño-onion variation, scatter the topping over the batter in the pan. Bake for 30 to 32 minutes, or until a toothpick or butter knife inserted through the middle comes out clean. Remove from the oven and let cool just a bit before serving.

SKILLET
CORN BREAD
& variations

MAKES 8 BIG SLICES / TIME: 35 MIN

Basic corn bread:

⅓ cup canola oil (plus more for skillet if making plain corn bread)

2 cups unsweetened nondairy milk

2 teaspoons apple cider vinegar

2 cups cornmeal

1 cup all-purpose flour

¼ cup organic sugar

2 teaspoons baking powder

½ teaspoon salt

VARIATIONS

JALAPEÑO-ONION CORN BREAD: 1 tablespoon canola oil, 1 medium-size yellow onion, sliced into 1 x ½-inch slices, 3 jalapeño peppers, seeded and sliced thinly, ¼ teaspoon salt

DOUBLE-CORN CORN BREAD: 1 cup fresh or frozen and partially thawed corn kernels, 1 tablespoon canola oil

SCALLION
FLATBREAD

MAKES 8 FLATBREADS /
TIME: 30 MIN

Flatbread:

1 cup all-purpose flour, plus more for
dusting

1 cup whole wheat flour

2 teaspoons organic sugar

¾ teaspoon salt

2 tablespoons neutral-tasting vegetable oil,
plus ½ cup for brushing

2 teaspoons toasted sesame oil

5 scallions, green parts only, sliced into ½-
inch lengths

¾ cup warm water

Dipping sauce:

3 tablespoons soy sauce

2 tablespoons rice vinegar

2 teaspoons organic sugar

½ teaspoon finely grated fresh ginger (use
a Microplane grater; it should resemble
almost pureed ginger)

1 teaspoon sesame seeds, lightly crushed or
left whole

This savory flatbread is a little like the love child between a flaky paratha (Indian grilled buttery flatbread) and a scallion pancake. Instead of deep-frying, we grill it on an iron skillet and serve with a sharp and savory soy dipping sauce. Include these in any Asian meal as an appetizer, in place of rice or as a side with thick curries.

Prepare the flatbread: In a large bowl, sift together the flours, sugar, and salt. Pour in the vegetable and sesame oils and mix until slightly crumbly. Add the chopped scallions and stir in ½ cup of the warm water, then add the remaining water 1 tablespoon at a time until a soft, nonsticky dough forms (add more water very gradually, if necessary).

Turn out the dough onto a lightly floured surface, kneading until smooth. Roll the dough into a thick rope and slice into eight equal pieces. Roll each piece into a ball, coat the surface of each ball with a little oil, and return to the mixing bowl. Cover with a damp, clean dish towel and let it rest for 10 minutes.

After the dough has rested, place a dough ball on a surface dusted with flour. Use a rolling pin, lightly dusted with flour, to roll the ball into a circle as thin as possible and brush with oil. Roll the dough into a tube, then tightly coil the tube into a circle. Flatten and roll the coil into a thin circle. Brush with oil and repeat the rolling and coiling, and roll into a circle again. Roll, coil, and roll out into a circle about 8 inches wide.

Repeat with the remaining dough. Be sure to sprinkle extra flour on top of the dough circles when stacking, or use pieces of waxed paper to separate.

Preheat a cast-iron skillet over medium-high heat. Lightly brush each flatbread with vegetable oil on each side, place on the heated skillet, and cook until the dough bubbles and rises, about 2 minutes. Flip once, pressing down with a spatula when it starts to bubble, and cook for another 1 to 2 minutes, until the bread is slightly puffed but not too hard. Some dark browned spots are good.

Stack the cooked flatbreads on top of one another, loosely wrapped with a clean dish towel. This will help keep the breads warm and soft. To serve, slice into triangles and serve with dipping sauce. The breads will toughen when cooled; to soften, wrap in a moist paper towel and microwave, or wrap the breads tightly in foil and warm in a conventional oven.

Prepare the dipping sauce: Combine all the sauce ingredients and serve with the hot flatbread.

There is nothing wrong with basic. In fact, recipes become basic for a reason: everyone loves them! And so, let's master this little triangle of perfection—the berry scone. Not too sweet, fluffy and crispy at once, bursting with beautiful fresh berries and perfect for dunking into coffee or tea. You can use any berry you like here; blues, rasps, sliced straws, or blackberry. If using frozen, the baking time will be a bit longer, so adjust it accordingly. If you're craving a little extra sweetness and crunch, sprinkle the scones with turbinado sugar before baking.

Preheat the oven to 375°F. Lightly spray a large, rimmed baking sheet with nonstick cooking spray.

In a measuring cup, whisk together the milk and vinegar and set aside to curdle.

Combine the flour, sugar, baking powder, and salt in a large mixing bowl. Add the coconut oil in small clumps, then use your fingers or a pastry cutter to cut it into the flour until the flour texture becomes pebblelike.

Create a well in the center and add the milk mixture and vanilla. Mix with a wooden spoon until about half of the flour is incorporated. Fold in the berries and mix until all the ingredients are just moistened, taking care not to overmix.

Place a piece of parchment on the counter. Divide the dough into two equal blobs. Shape each blob into a disk roughly 8 inches in diameter. Using a sharp knife, cut one disk in half. Then cut each of those halves into thirds, so that you have six cute triangles. Transfer the triangles to a baking sheet, then repeat with the other blob of dough.

Bake until the tops are lightly browned and firm to the touch, 22 to 26 minutes.

BASIC BUT BRILLIANT
BERRY SCONES

MAKES 12 SCONES / TOTAL TIME: 1 HR /
ACTIVE TIME: 30 MIN

Nonstick cooking spray, for pan

1¼ cups unsweetened nondairy milk, almond preferred

1 tablespoon apple cider vinegar

3 cups all-purpose flour

½ cup organic sugar

2 tablespoons baking powder

½ teaspoon salt

½ cup refined coconut oil

1½ teaspoons pure vanilla extract

2 cups fresh berries

BANANA-DATE
SCONES

MAKES 8 LARGE SCONES /
TIME: 40 MIN

Coconut oil, for oiling pans (if not lining)
and measuring cup

8 ounces pitted dates

1 cup plus 1 tablespoon all-purpose flour

2 tablespoons ground flaxseeds

⅓ cup unsweetened almond or coconut-
based milk

1 cup mashed, very ripe banana (about
3 bananas)

⅓ cup canola oil

3 tablespoons coconut palm sugar or
organic sugar

1¼ cups whole wheat pastry flour

2 teaspoons baking powder

1 teaspoon ground cinnamon

¼ teaspoon freshly grated nutmeg

½ teaspoon salt

½ cup chopped walnuts

TIP

This recipe makes large, drop-style scones, but
you can make them smaller by using an ice-
cream scoop and reducing the baking time by
about 5 minutes.

We made these fruity scones packed with dates and bananas with health food
in mind, but really they are just as delicious as dessert. We've since updated
the flavor profile by swapping out the health food store–era brown rice syrup
in favor of a touch of flavorful coconut palm sugar. Dates make these stay
fresh a little longer than most scones, but they really are excellent split and
toasted the next day with a dab of your favorite vegan butter and served with
plenty of black coffee.

Preheat the oven to 350°F and lightly oil two medium-size baking sheets, or line
them with parchment paper. Finely chop the dates, place them in a small bowl,
and sprinkle with the tablespoon of all-purpose flour. Toss the dates to thoroughly coat with the flour, breaking apart any clumps.

In a large bowl, whisk together the flaxseeds and milk. Whisk in the mashed
banana, canola oil, and coconut sugar. In a separate bowl, sift together the all-purpose flour, whole wheat pastry flour, baking powder, cinnamon, nutmeg, and salt.
Stir into the banana mixture and combine until the ingredients are just moistened;
the dough will be thick yet sticky. Fold in the chopped dates and walnuts.

Lightly oil a ½-cup measuring cup and scoop generous half-cupfuls of dough onto
the prepared baking sheets, leaving about 3 inches of space between the scones.
Gently pat down the tops of the scones and dab with a little milk, if desired. Bake
for 32 to 34 minutes, or until browned and firm. Transfer from the baking sheets
to a wire cooling rack to complete cooling.

These big, cakelike scones are almost like a pumpkin dessert but designed to reign supreme at brunch and saddle up to your best soy latte game. We've updated the recipe since its original version a decade ago with a little less sugar, a wholesome blend of canola and coconut oil, and easy-breezy yet always flavorful canned pumpkin. This recipe makes lots of big scones, so we think they would make a great addition to any fall brunch or Halloween tea party.

Preheat the oven to 350°F and line a large baking sheet with parchment paper. In a small plastic bowl, stir together canola and coconut oils. Transfer to the refrigerator and set aside for at least 20 minutes to cool and solidify for use.

In a large bowl, sift together all-purpose flour, pastry flour, baking powder, baking soda, brown sugar, granulated sugar, cinnamon, ginger, cardamom, cloves, nutmeg, and salt. Use a fork to crumble the cold oil mixture into chunks, toss into the flour mixture, and cut into the flour with a pastry cutter or the fork until the mixture looks crumbly. Make a well in the center of the flour mixture.

In a medium-size bowl, whisk together the ground flaxseeds, coconut yogurt, and pumpkin puree.

Fold the pumpkin mixture into the dry ingredients, then fold in the cranberries, if using. Stir only just enough to moisten all the ingredients and form a ball of soft dough.

Divide the dough into two equal portions. Transfer each portion to the baking sheet and flatten into a large circle just over 1 inch thick (leave at least 2 inches space between each circle). Brush each round with a little nondairy milk and sprinkle evenly with pepitas. Slice each round into six wedges.

Bake for 30 minutes, or until the scones are firm and lightly browned. Remove from the oven and let cool for 5 minutes before separating the scones and transferring to a wire cooling rack to complete cooling.

If you prefer a scone with a drier texture, after slicing the dough, gently pull each wedge apart and create about 2 inches of space between each scone before baking. Bake for another 8 to 10 minutes, until the bottoms of the scones are browned and feel firm to the touch.

PUMPKIN-CRANBERRY
SCONES

MAKES 12 LARGE SCONES /
TIME: 45 MIN

¼ cup canola oil

¼ cup virgin or refined coconut oil, melted

2 cups all-purpose flour

1 cup whole wheat pastry flour

4 teaspoons baking powder

1 teaspoon baking soda

½ cup organic dark brown sugar

¼ cup organic granulated sugar

2 teaspoons ground cinnamon

1 teaspoon ground cardamom

1 teaspoon ground ginger

¼ teaspoon ground cloves

¼ teaspoon freshly grated nutmeg

1¼ teaspoons salt

4 teaspoons ground flaxseeds

¾ cup plain coconut, almond, or your favorite nondairy yogurt

1½ cups canned pure pumpkin puree (not pumpkin pie mix)

½ cup dried cranberries (optional)

Unsweetened nondairy milk, for brushing

¼ cup shelled pepitas (shelled pumpkin seeds), for garnish

TIP

We love home-roasted pumpkin for soups and savory dishes, but after years of baking we agree that the drier consistency and concentrated flavor of canned pumpkin works better in baked goods than watery homemade pumpkin puree. Organic canned pumpkin is easier to find than ever, so give yourself a much-needed break and reach for the canned stuff for delicious scones every time.

BANANA–WHEAT GERM
MUFFINS

MAKES 12 MUFFINS /
TIME: ABOUT 40 MIN

Nonstick cooking spray, for pan

1 cup unsweetened nondairy milk

1 teaspoon apple cider vinegar

2 very ripe bananas

⅓ cup canola oil

⅓ cup organic sugar

1 teaspoon pure vanilla extract

1¼ cups whole wheat pastry flour or all-purpose flour

¾ cup wheat germ

1 tablespoon ground cinnamon

2 teaspoons baking powder

½ teaspoon salt

Wheat germ: not just for your grandma's oatmeal anymore! In the spirit of "muffins are not desserts," we present this no-nonsense, whole-grain muffin. They have lots of big banana flavor and a little bit of crunch provided by our friend wheat germ. A big scoop of cinnamon gives these guys what for.

Preheat the oven to 375°F. Lightly spray a 12-cup muffin tin with nonstick cooking spray.

Pour the milk into a measuring cup and add the vinegar to it. Set it aside to curdle.

Meanwhile, mash the bananas in a large mixing bowl. Add the milk mixture to the bowl along with the oil, sugar, and vanilla, and mix well.

In a separate bowl, mix together the flour, wheat germ, cinnamon, baking powder, and salt. Add this to the banana mixture and use a wooden spoon to gently stir the ingredients, until all the dry ingredients are just moistened.

Fill the prepared muffin cups three-quarters full and bake for 22 minutes. Remove from the oven and, once cool enough to handle, transfer to a wire cooling rack to cool the rest of the way. You can also serve them warm, if you like!

Another wholesome muffin recipe, updated and revised, too, because we care. Adding cooked whole grains is a convenient way to use leftovers, and we love how cooked quinoa adds crunchy, toothsome texture to these almond-scented muffins. So, next time you're cooking up a batch of plain quinoa for dinner, set aside some to make these muffins the next day and get excited for the next morning. Or if you need to make a batch from scratch, follow the package directions or the directions on page 39 and allow the quinoa to cool in the fridge for about an hour for firm, easier-to-use cooked quinoa.

Preheat the oven to 350°F and lightly spray a 12-cup muffin tin with nonstick cooking spray or line with paper liners.

In a medium-size bowl, whisk together the milk and ground flaxseeds. Allow to sit for 1 minute, then whisk in the oil, maple syrup, and vanilla and almond extracts.

In a large bowl, sift together the flour, almond meal, baking powder, baking soda, salt, and cinnamon.

Add the wet ingredients to the dry, mixing only just enough to moisten; a few small lumps are okay. Gently fold in the cooked quinoa and the apricots and mix until only the large lumps are gone.

Pour into the prepared muffin tin, scatter the tops with sliced almonds, and bake for about 24 minutes, or until a toothpick inserted into the center of a muffin comes out clean.

ALMOND-QUINOA
CRUNCH MUFFINS

MAKES 12 MUFFINS / TIME: 35 MIN, not including cooking quinoa

Nonstick cooking spray, for pan (optional)

1 cup unsweetened, plain almond, coconut-based, or soy milk

1 tablespoon ground flaxseeds

⅓ cup canola or olive oil

¼ cup pure maple syrup

½ teaspoon pure vanilla extract

½ teaspoon almond extract

1¼ cups all-purpose or whole wheat pastry flour

¼ cup almond meal

1½ teaspoons baking powder

½ teaspoon baking soda

½ teaspoon salt

½ teaspoon ground cinnamon

1¼ cups cooked and cooled red, white, or black quinoa

½ cup finely chopped dried apricots or dried cherries

¼ cup sliced or slivered almonds, for garnish

CARROT-PINEAPPLE
SUNSHINE MUFFINS

MAKES 12 MUFFINS /
TIME: ABOUT 40 MIN

Nonstick cooking spray, for pan (optional)

½ cup plain almond, coconut, or your favorite nondairy yogurt

⅔ cup unsweetened, plain almond, coconut-based, or soy milk

1 tablespoon ground flaxseeds

¼ cup canola oil

⅓ cup organic dark brown sugar

½ cup crushed pineapple, well drained

½ cup finely shredded carrot (about 1 large carrot)

1 heaping teaspoon finely grated orange zest (from 1 large orange)

½ cup golden raisins or finely chopped dried apricots

1⅓ cups whole wheat pastry flour or all-purpose flour, or a combination of both

1½ teaspoons baking powder

½ teaspoon baking soda

1 teaspoon ground ginger

½ teaspoon ground cinnamon

½ teaspoon salt

Bring some happy-fun-time-pineapple-carrot joy to your dismal-gray-sad morning with these muffins and slay breakfast sadness with each fruity bite. They really are like a burst of sunshine, only better because they freeze great and are much easier to shove into your face hole than sunlight. Like many of these recipes we've updated them to contain less sugar and let the fruity goodness of the ingredients shine through.

Preheat the oven to 350°F and lightly spray a 12-cup muffin tin with nonstick cooking spray or line with paper liners.

In a large bowl, whisk together the yogurt, milk, and ground flaxseeds. Whisk in the oil and brown sugar.

Squeeze the crushed pineapple to remove as much excess juice as possible and add the pineapple to the bowl. Add the carrot, orange zest, and raisins, and mix thoroughly. Sift in the flour, baking powder, baking soda, ginger, cinnamon, and salt. Stir only just enough to moisten the dry ingredients.

Scoop into the prepared muffin tin, filling to the top of each cup or a little bit above (the batter is chunky and these muffins don't rise very much). Bake for 24 to 26 minutes, or until a toothpick or a thin, sharp knife inserted into the center of a muffin comes out clean. Allow to cool for 5 minutes in the tin before transferring the muffins to a wire cooling rack.

TIPS These muffins don't rise very high, preferring to have a flat, crisp top instead. So don't be afraid to fill each muffin cup to the top, or even a little bit past that.

Fresh pineapple doesn't work so well in this recipe, so be sure to use only canned, crushed pineapple. The enzymes in fresh pineapple can interfere with the leavening process and cause uneven baking.

This is Isa mom's recipe, but we think it was originally from a Fannie Farmer cookbook from the '60s and has been tampered with over the years. This is a bake sale favorite. It smells just as lovely as it tastes!

Preheat the oven to 325°F. Lightly spray a 9 x 5-inch loaf pan with nonstick cooking spray.

In a large mixing bowl, mix together the milk, orange juice, oil, sugar, and vanilla.

Sift in the flour, baking powder, baking soda, salt, and allspice. Mix just until smooth. The batter will be thicker than a normal cake batter, so don't be alarmed!

Fold in the orange zest, cranberries, and walnuts. Spoon the batter into the prepared loaf pan.

Bake for about 1 hour or until a toothpick inserted into the loaf comes out clean. Remove from the oven and let the bread cool for about 15 minutes before inverting it onto a wire cooling rack. Flip it right side up to cool further.

CRANBERRY-ORANGE-NUT
BREAD

MAKES 1 LOAF / TIME: 1 HR 20 MIN,
not including cooling time

Nonstick cooking spray, for pan
½ cup unsweetened nondairy milk
¼ cup fresh orange juice
¼ cup canola oil
1 cup organic sugar
1 teaspoon pure vanilla extract
2 cups all-purpose flour
1¼ teaspoons baking powder
½ teaspoon baking soda
½ teaspoon salt
¼ teaspoon ground allspice
1 tablespoon freshly grated orange zest
1 cup chopped fresh cranberries
½ cup chopped walnuts

LOWER-FAT
BANANA BREAD

MAKES 1 LOAF / TIME: 1 HR 20 MIN,
not including cooling time

Nonstick cooking spray, for pan

1 cup mashed very ripe banana (about 3 bananas)

½ cup organic sugar

¼ cup applesauce

¼ cup canola oil

2 tablespoons molasses

2 cups all-purpose flour

¾ teaspoon baking soda

1 teaspoon ground cinnamon

¼ teaspoon freshly grated nutmeg

½ teaspoon salt

½ cup chocolate chips

TIP

Spray the measuring spoon with a little oil before measuring out the molasses; it will slide out very easily.

This bread is pure, unadulterated banana goodness. No one will know it's lower in fat, pinky swear.

Never use a hand mixer for banana bread because it makes it gummy; treat it like a muffin batter and mix with a wooden spoon just until the wet and dry ingredients are combined. In fact, if you would like to turn these into muffins, pour the batter into a greased muffin tin and bake for eighteen minutes.

Preheat the oven to 350°F. Lightly spray a 9 x 5-inch loaf pan with nonstick cooking spray.

In a large mixing bowl, combine the mashed banana, sugar, applesauce, oil, and molasses and whisk briskly to incorporate.

Sift in the flour, baking soda, spices, and salt. Use a wooden spoon to mix until the wet and dry ingredients are just combined. Fold in the chocolate chips, if using.

Transfer the batter to the prepared pan and bake for 45 to 50 minutes. The top should be lightly browned and a knife inserted through the center should come out clean. (If you're using the chips then of course some chocolate will come out on your knife.)

Remove from the oven and invert onto a cooling wire rack; flip the bread right side up and let cool.

In the first edition of *Veganomicon* we felt the need to explain oat bran: "Oat bran can be found in the cereals section; it's sold as a hot cereal but also leads a secret double life of lending plenty of heart-healthy fiber to baked goods."

By now everybody, and we mean EVERYBODY, knows that oat bran muffins, especially enhanced with apples, are about as honest as a muffin can get. We've enhanced the oat goodness of these muffins with flax seed and a dusting of oat bran, too. Enjoy this enduring throwback to a simpler breakfast, before we drank kale smoothies and coconut oil bullet coffee first thing in the morning, with these hearty cinnamon-laced muffins.

Preheat the oven to 350°F and lightly spray a 12-cup nonstick muffin tin with nonstick cooking spray.

In a large bowl, whisk together the milk, ground flaxseeds, applesauce, oil, and brown sugar.

In a smaller bowl, sift together the flour, oat bran, baking powder, baking soda, spices, and salt. Fold the dry ingredients into the wet; stir only to moisten and don't overmix. Fold in the raisins. Use an ice-cream scoop or measuring cup to scoop the batter into the prepared muffin cups. Sprinkle about a teaspoon of oat bran on top of each muffin.

Bake for 30 minutes, or until a toothpick inserted into the middle of a muffin comes out clean. Allow the muffins to cool in the tin for a few minutes, then transfer to a wire cooling rack to complete cooling.

APPLESAUCE 'N' RAISINS

OAT BRAN MUFFINS

MAKES 12 MUFFINS /
TIME: 45 MIN

Nonstick cooking spray, for pan

¾ cup plain, sweetened almond, coconut-based, or soy milk

3 tablespoons ground flaxseeds

1 cup applesauce

¼ cup olive or canola oil

½ cup packed organic dark brown sugar

1½ cups all-purpose or whole wheat pastry flour

¾ cup oat bran, plus more for topping muffins

1 tablespoon baking powder

½ teaspoon baking soda

2 teaspoons ground cinnamon

½ teaspoon freshly grated nutmeg

½ teaspoon salt

½ cup dark raisins or dried cranberries

MAPLE WALNUT
PINWHEELS

MAKES 12 TO 14 ROLLS /
TIME: ABOUT 2 HRS

Dough:

1¼ cups plain, unsweetened almond, coconut-based, or soy milk, plus more for brushing

¼ cup refined coconut oil, plus a little more for greasing (if using)

⅓ cup warm water

1 (¼-ounce) package active dry yeast

4 to 4¼ cups all-purpose flour, whole wheat white flour, or a combo of the two, plus more for dusting

⅓ cup organic dark brown sugar

1 teaspoon salt

½ teaspoon ground cardamom

½ teaspoon ground allspice

Filling:

2 tablespoons refined coconut oil, melted

2 tablespoons olive oil

2 tablespoons pure maple syrup

1 cup packed organic dark brown sugar

1 cup walnut pieces, toasted

Maple icing:

1½ cups organic confectioners' sugar, sifted

2 tablespoons refined coconut oil

2 tablespoons plain, unsweetened almond, coconut-based, or soy milk

1 teaspoon maple extract

½ cup toasted walnut pieces, for garnish

TIP

If you like, flip over the buns when hot, right out of the oven, so that the gooey stuff on the bottom is transferred to the top.

Sticky buns are the great equalizer: young, old, every economic stratum, every gender loves vegan sticky buns. We've since updated this *Veganomicon* favorite by taking out vegan margarine and adding the crunch of walnuts, as well as a deeper and richer maple flavor.

Prepare the dough: Heat the milk and coconut oil in a small saucepan over medium heat, stirring until the oil has melted. Remove from the heat and let cool until tepid.

In a measuring cup, sprinkle the yeast on the warm water. Set aside for 5 minutes and let the yeast foam. In a large mixing bowl, stir together the flour, granulated sugar, salt, cardamom, and allspice and form a well in the center. Pour in the milk mixture and the yeast and stir into a soft dough. If it's sticky, add extra flour a few tablespoons at a time.

Turn out the dough onto a lightly floured surface and knead for 2 minutes. Gather into a ball. Lightly grease the mixing bowl with a dab of coconut oil, add the kneaded dough, and turn the dough in the bowl to coat the surface with oil. Cover the bowl with plastic wrap, cover with a clean dish towel, and set in a warm, draft-free place to rise for about 1½ hours. The dough should double in size. While the dough rises, generously grease two 8-inch round cake pans or line with parchment paper.

Punch down the fully risen dough and fold a few times on a lightly floured surface. Use a rolling pin to shape the dough into an 11 x 18-inch rectangle that is ¼ inch thick. It helps to use your hands to gently stretch and pull the dough to shape.

Prepare the filling: Combine all the filling ingredients, except the walnut pieces, in a small bowl. Place the bowl in the freezer and chill for 10 minutes, or until the mixture has firmed up to a thick, easily spreadable mixture. Spread the mixture over the dough, keeping about 2 inches without filling along one of the long edges. Scatter the walnut pieces over the filling.

Roll the dough fairly tightly, starting from the filled long edge and move to the other bare edge (like rolling sushi or a jelly roll). If desired, seal the seam of the roll with a little nondairy milk and place the roll, seam side down, on a cutting board. With a sharp serrated knife, slice the roll into 1½-inch pieces and fit the slices into both cake pans (it will be a snug fit!). Cover the slices loosely with plastic wrap and then a kitchen towel. Move to a cool place and let rise another 30 minutes.

While the rolls are rising, preheat the oven to 350°F. If desired, brush the tops of the rolls with a little nondairy milk just before baking. Bake for 25 to 30 minutes, or until the tops are golden and the filling is bubbling. Transfer the pans to a wire cooling rack to cool for 10 minutes before flipping the buns onto serving platters to completely finish cooling before frosting.

Prepare the icing: In a medium-size bowl, cut the cold oil into the confectioners' sugar to form crumbs. Whisk in the milk and maple extract. Drizzle over the cooled buns and sprinkle with the walnuts.

CHAPTER TWELVE

COOKIES
&
BARS

**True story: over a decade ago when
we were developing the cookies and brownies for this very
section, lots of them with completely delicious
ingredients that are naturally vegan (chocolate, peanut
butter, pistachios, coconut, etc.), we'd occasionally
run into veteran vegans who admitted they hadn't eaten
a single cookie since going vegan.**

Not the best advertisement for would-be cookie-loving vegans!

Since those dark days superb vegan sweets and treats have blossomed into a full blown industry. There is SO much out there to choose from . . . dedicated vegan bakeries, vegan baked goods stacked up in coffee shops and cafés, and market aisles bursting with irresistible vegan grab-and-go treats. We even wonder whether anyone still makes great vegan cookies at home. Well, we certainly think they still do. You can't replicate the aroma and gloom-fighting powers in mixing up a batch of chocolate chip or oatmeal cookies on a rainy day, or the thrill of sharing homemade almond cookies and green tea ice-cream sandwiches with a future best friend. Or take it up a notch and introduce someone skeptical of delicious vegan sweets to blueberry brownies or apple caramel bars: vegan cookies can change hearts, minds, and perhaps even the world.

---------- ◆ ----------

VEGANOMICON
CHOCOLATE CHIP COOKIES

**MAKES ABOUT 24 (2-INCH) COOKIES /
TIME: 30 MIN**

¼ cup unsweetened almond milk or your favorite nondairy milk

2 tablespoons ground golden flaxseeds

½ cup organic dark brown sugar

3 tablespoons organic granulated sugar

⅓ cup canola or mild-tasting olive oil

⅓ cup virgin coconut oil, softened

2 teaspoons pure vanilla extract

½ teaspoon finely grated lemon zest

1½ cups unbleached all-purpose flour

½ teaspoon baking soda

½ teaspoon salt

¾ cup vegan chocolate chips

Nonstick cooking spray, for pans

1 teaspoon Maldon or other flaky sea salt

A decade later and countless meals made by readers across the world is a strange and startling time to realize a groundbreaking vegan cookbook lacks a recipe for the cornerstone of baked goods: an everyday chocolate chip cookie. Forgive us.

The bit of lemon in the batter doesn't make it taste lemony: the citrus weaves its way through the brown sugary dough and punches up all those chocolate chips. Is this the ultimate cookie? Who can say? But it's a damned good chocolate chipper with a very modern flourish of chunky sea salt.

In a glass measuring cup or small bowl, whisk together the milk and ground flaxseeds until smooth. Chill the mixture in the fridge while you prepare the other ingredients for the dough.

Use an electric mixer or a rubber spatula to cream together the brown sugar, granulated sugar, the canola or olive oil, and softened coconut oil in a large mixing bowl until thick and creamy. Scoop in the milk mixture, add the vanilla and lemon zest, and mix until smooth.

In a small bowl, sift together the flour, baking soda, and salt. Add half of the flour mixture to the wet ingredients and use a rubber spatula to mix together. Fold in ½ cup of the chocolate chips (setting aside the remaining ¼ cup to decorate the tops of the cookies) and the remaining flour mixture. The dough will be super-thick, so use the spatula or your fingers to press the chips back into the dough. Tightly cover the mixing bowl and chill the dough for 1 hour or overnight.

Preheat the oven to 350°F. Lightly spray two large, light metal baking sheets with cooking spray. Or even better, line with parchment paper to easily prevent any sticking.

For each cookie, scoop about 2 big tablespoons of dough and shape into a ball. Arrange about 2 inches apart on the prepared baking sheets, press a few chocolate chips on top, and flatten them with the palm of your hand to about 2½ inches in diameter. Sprinkle the top of each cookie with just a few crumbs of flaky sea salt.

Bake for 8 to 10 minutes, or until they are slightly browned around the edges. Allow the cookies to cool on the baking sheets for 2 minutes, then use a flat metal spatula to transfer to wire cooling racks.

COOKIE TIPS

Here's a cookie jar's load of helpful tips that apply to almost all the recipes in this chapter. Make yourself a cup of coffee and take a bite!

- **Wire cooling racks** are great for perfectly textured cookies; this way they won't brown too much on the bottom. But if, for whatever reason, you refuse to get cooling racks, you can turn the cookies upside down on a plate to let cool completely.

- **Store** completely cooled cookies in a tightly covered container and they should last for 3 to 5 days.

- **Silpat** is the brand name of a silicone baking surface that you can place over your cookie sheet, making greasing the sheet or baking parchment obsolete.

- However, if you're without Silpats or baking parchment paper, you can **lightly grease the cookie sheet:** spray with a light coating of nonstick cooking spray.

- We use **flaxseeds and starche**s to create chewy or crispy textures, and sometimes both, so you can toss out that dusty old box of "egg replacer." Instead, invest in the best-quality flours, oils, chocolate, and spices you can buy.

- **Go organic** if you can, especially when it comes to sugar! Organic sugar is almost always vegan.

- Of key importance is to get your hands on high-budget, **real vanilla extract.** Without butter or eggs to get in the way, you'll really taste every glorious note in these wholesome confections.

- Back in 2007, we used a lot of **brown rice syrup** in cookies! It creates a unique texture in baked goods, creating a pleasing spread and crisp yet chewy texture. While you can substitute the same amount of maple syrup or regular molasses in a recipe, the flavor and final texture will be very different from using brown rice syrup.

- **Love whole grains?** Replace up to half of the all-purpose flour in these recipes with whole wheat pastry flour with little change in the final results. We love the rich color; light, nutty flavor; and delicate texture that whole-grain flours add to cookies and other baked goods.

Pretty as a picture, these delectable disks are studded with jadelike pistachio nuts and are delicately scented with rose water. These cookies are a miracle of science, really; delicately flavored and somehow light and airy, chewy and crispy all at once. Lime juice and zest add a little citrus kick. A perfect end to your Persian feast, or even just some Middle Eastern takeout.

Preheat the oven to 350°F. Lightly spray two cookie sheets with nonstick cooking spray.

In a mixing bowl, whisk together the sugar, oil, milk, rose water, vanilla, and lime zest and juice. Add the cornstarch and whisk until dissolved.

Add the flour, baking powder, salt, and cardamom. Mix well.

Roll the dough into balls about 2 teaspoons in diameter (a bit smaller than a walnut) and dip into the chopped pistachios. Press down with two fingers; the dough will flatten a bit and the pistachios will adhere to the bottom (which will become the top!)

Place the cookies, nut side up, about 2 inches apart on the baking sheets. You should be able to fit sixteen on a standard baking sheet. Bake for 10 to 12 minutes; they will be soft but that's okay; they will firm up as they cool.

Remove from the oven and let cool on the cookie sheets for about 5 minutes. Transfer to a wire cooling rack to cool completely.

TIPS

The easiest way to chop pistachios is to pulse them in a food processor about twenty times. Otherwise, use a chef's knife on a cutting board and be gentle so that they don't shoot all over the place.

If you are aching to try these cookies but can't afford pistachios at the moment, replace them with chopped almonds.

PISTACHIO–ROSE WATER
COOKIES

MAKES 32 COOKIES / TIME: 35 MIN

Nonstick cooking spray, for pans

1¼ cups organic sugar

½ cup canola oil

3 tablespoons unsweetened nondairy milk, rice or soy preferred

1 tablespoon rose water

2 teaspoons pure vanilla extract

1 teaspoon finely grated lime zest

1 tablespoon fresh lime juice

¼ cup cornstarch

1¾ cups all-purpose flour

1 teaspoon baking powder

½ teaspoon salt

¼ teaspoon ground cardamom

½ cup shelled pistachios, coarsely chopped

CHEWY
CHOCOLATE-RASPBERRY COOKIES

MAKES 24 COOKIES / TIME: 35 MIN

Nonstick cooking spray, for pan
½ cup raspberry preserves
1 cup organic sugar
⅓ cup canola oil
1 teaspoon pure vanilla extract
1 teaspoon almond extract
½ cup plus 2 tablespoons unsweetened cocoa powder (sifted if clumpy)
1½ cups all-purpose flour
¾ teaspoon baking soda
¼ teaspoon salt

It's official—everyone loves the combination of chocolate and raspberry. These cookies are soft, dense, chewy, and just a little puffy. They're wonderful as ice-cream sandwich cookies.

Preheat the oven to 350°F. Lightly spray a cookie sheet with nonstick cooking spray.

In a large mixing bowl, stir together the raspberry preserves, sugar, oil, and vanilla and almond extracts.

In a separate mixing bowl, sift together the cocoa powder, flour, baking soda, and salt. Add the dry ingredients to the wet in three batches, mixing well with a fork after each addition. When you get to the last batch, you may need to use your hands to work the batter into a soft and pliable dough.

Roll the dough into walnut-size balls and then flatten them with your hands into 2½-inch-diameter disks. Place on the prepared cookie sheet (they need be only ½ inch apart because they don't spread out when baking). Bake for 10 minutes until they are puffy but soft.

Remove from the oven and let cool on the cookie sheet for 5 minutes. Transfer to a wire cooling rack to cool completely. You can also serve these cookies still warm over a scoop of ice cream. Or three.

You could call these Koala Noses because that's what they look like. Using turbinado sugar adds a slight brown-sugar taste and a little crunch because the crystals are bigger than normal sugar, but you can use regular old organic granulated if that's what you have; just cut back on it by two tablespoons or so. These cookies are crispy outside, chewy inside, and the anise pairs beautifully with the fruity figs. Plus, they will have your kitchen smelling like an Italian bakery.

Preheat the oven to 350°F. Lightly spray two baking sheets with nonstick cooking spray.

If using preground flaxseeds, place in a mixing bowl and beat vigorously with the milk. If using whole flaxseeds, grind them up in a blender and then add the milk. Blend until frothy. Place in the mixing bowl and proceed with the recipe.

Add the turbinado sugar and oil to the mixing bowl and beat until emulsified. Mix in the vanilla and anise extracts.

Add about 1 cup of the flour along with the baking powder and salt. Mix well. Add the remaining cup of flour and mix. Fold in the chopped almonds. At this point, a hand blender might not work, so use a wooden spoon or your hands.

Loosely roll the dough into golf ball–size balls, then flatten them with your hands into 2-inch-diameter cookies. Place on the prepared cookie sheets and gently but firmly smush a fig half, cut side down, into the center of each cookie.

Bake for 12 to 14 minutes. The fig should be soft and the cookies should be golden brown on the bottom. The tops don't brown much.

Remove from the oven and let sit on the baking sheets for about 5 minutes, then transfer to a wire cooling rack to cool completely.

-45

FIG SMUSHED

ANISE-ALMOND COOKIES

MAKES 24 COOKIES / TIME: 40 MIN

Nonstick cooking spray, for pans

2 teaspoons ground flaxseeds, or 1½ teaspoons whole

¼ cup unsweetened nondairy milk

1¼ cups turbinado sugar

⅔ cup canola oil

1 teaspoon pure vanilla extract

½ teaspoon anise extract

2 cups all-purpose flour

1 teaspoon baking powder

½ teaspoon salt

½ cup finely chopped almonds (start with slivers or sliced to make your life easier)

12 dried black Mission figs, rough stem removed, cut in half lengthwise

- - - - - -
TIP
- - - - - -

If you don't have flaxseeds, you can leave them out of the recipe. The cookies will be a bit less chewy but still yummy!

-45

TERRY'S FAVORITE
ALMOND
COOKIE

MAKES 24 COOKIES / TIME: 35 MIN

2¼ cups all-purpose flour

½ cup almond meal or ground almonds

1¼ teaspoons baking soda

½ teaspoon salt

½ cup canola or refined coconut oil, or a mixture of the two

¼ cup brown rice syrup

¼ cup unsweetened almond milk

1 cup organic sugar

1½ teaspoons almond extract

½ teaspoon pure vanilla extract

1 teaspoon toasted sesame oil

⅓ cup sliced, blanched almonds

TIP

This recipe makes large cookies (good for ice-cream sandwiches!). Make smaller cookies by using just 1 tablespoon of dough per cookie and reducing the baking time by 2 minutes.

Terry says, "Calling this cookie 'my favorite' makes it sound like I've been searching far and wide for the ultimate almond cookie. And I have! Almonds are still my favorite in desserts and/or snacks. These aromatic cookies are inspired by the kind one might find in their local Chinatown; sleek, crisp, with a distinctive almond aroma made without the obvious texture of chunky almonds. They rely on the subtle presence of almond meal and almond extract to give them that unmistakable almond flavor."

Preheat the oven to 350°F. Line two large cookie sheets with parchment paper.

Sift together the flour, almond meal, baking soda, and salt and set aside. In a large bowl, beat together the canola oil, brown rice syrup, milk, sugar, almond and vanilla extracts, and sesame oil. Add the flour mixture and mix until a firm dough forms.

Roll the dough into balls, using about 2 tablespoons of dough apiece. Press one side of each ball into the sliced almonds and place at least 2 inches apart, almond side up, on the prepared cookie sheets. Flatten each ball to about an inch thick (a flat-bottomed 1-cup measuring cup works great for this). Bake for 12 to 15 minutes, until just starting to turn golden on the edges.

Allow to cool for at least 10 minutes before removing from the sheets (the cookies will be very soft when first out of the oven but will firm up while cooling), then transfer to a wire cooling rack to cool completely.

Deep, dark, chocolaty, and nutty, this is a perfect (dairy-free) milk-and-cookies cookie for chocolate lovers. The recipe is incredibly versatile, so check out some of the variations.

Preheat the oven to 350°F and line two baking sheets with parchment paper.

In a large bowl, sift together the flour, cocoa powder, baking soda, and salt.

In a separate large bowl, mix together the oil and sugar. Add the flaxseeds, milk, and vanilla and almond extracts and mix well.

Fold in the flour mixture in batches. When the batter starts to get too stiff to mix with a fork, use your hands until a nice stiff dough forms. Add the chocolate chips and walnuts and mix with your hands again. Your hands will get covered in chocolate, but worse things have happened.

Wash your hands, roll the dough into 1-inch balls, and flatten into disks about 1½ inches in diameter. Place about an inch apart on the prepared cookie sheets.

Bake for 10 minutes. Remove from the oven and let cool for about 5 minutes on the cookie sheets, then transfer to a wire cooling rack to cool completely.

VARIATIONS

You can do so much with these!

WHITE CHOCOLATE CHIP–CHERRY–CHOCOLATE COOKIES: Replace the chocolate chips with vegan white chocolate chips and replace the walnuts with dried cherries.

ORANGE–CHOCOLATE–CHOCOLATE CHIP COOKIES: Omit the walnuts. Add 3 teaspoons of finely grated orange zest to the liquid ingredients.

CHOCOLATE-HAZELNUT COOKIES: Omit the chocolate chips. Replace ¼ cup of the milk with hazelnut liqueur. Replace the walnuts with chopped, toasted hazelnuts (see tip on page 112).

CHOCOLATE–CHOCOLATE CHIP–WALNUT
COOKIES

MAKES 36 COOKIES /
TIME: 30 MIN

2 cups all-purpose flour

⅔ cup unsweetened Dutch-processed cocoa powder

1 teaspoon baking soda

½ teaspoon salt

⅔ cup canola oil

1¼ cups organic sugar

4 teaspoons ground flaxseeds

½ cup unsweetened nondairy milk

2 teaspoons pure vanilla extract

½ teaspoon almond extract

¾ cup vegan chocolate chips

¾ cup walnuts, chopped small

OATY
CHOCOLATE
CHIP COOKIES

MAKES 18 COOKIES /
TIME: 45 MIN

1¾ cups oat flour

½ teaspoon baking soda

¼ teaspoon salt

1 tablespoon ground flaxseeds

¼ cup unsweetened nondairy milk

¼ cup organic dark brown sugar

½ cup organic granulated sugar

⅓ cup canola oil

1 teaspoon pure vanilla extract

¾ cup vegan chocolate chips

- - - - - - - -
TIPS
- - - - - - - -

Oat flour is available in many supermarkets, but if you can't find it or don't think you'll be using it much, you can make your own by whizzing rolled oats in a blender or food processor until they resemble flour.

These wheat-free cookies couldn't be any easier to make, unless you had someone else make them for you. Oat flour makes a dense and crumbly style of cookie that is perfect for all cookie monsters, not just those avoiding wheat. Note: Although oats do not contain gluten, some people with wheat allergies still avoid them. If you're making these for a celiac friend, ask whether they eat oats first, or whether subbing certified GF oat flour would do the trick.

Preheat the oven to 375°F.

Sift together the oat flour, baking soda, and salt.

In a small mixing bowl, whisk together the flaxseeds and milk. Add the brown and granulated sugars and stir, then add the oil and vanilla, and whisk vigorously until the mixture is emulsified, which takes about a minute.

Mix the wet ingredients into the dry; fold in the chocolate chips.

Drop the batter by the tablespoon onto an ungreased baking sheet, leaving 1½ inches of space between the cookies. Bake for 10 to 12 minutes until they are lightly browned on the bottom.

Remove from the oven and let cool for 5 minutes on the baking sheet. Transfer to a wire cooling rack to cool the rest of the way.

The peanut butter flavor in these tender, shortbread-like morsels is subtle, while chunks of candied ginger and a coating of crunchy sesame seeds make a big, bold statement. The perfect little dessert after a Chinese-inspired meal or great paired with a rich and smoky black or oolong tea.

Preheat the oven to 350°F and line two large cookie sheets with parchment paper.

Sift together the flour, baking powder, soda, salt, ground ginger, and cinnamon and set aside.

In a large bowl, use an electric mixer to beat together the coconut oil, peanut butter, rice syrup, sugar, milk, and vanilla and almond extracts until creamy, 4 to 5 minutes. Using a rubber spatula or wooden spoon, stir in the flour mixture, then add chopped candied ginger and stir until a very firm dough forms. You can use your hands toward the end to mix the dough.

Roll scant tablespoons of the dough into walnut-size balls. Roll each ball in either white or black sesame seeds (or a little of both), then roll in a little sugar and place on the prepared cookie sheets, leaving about 1½ inches of space between the cookies.

Flatten the balls just slightly (optional) and bake for 10 to 11 minutes for chewy cookies, or up to 14 minutes for firmer, crunchier cookies.

Remove from the oven and allow the cookies to remain on the cookie sheets for a few minutes before transferring to wire cooling racks to cool.

-45

PEANUT-GINGER-SESAME
COOKIES

MAKES 42 COOKIES / TIME: 35 MIN

2¼ cups flour, either all-purpose, whole wheat pastry, white whole wheat, or a combination of these

½ teaspoon baking powder

½ teaspoon baking soda

½ teaspoon salt

½ teaspoon ground ginger

¼ teaspoon ground cinnamon

⅓ cup virgin coconut oil, slightly softened

½ cup chunky peanut butter

¼ cup brown rice syrup

1¼ cups organic sugar, plus more for rolling

½ cup unsweetened almond milk

1 teaspoon pure vanilla extract

½ teaspoon almond extract

5 ounces candied ginger, diced finely

⅓ cup each white sesame seeds and black sesame seeds, or ⅔ cup of just one kind

RUMNOG
PECAN COOKIES

MAKES 24 COOKIES /
TIME: 45 MIN

Cookies:

⅓ cup canola oil

¼ cup unsweetened almond milk or your favorite nondairy milk

1 cup organic sugar

1 tablespoon molasses

2 tablespoons dark rum

1½ teaspoons pure vanilla extract

1¾ cups all-purpose flour

¼ cup cornstarch

1½ teaspoons baking powder

¼ teaspoon baking soda

½ teaspoon freshly grated nutmeg

½ teaspoon ground cinnamon

½ teaspoon salt

1½ cups coarsely chopped pecans

Frosting:

2 tablespoons refined coconut oil, softened

2 cups confectioners' sugar

2 tablespoons unsweetened almond milk or your favorite nondairy milk, or almond, soy, or coconut-based creamer

2 tablespoons dark rum

¼ teaspoon pure vanilla extract

Optional decoration:

Freshly grated nutmeg

Colored sugar sprinkles

This grown-up holiday cookie spiked with rum and nutmeg tastes like egg nog (can we say egg in a vegan cookbook?) in a rich and decadent cookie form. But it doesn't stop there: before baking, the dough is rolled in crunchy pecans, and after cooling, the cookies are topped with creamy, rum-infused icing and doused with happy fun-time holiday sugar sprinkles. The flavor improves after a few hours and the icing firms up, making them ideal for gift giving for people on your nice or naughty list, if you are the kind of charmingly creepy person that makes that kind of list.

Preheat the oven to 350°F and line two large cookie sheets with parchment paper.

Prepare the cookies: In a large bowl, combine the canola oil, milk, sugar, molasses, rum, and vanilla, and beat until slightly foamy. Sift in the flour, cornstarch, baking powder, baking soda, nutmeg, cinnamon, and salt and mix until a soft dough forms.

Roll the dough into walnut-size balls (about 1 heaping tablespoon), roll in the chopped pecans, and place about 2 inches apart on the prepared baking sheets. Bake for 10 to 12 minutes, until the cookies have puffed.

Remove from the oven and allow to cool on the baking sheets for 5 minutes before transferring to a wire cooling rack.

Prepare the frosting: Use an electric mixer to cream together the coconut oil and confectioners' sugar until smooth. Beat in the milk, rum, and vanilla. The frosting should have a consistency similar to that of buttercream frosting. If it's too thin, beat in more confectioners' sugar, 1 tablespoon at a time, until the desired consistency is reached. Spread 1 teaspoon or more frosting on each cooled cookie.

Add your ornaments: Sprinkle with nutmeg and colored sugar, if desired, while the frosting is still moist.

These are best when allowed to sit for a few hours so that the frosting becomes firm.

These chewy cookies are loaded with superwholesome flavors from cara-mel-like brown rice syrup, nutty whole-grain flours, and plenty of raisins. This recipe is as basic as a pair of jeans (but more straight-leg mom jeans than skinny jeans) and, we suppose, could be doctored with a handful of chocolate chips or shredded coconut, but why mess with perfection? These cookies are equally at home packed into lunchboxes or served with cold nondairy milk or a steaming cup of hot apple cider. Make them with either big, chunky old-fashioned oats or more finely textured quick-cooking oats for two different takes on this classic.

Preheat the oven to 350°F and line two large cookie sheets with parchment paper.

In a large bowl, combine the oil, brown rice syrup, milk, brown sugar, and vanilla and beat until smooth. Sift in the flour, baking powder, baking soda, cinnamon, nutmeg, allspice, and salt and beat just until a dough begins to form. Fold in the oats and raisins.

Roll the dough into walnut-size balls (about 1 heaping tablespoon) and place about 2 inches apart on the prepared baking sheets. Press the cookies down lightly with your fingers or the bottom of a glass dipped in water (to prevent sticking). Bake for 10 to 12 minutes, or until the cookies have spread and are lightly browned.

Remove from the oven and allow to cool on the baking sheets for about 2 minutes before transferring to a wire cooling rack. Let the cookies cool completely before storing in a tightly covered container.

CHEWY
OATMEAL-RAISIN COOKIES

MAKES 30 COOKIES /
COOKING TIME: 30 MIN

½ cup canola or safflower oil

⅓ cup brown rice syrup

⅓ cup unsweetened almond or coconut-based milk

¾ cup organic light brown sugar

1 teaspoon pure vanilla extract

2⅓ cups whole wheat pastry flour or all-purpose flour

½ teaspoon baking powder

¾ teaspoon baking soda

2 teaspoons ground cinnamon

½ teaspoon freshly grated nutmeg

½ teaspoon ground allspice

½ teaspoon salt

2 cups old-fashioned or quick-cooking oats

1½ cups dark raisins

ALMOND-ANISE
BISCOTTI

MAKE 18 COOKIES /
TIME: ABOUT AN HR

⅓ cup unsweetened almond or coconut-based milk

2 tablespoons ground flaxseeds

¾ cup organic sugar

½ cup canola oil

½ teaspoon pure vanilla extract

½ teaspoon almond extract

1⅔ cups all-purpose flour or whole wheat pastry flour

2 tablespoons arrowroot powder

2 teaspoons baking powder

2 teaspoons aniseeds

½ teaspoon salt

1 cup whole raw almonds

TIP

Can't find aniseeds? Then add ½ teaspoon of anise extract along with the vanilla and almond extracts. Or just pivot from the whole aniseed thing and make one of the awesome variant flavors instead!

VARIATIONS

ORANGE-CHOCOLATE CHIP: Substitute fresh orange juice for the milk. Omit the aniseeds and almond extract, and increase the vanilla to 1 teaspoon. Omit the almonds and add 2 tablespoons of packed, grated orange zest and ½ cup of vegan chocolate chips.

CRANBERRY-PISTACHIO: Omit the aniseeds and almonds. Add ½ cup each of dried cranberries and shelled green pistachios.

HAZELNUT: Leave out the aniseeds. Omit the almonds and use hazelnuts.

This is the classic twice-baked Italian cookie—not overly sweet, bursting with toasted almonds or chocolate or spices, with a defined crunch. It seemed like everyone in the 2000s was making biscotti, and we were (and still are) no exception. These flavorful and supercrunchy biscotti are ideal treats for tea time, coffee breaks, or packing into lunch boxes, especially lunch boxes for grown-ups. And, of course, these hold up perfectly when dipped into tea, a rainbow unicorn sparkling coconut milk latte, or whatever the drink of the moment may be. Try some of the variations as well, such as the Orange-Chocolate Chip and Cranberry-Pistachio.

Preheat the oven to 350°F and line two large cookie sheets with parchment paper.

In a large bowl, whisk together the milk and flaxseeds for about 30 seconds. Add the sugar, oil, and vanilla and almond extracts and mix until smooth. Sift in the flour, arrowroot, baking powder, aniseeds, and salt.

Stir to mix all the ingredients and, just as a firm dough starts to form, knead in the almonds. Knead the dough only briefly. Some of the almonds might pop out; just push them back in.

On the prepared cookie sheets, form the dough into a rectangle about 12 inches long and 3 to 4 inches wide. Bake for 26 to 28 minutes, or until slightly puffed and firm; the top may also be slightly crackled, which is okay.

Remove from the oven and allow to cool on the pan for 30 minutes, until very firm.

Increase the oven temperature to 375°F. Lift up the edges of the parchment paper and carefully transfer the baked dough to a cutting board. With a very sharp knife, slice the dough into ½-inch-thick slices. The best way to do this is in one motion, pushing down; don't saw the slices off (and don't use a serrated knife) or the slices could crumble. Be gentle when handling the biscotti at this time, as they are delicate.

Set the slices, on their cut side, on the cookie sheets, and bake for 12 to 15 minutes, or until your desired level of brownness and crispness is achieved. It's not necessary to flip these biscotti during the second baking. However, if you feel confident in your biscotti-making ability and want really crisp, firm cookies, try flipping them once during the middle of the second baking. Our fingers are made of asbestos, so we use those, but most normal people just use a small spatula.

Let cool for a few minutes on the cookie sheets before transferring the slices to a wire cooling rack. When completely cool, store in an airtight container.

From left to right: Almond-Anise Biscotti, page 372,
Chocolate-Hazelnut Biscotti, page 374.

CHOCOLATE-HAZELNUT
BISCOTTI

MAKE 18 COOKIES /
TIME: ABOUT AN HR

⅓ cup unsweetened almond or coconut-based milk

2 tablespoons ground flaxseeds

¾ cup plus 2 tablespoons organic sugar

½ cup canola oil

½ teaspoon pure vanilla extract

½ teaspoon almond extract

1½ cups all-purpose flour or whole wheat pastry flour

⅓ cup unsweetened Dutch-processed cocoa powder

2 tablespoons arrowroot powder or cornstarch

2 teaspoons baking powder

½ teaspoon salt

1 cup whole, raw hazelnuts

These are mouthwatering, dark chocolate biscotti chock full of crunchy hazelnuts. They are a chocolate and hazelnut lover's dream, so be careful if you start giving them away without a care or you will be flooded with requests for more and more.

Preheat the oven to 350°F. Line a large cookie sheet with parchment paper.

In a large bowl, whisk together the milk and flaxseeds, mixing for about 30 seconds. Add the sugar, oil, and vanilla and almond extracts and stir until smooth. Sift in the flour, cocoa powder, arrowroot, baking powder, and salt. Stir to mix and, just as the dough starts to come together, knead in the hazelnuts. Knead very briefly to form a stiff dough; if some of the nuts pop out, just push them back in.

On the prepared baking sheet, form the dough into a rectangle about 12 inches long and 3 to 4 inches wide. Bake for 28 minutes, or until lightly puffed; the top may also be slightly crackled.

Remove from the oven and allow to cool on the cookie sheet for 30 minutes, until very firm.

Increase the oven temperature to 375°F. Carefully transfer the baked dough to a cutting board. With a heavy, very sharp knife (don't use a serrated knife), slice ½-inch-thick slices. The best way to do this is in one pushing-down motion; don't saw the slices off or the slices could crumble. Be gentle when handling the biscotti at this time, as they are delicate.

Set the slices on the cookie sheet, cut side down, and bake for 12 to 15 minutes until your desired level of brownness and crispness is achieved.

Remove from the oven and let cool for a few minutes on the cookie sheet before transferring the slices to a wire cooling rack. When completely cool, store in an airtight container.

VARIATION

CHOCOLATE-HAZELNUT-ESPRESSO: Whisk 1 tablespoon of instant espresso powder into the liquid ingredients before adding the dry ingredients.

BARS &
A BROWNIE

◆

**And who can resist the charm of a
plateful of bar cookies?**

This chapter also includes our famous fudgy wudgy blueberry
brownies, which is surely the taste combination to usher us into the
next decade. We've also finally created the perfect lemon bar that
shines like a citrus-colored jewel. Meanwhile, apple lovers and peanut butter lovers can finally come to an agreement and end their
thousand years' war once and for all, with our apple bars topped
with peanut butter caramel.

These bars were created one autumn night when we were sitting around with our friend Paula, thinking about apples and peanut butter. Everyone loves peanut butter on apples, so why aren't there any treats dedicated to this combination? Could all the world's problems be solved if only we would take hold of our innermost desires? To the kitchen we went. The result is this bar: an apple pie filling inside a graham cracker crust, with a crumb topping and ribbons of luscious peanut butter caramel.

Preheat the oven to 350°F. Grease a 9 x 13-inch baking pan with coconut oil or spray with nonstick cooking spray.

Prepare the crust: Place the graham cracker crumbs in a mixing bowl. Drizzle with the oil and mix until moistened. Add the milk and vanilla and mix with your fingers; the crumbs should hold together if pinched. Press the crumbs firmly into the prepared baking pan to form a crust.

Prepare the topping: Combine the flour, sugar, spices, and salt in a mixing bowl. Drizzle 2 tablespoons of the coconut oil into the flour and mix with your fingertips until crumbs start to form. Keep tossing the mixture with your fingers; you want the crumbs to be fairly large for crumbs. Add more oil, if necessary.

Prepare the apple filling: Combine all the filling ingredients in a bowl, coating all the apples.

Assemble the bars: Layer the apples onto the crust and sprinkle with the crumb topping. The topping won't solidly cover the entire pan; just sprinkle it randomly over the top so that the apples are peeking through in places. Bake for 40 to 45 minutes, or until the apples are tender.

When the bars are almost done baking (at the 35-minute point), start preparing the peanut butter caramel: Mix all the caramel ingredients very well, with a fork, in a small saucepan. Heat over medium heat for about 3 minutes. The mixture should soften and slide off the fork in ribbons.

When the bars are done baking, drizzle the caramel in ribbons all over the top. Let cool completely before serving; you can place the pan in the fridge to hasten the cooling process. Slice into bars and serve.

TIP

If you can't find vegan graham crackers, vegan vanilla shortbread-style cookies or vegan speculoos cookies make a good substitution.

MAKES 12 BARS / TIME: 1 HR 15 MIN,
plus cooling time

Coconut oil or nonstick cooking spray, for pan

Crust:
3 cups vegan graham cracker crumbs

⅓ cup refined coconut oil, softened

3 tablespoons unsweetened almond or coconut-based milk

1 teaspoon pure vanilla extract

Crumb topping:
½ cup all-purpose flour

3 tablespoons organic sugar

¼ teaspoon ground cinnamon

¼ teaspoon ground ginger

¼ teaspoon freshly grated nutmeg

¼ teaspoon salt

3 tablespoons refined coconut oil, melted

Apple filling:
3 pounds Granny Smith apples (about 6), cored and sliced thinly (peeling is optional)

⅓ cup organic sugar

3 tablespoons all-purpose flour

1 teaspoon fresh lemon juice

¼ teaspoon ground cinnamon

¼ teaspoon ground ginger

Peanut butter caramel:
⅔ cup chunky peanut butter (the no-stir kind, not the kind that separates)

¼ cup pure maple syrup

3 tablespoons brown rice syrup

FUDGY WUDGY
BLUEBERRY BROWNIES

MAKES 16 BROWNIES / TIME: 50 MIN

Nonstick cooking spray, for pan

⅔ cup plus ½ cup vegan semisweet chocolate chips

10 ounces blueberry spreadable fruit

¼ cup unsweetened nondairy milk

¾ cup organic sugar

½ cup canola oil

2 teaspoons pure vanilla extract

½ teaspoon almond extract

1½ cups all-purpose flour

¼ cup unsweetened cocoa powder

¼ teaspoon baking powder

½ teaspoon baking soda

¼ teaspoon salt

1 cup fresh blueberries

- - - - - - - -
TIPS
- - - - - - - -

The highest-quality vegan chocolate chips will produce the highest-quality brownie. The only ingredients should be chocolate liqueur, sugar, cocoa butter, vanilla, and possibly lecithin. Avoid chips with high-fructose corn syrup as an ingredient.

Since the consistency of spreadable fruit varies from brand to brand, we used the kind that had no whole blueberries visible. If yours looks as if it does have whole fruit, no worries! Just pulse it in a blender a few times until smooth. You can add the recipe's measure of milk to it, if necessary, to make the blending easier.

These brownies are ridiculously fudgy. They better be, they're called fudgy wudgies. They have triple chocolate power—in the form of melted chocolate, cocoa powder, and then chocolate chips. And they have double blueberry power—in the form of blueberry spreadable fruit and plump, fresh blueberries, adding a tangy contrast to each sweet bite. The blueberry-chocolate combo is not the most popular one, but it should be! For a variation, try raspberry-chocolate by replacing the blueberry ingredients with raspberry ones.

Preheat the oven to 325°F. Lightly spray a 9 x 13-inch baking pan with nonstick cooking spray.

Heat a small pan of water over high heat until boiling. Place another small pan on top of that and place the ¾ cup of chocolate chips in that one. Use a rubber spatula to stir until melted. Remove from the heat and let cool just a bit while you prepare everything else. Or, if you want to melt the chips in a microwave instead, place them in a microwave-safe bowl (obviously) on high for 1 minute. Stir the partially melted chips and microwave again for another 30 seconds.

In a large mixing bowl, combine the blueberry spreadable fruit, milk, sugar, oil, and vanilla and almond extracts. Mix on high speed with an electric mixer until no large clumps of the spreadable fruit are visible. This could take 2 to 3 minutes.

Sift in the flour, cocoa powder, baking powder, baking soda, and salt. Stir until well mixed; we use a fork here because the batter is very thick and can clump up in a whisk or mixer. Mix in the melted chocolate as well.

Fold in the remaining ½ cup of chocolate chips and the fresh blueberries. Spread the batter in the baking pan (don't worry if it doesn't come to the very corners of the pan, because the batter will spread while baking and it will all work out). Bake for 45 minutes. You can't really do a toothpick test here because the chocolate chips will make the pick look wet and the top will appear soft and crinkly and not done when, we promise you, it is done.

Remove from the oven and let cool in the pan. Slice into sixteen squares (or whatever size you want). If you want to serve it warm, wait about 30 minutes, so it is still warm but not hot. For true decadence, serve with Vanilla Ice Cream (page 408) and a little bit of blueberry syrup, plus some fresh blueberries for good measure.

LEMON BARS

MAKES 12 BARS / TIME: 4 HRS,
most of that for chilling

Nonstick cooking spray, for pan

Crust:

1¼ cups all-purpose flour

⅔ cup confectioners' sugar, plus more to
decorate the finished bars

¼ cup cornstarch

1 cup refined coconut oil, softened

Filling:

3 tablespoons agar flakes

1 tablespoon finely grated lemon zest (from
2 large lemons)

⅔ cup fresh lemon juice

3 tablespoons arrowroot powder

1¼ cups organic granulated sugar

⅛ teaspoon ground turmeric

¼ cup unsweetened nondairy milk

Bet you thought you'd never have a lemon bar again in the land of vegan culinaria. Well, turn that frown upside down—café-style lemon bars are here! Lots and lots of tangy, creamy, jelled lemon topping blankets a shortbread crust. And with a sprinkling of confectioners' sugar, these are as pretty as can be.

Lightly spray a 9 x 13-inch baking pan with nonstick cooking spray.

Prepare the crust: Pulse the flour, confectioners' sugar, and cornstarch in a food processor. Add the coconut oil in spoonfuls and blend for 8 to 10 seconds, and then pulse until the mixture resembles coarse meal. Sprinkle the mixture in the prepared baking pan and press firmly into an even layer with slightly raised sides, so that it can hold in the filling. Refrigerate for about 30 minutes.

While the crust chills, preheat the oven to 350°F.

Bake the unfilled crust for 25 minutes, remove from the oven, and let cool in the pan.

Meanwhile, prepare the filling: In a saucepot, soak the agar in the 1⅓ cups of water for 15 minutes. Use the time while it soaks to zest your lemons and squeeze your lemon juice. Mix the arrowroot into the lemon juice to dissolve.

When the agar has been soaked for 15 minutes, turn on the heat and bring the mixture to a boil. Boil for about 10 minutes, or until the agar is completely dissolved. Add the granulated sugar and turmeric and boil until they have dissolved, about 3 minutes. Lower the heat to medium and add the arrowroot mixture, then add the lemon zest and milk. Whisk constantly until the mixture thickens, about 5 minutes. It should not be rapidly boiling, but low bubbling is okay.

Pour the mixture into the prepared crust. Let cool for 20 minutes and then refrigerate for at least 3 hours, until the filling is only slightly jiggly and has set. Use a sifter or a fine-mesh strainer to sprinkle the bars with confectioners' sugar. Slice into squares and serve.

ICE-CREAM SANDWICHES

What's better than a sandwich? A sandwich made of homemade ice cream smooshed between two freshly baked cookies. Okay, you might have a few other suggestions, but really what is better on a warm summer evening while you're walking around the city in your new flip flops?

Here's a quick and snappy list of some suggestions featuring some of the cookies in this book stuffed with ice creamy favorites. Use the basic Vanilla Ice Cream (page 408) recipe and create any of the variations listed. Or revel in your laziness and buy your favorite extra decadent nondairy ice cream.

For best results, allow ice-cream sandwiches to freeze for a minimum of two hours (or until frozen completely solid) before serving. Anything less and the ice cream won't have time to freeze firm and biting into a sammich will likely result in half-melted ice cream dripping all over your toes.

For maximum prettiness and decadence, roll the edges of your ice-cream sandwiches in pretty shredded coconut, chopped nuts, or shaved vegan chocolate. Place your rolling ingredients on a plate and roll the sammich like a tire across the plate before freezing.

THE GREEN TEA: Terry's Favorite Almond Cookie (page 364) with Green Tea Ice Cream

BLACK FOREST: Chocolate–Chocolate Chip–Walnut Cookies (page 367) with Cherry Ice Cream rolled in shredded coconut

THE MOCHA: Chocolate–Chocolate Chip–Walnut Cookies (page 367) with Coffee Ice Cream rolled in vegan chocolate sprinkles

CHUNKY MONKEY: Spread Chocolate–Chocolate Chip–Walnut Cookies (page 367) with Peanut Butter Caramel (page 377) and fill with Banana Ice Cream. Tuck in a few thin slices of ripe banana for kicks before smooshing halves together.

THE PERSIAN: Add a tablespoon of rose water to Vanilla Ice Cream, scoop into Pistachio–Rose Water Cookies (page 361) and roll in finely chopped pistachios.

OPEN SESAME: Peanut-Ginger-Sesame Cookies (page 369) filled with Peanut Butter Ice Cream and rolled in toasted sesame seeds. These make cute little tea sandwiches, because tea time should include ice cream.

THE PIRATE: Skip the frosting on Rumnog Pecan Cookies (page 370), spike Vanilla Ice Cream with rum or a tablespoon of rum extract, fold in raisins and roll in finely chopped pecans.

THE CLASSIC: Oaty Chocolate Chip Cookies (page 368) filled with Vanilla Ice Cream and rolled in shaved chocolate.

COCOA RASPBERRY: Chewy Chocolate-Raspberry Cookies (page 362) filled with Raspberry Ice Cream.

CHAPTER THIRTEEN

DESSERTS

**Desserts are usually listed at the end
of a cookbook, but we suspect that you've snuck a peek
and this is the first thing you are seeing.**

So, hi! Welcome to our cookbook! We talk a lot about how wonderful broccoli is but, at the end of the day, we know what really wins people over is a chocolate pie smothered in caramel and pecans.

Ten years after our first major dessert cookbook opus, *Vegan Cupcakes Take Over the World*, you know we've baked a lot of vegan sweets: cupcakes, cookies, and oh so many pies. While these still are our defaults when it comes to feeding an everyday sweet tooth, we know there are just some desserts that wow and awe crowds. Bundt cakes and bread pudding easily step out of the dessert spotlight for welcome tea time or brunch treats. Poached pears garnished with chocolate sauce and bountiful cobblers loaded with the season's freshest fruit are always stunning ends to any meal. But we wager you'll get everyone's attention with the simple pleasures of homemade vegan vanilla ice cream.

-------------- ◆ ----------------

TEA-POACHED PEARS

IN CHOCOLATE SAUCE

SERVES 4 / TIME: LESS THAN AN HR,
plus chill time

3 cups water

4 black tea bags

¼ cup organic sugar

4 firm Bosc pears, peeled, sliced in half lengthwise, and cored

Zest (strips) of ½ navel orange

1 teaspoon pure vanilla extract

8 ounces vegan bitter or semisweet chocolate, chopped (½ cup or so)

Vanilla ice cream (page 408) (optional)

Mint sprigs, for prettiness (optional)

TIP

To easily core the pears, slice them in half and use a melon baller or a round measuring spoon to scoop out the seeds in one fell swoop.

This dessert may seem like it should be served by your butler, but give him and your entire *Downton Abbey*–like ensemble the day off and make it yourself—it's incredibly easy. Pear halves are poached in strong black tea, and then the tea is used to make a soupy pool of chocolate sauce for the pears. A little orange peel gives these a subtle citrus kick. It's an especially good dessert after an Italian meal.

Bring the water to a boil in a medium-size saucepan. Once the water is boiling, turn off the heat, add the tea bags and sugar, and steep for 15 minutes. Remove the tea bags and stir to make sure the sugar is dissolved.

Bring the tea to a boil and add the pears, orange zest, and vanilla. Lower the heat to a simmer and cover. Let simmer for 15 minutes, remove the orange zest because it can get bitter, then simmer for another 20 minutes, or until the pears are tender.

Transfer the pears and liquid to a large bowl to cool. Remove a cup of the liquid from the bowl and place it back in the pot. Bring it to a simmer, then turn off the heat and add the chocolate. Whisk until completely dissolved. Let the sauce cool for the same amount of time as the pears, about an hour altogether. It tastes really good at room temperature.

To assemble: Ladle a good amount of the chocolate sauce, about ½ cup, into a small dessert bowl. Place one pear, cored side down, in the sauce, and another, cored-side down, perpendicular to it and overlapping. If desired, place a scoop of vegan ice cream on one side and garnish with a sprig of mint.

This warm, fruity dessert topped with a crumbly coconut topping could be easily summarized by that popular bumper sticker "Berries ♥ Coconut." Never saw that one? Oh well, at least here's a recipe that's way more fun than reading bumper stickers. Quick to make and not too sweet, this crisp is also gluten-free, to boot. If you don't want to make it gluten-free, go ahead and substitute ¾ cup of regular old gluteny flour for the quinoa and rice flours. We used blueberries and raspberries, but you can use whatever kind of berries you have on hand.

Preheat the oven to 350°F.

Prepare the topping: Mix together the flours, coconut, sugar, and nutmeg in a bowl. Add the coconut oil in spoonfuls and use a pastry knife to cut it into the flours until coarse crumbs form. Set aside.

Prepare the filling: Place the berries, tapioca, and cold water in an 8-inch square baking dish. Stir together to dissolve the tapioca. Add the sugar and coconut and vanilla extracts; stir to combine.

Sprinkle the topping over the berries. Bake for 45 minutes; the filling should be bubbly and yummy looking.

Remove from the oven and let cool for about 10 minutes. Serve in bowls with scoops of vegan vanilla ice cream.

BERRY-COCONUT
CRISP

SERVES 4 / TIME: LESS THAN AN HR

Topping:
½ cup quinoa flour
¼ cup white rice flour
¾ cup shredded unsweetened coconut
¼ cup organic sugar
½ teaspoon freshly grated nutmeg
5 tablespoons refined coconut oil, softened

Filling:
2 cups frozen blueberries, partially thawed
2 cups frozen raspberries, partially thawed
1 tablespoon tapioca flour
1 tablespoon cold water
¼ cup organic sugar
½ teaspoon coconut extract
½ teaspoon pure vanilla extract

For this dessert, juicy strawberries are made even more fragrant with a little rose water. The lemon-scented crust isn't plopped on as it is on most cobblers; here it's placed in lattice strips, to add a little down-home sophistication. It's so pretty and cheery that if you aren't already donning a '50s-style apron, you'll feel as if you should be.

Preheat the oven to 375°F. Have ready an 8-inch square baking dish or pan.

Prepare the filling: Mix together all the filling ingredients in a large mixing bowl. Stir to coat the strawberries and set aside.

Prepare the pastry: In a measuring cup, combine the milk, lemon zest and juice, and vanilla. In a bowl, stir together the flour, 2 tablespoons of the sugar, and the poppy seeds, baking powder, and salt. Sift together with a fork. Drizzle the oil into the flour mixture and stir with a fork until the mixture is crumbly. Add the milk mixture and mix with a wooden spoon just until the dough holds together.

Flour a flat work surface and your hands. Give the dough a quick knead in the bowl (like five times or so) and then turn it onto the work surface. If it feels very sticky, add a bit more flour. Gently flatten the dough into roughly the size of the baking dish you are using. With a floured pizza cutter or a knife, create seven or eight strips of dough, each about an inch wide.

Give the strawberry mixture another stir and transfer to the baking dish.

Now make a lattice on top of the cobbler: Gently lay four strips of dough in parallel across the top of the filled baking dish with some space between them. Then, lift the second strip and lay a new strip perpendicularly across underneath it. Lift the fourth strip and tuck your cross-strip under that one, too. So, now you have a kind of weave. Repeat with the next strip, this time lifting the first and third original strips. When all the strips are used, tuck in the edges around the strawberries.

Sprinkle the top with the remaining tablespoon of sugar and bake for 35 minutes, until the cobbler is bubbly and the dough is slightly browned.

Remove from the oven and let cool a bit before serving. You'll need to cut the cobbler with a serving spoon to get all the juices. For optimum presentation, serve each slice into a bowl, then lift the crust to preserve the lattice and spoon more strawberries and juice into the bowl. Don't forget the vegan ice cream!

STRAWBERRY–ROSE WATER
COBBLER
with Lemon–Poppy Seed Pastry

SERVES 6 TO 8 / TIME: 50 MIN

Filling:

3 pounds strawberries, hulled and cut into quarters

½ cup organic sugar

2 tablespoons tapioca flour

2 tablespoons rose water

1 tablespoon water

Pastry:

½ cup unsweetened nondairy milk

1 tablespoon freshly grated lemon zest

1 tablespoon fresh lemon juice

1 teaspoon pure vanilla extract

1 cup all-purpose flour, plus more for dusting

3 tablespoons organic sugar

2 teaspoons poppy seeds

1½ teaspoons baking powder

Generous pinch of salt

¼ cup canola oil

TIP

If you don't want to braid your lattice, just place some strips one way and others overlapping them the other way. Still cute!

STRAWBERRY-PLUM
CRISP

SERVES 6 / TIME: ABOUT AN HR

Filling:

2 pounds black plums (about 10 plums)

1 cup strawberries, hulled and sliced in half

1 tablespoon tapioca flour or arrowroot powder

¼ cup organic sugar

1 teaspoon pure vanilla extract

½ teaspoon ground cinnamon

½ teaspoon ground ginger

⅛ teaspoon ground cloves

Topping:

¾ cup rolled oats

½ cup all-purpose flour

¼ cup organic sugar

1½ teaspoons aniseeds

½ teaspoon ground cinnamon

Pinch of salt

3 to 4 tablespoons canola oil

Who ever thought that strawberries and plums could be such good buddies in this heavenly crisp? Tart, sweet, juicy plums are the star here, with a few strawberries in a supporting role. The oat topping is spiked with licorice-y aniseeds. A scoop of Vanilla Ice Cream (page 408) on top would be pretty awesome right about now, wouldn't it? Serve on a summer's night when plums and strawberries are in abundance.

Preheat the oven to 375°F.

Prepare the filling: Chop the plums by cutting around the pit (this gets a bit messy). Cut them into slices that are between ¼ and ½ inch thick. Place in an 8-inch square baking pan. Add the rest of the filling ingredients and stir to dissolve the starch. Set aside.

Prepare the topping: Toss all the topping ingredients, except the oil, into a mixing bowl and mix together with a fork. Drizzle in the oil by the tablespoon while tossing with a fork until the topping becomes crumbly and doesn't look too dry. If you've got it by 3 tablespoons of oil, more power to you; but you may need to add another few teaspoons up to a tablespoon to get the right consistency. Sprinkle relatively evenly over the plum mixture.

Place in the oven and bake for 45 minutes; the filling should be bubbly.

Remove from the oven and let cool for about 10 minutes. Scoop into bowls. Top with vegan vanilla ice cream.

Pandowdy is an old-fashioned American dessert that doesn't get much play these days. The concept reminds us of the kind of thing children might decide to do to their food, if they were industrious enough to roll out a pastry. It's simply a pie whose crust has been smashed into the fruit halfway through cooking. The appeal is in the texture; the top of the pastry stays flaky and crispy and the bottom is mushy and soggy with fruit. We love the sloppy beauty of it. This version is mango and pear with just a hint of ginger and cinnamon, but try the method with any pie you make.

Preheat the oven to 350°F. Have your piecrust rolled out and ready.

Combine all the filling ingredients, except the tablespoon of sugar, in a pie plate. Mix until the arrowroot is dissolved. Cover with the piecrust, tuck the edges around the filling, and sprinkle with the remaining tablespoon of sugar. Bake for 30 minutes, then remove from the oven.

Slice the crust into roughly 1-inch pieces, then use a spoon to smush the crust into the pie. Return to the oven to finish baking for 20 to 30 more minutes. The filling should be bubbling over and the crust should be browned.

Serve warm, with a scoop of ice cream if you are so inclined.

MANGO PEAR
PANDOWDY

SERVES: 8 / TIME: 1 HR 15 MIN

1 single Pastry Crust (page 409)

2 mangoes, peeled and cut into ½-inch dice

2 pounds Bartlett pears, cut into ½-inch dice

½ cup plus 1 tablespoon organic sugar

2 tablespoons arrowroot powder or tapioca flour

1 teaspoon ground ginger

1 teaspoon ground cinnamon

INDIVIDUAL HEART-SHAPED
APPLE GALETTES

MAKES 6 INDIVIDUAL GALETTES /
TIME: 1 HR 30 MIN

Crust:

2 cups all-purpose flour, or ½ cup whole wheat pastry flour and ½ cup whole wheat flour, plus more for dusting

1 tablespoon organic granulated sugar

1 teaspoon salt

⅓ cup refined coconut oil, softened

1 teaspoon apple cider vinegar

½ to ¾ cup very cold water

Apple filling:

2 Granny Smith apples, peeled, cored, and sliced very thinly (⅛ inch or less)

2 tablespoons organic light brown sugar

¼ teaspoon ground cinnamon

6 teaspoons apricot preserves

Canola oil spray, for pan and apples

- - - - - - - -
TIPS
- - - - - - - -

If you don't want to make hearts or are just scared of them (scared of love?), 8-inch circles will work, too!

If you don't have a pastry cutter, cut the coconut oil into the flour with two knives held together.

A galette is a thin, freeform pie. Although here we have forced them into the shape of hearts, so they are no longer free. A thin layer of sweet, tangy apricot preserves is spread onto each crust before baking. A little sugar and cinnamon are sprinkled on top of the apple, making a lovely, simple fruit dessert with a crisp, melt-in-your mouth crust for you and those you love. Or just you, six times.

Prepare the dough: In a large mixing bowl, combine the flour, granulated sugar, and salt. Add the coconut oil by the teaspoon in three batches, but you don't need to be precise about this; you just want to add it in small chunks. Cut the oil into the flour with each addition, until the dough is crumbly and pebbly.

In a measuring cup, combine the vinegar with ½ cup of cold water. Add the diluted vinegar to the flour mixture in three batches, gently mixing it into the dough with a fork, until the dough holds together when pinched. If need be, add up to ¼ cup more water.

Gather the dough into a ball and knead gently a few times until it holds together. Form again into a ball and flatten just a bit into a disk. Refrigerate for about 30 minutes. If you refrigerate it longer, that is fine; but in that case you may need to leave it out for 15 minutes or so until you can easily roll it.

Fifteen minutes before you are ready to prepare the galette, preheat the oven to 425°F, spray a baking sheet with canola oil spray, and slice your apples. Also, in a small bowl, mix together the brown sugar and cinnamon and lightly grease a baking sheet.

On a clean, lightly floured surface, roll out the dough into a 12 x 15-inch rectangle that is ¼ inch thick. It helps if you flour the rolling pin as well, so the dough doesn't stick. Use a butter knife to cut four 8-inch hearts from the dough. When you have done four hearts, place them on the prepared baking sheet, roll out your dough scraps, and create two more hearts. Place those on the baking sheet as well.

Roll in the edges of each heart to create a rimmed crust. You will have to do some pulling on top where the two curves meet, but it doesn't have to be too precise, as long as you get the general heart shape. Now, take a butter knife and score the rolled edges on a slight diagonal to create a pretty design. "Score" just means to press gently with the knife's edge. This not only makes the crust pretty, it also secures the rim in place.

Spread a teaspoon of apricot preserves in each crust. Starting from the top, place four apple slices on both sides of the heart, slightly overlapping, to create a fan effect. You might have to press them into the edges if there doesn't seem to be room; that is perfectly fine. The curved side of the apple slices should go along with the curve at the top of the heart.

Spray with a bit of canola spray to keep the apples from drying out, and sprinkle with the brown sugar mixture. Bake for 25 to 30 minutes, until the edges of the crusts are golden brown.

Serve warm, with a scoop of vegan ice cream, if desired.

Bread pudding is something of a miracle: stale bread and a few unassuming ingredients transform into an irresistible, old-fashioned treat that tastes great on a cold winter's night. Or breakfast, because bananas can be part of a healthy breakfast, or so we've heard. This version is unapologetically decadent, packing in plenty of deep, dark chocolate; creamy, sweet bananas; and a warming hint of cinnamon. This pudding makes the best use of leftover Home-style Potato Rolls (page 332), or any rustic bread with a mild flavor.

Preheat the oven to 350°F. Generously grease a 9 x 5-inch loaf pan with coconut oil.

In a large mixing bowl, whisk together ½ cup of the milk and the cornstarch until no lumps remain. Add the remaining 2 cups of the milk and the maple syrup, vanilla, cinnamon, and nutmeg and whisk to mix thoroughly. Fold in the stale bread cubes.

Set aside the bread and allow it to soak up the milk mixture, at least 15 minutes. The bread is ready when every cube of bread is saturated and there's a little bit of extra liquid in the bowl. The mixture should be mushy and somewhat wet.

Fold in the chocolate chips and bananas, mashing the bananas slightly (go ahead and use your hands for this part; it's fun!). Pour the mixture into the prepared loaf pan, patting the top until even and smooth.

Bake for 30 to 35 minutes, or until the top is puffed, slightly browned, and feels firm.

Remove from the oven and allow to cool slightly before slicing and serving.

TIPS — Try using an ice-cream scoop to scoop the pudding out from the pan and serve as pretty mounds.

Impatient types can make bread stale a little quicker by cutting it into cubes, spreading them on baking sheets, and letting them dry in a 300°F oven for 30 minutes, until the cubes are firm and rather dry. More patient types don't bother with the oven step and let that bread sit out on the counter for a few hours.

BANANA–CHOCOLATE CHIP
BREAD PUDDING

SERVES 6 TO 8 / TIME: ABOUT AN HR

Coconut oil, for pan

2½ cups plain or vanilla almond- or coconut-based milk

3 tablespoons cornstarch or arrowroot powder

½ cup pure maple syrup

1 teaspoon pure vanilla extract

½ teaspoon ground cinnamon

¼ teaspoon freshly grated nutmeg

6 cups (1-inch cubed) stale bread (about 1 pound)

1 cup vegan chocolate chips

3 large, ripe bananas, sliced ½ inch thick

CARAMEL
APPLE SPICE CUPCAKES

MAKES 12 CUPCAKES / TIME: ABOUT AN HR

2 tart, firm cooking apples, such as Granny Smith or Northern Spy

2 tablespoons organic dark brown sugar

1 tablespoon virgin coconut oil

1 cup unsweetened almond or coconut-based milk

1 tablespoon fresh lemon juice

⅓ cup canola oil

¾ cup organic granulated sugar

1 teaspoon freshly grated lemon zest

1 teaspoon pure vanilla extract

1½ cups all-purpose flour

½ teaspoon baking powder

1½ teaspoons baking soda

¼ teaspoon salt

1 teaspoon ground cinnamon

¼ teaspoon freshly grated nutmeg

Caramel-penuche frosting:

½ cup organic dark brown sugar

3 tablespoons virgin coconut oil

⅓ cup almond or coconut-based creamer

2 tablespoons coconut flour

Pinch of salt

2½ cups confectioners' sugar

1 teaspoon pure vanilla extract

½ cup chopped, roasted almonds or peanuts, for sprinkling

This is the ideal autumnal cupcake: it's bursting with caramelized apple chunks, just the right amount of spice, and topped with old-fashioned, fun-to-say penuche frosting with a light caramel flavor.

Preheat the oven to 350°F and line a 12-cup muffin tin with paper cupcake liners.

Leaving the skins on the apples, core and dice them into small pieces (about ¼-inch cubes), for about 1⅔ cups of diced apple.

Heat the brown sugar and coconut oil in a heavy skillet over medium heat, stirring, until the mixture begins to bubble. Add the apple pieces and stir to coat. Cook the apples, stirring occasionally, until almost all of the water has evaporated and the apples are lightly caramelized, about 12 minutes. Remove from the heat and allow to cool before proceeding.

In a large bowl, whisk together the milk and lemon juice, and allow to sit for a minute to curdle. Add the canola oil, granulated sugar, lemon zest, and vanilla, and beat well. Sift in the flour, baking powder, baking soda, salt, cinnamon, and nutmeg, then stir only until the dry ingredients are moistened. Fold in the sautéed apples along with any remaining juices.

Fill the cupcake liners three-quarters of the way with batter, and bake for 20 to 22 minutes, or until a toothpick inserted into the center of a cupcake comes out clean.

When the cupcakes are done, remove them from the oven and cool on wire cooling racks.

While they cool, prepare the frosting: Combine the brown sugar, coconut oil, creamer, coconut flour, and salt in a heavy-bottomed saucepan over medium heat. Stir and bring to a boil. Allow the mixture to boil and foam for 7 to 8 minutes, stirring occasionally. Remove from the heat.

When the frosting mixture has cooled slightly and is still a little warm, stir in ¾ cup of the confectioners' sugar and the vanilla, then beat with an electric mixer for 2 to 3 minutes, until creamy. Slowly beat in the remaining ¾ cup of confectioners' sugar until a thick, smooth, fudgelike frosting forms. (The frosting can be spread warm or slightly cooled, but too much cooling will make the frosting too stiff to spread. If this happens, just let it warm to room temperature.)

Frost the cupcakes and sprinkle with the chopped almonds or peanuts.

TIP If you demand cupcakes with a completely flat top, you will have a little extra batter. Make sure to have a few extra cupcake liners handy to bake a few extra cupcakes after you've finished the first batch.

PENUCHE

What is penuche and why would anyone put it on a cupcake? Penuche is actually a really old-fashioned American fudge candy, so old school in fact there's no chocolate or cocoa in it. Its deep, caramel flavor is achieved primarily by boiling brown sugar along with butter and maybe a little vanilla, but of course we do it better by leaving out the butter in favor of rich and delicious coconut oil. The texture of the frosting does indeed have a dense, smooth homemade fudgy quality that really delivers. The addition of coconut flour (found in natural food stores or "gluten-free" sections of supermarkets) is not traditional but helps thicken the texture of this frosting.

-45   SF

JELLY DONUT
CUPCAKES

MAKES 12 CUPCAKES /
TIME: ABOUT 40 MIN

1 cup unsweetened nondairy milk

1 teaspoon apple cider vinegar

2 tablespoons cornstarch

1½ cups all-purpose flour

¾ teaspoon baking powder

½ teaspoon baking soda

½ teaspoon freshly grated nutmeg

½ teaspoon salt

⅓ cup canola oil

¾ cup plus 2 tablespoons organic granulated
   sugar

2 teaspoons pure vanilla extract

About ⅓ cup raspberry jam or preserves
   (you can use strawberry or grape if you
   prefer)

2 tablespoons confectioners' sugar

TIPS

The cheaper your jam, the more authentic your donut will taste, so skip the organic spreadable fruit stuff here and go for the bright red, ambiguously "berry"-flavored supermarket brand. The cops down at the station will thank you for it.

The trick to these cupcakes is to leave them out in a cool place overnight, so make these a day ahead if you can, although it's fine if you can't wait.

Here is a treat that defies all logic: it's both a tender cupcake and sugared jelly donut at the same time. They're cute, yummy, and deceptively easy to make, too. No need to use a pastry bag to fill the cupcake to create its amazing jelly donut effect; the jam bakes right into it, doing all the work for you. Add a sprinkle of confectioners' sugar and you have yourself one heck of a cupcake moonlighting as a jelly donut.

Preheat the oven to 350°F. Pour the milk, vinegar, and cornstarch into a measuring cup and set aside. Line a 12-cup muffin pan with paper cupcake liners.

In a large mixing bowl, sift together the flour, baking powder, baking soda, nutmeg, and salt. Create a well in the center of the flour to pour your wet ingredients into.

Stir the milk mixture with a fork to dissolve the cornstarch, then pour into the flour mixture. Add the oil, granulated sugar, and vanilla. Stir until well combined.

Fill the cupcake liners about three-quarters full with batter. Place a heaping teaspoonful of jam on the center of each cupcake. You don't need to press down on the jam or do anything else; the baking will take care of all of that and it will sink in.

Bake for 21 to 23 minutes. You can't really do a toothpick test here because of the jelly filling, but the cupcakes should be done by this point. The tops should be firm.

Remove from the oven and let cool completely on wire cooling racks.

Once cooled, set them someplace cool and dry, and leave uncovered. If it's winter, leave them in your coldest room. If it's summer, leave them somewhere air-conditioned, if possible. If it's not possible, don't sweat it—just don't leave them anywhere very warm. Let them sit overnight and preferably up to 24 hours. This will make the tops dry and a little bit crispy and more donutlike.

Sprinkle with confectioners' sugar (using a sifter, if you have one). Serve with coffee.

VANILLA-YOGURT
POUND CAKE

MAKES 1 LOAF /
TIME: ABOUT 1 HR 30 MIN

Nonstick cooking spray, for pan

2 cups unbleached all-purpose flour, plus more for pan

½ cup vanilla almond, coconut, or soy yogurt

½ cup blended silken tofu (blend the tofu first, then measure it out)

¾ cup unsweetened nondairy milk

1¼ cups organic sugar

½ cup canola oil

2 teaspoons pure vanilla extract

½ teaspoon lemon extract, or ½ teaspoon freshly grated lemon zest

½ teaspoon orange extract, or ½ teaspoon freshly grated orange zest

3 tablespoons arrowroot powder

1½ teaspoons baking powder

½ teaspoon baking soda

½ teaspoon salt

TIPS

This cake has a very thick batter and requires a preheated oven at just the right temperature to rise properly. Allow the oven to heat for at least 20 minutes and, as always, use an oven thermometer.

For best results, use a pan that's no bigger than 9 x 5 inches. Using an 8 x 4-inch pan also works great.

Pound cake should be simple, just rich and buttery with a hint of vanilla, citrus, or other aromatic flavors, with a sturdy texture that lovingly delivers abundant calories directly to your thighs with each meltingly tender bite. Without the usual pound of butter and eggs, in this recipe we've made good use of vanilla nondairy yogurt and silken tofu to get the job done. The flavor and texture of this cake develops as it cools, so be sure to allow the loaf to cool completely to room temperature before slicing. And don't forget that pound cake loves to be adorned with fresh berries, or sliced and lightly toasted with a little dab of your favorite vegan butter.

Preheat the oven to 325°F. Lightly spray a 9 x 5-inch loaf pan with nonstick cooking spray and flour it. A metal pan with a dark finish is the best choice for this cake.

In a large bowl, combine the yogurt, blended silken tofu, milk, sugar, oil, and vanilla, lemon, and orange extracts. Use an electric mixer to beat until everything is smooth, about 2 minutes.

Sift in the flour, arrowroot powder, baking powder, baking soda, and salt. Stir with a rubber spatula to combine, then beat with the electric mixer for 1½ to 2 minutes, or until a very thick batter forms. Don't overmix.

Pour the batter into the prepared loaf pan. Use a rubber spatula to scrape all of the batter out of the bowl and smooth the top of the loaf. Bake for 60 to 65 minutes, or until a toothpick or thin sharp knife inserted into the center comes out clean (a little moisture is okay). Don't open the oven to peek for at least the first 45 minutes of baking!

Remove from the oven and let cool in the pan 10 minutes, then carefully transfer the loaf to a wire cooling rack to cool completely before slicing. Store the cake in an airtight container.

VARIATIONS

NUT, CHOCOLATE CHIP, AND/OR FRUITED POUND CAKE: Stir in ½ to 1 cup of any of the following: toasted chopped walnuts, vegan chocolate chips, raisins, dried sweetened cranberries, dried chopped cherries (if using cherries, omit the citrus extracts and use 1 teaspoon of almond extract instead).

LEMON POUND CAKE: Use lemon-flavor vegan yogurt and up the lemon extract to a full teaspoon. Reduce the vanilla extract to 1 teaspoon.

ROSE WATER POUND CAKE: Omit the orange and lemon extracts. Reduce the vanilla extract to 1 teaspoon. Add 1½ teaspoons of rose water.

This is a wonderfully rich chocolate Bundt with a delicate crumb. And it delivers big chocolate flavor without a whole lot of fat. Fresh brewed coffee and almond extract heighten all that chocolate, and applesauce stands in beautifully for most of the oil. This cake doesn't need a glaze or frosting, just a simple sprinkling of confectioners' sugar.

Preheat the oven to 325°F. Lightly spray an 8- or 10-inch Bundt pan with nonstick cooking spray.

Bring the coffee to a simmer in a saucepan over medium heat. Once it is simmering, turn down the heat and whisk in the cocoa powder until it has dissolved. Remove from the heat and set aside to bring to room temperature.

In a mixing bowl, whisk together the granulated sugar, oil, applesauce, and cornstarch until the sugar and cornstarch are dissolved, about 2 minutes. Mix in the extracts. Once the chocolate has cooled a bit, mix that in as well.

Sift in the flour, baking powder, baking soda, and salt. Beat until relatively smooth, about 1 minute with an electric mixer or 2 minutes with a whisk.

Pour the batter into the prepared Bundt pan and bake for about 45 minutes, or until a toothpick or butter knife inserted through its center comes out clean. If your pan is on the smaller side, it could take up to 55 minutes.

Remove from the oven and let cool for about 20 minutes, then invert onto a serving plate to cool completely. Once cool, sift confectioners' sugar over the top and enjoy.

DEEP CHOCOLATE
BUNDT CAKE

SERVES 12 / TIME: 70 MIN

Nonstick cooking spray, for pan

1¾ cups freshly brewed coffee

⅔ cup unsweetened Dutch-processed cocoa powder

1½ cups organic granulated sugar

⅓ cup canola oil

⅓ cup applesauce

¼ cup cornstarch

2 teaspoons pure vanilla extract

1 teaspoon almond extract

2 cups whole wheat pastry flour or all-purpose white flour

1½ teaspoons baking powder

1 teaspoon baking soda

½ teaspoon salt

2 teaspoons confectioners' sugar

TIP

Whole wheat pastry flour leaves the fiber of the wheat intact without sacrificing any of the texture, but if you can't find whole wheat pastry flour, then regular all-purpose flour will do the trick. But don't substitute *regular* whole wheat flour; it is different from pastry flour and will result in a rough and chewy texture.

How does moist, sublime, spiced pumpkin cake get better? A crummy mess of pecan streusel topping would get our vote any day. Perfect for autumn high tea.

Preheat the oven to 350°F. Lightly spray a 9 x 13-inch baking pan with nonstick cooking spray.

Prepare the streusel: In a small bowl, mix together the flour, brown sugar, and spices. Drizzle in the oil and mix with your fingertips until crumbs form. Add the chopped pecans and mix. Set aside.

Prepare the cake: In a large mixing bowl, combine the pumpkin, milk, oil, granulated sugar, molasses, and vanilla. Mix well. Add roughly half of the flour, the baking powder, salt, and spices, and use a fork to fold everything together. Add the remaining flour and mix gently until combined. Don't use an electric mixer for this, as pumpkin can get gummy if it's mixed too aggressively. Blending with a fork helps maintain the texture.

Pour the batter into the prepared baking pan and spread it out with a spatula. Scatter the streusel on top as evenly as possible. Bake for 45 to 50 minutes, or until a knife inserted through the center comes out clean.

Remove from the oven, let cool, and cut into squares.

Nonstick cooking spray, for pan

Pecan streusel:

¼ cup all-purpose flour

3 tablespoons organic dark brown sugar (organic granulated sugar is okay, too)

¼ teaspoon ground cinnamon

¼ teaspoon ground allspice

1 tablespoon canola oil

1 cup coarsely chopped pecans

Cake:

1 (15-ounce) can pure pumpkin puree (not pumpkin pie mix)

¾ cup unsweetened nondairy milk

¾ cup canola oil

1½ cups vegan granulated sugar

3 tablespoons molasses

2 teaspoons pure vanilla extract

2⅔ cups all-purpose flour

1 tablespoon baking powder

1 teaspoon salt

1½ teaspoons ground cinnamon

¾ teaspoon freshly grated nutmeg

¾ teaspoon ground ginger

½ teaspoon ground allspice

⅛ teaspoon ground cloves

BUNDT CAKE

SERVES 10 / TIME: 1 HR 30 MIN

1⅔ cups vegan granulated sugar

⅔ cup canola oil

1 (14-ounce can) full-fat coconut milk

¼ cup unsweetened nondairy milk

3 tablespoons finely grated lemon zest

¼ cup fresh lemon juice

2 teaspoons pure vanilla extract

3 cups all-purpose flour

2 teaspoons baking powder

1 teaspoon baking soda

1 teaspoon salt

1½ cups shredded unsweetened coconut

Several tablespoons confectioners' sugar,
   for sprinkling

Bundt is a hilarious name for this variety of cake. Get past the silliness with the enticing combination of tangy, bright lemon and irresistible chewy shredded coconut, made extra moist with plenty of coconut milk. No need for an icing on this cake, which is bursting with extreme flavor. It's so simple and good—just "slice and go"—but sprinkle with a little confectioners' sugar to dress it up.

Preheat the oven to 350°F. Lightly grease an 8- or 10-inch Bundt pan.

In a large mixing bowl, combine the granulated sugar, oil, canned coconut milk, milk, lemon zest and juice, and vanilla. Stir to combine.

Sift the flour, baking powder, baking soda, and salt into the wet ingredients in batches, mixing well after each addition. Fold in the coconut.

Pour the batter into the prepared Bundt pan. Bake for 1 hour, or until a knife inserted through the cake comes out clean.

Remove from the oven and let cool for about 10 minutes, then place a cutting board over the cake pan, gently flip over, and release the cake from the pan. Let cool completely. One cooled, sift a sprinkling of confectioners' sugar over the top. Slice and serve.

This pie was inspired by the question "What would Paula Deen bake if she were vegan?" It's a rich yet airy chocolate pie, smothered in peanut butter caramel, studded with maple candied pecans, and finished off with a chocolate drizzle for good measure. We use a graham cracker crust, but a chocolate cookie crust would be nice and decadent, too. The pie filling is gluten-free, so if you have a recipe for a gluten-free crust, you celiacs are good to go. If you don't want to go through the trouble of making the toppings, the pie by itself is pretty yummy, too! Top it with nondairy whipped cream if you've got it.

Preheat the oven to 350°F. Spray a 10-inch pie plate with nonstick cooking spray.

Prepare the crust: Place the grahams in a food processor and process into fine crumbs. Place them in a bowl and drizzle the oil on them. Use your fingertips or a fork to mix in the oil until all crumbs are moistened; sprinkle in the milk and mix again. Pour the crumbs into the pie plate and firmly press them to the bottom and sides of the plate. Set aside.

Prepare the filling: First, melt your chocolate. Crumble the tofu into a blender or food processor. Add the liqueur, vanilla, and arrowroot to the tofu and blend until completely smooth. Scrape down the sides to make sure you get everything. Add the melted chocolate and blend again until completely mixed. Pour the filling into the piecrust and bake for 40 minutes. The center may still be jiggly, but that's fine.

Remove from the oven and let cool on a wire cooling rack for 10 minutes, then chill in the fridge for at least 3 hours. The top of the pie should be firm to the touch.

Meanwhile, prepare your candied pecans: Cover a large plate with baking parchment. Heat a dry, heavy-bottomed skillet over medium heat. Add the pecans and stir them very frequently for 3 minutes, until they start to brown. Stir constantly for 2 more minutes, until they are a few shades darker and relatively uniformly toasted. (If a few don't look toasted, don't worry about it. That's better than having them burn.)

Add the oil and salt and stir for another minute. Add the maple syrup and stir constantly for about a minute. The maple syrup should get bubbly and dry. Use a spatula to transfer the pecans to a plate and spread them out as much as you can; it's best if they aren't touching. Place in the fridge until ready to use.

Once the pie has been chilling for at least 3 hours, prepare the peanut butter caramel and chocolate drizzle. Have your pie out and ready to be assembled.

Recipe Continues

SMLOVE PIE

SERVES 8 / TIME: 1 HR,
plus 3 hrs for chilling

Nonstick cooking spray, for pan

Graham cracker crust:

12 graham crackers, or 1¾ cups graham cracker crumbs

¼ cup canola oil

1 tablespoon unsweetened nondairy milk

Chocolate pie filling:

12 ounces bittersweet vegan chocolate, melted (see tip below for melting chocolate)

1 pound silken tofu (not the vacuum-packed kind), drained

¼ cup hazelnut liqueur (other liqueurs would work, too, such as coffee or chocolate, or just use unsweetened nondairy milk)

2 teaspoons pure vanilla extract

2 tablespoons arrowroot powder

Maple candied pecans:

1 cup pecans

2 teaspoons canola oil

⅛ teaspoon salt

2 tablespoons pure maple syrup

TIP

Obviously you don't have a double boiler so take a small sauce pan and fill it halfway with water. On top of that place a small sauté pan. Fill the sauté pan with chocolate chips and bring the water to a boil. Use a rubber spatula to mix the chocolate as it melts. Once melted, remove pan from heat and let cool for 5 more minutes, stirring occasionally.

Peanut butter caramel:

⅓ cup natural peanut butter, smooth or chunky, at room temperature

3 tablespoons pure maple syrup

2 tablespoons brown rice syrup

Chocolate drizzle:

¼ cup unsweetened nondairy milk

4 ounces vegan bittersweet chocolate, chopped, or ¼ cup vegan chocolate chips

Prepare the peanut butter caramel: Stir all the caramel ingredients together in a small saucepan. Gently heat everything over low heat, stirring constantly with a fork, just until smooth and heated through. It should fall from your fork in ribbons. If it seems stiff, turn off the heat immediately and add a little extra brown rice syrup until it's fluid again. (This happens because different peanut butters have different amounts of moisture.)

Pour the caramel over the center of the pie, leaving an inch or two bare at the edges because it spreads. Take your pecans out of the fridge and place them on top of the caramel, pressing them in firmly. You may have to break the pecans apart from one another if they cooled touching.

Prepare the chocolate drizzle: In a small saucepan, heat the milk to boiling, then add the chocolate and turn down the heat. Use a fork to stir until completely blended. Turn off the heat and let cool for 5 minutes, stirring occasionally.

You can drizzle the chocolate over the pie with a spoon, but we like to put it in a pastry bag fitted with a wide writing tip and drizzle it that way, in stripes. Chill the pie for at least 10 minutes before serving, so that the chocolate firms up a bit.

Lost, literally. That is, the recipe for this pie (which once appeared in an episode of *The Post Punk Kitchen*, our public-access cooking show) melted into the shadows soon after that episode was filmed and hasn't been seen for years. Yeah, we could have actually just rewatched the show and maybe paid attention to how the pie was made, but where's the fun in that?

But, whatever. This new and improved version of the recipe is better than ever: more fresh coconut flavor from more luscious coconut milk. Not to mention it's now soy-free, with the inclusion of rice milk or, new for 2017, almond milk or coconut milk beverage. Because this pie originated as a dessert for Passover, we've included its "traditional" matzo crust. But swap graham cracker crumbs (or a prepared prebaked pastry crust) for matzo meal and this cool, sweet, and creamy dessert is the perfect finish to any summertime BBQ or Caribbean-themed meal. Serve it up with slices of fresh pineapple, mango, kiwi, or your favorite seasonal fresh berries.

Prepare your desired crust, bake it, and set aside.

Prepare the filling: In a small bowl or measuring cup, whisk together ½ cup of the nondairy milk with the arrowroot powder. Set aside.

In a large, heavy-bottomed saucepan, whisk together the remaining ½ cup of nondairy milk with the agar powder. Over medium-high heat, bring the mixture to a boil, stirring constantly. Allow it to boil for about 1 minute, then lower the heat to medium-low. In a slow, steady stream, pour in the arrowroot mixture (you might need to give it a brief stir before pouring), stirring this mixture constantly.

Pour in the coconut milk, lemon juice, and sugar. Using a wire whisk, stir constantly as the mixture cooks until thickened, 3 to 5 minutes. Remove from the heat and stir in the vanilla, coconut extract, if using, salt, and shredded coconut. Immediately pour into the baked piecrust. If you have any leftover filling, pour that into a small serving dish and there you go, bonus coconut custard! Allow the pie to cool on a countertop for 15 minutes, then carefully transfer to the refrigerator and allow to chill for at least 2 hours. Cover tightly in plastic wrap until ready to serve.

LOST
COCONUT CUSTARD PIE

SERVES 6 TO 8 / TIME: ABOUT 45 MIN, plus chill time

1 single Pastry Crust (page 409), rolled, shaped, and baked, or Crumb Crust (page 409), prepared with matzo meal or vegan graham cracker crumbs

Filling:

1 cup unsweetened rice, almond, or coconut-based milk (see headnote)

2 tablespoons arrowroot powder or cornstarch

½ teaspoon agar powder, or 1½ teaspoons flakes

1 (14-ounce) can full-fat coconut milk, preferably Thai coconut milk

1 tablespoon fresh lemon juice

1 cup organic sugar

1½ teaspoons pure vanilla extract

1 teaspoon coconut extract (optional but good)

Pinch of salt

¾ cup shredded, unsweetened coconut

Optional garnishes: additional shredded coconut or slices of fresh mango, sliced pineapple, sliced strawberries (sprinkle with lemon juice first before topping), or any fresh, sliced fruit or berry

VANILLA ICE CREAM

MAKES 1½ PINTS ICE CREAM /
TIME: 10 MIN for prepping
and OVERNIGHT for chilling

½ cup cream of coconut milk (see tip)
1 cup unsweetened nondairy milk
¾ cup vegan sugar
6 ounces silken tofu
1 tablespoon pure vanilla extract

- - - - - - - -
TIPS
- - - - - - - -

We actually just used the cream from a can of coconut milk. Place the can in the fridge overnight and the cream will rise to the top. Open the can carefully and scoop out ½ cup of the cream. Freeze the rest for use in a soup or another recipe some other time.

If you are not even considering making your own ice cream, we recommend trying Temptation Ice Cream, from a vegan-owned and -operated company in Chicago.

Making your own ice cream gives you such a feeling of accomplishment, like you just passed the bar exam or climbed a mountain. But it also gives you something even more important . . . ice cream! Coconut milk and pureed silken tofu make this ice cream extra thick and supercreamy, like it should be. Because ice-cream makers vary by manufacturer, our directions basically say to follow the directions your ice-cream maker came with. Basically, you add the ice cream to the container of your ice-cream maker, and then it churns away to keep your ice cream from forming ice crystals. Remember to make sure all your ingredients are cold by keeping them refrigerated overnight the day before your big ice-cream event. Also, prep your ice-cream bowl by keeping it in the freezer overnight. You want everything as cold as can be.

Puree all ingredients in a blender or food processor until smooth. Pour into your ice-cream maker and follow the manufacturer's instructions.

VARIATIONS

GREEN TEA ICE CREAM: Add 2 tablespoons of matcha green tea powder when blending.

ANY BERRY ICE CREAM: Try raspberries, blueberries, cherries, or blackberries, coarsely chopped. If using strawberries, hull and slice them thinly.

You will need ¾ pound of berries. Place half of them in a saucepan with ¼ cup of water, 1 tablespoon of arrowroot powder, and 2 tablespoons of organic sugar. Bring to a boil, then turn down the heat to low and simmer. Simmer for about 7 minutes until slightly thickened, stirring often, then let cool completely.

Once cooled, proceed with the Vanilla Ice Cream recipe, adding your cooled mixture to the blender. Once you pour it into the ice-cream maker, add the remainder of the sliced berries and stir. You can also add a cup of chocolate chunks at this point.

BANANA ICE CREAM: Place two large ripe bananas in the blender with the Vanilla Ice Cream ingredients and proceed with the recipe. If you like, mix in ½ cup of chopped walnuts and ½ cup of vegan chocolate chips when you transfer the mixture to the ice-cream maker.

COFFEE ICE CREAM: Replace ½ cup of the milk with ½ cup of strong, cold espresso, or add 2 tablespoons of coffee extract to the blender.

CHOCOLATE ICE CREAM: Reduce the sugar by ¼ cup. Add 8 ounces of cooled, melted vegan semisweet chocolate to the blender.

PEANUT BUTTER ICE CREAM: Increase the sugar to 1 cup and stir ½ cup of your favorite creamy or chunky all-natural peanut butter into the blender.

PISTACHIO-ANISE ICE CREAM: Stir 1 teaspoon of almond extract, ⅔ cup of coarsely chopped, roasted pistachios, and ½ teaspoon of anise extract into the blender.

If using graham cracker crumbs, for best results purchase whole crackers and smash them up yourself. We know it's a real pain in the butt these days to find vegan graham crackers (stupid honey in everything), so feel free to spare yourself a quest for the nearly impossible and use matzo meal, vanilla cookies, or any kind of dry, crumbly cookie such as ginger snaps or even speculoos cookies.

Preheat the oven to 350°F.

Combine the shredded coconut, matzo meal, and sugar in a large bowl. Pour in the melted coconut oil and toss to create soft crumbs. Add the creamer, a tablespoon at a time, until the mixture is moist and holds together if squeezed. Gently but firmly pat the mixture into a 9- or 10-inch deep pie plate, pressing the mixture up the sides, and form a slight lip if desired. Bake for 12 to 15 minutes, or until the coconut and matzo are lightly toasted and the crust is firm. Remove from the oven and allow to cool on a wire cooling rack before filling.

-45

CRUMB CRUST

MAKES 1 CRUST / TIME: 25 MIN

½ cup unsweetened, shredded coconut

1¾ cups matzo meal, vegan graham cracker crumbs, or vegan vanilla cookie crumbs

2 tablespoons organic sugar

3 tablespoons virgin coconut oil, melted

3 to 5 tablespoons soy or coconut milk creamer

An olive oil–coconut oil blend produces a beautiful flaky crust. Apple cider vinegar helps tenderize the flour. The secret is to have very cold flour and olive oil, while the coconut oil is softened but not cold, so that it works easily into the dough.

In a large mixing bowl, sift together the flour and salt. Drizzle in the coconut oil and mix with your fingertips to form crumbs. Working quickly, add the olive oil by the tablespoonful, cutting it into the flour with your fingers or a pastry cutter, until the flour appears pebbly.

In a cup, mix the ice water (start with the smaller quantity) with the apple cider vinegar. Drizzle the liquid into the flour mixture and use a wooden spoon or rubber spatula to stir it into the dough, adding more ice water a tablespoon at a time until it holds together to form a soft ball. Take care not to overknead the dough.

If you're making a double crust, divide the dough in half. Press one portion of dough into a disk about 1 inch thick and place it between two 14-inch-long pieces of waxed paper. Use a rolling pin to roll the disk into a circle about ¼ inch thick. For a more even, uniform circle of dough, roll the pin one or two strokes outward away from you, rotate the dough a few degrees, roll a few more times, and repeat all the way around. Repeat with the other dough disk if you're making a double crust. Refrigerate the rolled dough wrapped in the waxed paper until ready to use.

PASTRY CRUST,
SINGLE & DOUBLE

TIME: 20 MIN, plus chill time

Double crust:

2½ cups all-purpose flour

¾ teaspoon salt

¼ cup refined coconut oil, softened

⅓ cup very cold olive oil

4 to 8 tablespoons ice water

1 tablespoon apple cider vinegar

Single crust:

1½ cups all-purpose flour

½ teaspoon salt

¼ cup refined coconut oil, softened

¼ cup very cold olive oil

2 to 5 tablespoons ice water

1½ teaspoons apple cider vinegar

ACKNOWLEDGMENTS

TERRY AND ISA WOULD LIKE TO THANK

Katie McHugh, our beautiful and patient editor at Perseus back in 2007, and Renee Sedliar of now 2017

Matthew Lore, our publisher at Perseus who took a chance on us in the first place

Christine Marra, our other editor at Perseus, for calling us every 5 minutes

Marc Gerald, our super-agent at United Talent Agency

Julia Moskin at the *New York Times*, who made us famous

ISA WOULD LIKE TO THANK

Justin Field, for building me shelves and keeping the cats at bay.

My mom, Marlene Stewart, for transitioning to veganism and loving tempeh.

Josh Hooten for finally admitting that I am the new face of veganism and he is a washed up old man who listens to Les Savy Five and wonders what might have been. And his beautiful wife Michelle for publishing *Herbivore Magazine*.

Amy Sims, for being muh guh, (lylas!)

The Post Punk Kitchen forum mods; Paula, Eppy, Angela, Katie and Brian, for deleting spam and threads about honey and dating omnis, thus freeing up my time to play scrabble and write cookbooks.

Erica Levine because I have to thank her in every book or else she headbutts me (someone please help!)

Michelle Moskowitz-Brown for being my sister, even if she doesn't name the new baby after me. Also, Max for being cute and Aaron Brown for having good genes. (There is still time to name the baby after me.)

Gorilla Coffee in Brooklyn, for having free wi-fi and keeping the soy milk out in a thermos. I spent many, many hours there doing most of the writing and editing for *Veganomicon*.

The Brooklyn Public Library at Grand Army Plaza for being a glorious place with air conditioning, free wifi, and, oh yes, so many books! Also, for being around the corner.

Thank you, too, to the vegan community for embracing our big little cookbook as your cooking bible! So many books have come and gone since then, but this one will always be home.

TERRY WOULD LIKE TO THANK

John Stavropoulos, who gives great hugs, isn't afraid to tell me if he doesn't like something and breaks for seitan. And his mom Eleni for bringing me oregano from Greece that she picked herself from the side of a mountain in Sparta. Now that's hardcore.

My parents, Teresa and Nerio, who will make every recipe in this book (even if they don't know this yet).

The Forest Hills crew for keeping me company in the kitchen back in 2007 and being awesome: Erica, Keren, Evelyn, Paula, Frank, Jim and Jason. And the vegan food pals beyond Queens in 2017: Russel, Dawne, Rudy, Jacob & Dawn, Miss Rachel, Sara P., Karen at Like No Udder, and so many inspiring people in NYC, Philly, and New England making great food and doing great things for the animals.

Drozdal for his evil insight (the title of this tome you hold in your hands).

Woodstock Farm Animal Sanctuary, for being the greatest of friends to the animals.

Derrick Hachey, for all our long coffee walks and recipes for the next big adventure.

Our recipe testers guided our way throughout this cookbook. Not only did they tirelessly test our recipes, find our typos, help us clarify directions and hold our hands, they also let us know what foods they were craving and gave us endless ideas and inspiration. They let us know what they wanted in a cookbook, so while we would love to take full credit for being psychic culinary geniuses, we'll pull back the curtain and give them big fat hugs. Thank you guys so much, we love you all!

Amanda Sacco tested over 100 recipes. No sooner did we post something than Amanda had tested it. We think she might be a vegan robot. But aren't all robots vegan?

Erica Johnson
Lisa Coulson
Raelene Coburn
Jayne Ott, Nadia and Brigit Wendt
Webly Bowles
Megan Duke
Julie Farson
Anna Hood
Abby Wohl
Andrea Zeh
Michelle Gardinier
Carrie Lynn Morse
Rachel Bavolar
Keren Form
Allicia Cormier
Mike Desert
Connie Leonard

Kim Cannard
Jessica DeNoto
Katie Marggraf
Molly Tanzer
Eryn Hiscock
Amanda Sacco
Mike Crooker & Liz Bujack
Shanell Dawn Williams
Lauren Ulm
Deborah Diamant
Jenna Mari Brooks
Lucy Allbaugh
Joanna Vaught
Kim Carpenter
Paula Gross
Karla E. Nolt
Jordan Faulds
Mat Winser
Michele Thompson
Terri Kruse
Jessica Scoles
Val Head
Erica Manney
Jill Murray
Angelene Gaal
Drew Blood
Cassondra Herman-Zajac
Elizabeth Ryan

RECIPES BY ICON

SOY FREE RECIPES

GLUTEN FREE RECIPES

VEGANOMICON

Appendix: Recipes by Icon

LOWER FAT RECIPES

RECIPES UNDER 45 MINUTES

SUPERMARKET FRIENDLY RECIPES

VEGANOMICON · Appendix: Recipes by Icon

METRIC CONVERSIONS

The recipes in this book have not been tested with metric measurements, so some variations might occur.

Remember that the weight of dry ingredients varies according to the volume or density factor: 1 cup of flour weighs far less than 1 cup of sugar, and 1 tablespoon doesn't necessarily hold 3 teaspoons.

GENERAL FORMULAS FOR METRIC CONVERSION

Ounces to grams	→	ounces × 28.35 = grams
Grams to ounces	→	grams × 0.035 = ounces
Pounds to grams	→	pounds × 453.5 = grams
Pounds to kilograms	→	pounds × 0.45 = kilograms
Cups to liters	→	cups × 0.24 = liters
Fahrenheit to Celsius	→	(°F – 32) × 5 ÷ 9 = °C
Celsius to Fahrenheit	→	(°C × 9) ÷ 5 + 32 = °F

VOLUME (LIQUID) MEASUREMENTS

1 teaspoon = ⅙ fluid ounce = 5 milliliters

1 tablespoon = ½ fluid ounce = 15 milliliters

2 tablespoons = 1 fluid ounce = 30 milliliters

¼ cup = 2 fluid ounces = 60 milliliters

⅓ cup = 2 ⅔ fluid ounces = 79 milliliters

½ cup = 4 fluid ounces = 118 milliliters

1 cup or ½ pint = 8 fluid ounces = 250 milliliters

2 cups or 1 pint = 16 fluid ounces = 500 milliliters

4 cups or 1 quart = 32 fluid ounces = 1,000 milliliters

1 gallon = 4 liters

LINEAR MEASUREMENTS

½ inch = 1½ cm

1 inch = 2½ cm

6 inches = 15 cm

8 inches = 20 cm

10 inches = 25 cm

12 inches = 30 cm

20 inches = 50 cm

OVEN TEMPERATURE EQUIVALENTS, FAHRENHEIT (F) AND CELSIUS (C)

100°F = 38°C

200°F = 95°C

250°F = 120°C

300°F = 150°C

350°F = 180°C

400°F = 205°C

450°F = 230°C

WEIGHT (MASS) MEASUREMENTS

1 ounce = 30 grams

2 ounces = 55 grams

3 ounces = 85 grams

4 ounces = ¼ pound = 125 grams

8 ounces = ½ pound = 240 grams

12 ounces = ¾ pound = 375 grams

16 ounces = 1 pound = 454 grams

VOLUME (DRY) MEASUREMENTS

¼ teaspoon = 1 milliliter

½ teaspoon = 2 milliliters

¾ teaspoon = 4 milliliters

1 teaspoon = 5 milliliters

1 tablespoon = 15 milliliters

¼ cup = 59 milliliters

⅓ cup = 79 milliliters

½ cup = 118 milliliters

⅔ cup = 158 milliliters

¾ cup = 177 milliliters

1 cup = 225 milliliters

4 cups or 1 quart = 1 liter

½ gallon = 2 liters

1 gallon = 4 liters

INDEX

ABOUT THE AUTHORS

© RANDY EDWARDS

© LUKE ALBERT

ISA CHANDRA MOSKOWITZ is the bestselling author of *The Superfun Times Vegan Holiday Cookbook*, *Isa Does It*, and *Vegan with a Vengeance*, and more. She created the beloved website Post Punk Kitchen (now IsaChandra.com) and her restaurant, Modern Love, has locations in Omaha and Brooklyn.

TERRY HOPE ROMERO is the author of several bestselling and award-winning cookbooks, including *Salad Samurai*, *Vegan Eats World*, and *Viva Vegan!* Terry lives, cooks, and eats in Queens, NYC.

Together, Isa and Terry masterminded the vegan desserts revolution (*Vegan Cupcakes Take Over the World*, *Vegan Cookies Invade Your Cookie Jar*, and *Vegan Pie in the Sky*). All of their recipes will make you five times more awesome.